Yellow Light

In the series
Asian American History and Culture *edited by Sucheng Chan,*
David Palumbo-Liu, and Michael Omi

Yellow Light

THE FLOWERING OF
ASIAN AMERICAN ARTS

Edited by Amy Ling

TEMPLE UNIVERSITY PRESS
PHILADELPHIA

For my Asian American
son and daughter,
Arthur Ling Hinds
and Catherine Ling Hinds,
and the next generation of Asian Americans

Temple University Press, Philadelphia 19122
Copyright © 1999 by Temple University
All rights reserved
Published 1999
Printed in the United States of America

Text design by Anne O'Donnell

♾ The paper used in this publication meets the requirements of the American
National Standard for Information Sciences—Permanence of Paper for Printed Library
Materials, ANSI Z39.48-1984

Library of Congress Cataloging-in-Publication Data

Yellow light : the flowering of Asian American Arts / edited by Amy Ling.
        p.   cm. — (Asian American history and culture)
    ISBN 1-56639-670-0 (cloth : alk. paper)
    1. Asian American arts.   2. Arts, Modern—20th century—United States.
    I. Ling, Amy.   II. Series.
    NX512.3.A83C74   1999
    700′.92′3951073—dc21   98–29511

The permissions for reprinted material appear on pp. 373–74, which are an extension of the copyright page.

Contents

Acknowledgments   ix
Introduction: What's in a Name   1

PART I
The Written Word

C. Y. Lee, Novelist   11
*The Short-Short That Changed My
    Fate*   16

Kim Yong Ik, Novelist   19
"Home Again, 1945" (from *Gourd Hollow
    Dance*)   23
From *Elegy* by Kim Udam   27

Mitsuye Yamada, Poet   28
That Man   34
In Some Countries   35

Diana Chang, Novelist and Poet   37
The Oriental Contingent   40

Sook Nyul Choi, Memoirist and
    Novelist   46
From *Year of Impossible Goodbyes*   48

Maxine Hong Kingston, Memoirist and
    Novelist   55
From *Tripmaster Monkey*   60

Peter Bacho, Novelist   66
A Family Gathering   69

Arthur Sze, Poet   73
In Your Honor   76
The Redshifting Web   77

Meena Alexander, Poet, Novelist, and
    Memoirist   83
Imagining Dora   85

Darrell Lum, Fiction Writer and
    Playwright   92
Paint   98

Garrett Hongo, Poet   103
Ministry: Homage to Kilauea   110

David Mura, Poet, Memoirist, and
    Performance Artist   112
The Colors of Desire   120

Karen Tei Yamashita, Novelist   126
Siamese Twins and Mongoloids   127

Chitra Banerjee Divakaruni, Poet and
    Fiction Writer   136
Clothes   139

Kirin Narayan, Anthropologist and
    Novelist   149
"Firoze Ganjifrockwala" (from *Love, Stars,
    and All That*)   153

Katherine Min, Poet and Fiction
    Writer   156
The Brick   159

Stewart David Ikeda, Novelist   165
Roughie   172

PART II
Images, the Spoken Word,
Dance, and Music

Flo Oy Wong, Artist   179
Made in USA: Angel Island Shhh   183
My Mother's Baggage   184
Baby Jack Rice Story: The Corner Beckoned
    186

Munio Makuuchi, Artist and Poet   192
From Lake Minidoka to Lake Mendota   193
Black Diamond, Rooting for Coal   200
Fairgrounds Called Camp Harmony?   201
*Gathering the Lost Tribes under Blue-Spot-
    Tailed Golden Eagle Wings*   202
*Diane as Victory Garden—Even 1/16
    "Japanese" Blood*   203

Ping Chong, Playwright   204
98.6—A Convergence in 15 Minutes   206

Genny Lim, Poet and Playwright   213
From *La China Poblana*   216

David Henry Hwang, Playwright   222
Trying to Find Chinatown   227

Velina Hasu Houston, Playwright and
    Poet   236
From *Tea*   241

Dwight Okita, Playwright and Poet   250
Richard Speck   256
Asian Men on Asian Men: The Attraction
    258
In Response to Executive Order 9066   259

Dan Kwong, Performance and Installation
    Artist   261
*"Song for Grandpa" (from Monkhood in 3
    Easy Lessons)*   266

Slant, Performance Group   270
    Richard Ebihara   271

Wayland Quintero   272
Perry Yung   275
*"No Menus Please" (from Big Dicks, Asian
    Men)*   278
*"Diary of a Paper Son" (from The Second
    Coming)*   279

Christine Choy, Filmmaker   281
Stills from *Who Killed Vincent Chin?*   284

Renee Tajima-Peña, Filmmaker   287
Stills from *My America . . . or Honk if You
    Love Buddha*   292

Eric Koyanagi, Filmmaker   295
Stills from *hundred percent*   297–99

Garrett Richard Wang, Actor   301
Response   301

William David "Charlie" Chin, Musician,
    Composer, and Writer   309
Johnson's Store   315

Chris Iijima, Lawyer, Singer, and
    Songwriter   319
Asian Song   322

Nobuko Miyamoto, Dancer, Singer, and
    Songwriter   324
To All Relations/Mitakuye Oyasin   328
What Is the Color of Love?   330
The Chasm   331

Peggy Myo-Young Choy, Dancer and
    Choreographer   334
Response   334

Jon Jang, Composer and Pianist   339
From *Island: The Immigrant Suite
    No. 2*   345–46

Fred Ho, Musician and Composer   347
Response   347

Jamez Chang, Hip-Hop and Rap
    Artist   355
Indiana Jones Chang   358
Longing for Home   358
Sai–i–ku, April 29   360

Tou Ger Xiong, Hip-Hop and Rap Artist
    362

Go Hmong Boy Go Hmong Boy Go: A Rap
    367
We Are Hmong: A Rap   368

Permissions   373

Acknowledgments

This book began as the "bee in the bonnet" of my University of Wisconsin (UW) English Department colleague Gordon Hutner and with the early collaboration of Amit Bhargava, then president of the UW Asian American Student Union. Initially my purpose was to showcase the Asian American writers and performance artists who had visited our Madison campus, but the project grew. Stewart Ikeda, formerly lecturer in the UW Asian American Studies Program, invited and interviewed some of the writers; Miseong Woo and Tom Robertson, the program's assistants, interviewed a few others and helped prepare the manuscript. A $2,500 grant from the C. J. Huang Foundation of New York enabled me to offer a modest honorarium to participants in the early years of the project, but without the generous cooperation of all the contributors, this book would not have been possible. My thanks to Garrett Hongo for permitting me to use the title of his first book of poetry: *Yellow Light*. Finally, I thank Gelston Hinds Jr. for reading drafts, suggesting improvements, cleaning and organizing copy, and for his unflagging love and support throughout the years.

Introduction

WHAT'S IN A NAME?

Amy Ling

What is Asian America?
a place?
a race?
a frame of reference?
a government-imposed expedient?
a box to check on a form?

It's a dream in the heart
like Bulosan's claim,
a tug in the gut,
a gleam of recognition:
Asian ancestry
American struggle.

I've been given many labels in my life, but "Asian American" is the most recent and the most comfortable. Because others may find resonance in my story and parallels with their own experience, I'd like to tell how I came to embrace this name.

Each January when I was a girl, the radio would announce that all "aliens" had to report to the Immigration and Naturalization Services (INS). My heart would sink. My family and I were living in Mexico, Missouri, on expired visitor's visas; so my father didn't report. One day I was taken out of school, driven to St. Louis, and fingerprinted—like a criminal. The INS had caught up with us, stamped us "illegal aliens," and ordered us to return to China. However, before we could obtain passage, the Communists won China's civil war, and by an act of Congress, we were relabeled "political refugees" and no longer deportable. (I'm relieved that "aliens" nowadays are extraterrestrials instead of Chinese.)

Born in Beijing in 1939 and brought to the United States at age six, I grew up in small towns where we were the only Asian family. Little wonder that we sought a low profile, for as the Japanese saying goes, "The nail that sticks out gets the hammer." Even when we moved to Brooklyn and became citizens (Asians were not permitted to become naturalized citizens until 1954), we kept to ourselves. We lived in the white man's world, and it did not occur to us that we should have any real voice in this country. Our rights were tenuous at best. I remember vividly one incident in Mexico, Missouri, when my father wanted to give the family a treat: dinner out at the best restaurant in town. But we were met by a sign on the restaurant door, "For Whites Only." Red-hot with shame, I wanted to leave, but my father insisted we enter. We seated ourselves and waited for what seemed an eternity before the waitress brought us a menu, and another eternity before we got our food.[1]

My parents were very westernized—both graduates of an American missionary college, both Christian, and fluent in English. In fact, my mother at age two had been adopted by an American missionary nurse to China. Nonetheless, when I was about to graduate from high school, my father shocked me by saying, "Amy doesn't need to go to college. She's only a girl." Fortunately, mother disagreed, and Queens College, a fifteen-minute bus ride, was tuition free.

An avid reader, I found a exciting new world of ideas in college. The curriculum was broad and rigorous, with two years of required liberal arts subjects and long comprehensive examinations at the end of each set of courses. Our professors had a clear idea of what a college-educated person should know, and their job was to transform these poor but bright, largely working-class and immigrant youths into polished, cultured citizens of the world. With uniform testing, they could ensure high standards and an undiversified foundation of great books, great thought, and great culture. They pursued their task with unswerving zeal, and we, believing we were being admitted to the empyrean heights, worked hard and enjoyed the challenge. Just turned twenty, I was bookish and socially immature when I graduated.

Finding the outside world indifferent to my academic accomplishments, I returned to school, obtained a master's degree in English, then taught for a year in Taiwan before working as a bilingual secretary in Paris, all the time searching for a place to call home. Back in New York in 1965, at a Chock Full O' Nuts, I chanced to sit opposite Toni Cade (Bambara), a good friend from Queens College, who told me about teaching positions in the SEEK Program at City College. I applied and got a job. Our students were inner-city kids, mostly Black and a few Latino, who had the motivation but not skills to survive in college. Our task was to prepare them to compete successfully and to graduate. We drilled them in grammar, basic writing skills, and literary analysis. The SEEK Program faculty were deeply engaged with the students, and with their own projects. Toni Cade was doing an unprecedented thing: writing stories in Black dialect. Addison Gayle was writing a book on the Black aesthetic and urging me to read W. E. B. Du Bois. Barbara Christian had discovered Ralph Ellison's *Invisible Man*

and presented a stunning paper at our faculty colloquium. The program's second director, Mina Shaughnessy, hired more writers to inspire our students: Audre Lorde, Adrienne Rich, Larry O'Neal. I found myself surrounded by an enormously talented group engaged in a wonderful cause.

But as the only Asian in the middle of an Afro-American whirlwind, I again felt alien. Trained in the Euro-American literary tradition, I was not prepared to give untraditional students what they demanded and needed: writers of color. With "enemy outposts" in my own head, I needed a complete reeducation. I was stunned by the slogan "Black Is Beautiful." Why had I believed that only blue-eyed blonds were beautiful? And what damage had this notion, imbibed since childhood, done to my own psyche? I was astounded to read in *The Autobiography of Malcolm X* that the squeaky wheel gets the grease. If we kept quiet, as I'd been taught, we would simply be ignored, for no one in this society was trained to anticipate needs before they were spoken.

I felt I'd been hit by a bolt of lightning and suddenly awakened when I wasn't even aware of having been asleep. But translating these new ideas into action in my own life was another matter. I was by this time working on my doctorate in Comparative Literature, desiring to bring my two disparate cultural heritages together. However, none of the professors in my department at New York University knew any Asian languages, and my own proficiency in Chinese was insufficient for meaningful research. By default, I chose to write my dissertation on the painter in the novels of William Thackeray, Émile Zola, and Henry James. And having begun down this path, I followed it doggedly to its end; all the while a maelstrom was swirling around me.

Told I had to write a book if I wanted to continue teaching in college, I decided to write the book I would have liked to read, one that would answer the question "What have women who look like me contributed to the literature of this country?" Because the concept of Chinese American women as writers of American literature had never occurred to anyone before, I found myself doing literary archaeology with no bibliographic aids and little previous scholarship to rely on. Combing used bookstore shelves and checking the National Union catalog under Chinese surnames, I eventually discovered more than three dozen writers, many of whom were excellent. Among the most fascinating were the two earliest, Eurasian sisters Edith and Winnifred Eaton, who published fiction at the turn of the century under the pseudonyms Sui Sin Far and Onoto Watanna. My author's query in the *New York Times Book Review* brought a response from Winnifred Eaton's grandson, who introduced me to other family members, all of whom graciously shared with me family lore. I found the entire project, which resulted in my book *Between Worlds: Women Writers of Chinese Ancestry,* exhilarating, affirming, totally engaging. I felt as though I'd found my real home.

However, with this book manuscript and twelve years of teaching at Rutgers, I was denied tenure. The majority thinking in the academy in the early 1980s and in the English Department at Rutgers was that the work of peoples of color, like that of women, had not been taken seriously because it was not very "good." All "good" work, like cream, rises to the top. Since texts by women writers of color were unknown, they obviously couldn't be any good, precisely because the experts didn't know about them. (The circularity of this reasoning escaped notice.) The fact that nearly all the arbiters of "taste" and "quality" were white and male had nothing to do with their "objectivity," for they were trained experts, and who could argue with

the experts? That new experts were disagreeing with old experts merely testified to the inferiority of the new experts, who were unable to be objective because they had too much of a personal stake in this scholarship; after all, they were studying literature written by people who looked like them. (That white male scholars had been doing the same thing for generations also escaped notice.) Friends later told me the department discussion on my work concluded that literary criticism couldn't be done on texts that no one knew anything about, and that literary history counted for nothing, for there was no value in unearthing "third-rate authors." Moreover, as one colleague told me, he couldn't support a Chinese expert because the department didn't have any Chinese students. I asked him how many sixteenth-century Englishmen we had as students.

Despite, or perhaps because of, this resistance, I became more confirmed in my conviction that I was on the right path. I realized that in any revolution, the old guard fights hard to retain its privileges. Although my colleagues in New Jersey in 1984 could not accept Chinese American writers as a part of American literature, in California, Asian American Studies had been established eighteen years before, as one of the results of the nine-month-long Third World Student Strike at San Francisco State. What had been hitherto an "airy nothing," to borrow from Shakespeare, had been given "a local habitation and a name."[2] The naming of this space allowed scholars to dig into the past, to recover forgotten history. At the same time, it created a space for new life, encouraging contemporary writers and artists "to sing their own song," as Korean American writer Kim Yong Ik has put it. Asian American writers have since been garnering such prizes as the National Book Critics Circle Award (Maxine Hong Kingston's *The Woman*

Warrior: Memoir of a Girlhood among Ghosts in 1976), the Yale Younger Poets Award (Cathy Song's *Picture Bride* in 1982), the Tony Award for Best New Dramatic Play on Broadway (David Henry Hwang's *M. Butterfly* in 1988), and two Lamont Poetry Awards (Garrett Hongo's *River of Heaven* in 1988 and Li Young-lee's *The City in Which I Love You* in 1990). Amy Tan's best-selling novel *The Joy Luck Club* became a feature-length Hollywood film in 1993, the first with a nearly all-Asian cast since C. Y. Lee's *The Flower Drum Song* in the late 1950s.

Asian American culture is emerging, as Lisa Lowe has put it, "as alternatives to national cultural forms . . . a mediation of history, the site through which the past returns and is remembered, however fragmented, imperfect, or disavowed."[3] The Asian American perspective on the building of the railroads, the Asian Exclusion Acts, and more recently the Golden Enterprise and the Democratic National Committee's interrogation of every campaign contributor with an Asian name is different from the dominant view. The value of an Asian American perspective, however uncomfortable and unwanted by some, is that it calls to account those in positions of power and shines a light on the discrepancy between word and deed, between democratic ideals and discriminatory practices. If we dismiss minority perspectives as "victim studies" and turn a deaf ear, we will simply be perpetuating "tyrant studies," the glossing over of raw past wrongs in favor of a cooked myth of rightness. We cannot learn to avoid mistakes of the past, if we do not know what they were.

Yet Asian American culture is not just about reacting to our treatment at the hands of the dominant society. It is about recapturing various histories differentiated by the specificities of each group, histories of survival and endurance, stories of love and hero-

ism, which would otherwise be lost. It's about enjoying the legacy of the civil rights and feminist movements of the 1960s and 1970s, which now, looking back, seems a social revolution whose impact was as enormous as Galileo's discovery in the sixteenth century. White men were not, after all, the sun around whom the galaxy revolved, but only one of the many planets. We women and people of color were planets as well. Our stories and perspectives had been ignored because few of us had been in positions to create or disseminate knowledge. Somehow, between 1984 and 1991, when I found my professional home as professor of English and director of the Asian American Studies Program at the University of Wisconsin, the world did an about-face, and multiculturalism became a desirable educational goal. More and more colleges are now establishing Asian American Studies programs and requiring ethnic studies courses.

This book was conceived when my colleague, Gordon Hutner, suggested an interesting volume could be made from responses to a set of questions posed to prominent Asian American writers who had visited the Madison campus. But like Harriet Beecher Stowe's Topsy, it "jes grew" to include makers of culture regardless of whether or not they had visited Wisconsin. This book presents the persons behind the words, the thoughts and feelings behind the images, and a sampling of the creative work of some representative artists creating Asian American culture today. Addressed to the general reader, it spans three generations—from C. Y. Lee, whose novels were published in the 1950s before the creation of Asian American Studies, to Tou Ger Xiong, Hmong American rap artist born in 1973. It presents people from a variety of Asian backgrounds and racially mixed ancestry, who work in a variety of media. Contributors from the world renowned to the newly emerging are arranged more or less chronologically by birth year (when divulged) within generic categories. The book is divided into two sections: Part I, "The Written Word," including novelists, short story writers, and poets, and Part II, "Images, the Spoken Word, Dance, and Music," including painters, dramatists, performance artists, filmmakers, dancers, and musicians. A few who are known in one genre have chosen to be represented by work in a different genre.

Initially, I sent out the following eleven questions:

1. What are the origins/genesis of your work?
2. For what audience do you create your work?
3. Which writers/artists/filmmakers/musicians/dancers have most influenced your work?
4. Do you see yourself in a tradition of American artists, Asian American artists, artists of color, émigré or immigrant artists? Are these distinctions meaningful or even separable?
5. Is there an "authentic" Asian American sensibility? If so, how would you define it?
6. What is the role of Asian American artists in the larger American society? What are we in a position to contribute to this society?
7. Are there risks and challenges peculiar to Asian American artists? If so, how do you attempt to resolve them?
8. A common belief is that the dominant society has emasculated the Asian male, commodified the Asian female, and exoticized Asian culture in general. Do you agree?
9. Is this a particularly receptive moment for Asian American artists? If so, what

circumstances (historical, political, social, or other) have shaped this moment?
10. How would you characterize the reception of your work? What has been most lacking in this reception? For what are you most grateful?
11. What words of advice do you have for aspiring Asian American artists?

As the project evolved, I included an additional set of six questions, which Stewart Ikeda told me assumed less and were more interesting:

12. Must the multicultural writer/artist be answerable solely to his/her ethnic community, the community's spokesperson, or can s/he claim the right to express an individual vision and personal concerns and to modify the group's myths and legends for artistic purposes?
13. If Asian Americans write about subjects other than their identity and our common cause—justice and equality (Diana Chang and Kazuo Ishiguro, for example, have peopled certain novels with only Caucasian characters)—can they still be called Asian American writers? In other words, do we identify an "Asian American" work by the racial ancestry of its producer or by its subject matter?
14. Do we, as Asian Americans, claim exclusive rights to our history, our culture, or can writers/artists of other backgrounds use our material and tell our stories?
15. If an Asian American writer/artist attracts a wide audience of non–Asian Americans, is this general acclaim *in itself* to be taken as evidence that the writer/artist has "sold out" and has become overly assimilated?

16. Does an "ethnic" writer become more readily admitted into the general "canon" when s/he becomes less a writer with a cause (with content that is disturbing to the "majority") and more a writer with a style, a form, that is intricate enough for scholars to sink their critical teeth into?

17. What happens to a writer whose very identity is defined by his/her marginality when s/he becomes "canonized" or "central" and is no longer on the periphery? Does s/he lose this identity?

To save space, I have chosen not to restate each question in each contributor's section (except where necessary) but instead have tried as much as possible to highlight each person's own words. Some respondents chose to answer the questions in order; others selected a few as launchpads for creative essays, such as Karen Tei Yamashita's academic satire on the pitfalls of ethnic identity. Meena Alexander's visit to Wisconsin and her conversation with Japanese American artist Munio Makuuchi (also in this collection) inspired her to write "Imagining Dora," demonstrating how the landscape and people surrounding an artist become food for her imagination and subject matter for her pen.

The contributors to this volume are people whose work I know and admire, whose paths have crossed mine, and who responded positively to my invitation. I regret that many other people whose work I also admire are not included in this far-from-comprehensive volume for a variety of reasons, mostly time and space constraints. I hope that readers will be enticed by what they find here to explore further the field of Asian American culture. For those curious about Asian American filmmakers, Russell Leong's *Moving the Image* is a useful anthology; for Asian American artists, read the essays of Margo Machida and Yong Soon Min. For more poetry and fiction by South Asians, look for *Living in America,* edited by Roshni Rustomji-Kerns, and *Contours of the Heart,* edited by Suanina Maira and Rajini Srikanth. The Asian American Writers Workshop in New York has recently published anthologies of Vietnamese American and Filipino American work—respectively, *Watermark: Vietnamese American Poetry and Prose,* edited by Barbara Tran and others, and *Flippin': Filipinos on America,* edited by Luis H. Francia and Eric Gamalinda—and often holds workshops and readings.

One unique feature of this book is the inclusion of Asian American musicians, and I was particularly delighted to discover and include the Peter, Paul and Mary of Asian American folk music: William David "Charlie" Chin, Chris Iijima, and Nobuko Miyamoto. As singer-songwriter Miyamoto has remarked, Asian American writers have received a good deal of attention and their work is available elsewhere, but the work of dancers, musicians, and performance artists is more ephemeral—although the musicians' CDs are certainly available.

Despite the unity I claim in my poem at the beginning of this Introduction, some invitees informed me that my questions made assumptions they didn't share, for instance, that the label "Asian American" was a comfortable "fit" and an identity they embraced. For example, Ang Lee, director of *The Wedding Banquet* (1993) and *Sense and Sensibility* (1995), who came to the United States for graduate studies and has been living here for eighteen years, liked the project but declined involvement, explaining: "I find it difficult to define myself as an 'Asian American' artist per se. I am a Taiwanese filmmaker currently working in America perhaps, but I don't know what that means for my work. This is not to say that my background is not important to me; but I create out of individual experience and interests rather than any specific ideas of identity and community." Ang Lee is hardly alone in his discomfort with the term *Asian American;* it is apparent also in the responses that Kim Yong Ik gave to my questions. In general, people who have immigrated to the United States after reaching adulthood identify themselves as Asian specific, while those born in the United States or who came as young children tend to be more comfortable with the term *Asian American.*

Thus, creating unity and community out of diversity and individuality is no easy matter. While it may be true that art needs to be grounded in specificities, in life these may divide rather than unite. For example, as an Asian American, I sympathize totally with Japanese American former internees and feel deeply the injustice they have suffered. Paul Fussell wrote in *The New Republic* years ago that the bombing of Hiroshima was right because it saved American lives, adding that an American naval officer remarked "those were the best burnt women and children I ever saw";[4] I was incensed and wrote him to recommend that he read Hanama Tasaki's moving novel *Long the Imperial Way.* But as one whose earliest childhood memory is of running to air-raid shelters in Chongqing to escape Japanese bombs, I cannot help resenting the Japanese who purchased Universal Studios and cut out scenes showing Japanese massacring Chinese in Nanjing from Bernardo Bertolucci's *The Last Emperor* (1987). Yet, I held my tongue recently when a Japanese American colleague from the business school confided to me her discomfort when a student said, "Oh, those Japanese!" in response to the Japanese purchasing of American businesses. I empathized with the professor, but I also agreed, secretly, with the student. My American-born colleague may well have understood my feelings, since she is married to a Chinese from Hong Kong. Thus, life is extremely complex, identity is ever fluid, and the "Asian American" rubric makes strange bedfellows. However, this fluidity and these strange bedfellows may be all to the good.

It is striking how many of the Asian American artists in this book found inspiration for their sense of identity in the African American movement, and how many are actively collaborating across racial and cultural lines. Genny Lim crossed the border to uncover La China Poblana, while Nobuko Miyamoto found inspiration in a Lakota ritual for her song "To All Relations/Mitakuye Oyasin." David Mura tells how his father, in the 1940s, when invited by Whites to sit in the front of the bus and by Blacks to sit in the back, chose to be an honorary White; but in the 1990s, Mura, aware of a common history of racism, is allying himself with Blacks for creative work. The crossing of ethnic boundaries is particularly noticeable in the "Afro-Asian new American multicultural music" of composers Jon Jang and Fred Ho, the dialect Stewart David Ikeda chose for his story "Roughie," the artwork of Flo Oy Wong, the personal life and songs of Nobuko Miyamoto, and the rhythms of hip-hop/rap artists Jamez Chang and Tou Ger Xiong.

For some, the term *Asian American* is in a formative, contested state, with many questions still unresolved. How is an Asian American artist defined—by subject matter? by place of birth? by place of burial? by blood and race, and what percent? by culture? by self-definition? by length of time in the United States, and how long? by political intent? Must one's own identity always be the subject of one's work? (Of course not.) But isn't the work that emerges from one's heart and gut, from what one knows best, the most moving and effective? (Yes, of course.)

But doesn't imagination come into play in the best work, and isn't it true that the imagination knows no boundaries? (Yes, again.) Are we forgetting, as Chris Iijima reminds us, that the Asian American movement came out of political action within the community and that our concern should be to give back to the community, to right wrongs, to create social change? (But to quote Miyamoto, "What can a song do?") Finally, what, after all, is one's community—those from the same racial and national background? those who have suffered? all of humanity? (To quote Ping Chong, "I detest exclusivity.")

Granting all these contradictions and ambiguities, I nonetheless believe in this project and have worked four years to bring it to fruition. I think of it as my brag book, a family album, showcasing the ideas and creations of people I proudly consider family (in fact, one *is* family—my nephew Garrett Wang, my first cousin's son) because of their Asian ancestry and regardless of their particular Asian ancestry. Some may question whether a gathering of such disparate voices can create a coherent and harmonious whole. Perhaps it doesn't. But having trained exclusively in the Eurocentric, masculinist tradition, I, for one, delight in the novelty of hearing a variety of Asian American voices singing of hardship and heroism, of endurance and survival, of solidarity with other minority peoples, and of universal principles such as justice, dignity, and self-respect. I believe that in people, as in nature, the borderland is the place of the richest diversity and the most nurturing of creativity. Asian America is a "borderland," rich in its variety of permutations of ethnicity, race, and culture and in the paradoxes of multiculturalism, multivocality, and multinationalism. These voices and images speak to and for me, as I hope they will speak to you.

NOTES

1. A happy postscript to my incident is that in July 1997, I was back in Mexico, Missouri, and had dinner in the same airport restaurant. This time the hostess seated us without blinking an eye, and as we were leaving, smiled and said, "Y'all come back now, y'hear?" Some things have changed.

2. From William Shakespeare, *A Midsummer Night's Dream* Act V, scene i: "And as imagination bodies forth / The forms of things unknown, the poet's pen / Turns them to shapes, and gives to airy nothing / A local habitation and a name."

3. Lisa Lowe, *Immigrant Acts* (Durham, N.C.: Duke University Press, 1996), x.

4. Paul Fussell, "Hiroshima: A Soldier's View," *New Republic*, August 22 and 29, 1981, p. 27.

The Written Word

C. Y. Lee

NOVELIST

Born in China in 1917, C. Y. Lee came to the United States in 1944 and earned a master of fine arts at Yale University. He is best known for his 1957 novel, The Flower Drum Song, *which became a Broadway musical in 1958 and a Hollywood film in 1962. He is the author of nine novels and two nonfiction books, including* Lover's Point *(1958),* Sawbwa and His Secretary *(1959),* Madame Goldenflower *(1960),* Cripple Mah and the New Order *(1960),* The Virgin Market *(1964),* The Land of the Golden Mountain *(1967),* The Days of the Tong Wars *(1970),* China Saga *(1987),* The Second Son of Heaven *(1990), and* Gate of Rage *(1991).*

Lee has received numerous awards for his writing. Although past eighty, his energy seems unflagging. He is currently working to establish a theater for Chinese and Chinese American drama at California State University, Los Angeles, and is writing a collection of short stories. His papers are being collected in the C. Y. Lee Archive at Boston University's Mugar Memorial Library. Following his response is a short essay about the fortuitous beginning of his writing career.

RESPONSE ⟿

I was born in 1917 in Hunan, Hsiang-t'an, China. My father was a gentleman farmer and my mother, a homemaker. My family had eleven children (eight boys and three girls), and I was the youngest of all. When I was twelve years old, I left my native province

11

to go to Peking (Beijing) to a middle school and senior middle school run by Presbyterian missionaries. I studied English and French. My teachers were British-educated Chinese who had peculiar accents, but British-educated English professors seemed to have more prestige. When I first came to this country, no one could understand me and I didn't understand them.

In 1943, during World War II, I went to the Southwest Associated University, which was a combination of three refugee universities. I majored in Comparative Literature and English. After graduation, I answered an ad and applied to be a secretary for the *sawbwa* [ruler] of Mangshih on the China-Burma border. Friends tried to dissuade me by telling me about poisonous vapors there that caused a trembling disease, but I went anyway. The place was beautiful, and the Shan people were clean and healthy. There were no fights and quarrels, and the air was not poisonous. I stayed for one year, the happiest year of my life. My duties were light. I translated a few English letters into Chinese and played badminton with the *sawbwa*'s nineteen-year-old Eurasian wife.

When the Japanese invaded Burma, the *sawbwa* gave me some silver coins, a typewriter, a Parker 51 pen (a status symbol in those days), and a watch. I escaped to Chungking, only to find the city constantly bombarded by the Japanese. My brother told me the government was encouraging students to leave the country. Since we were given a highly favorable rate of exchange, I sold some of the things the *sawbwa* had given me—a Western suit, a typewriter—and received $2,000 U.S. in exchange. I obtained passage on an American army transport ship across the Pacific from Bombay, through Hawaii to Los Angeles. We had to follow a zigzag route to avoid Japanese torpedoes. The crossing took more than one month. I arrived in Los Angeles in 1944 and didn't know a soul.

I decided to take a train across the country and enrolled in Columbia University, majoring in Comparative Literature and living in the dormitory. Unfortunately, it was a waste of six months. I was always sleepy in the classroom because the temperature was too warm, and I had language difficulties. Mr. Loo, a film producer from China, told me to study writing so I could go back and work for him. He was the head of the China Film Company in Chungking. I still had $1,200 of my $2,000 and since Yale's class of 1949 was famous for playwriting (Eugene O'Neill was a member of that class, and Professor George Pierce Baker was very famous, but he unfortunately died before I got there), I enrolled at Yale and studied with Walter Pritchard Easton. I told him I had a problem following lectures, and he was very understanding. He asked me to write more plays. In China, I had written and published essays, articles, and short stories; I drew and published some cartoons as well. I stayed in Yale for three years on a China Institute scholarship and received an M.F.A. in playwriting.

Chinese students were applying for interpreter jobs at the United Nations because it was considered to be the best job in the world at that time; there was no income tax. I applied too, but I was overqualified. I would have been accepted if I had only a B.A. degree. However, luck works both ways. Those who had gotten the jobs reported to me decades later, "It's a job that is tasteless to eat and yet a pity to throw away."

I returned to Los Angeles to get ready to go home, since I was on a student visa. At a rooming house in old Chinatown, I ran out of money, and immigration officials were trying to drive me out; so I waited for them to deport me, to save on the airline ticket. Then a Chinatown newspaper in San Francisco, *Chi-*

nese World, offered me a job. They served wonderful Cantonese meals. I sunned myself after lunch and started writing *The Flower Drum Song*. The generation gap interested me. I invented a character from the Old World, developed a conflict between him and his young son, who became involved with a nightclub singer, and a picture bride from China. Richard Rodgers and Oscar Hammerstein further developed the love triangle.

I directed my writing to a mainstream audience, but I also wanted to show Chinese life. I exaggerated it a little, perhaps, made it a little more quaint. The old man in the novel is very old-fashioned, but actually, I knew some men at the newspaper who were even more old-fashioned. These people had lived forty to fifty years in the United States but didn't speak a word of English and didn't even step out of Chinatown. One old man kept his entire life's savings in his mattress. Old Master Wang in *The Flower Drum Song* is reluctant to go to the bank. He doesn't trust banks with his money, just as he doesn't trust other men with his wife.

Some readers criticized me, saying I was showing the stupidity of my own race, but I don't think that's true. When I published a book about the California gold rush, some criticized me for writing stereotypes of Chinese with pigtails and bound feet, but that's history. I wanted to point out things to a Western audience that they didn't know before. *Lover's Point,* my second novel, is set in Monterey/Pacific Grove. I think it's a better book than *The Flower Drum Song*. The characters, drawn from people I know, seem more real. The book tells a poignant story of some displaced people. A friend of mine lived in a garage to save money, like the main character in that novel. He was offended, the City of Monterey was offended, but everybody was happy at the end. *Lover's Point* is my favorite book.

My latest novel, *Gate of Rage,* is a sequel to *China Saga* set in mainland China. *China Saga* is about four generations of a family going through one hundred years of political and social upheaval in China, beginning with the Boxer Rebellion and extending through the Chinese Revolution, the Communists' so-called liberation and the Cultural Revolution. *Gate of Rage* is about Do Do and Jimmy, the fourth generation. The story ends with the Tiananmen Square massacre in 1989. It's not exactly a historical novel but a family story with a historical background.

I want to make readers more aware of history. Out of my eleven books, I've written two historical novels, *Madame Golden Flower* and *The Second Son of Heaven;* the latter is about the Taiping Rebellion and General Charles George Gordon, the British vagabond who became a Chinese general. *The Second Son of Heaven* is another favorite of mine because the two main characters, Hung and Gordon, are fascinating, real people. But one critic thought it was dull. The readers will have to decide. For facts and background material, I read a lot of books, magazine articles, Hong Kong magazines in Chinese.

I became an American citizen forty years ago, but as a Chinese American, I have one foot in China, one foot in this country. Some things you just can't get rid of, for example, my liking for Chinese food and my Chinese accent. I have no objection to the term *Asian American,* however. I would be comfortable with the term.

In America, people are a little more straightforward, and there's a little less guesswork in your relationships. There's more freedom in America. China was never very comfortable. During my childhood in China, I was afraid of many things—bandits, defeated soldiers. I was also afraid of high government officials and their children. The government officials' children rode thunderous motorcycles, and if one of their motorcycles hit you, their bodyguards would kick you, saying, "Are you blind? You could have hurt the motorcycle!" There was crowding, poverty, sickness, constant war. In the refugee university, we didn't even have tables. We drew a circle on the floor for a table and pretended we were having a feast. Pork skin floating in a thin soup was a treat.

Thirty-three years ago, in 1962, I married an American woman, Joyce Lackey, a writer. We met at James Wong Howe's; he was a Chinese American cameraman in Hollywood who won three Academy Awards. In China, I fell in love with a girl and wrote love letters without signing my name. I was afraid she'd discover my identity and spit on me. At Yale, the School of Drama was full of young women, but I never had a date with any of them; I was too shy. James Wong Howe hosted parties. Sonara, Howe's Caucasian wife, often invited me to the writers group meetings at their house. People brought stories to read. I asked for a volunteer to read mine. Joyce volunteered, and one thing led to another.

Chinese cigarettes always had a card inside—a voluptuous girl, big-busted and big-hipped. I used to collect cigarette cards, and I developed a liking for that kind of woman, nineteenth-century saloon-type ladies. So Caucasian women attracted me. When my shyness gradually went away, I became quite aggressive.

On the whole, I've been treated very well by Americans. I came to this country with nothing. The years I've spent here have been very satisfying. There have been ups and downs, of course. I had only one experience of racial discrimination. It was years ago at Yale. I saw a sign, "Room for Rent," and I went to rent the room. The landlady said, "No, the room is already rented," and took down the sign. Half an hour later, the sign

was up again. Otherwise, either it's been hidden very well or I haven't been very sensitive.

In fact, I've experienced reverse discrimination. A friend from Taiwan came to Los Angeles and he wanted to buy some Gucci shoes. I took him to Beverly Hills. There I saw a Caucasian couple wanting to go into the store. The clerk shook his head, motioned with his hands, and said, "No, you're too late." I shouted, "I have a friend who traveled six thousand miles and wants to buy a pair of shoes." They opened the store for us, probably thinking Asians are loaded. So the American couple came in too, saying, "We're with them."

Some people are offended by Charlie Chan. I think Charlie Chan is respectable, clever, superior to many of the other characters in the same story. He's the boss, cleverly solving problems. I don't see that this Charlie is damaging to our image. In the 1920s, most characters were caricatured and stereotyped. Exaggerated speech was a pattern. This character spoke with wisdom, which is better than gangster talk. Was he emasculated? Well, he's not physical, not macho, but a lot of detectives are not macho. The Western sheriff with a big beer belly, talking out of the corner of his mouth, is just another stereotype. Nobody criticized that. Audiences are used to certain types. Gangsters can't be depicted as scholars. They were usually dark and Italian. Audiences enjoy seeing that type of thing. No matter what you do, someone will criticize you. *The Flower Drum Song* corrected some old stereotypes. For example, the younger generation talked American slang and walked and acted like ordinary Americans. I was breaking stereotypes. Only old Master Wang was old-fashioned.

I've been satisfied with the reception of my work. My main frustration is that I didn't get my movies off the ground. I went to China and Taiwan with an American investor. I wanted to make a film about the railroad building—the Chinese contribution to California. It hasn't been done. There are a lot of stories about the Chinese participation in the California gold rush, too. One was a young girl who disguised herself as a boy; I wrote about it in *The Days of the Tong Wars*. Also, *Madame Golden Flower* should be a movie. She saved Peking from complete ruin. Chinese filmmakers objected to glorifying the life of a prostitute, but I was trying to tell a story of a patriot who saved Peking at great personal sacrifice. The movie studios in China are all government owned. American investors must have their cooperation; otherwise, the expense would be prohibitive. The railroad-building film would have needed a cast of thousands. Government studios could have easily mobilized army troops to play railroad workers, but high-ranking government officials didn't want to show Chinese with pigtails working like slaves, so the film project fell through.

About Asian American culture, Amy Tan's *The Joy Luck Club* (1989; film version, Wayne Wang, 1993) is aimed at an American audience. Some people think things are too exaggerated—perhaps about the same amount as I exaggerated my characters. I don't see any harm as long as we're not insulting to our race. Some customs are very, very old-fashioned. For example, the foot massage shown in *Raise the Red Lantern* (Yimou Zhang, 1991) did exist, though I never saw it. *Chan Is Missing* (Wayne Wang, 1982) I thought was very ordinary, nothing exciting, nothing new. I explain its popularity by the window theory: it's a window allowing others to peek through, to reveal Chinese life unfamiliar to the Americans. A lot of people are ignorant of other cultures. As a result, they enjoy seeing anything different—lifestyles, tribes, animals, social life, customs, and so forth. There's the ethnographic appeal of something different. The purpose is to draw us closer and enhance understanding.

A few years ago, I discovered a huge Chinese community in Monterey Park/Alhambra where the people speak Mandarin, so I feel at home there. It's a rich source of material for me right in Los Angeles. I've been spending a lot of time there for social events.

I'm involved in another project as well. Philanthropists Mr. and Mrs. [Charles and Harriet] Luckman spent $12 million to build an arts complex at California State University in Los Angeles, including the Luckman Theatre with twelve hundred seats. The university is also building an intimate theater next door. The state has pledged $4 million. It needs $2 million more to complete. I'd like to see the intimate theater used to help Chinese dramatists break into the international market. Even if a play is written in Chinese, we can easily translate it, since plays are generally only 120 pages or so. Now the job is to raise $2 million to finish the theater. The university will even name the theater for the donor. Then we shall have a play contest once or twice a year; the prize will be a professional production. Right now, I've established only a creative writing contest, with cash prizes. But the ultimate goal of a writer is publication or production. If we have a theater, we'll concentrate on production.

I haven't planned my next book, but I'm thinking about a collection of short stories set in Taiwan, Hong Kong, all over the world—maybe in the new Chinese community in Los Angeles, which is like a little China, full of interesting stories. I'm also working on a musical in Chinese language—about a woman from China who migrated to this country and her struggles to realize her American dream.

The most important thing for young writers is determination. Talent is curiosity and the ability to invent. Some people have tremendous ability to memorize, to figure things out, but creativity and curiosity, plus luck, makes a writer. Two things I never learned well: typing and driving. So I still write in longhand and always try to bum a ride. My son drives well. My wife never in her life got a traffic ticket. I guess they have those abilities built in their genes.

EDITOR'S NOTE: This response is compiled from an interview I conducted with C. Y. Lee on April 6, 1995, in the Grand Hotel, Taipei, Taiwan.

The Short-Short That Changed My Fate

I used to believe that "apply the seat of the pants to the seat of the chair," was the only formula for writing. Now I believe that hard work alone is not enough. A writer needs some natural ability and a lot of luck.

Everyone has a few lucky stars and some blessings in disguise in life. My lucky stars were a short-short published in *Writer's Digest,* and an elderly gentleman I never met.

When I finished Yale in 1947, life became unbearable. Staying in a rooming house near Los Angeles' Old Chinatown, I survived on two bowls of noodles a day. In those days a bowl of barbecued pork noodles cost twenty-five cents, plus free tea and all the Chinese language newspapers you could read.

When my funds were down to the last few bowls of noodles, I wangled a job at a corner drug store, but was unceremoniously sacked a week later for breaking a few bottles. That afternoon I asked myself, "What am I doing here, a man with a master's degree from Yale University, starving in the slums while all kinds of prestigious jobs are waiting in China?"

Before I went to wire for funds to go home, I dropped in at the restaurant to have my last bowl of noodles. While there, I saw a small ad in *The Chinese World,* a San Francisco Chinese-language newspaper, looking for a columnist for its English edition. I submitted three columns. Almost by return mail the paper sent me $5.00 for each, and ordered five more every week. Suddenly I saw a lot of noodles and changed my mind about going back to China.

My column, "So I Say," seemed to please the editor. When he offered me a full-time job, I accepted with gratitude and moved to San Francisco. A few weeks later the Immigration Service called and gave me two weeks to leave the country for violating my student status. At the end of the two weeks, a man with a gravelly voice phoned and started asking me questions. I said, "Officer, I'm all packed. Deport me any time."

It turned out that the caller was the editor of *Writer's Digest,* who said that I had won the first prize in their short-short contest. He wanted to make sure that I was the right Lee before he sent the prize money of $750. He added that *Ellery Queen's Mystery Magazine* had already bought the reprint rights. The entry, "Forbidden Dollar," also appeared a year later in Robert Oberfirst's *Best Original Short Shorts*. The five-page story brought me almost as much as a whole year's salary at *The Chinese World*.

After my "Forbidden Dollar" launched my writing career, a long period of struggle began. My first novel, *Flower Drum Song*, was turned down by almost every major publisher in New York. My agent hinted that after one more rejection, she would return it and that I should think of another line of occupation. A few weeks later she called again and said, "Keep writing. A highbrow publisher, Farrar, Straus and Cudahy, has bought the book." She added that the publisher liked it because it was quaint and episodic, the very reasons for which the other publishers had turned it down.

According to John Farrar, my editor and the senior partner of the publishing house, the manuscript had at first landed on the sick bed of an 80-year-old reader. The elderly gentleman, having finished the book, didn't have enough energy to write a detailed critique. With his last bit of strength he scribbled on the dog-eared cover, "Read this," and died.

The book opened many doors for me. It climbed onto *The New York Times'* best seller lists; it became a Rodgers and Hammerstein musical, and later, a Universal film. A series of events followed that provided me the opportunity to do some blatant name-dropping among my peers.

First, I was invited to accompany Gene Kelly on his search for talent for the Broadway production of *Flower Drum Song*, which he directed. Then I received a letter from Groucho Marx, who told me that he didn't know if I was Mr., Mrs., or neuter, but after he had read the first chapter of the book in *The New Yorker* he felt compelled to write to me. He invited me to meet him in San Francisco. I went nightclubbing with him and his young wife. With Marx, every minute was a comedy feast. I listened to him bantering with the Andrews Sisters and almost fell off my chair laughing.

I shared the podium with Phyllis Diller at the San Francisco Press Club, and while receiving the club's black cat award, she asked me about my sex life. The audience howled, drowning my awkward answer; for that I was grateful.

My name also wormed its way into many gossip columns. Walter Winchell first reported that Rodgers and Hammerstein's next musical had an odd title . . . "Flower *Drum Song* . . . probably about a pansy and a bongo player." The celebrated San Francisco columnist, Herb Caen, probably fishing for tidbits, took me to Senator S. I. Hayakawa's dinner party in Mill Valley. Sitting beside the editor of *Playboy*, I wondered if I should sell him a story about two Shanghai sisters who murdered a young man with sex for insurance money—a perfect crime. But I never worked up the courage to tell it.

Joseph Field, the Broadway producer, introduced me to the glamorous world of Hollywood. At Lana Turner's house, I met Edward G. Robinson, who pointed a stubby finger at me and said, "Listen, I wanna play that old man in your book." I watched in fascination while Fritz Loewe played the piano and sang his latest creation, "Gigi," interrupting himself to say how much he hated parties. In the same year, Twentieth-Century Fox gave me an office and a secretary and asked me to write a film called *The Buddha Story*, which they shelved as soon as the Japanese released a flop on the same subject.

Then I went to London and shook many bejewelled hands, including Princess Margaret's, during *Flower Drum Song*'s London production. I toured the Orient twice as the guest of the American President Line and Japan Airlines. Back in Hollywood, Lisa Lu took me to one of Marlon Brando's private screenings, where he personally served McDonald's hamburgers. In Steve Allen's home, I listened to Shirley MacLaine's weird ideas, which later became the basis for her famous books on mysticism and reincarnation.

To top it all, San Francisco declared *Flower Drum Song* Day, and Mayor George Christopher presented me with the key to the city after a parade on a rainy day in 1959. Governor Goodwin Knight sent me a personal warm letter of congratulation. At a big Chinatown banquet, the Chinese Chamber of Commerce presented me with a scroll and a gold tie pin. The Chinatown queen tried to fasten the pin on me, but I was wearing a bow tie. It gave everybody a belly laugh that helped us digest the twelve-course shark's fin dinner.

Did I enjoy those glamorous days? Not really. I was an introvert writer, self-conscious and uncomfortable among celebrities. When I remember how I swallowed hard and secretly wiped my sweating hands on my trousers, I'm glad that those days were fleeting. I think they are rather like ribbons on gift packages—they are discarded soon after the gifts are unwrapped. But still I owe everything to my two lucky stars. Without "Forbidden Dollar," and that dying old gentleman's two words, "Read this," I might have gone back to China long ago.

Kim Yong Ik

~~~~~~

NOVELIST

Born in 1920 in the scenic South Korean seaport Choong Moo, Kim Yong Ik studied English literature at Aoyama Gabuin College in Tokyo. In 1948, he came to the United States and studied at Florida Southern College in Lakeland, the University of Kentucky, and the Iowa Writers' Workshop. From 1957 to 1964, he taught at Korea University and Ewha Women's University. Back in the United States in 1965, he taught at the University of California, Berkeley, and at Duquesne University in Pittsburgh until his retirement in 1990.

Kim published nonfiction, novels, and collections of short stories about life in Korea: Moons of Korea *(1959),* The Happy Days *(1960),* The Diving Gourd *(1962),* Blue in the Seed *(1964),* Love in Winter *(1962),* The Shoes from Yang San Valley *(1971),* The Wedding Shoes *(1984). His stories have appeared in* Atlantic Monthly, The New Yorker, The Hudson Review, *and* Harper's Bazaar. *Two stories, "From Below the Bridge" (1958) and "Village Wine" (1976), were collected in Martha Foley's* Best American Short Stories. *"Crown Dick" won the PEN Syndicated Short Fiction Project in 1984 and was made into a TV film (PBS).*

Kim had numerous residencies in artists' colonies and two fellowships from the National Endowment for the Arts (NEA). He was awarded the first overseas Korean Literature Prize from the Korean Writers' Association in 1990, as well as a cultural award from his birthplace. He returned to Korea in March 1995 to teach one semester at Korea University and suddenly passed away on April 11, 1995.

RESPONSE ⟳

I wrote before I could write. On the way to school, I entertained myself making up stories. Often I found myself taking the wrong path. The length of each story depended on how long I walked that day. Weekends I "wrote" much longer stories, as I walked six miles to visit my parents in a rural village where my father worked as an administrator of six or seven surrounding villages. At that time I stayed with my grandparents. Later, in America, homesick, I fashioned my fiction from the long, strong fibers of Korean culture.

When American soldiers came to Korea, they looked down on Koreans, and as a Korean, I didn't like it. So I started to write descriptions of Korean village life, Korean customs, for the GIs, and then some educated GI edited my English. And in America, I got so homesick for Korea, I began to write about it. I always write about Korea, especially the poorer people I grew up with. I felt very sad. They used to come to my mother and tell the saddest stories, and I remember them, every one. My memory is always, always good. That's why I write sad stories, rather than cheerful, happy ones about businesspeople, advancing culture, and so on. In that sense, my writing is about the rural area. It's always about old Korea. Through my stories, you can have a glimpse of old Korea, an old Korea that's very peaceful.

I didn't write about the Japanese occupation because the Japanese were more or less city people. They occupied the cities, and they didn't come to the rural areas. At that time, Japanese policemen only once in a while came to rural areas to arrest Koreans, to bother Koreans; but they didn't come often, so in my writing I left them out. I didn't write about toilets, either. That could be considered political writing. I dealt with the pastoral.

I write for myself. There is an audience in me. I often enjoy reading my work, but in 1945 when Americans first came to Korea, I wrote in English for them. My first book was *Moons of Korea*, a study of Korean village life. You see, the thing is—I am a little complex. In a way, as a writer, I can call my writing a song of beauty, but at the same time, I'm a businessman, too. If I want to survive in this culture, then I have to write in English. When I had the luck of selling my first short story, "The Wedding Shoes," I collected about $250 from *Harper's Bazaar*. In those days, $250 was big money. That was beginner's luck. Everybody liked that short story. That's why I wrote in English, because I could sell.

But I studied hard. I was always a good student of English. My high school teacher always wanted us to memorize English lessons. I read Dostoyevsky and Yeats. If sentences are good, then I always memorize. Even now I can remember, "How we had our straight shoes on toward the boundless beautiful blue horizon and wept and wept"—that line was so moving, so I enjoyed it, even "fly . . . butterfly . . . where to fly . . . but I, I'm lost." I remember beautiful sentences.

I used to read Tu Fu, Li Po, and W. B. Yeats. I admire a highly talented Korean story writer, Kim Yoo Jung, who died young in his thirties. This morning before you [Amy Ling] telephoned me, I remembered Kim Yoo Jung's "Camellia Flower" and "Spring Spring" stories. Sometimes his stories make me weep. Some are two-handkerchief stories; some are one-handkerchief. And also, I like *Strayed Bullet*. This is very intense, good writing, a masterpiece. The Korean title is *O Bal Tan*; in English, it's *Strayed Bullet*, translated by Marshall Phil, who taught at Harvard. I went to his office to congratulate him. That's good modern writing—good, deep writing. I enjoy it.

My life has been affected by my reading.

When I was in America, I saw one boy in Maine who reminded me of Dostoyevsky's Idiot. I went to talk with him. He happened to be a rich boy with a mental problem. I became his summer companion. I was hired by his family. From this experience, I wrote "Sheep, Jimmie, and I"; when I wrote "Sheep, Jimmie, and I," of course, I changed their names. I didn't want to hurt their feelings. He was very friendly with me, and every summer for three or four years I went to Maine. I stayed in a gorgeous home and was at the family table every night. I heard every conversation they had. When I stayed in that home, I felt that I had come from the slums almost. They were multimillionaires and gave me time to write. I was lucky in that regard.

Then I started publishing. When the boy's mother saw the "Wedding Shoes" and my picture in *Harper's Bazaar*, she couldn't believe it. She wired me her congratulations right away. And I was a little embarrassed, so when I started to sell stories to *The New Yorker* or *Mademoiselle*, I told them that in the summertime I was busy—I gracefully bowed out. After ten years of writing, I broke into publication in *Harper's Bazaar*. That was what I described in "A Book-Writing Venture," which you [Amy Ling] included in *Visions of America* (ed. Wesley Brown and Amy Ling, 1992).

Am I Asian American? It depends on how you interpret "America." I write about minorities (Korean people) and forgotten people. I never think about Asian American. You know, I'm a little bit of a loner. Essentially, I want to sing my own song; I love to sing songs. I sing only at midnight—even now I sing a song at midnight; you know, a sad, wistful song. And my daughter says, "I don't like your singing at midnight. Keep quiet." And I keep quiet. But essentially, I want to sing my own song, a little sad song, in my own way.

Q: You don't see yourself as part of a group of Asians in America?

I'm Asian American, but uh—critics might say that—but my writing is a little different from other people's writing.

Q: How about Korean American? Do you see yourself as a Korean American writer?

Korean American, uh, maybe—when someone asks me, I introduce myself as Korean American, because . . . I use the Korean language. Some Korean expressions are beautiful. So I use them. Like in "Wedding Shoes," we don't say "sowing wild oats," we say "chasing the spring wind."

Q: That's very poetic. Do you think of yourself as an émigré from Korea, not an immigrant coming to live here permanently, but an émigré, then, a person in exile?

I enjoyed reading a story set in a far-off country, about dark monkeys crying, saying that they are very homesick. I read it and I enjoyed the intense poetry of it. So in that sense, yes: I'm a Korean émigré, yes.

Q: What brought you here, in 1948?

I received a scholarship from Florida, Florida Southern University. I wanted to study a little more. I wrote an academic book, a study of Korean village life, *The Moons of Korea*. I wanted to sell that story, but no one believed that beautiful story. And they didn't want to publish it . . . so with that as background I started to write a short story. I decided to use that Korean village life as background for a fictional story. One of the courses I took at Florida Southern University was Children's Literature. When I saw that there were Japanese children's stories, but there were no Korean stories, I decided to write juvenile stories.

Q: Why did you stay in this country rather than go back to Korea?

The thing is when you start to write, you

keep on writing. Then I told myself, after I finish this story I'll go home. I'd finished, and then I found myself putting off departure. I would write a book, like *Happy Days,* then I had to get it published. And then I would take a tour for three years. Then I started another story. I kept on writing. My writing kept me here. When you write, you don't know time is passing by. Someone said, "Time is the enemy of creation." When I write, I don't know that time is passing. Suddenly I find myself old, and it seems like yesterday when I came to this country. And it seems I'm always thinking about the past.

Q: Are you a citizen now? An American citizen?

Oh, I am, I am a citizen now—because it's easier to travel with an American passport. I became a citizen about twenty years ago.

What brought me here? When people asked me, I said because I received a scholarship, but nowadays I joke about it—I was young and foolish, that's why I came here. Because the best thing maybe would have been to stay in Korea and to teach. I am a little bit of a misfit everywhere I go. Even in America I don't have a car, and for a while, I didn't have a telephone either. If anyone wanted to call me, they had to get in touch with my landlady. Or they'd have to come themselves in a car. Friends would come in their car and ask, "What are you going to do tonight? We have enough food—let's go to my home to have supper." I enjoyed them, even though some of them are Christians. You see, I'm originally Buddhist. So their idea of Christianity I didn't buy, but I enjoyed food so much. I had a great appetite. So that's the way I felt. A lot of people assume that I'm a Christian. But deep inside, I'm not. I prefer Buddhism. It was the religion of my childhood, of my mother. In that sense, I'm little bit of a misfit.

Oh, there are Buddhists in this country, but I don't go to Buddhist temples here. When I go to Korea, I visit a Korean Buddhist temple. I enjoy their surroundings. There, it's not citified.

Q: But if you had stayed in Korea, you would not have been able to play the role you have played, which is to introduce Korean life to American readers, to English readers.

Yes, but the thing is if I had stayed in Korea . . . maybe . . . but I don't want to think about [it]. When you think about it too much, it gets too complicated.

Q: Have you found any particular challenges, in writing for an American audience?

A lot of people think that English writing is difficult, but I'm a daydreamer. When I determined to do something, I always think about the goal, I think I can do it. A lot of people give up, but—once I start something, I have a tendency to finish it.

Q: Have you done any writing in Korean as well?

Yes. After I write in English, I translate my work into Korean. My wife is Korean and she reads Korean. She's a linguist, as well. My wife says, "Oh, you're a Korean, but you don't know Korean well." She also corrects my English spelling. When my translation goes out, she goes back over my Korean expressions. I publish in Korean rather extensively. My book *The Wedding Shoes* in Korean is called *Flower Shoes.* They gave me an overseas Korean literature prize. When I went to my birthplace, they gave me a cultural award.

Q: I liked your story "They Won't Crack It Open" very much and it's one that many readers of Imagining America *(ed. Wesley Brown and Amy Ling, 1991) particularly enjoy. Since it tells of a friendship between a Korean teacher and an American soldier, I wondered if you had much experience with the American military.*

Every story I write is more or less an autobiographical story. Some Koreans who know English read this story and get a kick out of it—because it's so Korean, they think. There are expressions that are exactly folk village customs. It's so humorous.

Q: Did you have much experience with the American military in Korea?

I've had unhappy experiences with the Japanese military. When Japanese gave me military training, I was terrible in that. I did not know how to tie shoes, and all these Japanese soldiers would come over to me, "You're untidy," they'd say and scold me. I don't like the military—I don't like . . . military uniformity. I'm different. The military—I stay away from them.

In Japan, I was unhappy. I stayed three years and a half. During the wartime, the Japanese tried to send me to a coal mine, so I was hiding—in my own house. In the daytime, I wouldn't go out. I read books, always. And at the night, I would go up to the hill. I never went out.

I was in jail in Japan, you know. Because I told them, "You Japanese are obsolete." The Japanese didn't like it. Then they started to insult the Koreans, "You Koreans don't understand our Japanese spirit." I got mad. I almost quarreled with [the man who said that]. Later, a Japanese detective arrested me. And I was real scared. In hindsight, life in prison for a few weeks in Japanese winter gave me a deep insight into certain people. If you're a writer, any experience counts. That's good.

I'm grateful to you for including my short story in *Imagining America* and "Book-Writing Venture" in *Visions of America.* When people tell me they've read my story, I am a little surprised, since I'm a little bit cynical about reading. Nowadays, people don't read. They watch television, mostly. But when they read my work, and they ask if they can include it in another textbook, that's good. And I'm happy.

Any inspiring words for aspiring young writers? I don't give any advice to young Americans. If I give it, I make a joke. I'll say, "People will tell you: 'Oh, you go to Harvard, study English literature there; get a Ph.D. Then you become a writer, and you'll be comfortable.'" I tell them, "You listen to them, then do the exact opposite of the things that they tell you to do." This money culture tries to reduce you to zero. One should assert himself as an individual by singing his own song. Then, you'll become a writer. If you want to be a writer, you must write what you want to write. Sing your own song.

EDITOR'S NOTE: Perhaps in response to my questions about why he didn't write about Korea under Japanese colonial rule, Kim Yong Ik sent me the following chapter from an unpublished novel, *Gourd Hollow Dance,* which gives the dark side of Korean village life in the aftermath of war.

Home Again, 1945

Water Root in the rain, Water Root in the sun—the poplars against the sky—I was home again. In the Tokyo jail, scratches of fingernails, cracks in the cell wall had turned into the waving trees. Warm water in the throat, a little food, at such moments I saw in the scratches and cracks the road to the sky by Water Root.

Released from the jail because of my illness, I had returned to the Hollow. Jin Sam was the only one of my friends home again. I saw him only a few times at the old dock, but I heard about him everywhere I went. He was the leading topic of gossip among the villagers. Jin Sam had run away with folksinger Soyun to the Manchurian wilderness where the Japanese Army was fighting the Chinese. Then a year ago he came home without Soyun but with her little daughter and married my sister Lan, a marriage arranged by my father and his. With the money that he brought from Manchuria, he built a house below Water Root and bought a ferryboat to go from the Hollow to the Harbor. The Japanese Navy in the Harbor, short of boats, confiscated all the large motorboats in the neighboring villages, but not Jin Sam's. Some said his boat was spared because he had a Japanese battalion commander's citation for cooperating with the Japanese Army in Manchuria. The villagers talked about beating him up, but they were afraid of the Japanese officers who saluted him. However, the American planes, often flying over the coast, did not spare Jin Sam's boat, which was eventually bombed and sunk. Avoiding the relatives of the dead crewmen of his boat, he often stayed in the Harbor, but I did not seek him out, seeing my sister only at our father's house.

. . . The night grew chilly. I was about to go into my room when I saw what looked like a small boy, limping hurriedly into the yard to hold himself against the porch pillar. It was Jin Sam. Out of breath, he could not say anything at once. He had no cap on. No wonder he looked like a child.

"Let me talk to you inside the house. In the dark, people are gathering before my house. I slipped out by the back door." He was panting.

"Tell me where Soyun is." I demanded. "If you don't, I will tell everyone where you are."

"Let me go inside first," he begged. In the room I did not light the lamp. I did not want to see him. He cleared his throat many times. "When I went to Manchuria with Soyun . . . Do you have some wine, Yang Ho?" he asked.

I left and returned with a pitcher of wine my father had kept. Jin Sam drank; I did not. He smacked his lips and shook the pitcher to see if there was more. Suddenly, I remembered he had used Soyun to sell wine to the Japanese soldiers. I became angry. "Leave at once. I want to hear nothing. Leave."

"Are you asking your old friend to leave? Your brother-in-law?" he asked and finished the remaining wine. "I left with Soyun to run a wineshop. Why in Manchuria? To make money, yes, but I have always wanted to see the north beyond the Yalu River. You know I loved the Japanese song, 'Border Town.'"

I reached out to slap his face, but my palm landed on the back of his quickly raised hand. "You are talking of songs when you used the small waist of a child in smuggling."

"For her I quit the silk smuggling and had to leave the border town where Koreans lived," he said. He hit my hand sharply. "Can we talk without that hand of yours? After Soyun gave birth to Naja, everyone denied being the father. Soyun was very unhappy. I volunteered to announce that I fathered her girl. Don't tell me I used her child."

I backed away from him and sat, leaning against the wall.

"All right, I admit that with money from smuggling silk, we set up a wineshop near a Japanese army barracks," he resumed angrily. "The soldiers broke bowls, tables, and chairs. Some threatened to hit me when I asked them to pay. The soldiers wanted Soyun, but I ran a wine house, not a girl house. I lost money until the battalion commander became our customer. When the soldiers saw him, many of them started to leave, but we made money from those few quiet customers who remained. In the evening, he brought his shakuhachi flute, and played always the Japanese folk song 'Sakura' sadly—Colonel Oki was a one-song man. Whenever the shop was crowded, he and his aide drank sake in our private room. One summer night like this, after I shielded the kerosene lamps against possible air or guerrilla attacks, Colonel Oki came alone and stayed late, drinking in our room. He was quieter than usual. I boarded up the wine stall, deliberately making loud noises to let him know we were ready to sleep. When he finally left, Soyun did not come out of the room to see him off. She did not rise to clear the wine table but sat without moving. 'How much did he pay?' I asked. She did not answer. Her unfaded lipstick and neat-looking hair assured me that nothing had happened.

"She gave a long, long sigh. 'The colonel has asked to have me. On bent knees he asked me. . . . He said he would be leaving soon for the battleground and would never see me again. His sad face grew into—I don't know what—not gentle, not fierce, but with so much desire, I was frightened. I could not say no to that face, so I told him I would ask you.' Her calm bothered me. Any entertaining house for soldiers had to be approved by the commander. Everything we had was by his approval—the kerosene for the lamps, the sugar and rice rations, all that would be cut off.

"I asked Soyun, 'What do you think? Shall we go home?'

" 'Home?' she asked weakly. 'Do I have a home?' But a soldier, a Japanese soldier, sleeping with her—I could not think of that.

" 'We are going home,' I said. The next day I drank heavily and we did not pack our things. Then I left the wine house and drank some more in a Chinese village."

I sat up straight and shouted, "You didn't shove that flute down his throat? You didn't murder him?"

"I didn't go deep into Manchuria to watch a movie and come home weeping. Jin Sam is not Yang Ho," he shouted back.

After a long pause he resumed his story. "I pushed opened the door. Soyun was alone, her cheek on the wine table, waiting. She did not cry, nor even raise her hand. She looked listless, calm, but her arm was shaking. I heard a ticking sound, and there lay a gold watch and a pile of money. Soyun hid her face. I held her shaking arm, comforting her, 'Oh well, no one else knows. It won't happen again!'

"I counted the money; it was seven hundred yen altogether, new, green money, not the old, shrunken notes you see in the Hollow. I put them in the iron stove where no fire would touch them.

"Before Colonel Oki and his soldiers left for the front, his aide brought the commander's letter of gratitude." Jin Sam took off his trousers and examined the bruises on his legs. "Then a new commander started to come to our wine house and demanded that Soyun sleep with him. This time, the request was very sudden so we knew he had heard of her from Colonel Oki. I drank wine in the Chinese village and returned to comfort Soyun. Several army commanders passed our way; well—money piled up in our iron-stove bank." He halted, as though he expected another outburst from me. All the time I wanted to stop him but couldn't utter a word. He asked, "Are you asleep?" I didn't answer. As his hand felt my foot in the dark, I quickly drew up my knees.

"Once, once—" he stuttered a few times and went on. "While in a Chinese village, I heard earth-shaking explosions. Black smoke rose above the barracks. Chinese were laughing and cheering, 'Ho, ho, Ting ho.' Running away from the Chinese, I bicycled as fast as I could to return to the wine house.

"Faster than forest fire, the whole area of the barracks was burning. I looked for my wineshop but couldn't find a trace of it. Guerrillas had attacked the barracks. An ammunition dump had exploded, killing their own soldiers and setting the fields on fire. The fire had a three-day feast. When it had burned out, I poked among the ashes that had been the wineshop—and found the iron stove and green money still good. Before taking it out, I looked around. There Soyun stood, still barefoot, her hair over her ears—like a ghost among the unburied corpses. Each of us suspected that the other had come back just to look for the money."

Jin Sam didn't go on. I lit the lamp. "You didn't come back with Soyun?" Looking at his eyes, I asked.

"Manchuria was not a place for her child. Soyun told me to take her daughter back to the Hollow and wash my feet in the stream water and marry a Hollow woman who would be good to her daughter. When I promised Soyun to take care of her child, she wept and later disappeared, without taking her share of the stove money." He now blinked as though light was too bright, and he asked, "Anything to eat?"

I went to the kitchen and brought a leftover mixture of more barley and less rice, and kimchi. Eating greedily, he looked curiously at my concise English-Korean dictionary on the shelf. "The language of an occupying army is a meal ticket, you know," he smiled faintly.

The food was gone; licking his empty spoon, he asked for more. I told him that was all the food I had at home. He nodded weakly and knowingly as a good son of a poor farmer should, then he turned to the wall and slept immediately.

Jin Sam asleep looked even smaller, one hand serving as a pillow and the other deep into his groin. This was the friend I remembered from a long time ago. I slipped my pillow under his head and covered him with a quilt. I left quietly to tell my sister Jin Sam was with me.

~~~~~~

From Elegy by Kim Udam (Mrs. Kim Yong Ik), April 19, 1995

His universe has been closed; his shell is now resting at a sunny hillside family plot near his beautiful hometown. From not too far down, the blue oh-so-blue inland sea sends up the faintly sea-scented breeze toward the hill. The pines green oh-so-green stand sentry on the hill. And the two are singing an eternal lullaby in harmony on that sunny hill.

He is now with his truly beloved.

He often talked about a poem by T. S. Eliot, "the end of a journey is to arrive at the place where it began, as if for the first time." He was yearning to do just that, longing for his childhood home.

His song:

I left my hometown long long ago,
I blew a willow whistle in spring,
I flew the big-eye kite in winter,
Those were the happy days.
Those were the happy days . . .

Photo courtesy Mitsuye Yamada

Mitsuye Yamada

~~~~~~

POET

Born in Kyushu, Japan, in 1923, Mitsuye Yamada grew up in Seattle, Washington. During World War II, she was interned in Camp Minidoka in Idaho. Her chapbook Camp Notes and Other Poems *(1976) recounts this experience, which profoundly shaped her commitment to human rights and peace issues and to her work as a member of the board of directors of Amnesty International USA (1987–1991). She earned a B.A. in English and art from New York University in 1947 and an M.A. from the University of Chicago, and she studied linguistics at Columbia University. From 1966 to 1989, Yamada taught at Cypress College in Orange County, California. Although "retired," she continues to teach poetry workshops, Asian American literature, and women's studies classes as a visiting professor in southern California colleges and universities.*

Yamada is the author of two books of poetry: Camp Notes *(1976) and* Desert Run: Poems and Stories *(1988). She has edited three anthologies of work by women writers of color:* The Webs We Weave *(1986),* Sowing Ti Leaves *(1990), and* Scaling the Chord *(forthcoming). Her work has appeared in numerous anthologies; her poems and short stories have been translated into Japanese, and she and poet Nellie Wong were the subjects of a documentary film,* Mitsuye and Nellie: Two American Poets *(1981).*

RESPONSE ⌐

My father, an Issei (Japanese immigrant) pioneer in Seattle, Washington, was the first poet I ever knew. Around 1930, he founded a poetry society called the Senryu Kai, of which he was president until the outbreak of World War II. The poets, about twenty in number, met at our house every month to compose and discuss poetry, sitting around the long table in our dining room. As a child, I was especially intrigued by the calligrapher, who brushed the poems with black ink on a long butcher paper tacked on the wall as the poets would recite their work. After all the poems were written up, there followed a discussion. Someone would say, "Number twelve is *suteki* (spectacular)," and give his or her (there was only one woman in the group through all those years) reasons why. The calligrapher would draw a circle in red over the chosen poem.

Someone would agree with this person, and a second circle would be drawn around the first one. Another poem would be chosen for a short discussion. Soon, about half the senryu poems on the wall would have multiple red circles over them. The one with the most circles was declared the "winner." I grasped only a word or two in each of the poems and about half the discussion going on, but I did understand that poems are written somewhat spontaneously, about everyday matters. This must have been my "genesis" as a poet.

My interest in writing and literature led me to major in English in high school and college. Unfortunately, I discarded very quickly whatever lessons I had absorbed from my father's group and began to write formulaic "academic" poems and objectified prose. In retrospect, I can only conjecture that I learned poetry is written metaphorically about "large" subjects. It was only after publishing the short poems I had written in the camp in Minidoka during World War II that I became aware of my father's role in my life as a poet.

Most poets claim to write foremost for themselves. I am no exception, but in the be-

ginning I wrote stories and poems for my father, for his approval. The lesson of my father's Senryu Kai (that poems are written "in community") must have remained in my subconscious, for later on, in my creative writing classes in high school, I wrote for my classmates. However, I kept a journal in camp, which I showed no one. (My father was incarcerated by the FBI and was held in a POW camp for the duration of the war.) These "camp poems" were eventually published in *Camp Notes and Other Poems* decades later, in 1976.

My work was first recognized and accepted by several women's groups in this country in the late 1960s. What I was saying resonated in their struggle to gain their place in this patriarchal society. The women's movement of those early years has been the most significant factor in bringing together women of all cultures, nationally and globally. At first we were "tokens" (and in many respects we still are), but it was the breakthrough that I needed. The organizers in the women's movement gave me a platform by asking me to read at their functions and created a receptive audience of women for my work. It was they who saw the need for recognition of more ethnically diverse voices within the movement. For instance, in the 1970s when a filmmaker, Allie Light, and poet, the late Lynn Lonidier, could find no films about Asian American women writers for their festival of films about women writers, they decided to give the audience live performances by Asian American women poets. It was this event that gave birth to the film *Mitsuye and Nellie; Two American Poets*, by Allie Light and her husband, Irving Saraf. During those early years after the publication of my first book of poems, most of the critical reviews appeared in small women's publications. I am also grateful for the encouragement of gay poets who read my work on public radio and acknowledged my poems during their own readings.

Poets write for themselves for many different reasons. I often write poems when I am trying to make "sense" out of what I am feeling or what is happening around me. I try to deal with the many contradictions that have become part of my life and tell the truth, as honestly as I know, about how my past clings to me and informs my present in spite of myself. My writings then become a public "sorting out." However, the poems *are* written and then published in hopes that, by chance, the words may resonate in some person "out there." In that sense, writing may be a way of looking for a community. I feel a great sense of satisfaction and pleasure when I hear from someone in some (to me) remote area of the country.

I spend too much time writing internal essays or letters to the editor on current issues, writing policy papers, memos, and so forth, in connection with Amnesty International (AI) or women's groups that I am actively involved in. Because one of my brothers is intensely involved in issues concerning political prisoners in the United States (my Amnesty work is international, since AI has a policy not to work on one's own country), I am becoming concerned about these prisoners, who are no longer just names but personal friends serving life sentences for their political activities. These activities on behalf of political prisoners keep me from doing "my creative work." I seem to feel guilty if I do (get distracted from my writings) or if I don't. I periodically analyze this part of my life, because I am plagued by the thought that these activities keep me from my "real writing." Somehow, I have developed a habit of mind through these years that poems of intensely personal matters are written for oneself and essays of a political nature are addressed to specific audiences so that issues can be raised and brought forward

for discussion. It is the age-old issue of separation of art and politics, or the quarrel between the "universal" and the "particular" that some of us who went through the educational system from the 1930s to the 1950s are still saddled with.

Writers that we are exposed to very early in our lives remain with us forever. (There might be a pitch here for more of us Asian American writers to write for children of all ages.) I still love Christina Rossetti's poems, for sentimental reasons. My father gave me a collection of her poems when I was about twelve years old. I loved the feel of her words, the voluptuousness of her images. I also treasured the beautiful soft leather cover, the title embossed on it in gold letters and gilt-edged pages. It was discarded, apparently, with other personal possessions when we were evacuated from the West Coast. Only a few lines I had memorized as a child remain with me.

My favorite writers during my undergraduate years at New York University were Gertrude Stein and William Blake. Though I didn't always understand what Stein's writings were about, I was fascinated by her experiments with language and remember attending a rare theater production of *The Mother of Us All* (1947), an opera which is her collaborative work with the composer, Virgil Thomson. As a nursing mother, I read Gertrude Stein's poetry and prose work "A Rose Is a Rose" aloud to my babies. I suppose I should mention the poets and writers I did admire at one time and spent many, many hours studying: Shakespeare, John Keats, Henry James, and T. S. Eliot. I still appreciate them to some extent for teaching me something about craft.

I have been an avid but passive reader for as long as I can remember, but it was only in the past three decades that I became a different kind of reader. As a literature student, my usual habit was to compare writing styles:

this is like a Faulkner, a Whitman, a Frost, a Robinson Jeffers, and so forth. When I was a full-time mother, my four children and I took weekly trips to the local library, where I first discovered Tillie Olsen's "Tell Me a Riddle" (1961) in an O. Henry collection of short stories. I had never heard of Tillie Olsen, but I knew immediately that I wanted to write like her. Because the circumstances of my life at the time threatened to overwhelm me, the story had an electrifying effect on me.

I had been told about a year before that I had terminal emphysema. At the time, my four children ranged from two to twelve years old, and my mother, whom I never got along with throughout my growing up years, had come to live with us. My only thought was that I needed to write something for my children so that they would not forget me. I wanted to prepare them for a life with their father and my mother. As it turned out, seven years later I learned that I had been misdiagnosed, and I never did learn to "write like Tillie Olsen." But somehow I managed to find my own voice, even after the urgency to "leave something concrete for the children" had passed. How can I ever forget my debt to this great woman for publishing her powerful story and for becoming a source of inspiration to me at a very critical period of my life?

Since then, there were many women poets whom I became aware of because they reached out to me in ways that the traditional poets I had been studying for years had not. Among those that I most admired were Joy Kogawa, Alta, and Audre Lorde. I read Joy Kogawa's poetry in the *Chicago Review.* Her poems were unaccountably included with translated poems by Japanese poets in a special edition of the journal titled "Anthology of Modern Japanese Poets." I remember her poems vividly because of what seemed to me the oddity of finding this Japanese Canadian Nisei's work in this collection. [A Nisei is the son or daughter of Japanese immigrants, educated in the new country.] I was particularly struck by her poem "What Do I Remember of the Evacuation," because I had never known anyone else writing poems about the "evacuation." I now admire the artistry and music in her novel, *Obasan* (1981).

Alta was introduced to me in the late 1960s. I had never met a poet to whom hardly any subject matter was off limits. I admired her openness and indomitable spirit. In addition, she gave me the courage to publish my first book, *Camp Notes and Other Poems.* Audre Lorde was another writer whose fire and political force stirred me. Her personal courage and the clarity of her vision still move me when I think of her. I will always treasure my personal relationship with her.

I see myself as a woman writer first of all; second, a woman writer of color; and third, an Asian American woman writer. As a small child, in the context of my own family, the first awareness was that I was a girl, different from my three brothers. Little girls grow up with acute awareness of their femaleness: You are a girl, you must talk in a soft voice, sit with your knees closed and ankles crossed, come inside before dark, wait until everyone else is served. On the other hand, as the only girl, I was pampered and "looked after." My brothers pulled me on the wagon, held my hand to cross the street, covered me with a towel at the beach.

I began to suspect that "men think differently than women" when I joined a small group of poets in a writing workshop during those "lost seven years." (I was in need of something to keep my mind occupied and also took up sculpting!) It was during the Vietnam War, and the poets, mostly men, were antiwar activists and budding environmentalists. They brought poems full of images of the woman's body as metaphor for their antiwar and pro-environment poems. They argued that they were demonstrating the brutality of war and the shame of environmental destruction, but I felt that if metaphors were supposed to "clarify" the image, these attacks on the woman's body were not working for me. "These images have been around since *Beowulf,*" they claimed. In those days, I did not have the vocabulary to argue with them. I knew only that there was something fundamentally wrong with their thinking, and that it was more than my "prissiness" about sexual matters that was making me uncomfortable with their writings.

When I discovered a community of women writers whose words spoke to me, I knew that I was not alone. When I met some Asian American women writers, I knew they were my sisters. I became aware of women's issues before I was aware that ethnicity was a "problem" in this country; this, oddly enough, in spite of having been thrown into a concentration camp during World War II. My parents, especially my father, protected us from the outside world and led us to believe that we could do anything in this democratic society. Before World War II, and perhaps even after, in spite of the fact that he was arrested by the FBI and labeled "dangerous enemy alien," my father was a true idealist who believed in the American dream and instilled in us the notion that the government will respond to its citizens. (The wartime behavior of the U.S. government he saw as an aberration.) As a child, if I complained about anything (the city bus schedule, for instance), he said, "Well, don't complain to me, write a letter to City Hall."

I became an American citizen in 1955. The oddity of my having to become naturalized because I was "unnatural" before gave me pause. By that time, I had spent most of my thirty-some years in this country and considered myself thoroughly "Americanized." My invisibility as a Japanese American in American culture occurred to me with unusual force at that time. I am an Asian American woman writer all rolled into one, after all.

"Authentic" Asian American sensibility? Does that imply that there is only one way an Asian American *should* respond to certain facets of American culture? In that case, the answer is no; but of course, there most certainly is an Asian American sensibility. It could simply be a state of knowing that one is an Asian, or it may be a consciousness or an awareness that one has had an ancestor who lived somewhere in Asia at one time. Insofar as "an attitude" (even unconsciously positive or negative) toward Asians in White America exists, we respond to it in many different ways, depending on our past experiences. For some of us, the sensibility might extend to the acute awareness that White America had considered Asians unworthy of citizenship in the United States until 1954. We were almost the last among others who were similarly excluded: the American Indians, Africans, women, the criminals, and the insane. Now, only the latter two remain excluded. Many Asians in America are aware that Asians were and still may be considered (unlike the Europeans) unassimilable. Even a person of mixed ancestry who is "passing" because she or he does not "look Asian" must respond emotionally and defensively in some way to the plethora of Asian stereotypes that exists in American culture. This internal response is the Asian American sensibility.

Having said this, there *is* a difference in sensibility between more recent Asian immigrants and Asian Americans. Asian Americans have a greater responsibility in convincing the mainstream culture that we are not exotics from another country trying to assimilate into this "host culture" but are homegrown and have every right as Americans to speak out.

There are several pressing burdens we face today: (1) Asian American writers are often relegated to being "representative voices" of all Asian Americans; (2) Asian American writers have a sense that they are expected to write only about Asian American issues; (3) Asian American writings about their "place" in the United States are often considered to be historical or sociological writings rather than "art," and therefore aesthetically inferior; (4) in the past, Asian Americans themselves have continued to simulate "mainstream" attitudes and have not fully supported their own writers; and finally (5) as we push for greater solidarity (e.g., by trying to establish more Asian American Studies programs in colleges and universities), there has been a backlash, for we are again being accused of being "separatist."

No writer should be expected to represent a group of people as diverse as Asian Americans. We are not a monolithic group, and more writings by different ethnic Asians are needed to dispel this notion. More writings by new immigrants themselves, as well as by descended Asian Americans, are needed to close the gap between these two subgroups in Asia America.

Asian American writers face existing attitudes that impact on the acceptance of their work. During the 1970s and 1980s, when Nellie Wong, Merle Woo, and I, billed as "Asian American Women Speak Out," did readings together, we were asked why we write about the Chinese, Korean, or Japanese American experience. Why don't we write about "ordinary people"? We lack outlets and an audience because the Asian American experience is still considered to be "different" and not part of the greater American tradition. While it appears that we are expected to write only about Asian American issues, when we do, we are perceived as being separatist.

The notion that political issues in poems reduce the aesthetic value of the work is still prevalent in literary circles. This makes being overtly political difficult for many ethnic writers. The division of politics and art is an age-old issue with artists. Fortunately, this has been changing in the past two decades.

The responsibility that Asian American writers face today is to tell the truth about Asians in the United States, even at the risk of causing discomfort in one's own community as well as in the dominant society. We, the Asian American community, have not been kind to our own writers who have been on the cutting edge of speaking about our experiences. *No-No Boy* (by John Okada, 1957), for example, was not generally accepted by Japanese Americans for decades after it was published, because of "negative portrayals" of the Japanese that we do not want to acknowledge.

When a writer as distinguished and "liberal" as Arthur Schlesinger begins to warn America of the dangers of separatism, and as more "assimilated and successful" Asian Americans begin to agree with him, we have a problem that will not easily go away.

Asian American writers have challenged all the points raised above, but there are risks involved in doing so. The risks the Asian American writers face in telling the truth about their own culture may not be any different from those encountered by other ethnic American writers: the risk of being accused of exposing "dirty laundry" in one's culture and thereby contributing to the prejudice against Asians in the country. There is the risk of playing into the hands of the dominant culture, with all its prejudices. The challenge is to uncompromisingly tell what has to be told, regardless of the risks.

Have we been commodified, exoticized? This is a disturbing question. Why do we ask such questions of each other? They give credence to the "common beliefs" of the "dominant society" and codify them, exactly what we are trying to avoid. Most Asian American writers grapple with these "common beliefs" within ourselves, because if they exist in the "dominant society," they exist in us.

I definitely think this a particularly receptive moment for Asian American writers. Asians and Asian Americans, recent immigrants and longtime residents and citizens alike, are becoming more attuned to each other's situations than they were even ten years ago. As recent immigrants emerge to write about their experiences, I feel a hope for a more common ground of acceptance. The logical order may be that first we accept ourselves, then we are accepted by our local communities, then by the larger community, and ultimately by the global community. But very often, the process is the reverse. We need to support and promote Asian American writers who do not stereotype us further.

Asian American writers are beginning to write for themselves, for each other, as we search for the commonality of our roots and define the condition of our lives as Asian Americans. We are no longer simply in the business of explaining ourselves for acceptance by the "dominant" culture.

My advice to young Asian American poets—take yourself seriously as a poet and aspire to be as great a poet as you can. Seek out other aspiring poets with a vision similar to yours, and keep a conversation going among yourselves. Remember, you are part of a continuum in the great American literary tradition, and you have a historical responsibility for its qualitative growth.

All writers, especially ethnic American writers because our experiences are not reflected in the general culture around us, need the affirmation of at least one, maybe two kindred souls. On a more practical note, you need to encourage each other to send your works out to publications. Do not be afraid of rejections. Remember that just because your poem was not acceptable to some editor with a limited vision, that doesn't mean the poem is not worthy of publication. On the other hand, being published doesn't mean, necessarily, that the poem is great. But taking the risk of opening your poems up to public scrutiny is a good beginning.

A young student asked me recently, "How do I know that my poems are good?" I don't know whether or not my own poems are good. I know only that my experiences as an Asian American poet must be told, and that we must be heard. I know that our growing collective voices are important in the context of American culture. We must become more of a presence on that landscape. Toward that end, we must continue writing, writing, writing.

That Man

Eyes attentive
heads nodding
she in a warm glow
after her last poem
smiles.
That man in the last row
raises his hand
from a crumpled

sheet of paper
reads:

I am touched by your camp poems
about the Japanese American Internment
such powerful images
so tragic, poignant
full of nostalgia.

She leans forward—yes? yes?
That man continues:
I for one am ashamed of what *my* government
has done to *your* people
but we have already apologized to you
haven't we?
Why so much anger after all these years?
why not forgive and forget
why dwell on the past
why not let bygones be bygones
and get on with your life? And why
why do you write only about
the Asian American experience?
why if you want to belong
why not write about
the human condition of
ordinary people?

In Some Countries

In some countries poets are
taken seriously in high places
and writing poems
may be a crime.
In these countries
poems are cryptograms
codes to be skinned and probed
offending poets like Mila Aguilar
are arrested and tortured
undercover bloodhounds
expose metaphors.

In some countries
writing poems
is deadly business.

In my country
poets are free
to read poems in bookstores,
cafes, bars and other low places
Trotted out as window dressing
at presidential inaugurations
But most of the time poets could be
speaking in tongues
about truth and beauty
In my country poets
like Pat Parker
are ignored to death.

Diana Chang

NOVELIST AND POET

Primarily a novelist, Diana Chang has also published poetry and short stories and exhibited her paintings. Born in New York to a Chinese father and Eurasian mother, she was taken to China as an infant and educated in American schools in Shanghai; she returned to the United States for college. She has lived in the New York area ever since. Chang has taught creative writing at Barnard College in New York, edited the American Pen, *and worked in publishing. She has received numerous awards, including a Fulbright Fellowship, a John Hay Whitney Opportunity Fellowship, and a grant from the New York State Council on the Arts.*

Her first novel, The Frontiers of Love *(1956; 1995), explored the identities of three young Eurasians living in Shanghai at the end of World War II. Her other novels include* A Woman of Thirty *(1959),* A Passion for Life *(1961),* The Only Game in Town *(1963),* Eye to Eye *(1974), and* A Perfect Love *(1978). Chang has published three poetry chapbooks:* The Horizon Is Definitely Speaking *(1982),* What Matisse Is After *(1985), and* Earth, Water, Light *(1991). Her stories and poems have appeared in many anthologies.*

RESPONSE 〰

It is hard to know where to begin when considering identity, one's own, that is. We know who *They* are—sure we do. And certainly they think they know who *We* are.

Almost anything you say about identity is an oversimplification. I'm no pundit, and many others have explored aspects of our elusive Asian American identity exceedingly well. Take, for example, Mitsuye Yamada's and Stewart Ikeda's contributions to this very book of Amy Ling's—I admire their articulateness and clarity about our condition; about our past in this country; about multiculturalism and where it stands now, though where it "straddles" now may be a more accurate way of putting it. I have been enlightened and enriched by so many people's consideration of Asian Americanness in what I have read and heard over many years.

Interestingly, here we are engaged in defining our differences when all of us are—on the global scene—growing more and more alike. In mainland China, even in an obscure town like Lijiang in Yunnan Province, teenagers dance to rock music in discos and get into trouble with drugs. In an Australian film, a mirror of current life, folks in drag traverse the outback in a bus called Priscilla and encounter Aborigines who take this White minority in stride. What the world was coming to has arrived. Everywhere is littered with Coke bottles, sandwashed knockoffs of Calvin Klein jeans, the machinery and obsolescent detritus of technology, and a shared loss, perhaps a nostalgia, for what used to be, and often never was.

Being neither one thing nor the other, I'm confusing and confusable, but not perplexed. Am I neither-nor or both? I prefer both. But no real Chinese takes me for Chinese. They can't be hoodwinked. Even my body language is suspect. Yet I can't pretend to be more Chinese than I am, or less American.

I hear I am a Chinese American novelist and poet. But if one belongs to one's language (verbal and body), I must be an American writer who sometimes, not always, draws on her ethnic background. (Of my six published novels only two draw on my own

identity; and of my many short stories and poems, perhaps ten in all.) Yet to be accurate, this statement must be qualified too.

I not only spent part of my childhood in China but was also raised by a Eurasian mother and a Westernized Chinese father. My actual identity, then, is more particular than the term *Chinese American* may suggest. I am making the point that a member of a minority is as much an individual as someone of the majority, a fact that will not be surprising or news to any of us Asian Americans. (I hope, however, *They,* those Others I mentioned in my first paragraph, will read this, too.) Individuals may be a bother, but it is a serious writer's business to remind us of them and to subscribe to their differences.

I realize you know all of this backward and forward, and I go on like this only when I am asked to consider identity. I also realize that my reflections on ethnicity aren't "collective" or ideological and therefore probably are not politically useful.

In preparing to answer Amy Ling's excellent questions, at first I intended to look up various talks I've given—say, at an MLA event in Washington, D.C., or at the Hilton Hotel in New York City—or to reread remarks I've made in published interviews, but something in me balks at going over old ground, especially when it's my own. I seem to use up where I've once been, what I once felt, saying what I did then.

Therefore, I'll be less thorough and more personal. I am a multicultural individual, and would be even if my background were not Chinese, even if I did not live my life in the United States. In Hong Kong, in Beijing, in Bombay, in Beirut, in Sydney, in London, in Paris, in Madagascar, I would be/am a multicultural soul. And these days, so is almost everyone else, whether they realize it or not, want it or not. The mass media; the corporate hegemony; the import/export of ideas, attitudes, lifestyles and technology; the porousness of even closed societies—because of faxes, E-mail, and the like—these affect our lives and minds and values, for better and for worse.

Let me come clean on two counts. I was in the doghouse once. My first novel, *The Frontiers of Love,* originally published by Random House, aroused the ire and condemnation of several literary Asian Americans, the group who defined our condition with a groundbreaking anthology, *Aiiieeeee!* (ed. Jeffery P. Chan et al., 1974). My book was misread as having to do with growing up and living as a minority person in this country, when what I wrote was about three young Eurasians (people of mixed race) living in Shanghai, China. It was about the Eurasian identity problem and not about ethnicity in the United States. The mainstream press accepted the book (to many rave reviews) as a literary novel only but also seemed to miss a point or two, such as what it queries—national, racial, class, and gender categories.

Recently, the University of Washington Press in Seattle reissued *The Frontiers of Love* in a trade paperback. Shirley Geok-lin Lim's erudite, postmodern introduction to this edition is much more than a vindication—so welcome to me—of the novel. Among other perspicacious features of her critique, it offers several ways of reading and of teaching the book.

And Frank Chin, one of the editors of *Aiiieeeee!* who may not remember that he had threatened to "badmouth" me "from coast to coast" in his then-youthful zeal, quite unexpectedly made an about-face two or three years ago. He now declares that my book was "prescient." I am charmed by this reversal and favorable assessment, and by the evidence that he is reasonable and pervious to different and new realities. There *are* other stripes of Chinese Americans, other kinds of Asian American experiences. We cannot be stereotyped. I am relieved and delighted to have been reinstated into the fold of Asian American literature.

I've never been a spokesperson and cannot hope to be representative of any group. I'm not an "opinion" person. The characters I create in my novels and short stories do have opinions. They have to, to be vivid, to fulfill their function in the work.

To me, as a person and as a writer, nothing human is alien. In fact, my own frames of reference are diverse enough to make me feel almost amorphous at times, seeing and empathizing with both sides of almost any question; susceptible to character and personality, to other people's consciousnesses, to their situations, to their plights and triumphs. These matters are not ideological, and political correctness or incorrectness does not apply. (In one respect, I find that ideology often resembles fashion—in its dictates, nothing is more old-fashioned than the recently out-of-date.)

As F. Scott Fitzgerald said, and I am paraphrasing, a novelist or playwright must be able to hold two opposing points of view without cracking up. He wrote this in his book *The Crack-Up* (1956). I haven't cracked up yet, being able to entertain the thought that everyone is right for him- or herself. We all have our reasons. Incidentally, as a writer, it is helpful to bear this evenhandedness in mind in order to create necessary conflict between characters in a novel or play.

To change the subject now, and at the risk of being in the doghouse again, I'll venture to say that self-esteem must be achieved in several ways. One of them, of course, is through self-definition and self-assertion, through knowledge of and identification with our ethnic backgrounds and cultures, which lead to pride in one's racial and gender identities. But these are a partial measure, and categorizing and separatism should be avoided. Each individual must find him- or herself in personal achievement, *and* it is society's job to make that possible through educational and job opportunities.

It's another way of saying what Mary McCarthy once remarked, if I remember it correctly: "Instead of looking for oneself, one must create oneself." It's the opportunity to do that—for everyone—that one must struggle for politically.

As a member of a minority group, I find that the challenge lies in not allowing oneself to be defined by others—either by the majority or by people of different persuasions within one's own collective group. Don't lend yourself to their idea of you, if what they see is false and limiting. The challenge is not simple or easy, but then, what is? However, in this life we undertake, almost everything turns out to be surpassingly interesting.

The Oriental Contingent

Connie couldn't remember whose party it was, whose house. She had an impression of kerosene lamps on brown wicker tables, of shapes talking in doorways. It was summer, almost the only time Connie has run into her since, too, and someone was saying, "You must know Lisa Mallory."

"I don't think so."

"She's here. You must know her."

Later in the evening, it was someone else who introduced her to a figure perched on the balustrade of the steps leading to the lawn where more shapes milled. In stretching out a hand to shake Connie's, the figure almost fell off sideways. Connie pushed her back upright onto her perch and, peering, took in the fact that Lisa Mallory had a Chinese face. For a long instant, she felt nonplused, and was rendered speechless.

But Lisa Mallory was filling in the silence. "Well, now, Connie Sung," she said, not enthusiastically but with a kind of sophisticated interest. "I'm not in music myself, but Paul Wu's my cousin. Guilt by association!" She laughed. "No-tone music, I call his. He studied with John Cage, Varèse, and so forth."

Surprised that Lisa knew she was a violinist, Connie murmured something friendly, wondering if she should simply ask outright, "I'm sure I should know, but what do you do?" but she hesitated, taking in her appearance instead, while Lisa went on with, "It's world-class composing. Nothing's wrong with the level. But it's hard going for the layman, believe me."

Lisa Mallory wore a one-of-a-kind kimono dress, but it didn't make her look Japanese at all, and her hair was drawn back tightly in a braid which stood out from close to the top of her head horizontally. You could probably lift her off her feet by grasping it, like the handle of a pot.

"You should give a concert here, Connie," she said, using her first name right away, Connie noticed, like any American. "Lots of culturati around." Even when she wasn't actually speaking, she pursued her own line of thought actively and seemed to find herself mildly amusing.

"I'm new to the area," Connie said, deprecatingly. "I've just been a weekend guest, actually, till a month ago."

"It's easy to be part of it. Nothing to it. I should know. You'll see."

"I wish it weren't so dark," Connie found herself saying, waving her hand in front of her eyes as if the night were a veil to brush aside. She recognized in herself that intense need to see, to see into fellow Asians, to fathom them. So far, Lisa Mallory had not given her enough clues, and the darkness itself seemed to be interfering.

Lisa dropped off her perch. "It's important to be true to oneself," she said. "Keep the modern stuff out of your repertory. Be romantic. Don't look like that! You're best at the romantics. Anyhow, take it from me. I know. And I like what I like."

Released by her outspokenness, Connie laughed and asked, "I'm sure I should know, but what is it that you do?" She was certain Lisa would say something like, "I'm with a public relations firm." "I'm in city services."

But she replied, "What do all Chinese excel at?" Not as if she'd asked a rhetorical question, she waited, then answered herself. "Well, aren't we all physicists, musicians, architects, or in software?"

At that point a voice broke in, followed by a large body which put his arms around both women, "The Oriental contingent! I've got to break this up."

Turning, Lisa kissed him roundly, and said over her shoulder to Connie, "I'll take him away before he tells us we look alike!"

They melted into the steps below, and Connie, feeling put off balance and somehow slow-witted, was left to think over her new acquaintance.

"Hello, Lisa Mallory," Connie Sung always said on the infrequent occasions when they ran into one another. She always said "Hello, Lisa Mallory" with a shyness she did not understand in herself. It was strange, but they had no mutual friends except for Paul Wu, and Connie had not seen him in ages. Connie had no one of whom to ask her questions. But sometime soon, she'd be told Lisa's maiden name. Sometime she'd simply call her Lisa. Sometime what Lisa did with her life would be answered.

Three, four years passed, with their running into one another at receptions and openings, and still Lisa Mallory remained an enigma. Mildly amused herself, Connie wondered if other people, as well, found her inscrutable. But none of her American friends (though, of course, Lisa and she were Americans, too, she had to remind herself), none of their

Caucasian friends seemed curious about backgrounds. In their accepting way, they did not wonder about Lisa's background, or about Connie's or Paul Wu's. Perhaps they assumed they were all cut from the same cloth. But to Connie, the Asians she met were unread books, books she never had the right occasion or time to fully pursue.

She didn't even see the humor in her situation—it was such an issue with her. The fact was she felt less, much less, sure of herself when she was with real Chinese.

As she was realizing this, the truth suddenly dawned on her. Lisa Mallory never referred to her own background because it was more Chinese than Connie's, and therefore of a higher order. She was tact incarnate. All along, she had been going out of her way not to embarrass Connie. Yes, yes. Her assurance was definitely upper crust (perhaps her father had been in the diplomatic service), and her offhand didacticness, her lack of self-doubt, was indeed characteristically Chinese-Chinese. Connie was not only impressed by these traits, but also put on the defensive because of them.

Connie let out a sigh—a sigh that follows the solution to a nagging problem . . . Lisa's mysteriousness. But now Connie knew only too clearly that her own background made her decidedly inferior. Her father was a second-generation gynecologist who spoke hardly any Chinese. Yes, inferior and totally without recourse.

Of course, at one of the gatherings, Connie met Bill Mallory, too. He was simply American, maybe Catholic, possibly lapsed. She was not put off balance by him at all. But most of the time he was away on business, and Lisa cropped up at functions as single as Connie.

Then one day, Lisa had a man in tow—wiry and tall, he looked Chinese from the Shantung area, or perhaps from Beijing, and his styled hair made him appear vaguely artistic.

"Connie, I'd like you to meet Eric Li. He got out at the beginning of the detente, went to Berkeley, and is assimilating a mile-a-minute," Lisa said, with her usual irony. "Bill found him and is grooming him, though he came with his own charisma."

Eric waved her remark aside. "Lisa has missed her calling. She was born to be in PR," he said, with an accent.

"Is that what she does?" Connie put in at once, looking only at him. "Is that her profession?"

"You don't know?" he asked, surprised.

Though she was greeting someone else, Lisa turned and answered, "I'm a fabrics tycoon, I think I can say without immodesty." She moved away and continued her conversation with the other friend.

Behind his hand, he said, playfully, as though letting Connie in on a secret, "Factories in Hongkong and Taipei, and now he's—Bill, that is—is exploring them on the mainland."

"With her fabulous contacts over there!" Connie exclaimed, now seeing it all. "Of course, what a wonderful business combination they must make."

Eric was about to utter something, but stopped, and said flatly, "I have all the mainland contacts, even though I was only twenty when I left, but my parents . . ."

"How interesting," Connie murmured lamely. "I see," preoccupied as she was with trying to put two and two together.

Lisa was back and said without an introduction, continuing her line of thought, "You two look good together, if I have to say so myself. Why don't you ask him to one of your concerts? And you, Eric, you're in America now, so don't stand on ceremony, or you'll be out in left field." She walked away with someone for another drink.

Looking uncomfortable, but recovering himself with a smile, Eric said, "Lisa makes me feel more Chinese than I am becoming—it is her directness, I suspect. In China, we'd say she is too much like a man."

At which Connie found herself saying, "She makes me feel *less* Chinese."

"Less!"

"Less Chinese than she is."

"That is not possible," Eric said, with a shade of contempt—for whom? Lisa or Connie? He barely suppressed a laugh, cold as Chinese laughter could be.

Connie blurted out, "I'm a failed Chinese. Yes, and it's to you that I need to say it." She paused and repeated emphatically, "I am a failed Chinese." Her heart was beating quicker, but she was glad to have got that out, a confession and a definition that might begin to free her. "Do you know you make me feel that, too? You've been here only about ten years, right?"

"Right, and I'm thirty-one."

"You know what I think? I think it's harder for a Chinese to do two things."

At that moment, an American moved in closer, looking pleased somehow to be with them.

She continued, "It's harder for us to become American than, say, for a German, and it's also harder not to remain residually Chinese, even if you are third generation."

Eric said blandly, "Don't take yourself so seriously. You can't help being an American product."

Trying to be comforting, the American interjected with, "The young lady is not a product, an object. She is a human being, and there is no difference among peoples that I can see."

"I judge myself both as a Chinese and as an American," Connie said.

"You worry too much," Eric said, impatiently. Then he looked around and though she wasn't in sight, he lowered his voice. "She is what she is. I know what she is. But she avoids going to Hongkong. She avoids it."

Connie felt turned around. "Avoids it?"

"Bill's in Beijing right now. She's here. How come?"

"I don't know," Connie replied, as though an answer had been required of her.

"She makes up many excuses, reasons. Ask her. Ask her yourself," he said, pointedly.

"Oh, I couldn't do that. By the way, I'm going on a concert tour next year in three cities—Shanghai, Beijing and Nanjing," Connie said. "It'll be my first time in China."

"Really! You must be very talented to be touring at your age," he said, genuinely interested for the first time. Because she was going to China, or because she now came across as an over-achiever, even though Chinese American?

"I'm just about your age," she said, realizing then that maybe Lisa Mallory had left them alone purposely.

"You could both pass as teenagers!" the American exclaimed.

Two months later, she ran into Lisa again. As usual, Lisa began in the middle of her own thoughts. "Did he call?"

"Who? Oh. No, no."

"Well, it's true he's been in China the last three weeks with Bill. They'll be back this weekend."

Connie saw her opportunity. "Are you planning to go to China yourself?"

For the first time, Lisa seemed at a loss for words. She raised her shoulders, then let them drop. Too airily, she said, "You know, there's always Paris. I can't bear not to go to Paris, if I'm to take a trip."

"But you're Chinese. You *have* been to China, you came from China originally, didn't you?"

"I could go to Paris twice a year, I love it so," Lisa said. "And then there's London, Florence, Venice."

"But—but your business contacts?"

"*My* contacts? Bill, he's the businessman who makes the contacts. Always has. I take care of the New York office, which is a considerable job. We have a staff of eighty-five."

Connie said, "I told Eric I'll be giving concerts in China. I'm taking Chinese lessons right now."

Lisa Mallory laughed. "Save your time. They'll still be disdainful over there. See, they don't care," and she waved her hand at the crowd. "Some of them have been born in Buffalo, too! It's the Chinese you can't fool. They know you're not the genuine article—you and I."

Her face was suddenly heightened in color, and she was breathing as if ready to flee from something. "Yes, you heard right. I was born in Buffalo."

"You were!" Connie exclaimed before she could control her amazement.

"Well, what about you?" Lisa retorted. She was actually shaking and trying to hide it by making sudden gestures.

"Westchester."

"But your parents at least were Chinese."

"Well, so were, so are, yours!"

"I was adopted by Americans. My full name is Lisa Warren Mallory."

Incredulous, Connie said, "I'm more Chinese than you!"

"Who isn't?" She laughed, unhappily. "Having Chinese parents makes all the difference. We're worlds apart."

"And all the time I thought . . . never mind what I thought."

"You have it over me. It's written all over you. I could tell even in the dark that night."

"Oh, Lisa," Connie said to comfort her, "none of this matters to anybody except us. Really and truly. They're too busy with their own problems."

"The only time I feel Chinese is when I'm embarrassed I'm not more Chinese—which is a totally Chinese reflex I'd give anything to be rid of!"

"I know what you mean."

"And as for Eric looking down his nose at me, he's knocking himself out to be so American, but as a secure Chinese! What's so genuine about that article?"

Both of them struck their heads laughing, but their eyes were not merry.

"Say it again," Connie asked of her, "say it again that my being more Chinese is written all over me."

"Consider it said," Lisa said. "My natural mother happened to be there at the time—I can't help being born in Buffalo."

"I know, I know," Connie said with feeling. "If only you had had some say in the matter."

"It's only Asians who haunt me!" Lisa stamped her foot. "Only them!"

"I'm so sorry," Connie Sung said, for all of them. "It's all so turned around."

"So I'm made in America, so there!" Lisa Mallory declared, making a sniffing sound, and seemed to be recovering her sang-froid.

Connie felt tired—as if she'd traveled—but a lot had been settled on the way.

Sook Nyul Choi

MEMOIRIST AND NOVELIST

Born in Pyongyang, North Korea, Sook Nyul Choi came to the United States to attend Manhattanville College in Purchase, New York, earning a B.A. in European history. For nearly twenty years, she taught in New York City schools and reared two daughters. She now lives and writes in Cambridge, Massachusetts. Choi has published a three-volume semi-autobiographical novel sequence. The first volume, Year of Impossible Goodbyes, *won the 1991 Best Book for Young Adults and has been translated into Korean and French. It tells the story of Sookan, a ten-year-old girl living in North Korea under Japanese rule and escaping across the Thirty-eighth Parallel when the Russians take over her country.* Echoes of the White Giraffe *(1993) follows Sookan into South Korea, where the war forces her family to become refugees*

again. The last volume, A Gathering of Pearls *(1994), brings Sookan to college in the United States. In 1992 Choi received the Judy Lopez Award from the Women's National Book Association. With illustrator Karen Dugan, Choi has published two children's picture books,* Halmoni and the Picnic *(1993) and* Yunmi and Halmoni's Trip *(1997).*

RESPONSE

The genesis of my work to date has been my own experiences and my own observations, and my desire to share these thoughts and experiences with others. Upon emigrating to the United States in the 1950s, I was struck by how little was known about Korea, its culture and its history. As an educator in the United States, I was astounded at the lack of information available about Asia in general, through textbooks, storybooks, or novels. Having a deep love and respect for Korean culture, and having grown up in Korea during a very turbulent time in its history, I wanted to share my knowledge and bring the culture and history of my native land to life for Americans. Now, having lived in the United States for over thirty years, I also want to share with other Asian Americans, and with the American population in general, my observations and experiences as an Asian American. For me, the way to bring these experiences to life and to touch others was to write.

I would like to think that I write for people of all ages, of all ethnic backgrounds, and of all nationalities. *Year of Impossible Goodbyes* and *Echoes of the White Giraffe* are written for young adults. The picture books *Halmoni and the Picnic* and *Yunmi and Halmoni's Trip* are for younger readers. Having been an educator for twenty years, I have always been aware of how interested and inquisitive young people are about the world around them. I wanted to give them the opportunity to learn about Asian culture and history, to make Korean culture and history accessible to them. Given the growing number of Asian Americans, I feel it is important to foster a better understanding of Asia and of Asian Americans. I also feel it is important to create literature about Asia and about Asian American experiences for young Asian Americans to learn about their heritages and to feel that there is a voice for them to relate to.

I have been very pleased to have so many universities and women's study groups interested in my work. I am delighted that it is being translated into several different languages. My hope has always been that my work can help forge greater understanding of

Korean culture and history, among all age groups and across many different cultures.

There is a voice deep within me full of stories to tell, a voice shaped by all my thoughts, experiences, and feelings. It is my own, very individual voice that prompts me to write. When I write, I don't think of myself as part of any particular literary tradition. On reflecting on your [Amy Ling's] question about which tradition I see myself in—American, Asian American, or writers of color—I think I am part of each of these traditions. I think there is significant overlap in these categories, and I find it very difficult to classify a single author or a single work into any single category.

It is extremely difficult to tackle the question of an "Asian American sensibility." When we speak of "Asia," we are referring to such a vast geographic area encompassing so many diverse cultures. So to speak of a single, monolithic Asian American sensibility is virtually impossible in my mind. However, I do think that since Asian cultures are very different from Western cultures, there is a different sensibility in terms of aesthetic, manner of communication, and interaction. So in a broad sense, I think there is an Asian American sensibility that we share. However, I also think this Asian American sensibility is in a constant state of flux and development.

As more attention is focused on Asian American writers, I feel that one of our most pressing responsibilities is to heighten awareness of our rich and unique heritages and our individuality. Another challenge as an Asian American writer is to be viewed as an artist and writer in one's own right, more than just a conduit for providing a revelation about "the" Asian American experience. Perhaps people pick up one of my books to learn about Korea or about the Asian American experience, but I hope they will come away with more. My hope is that they will come to understand the characters in my books and experience their sorrows and joys and challenges. In getting to know these characters, they will gain a better understanding of Asians and Asian Americans.

I think the dominant society has long misunderstood Asian culture. I attribute this to a lack of knowledge about Asians and Asian cultures, and a lack of Asian voices to dispel misunderstandings and misconceptions. I am delighted that an increasing number of Asian American writers have been published and believe this will help remedy the misunderstandings, which can be so detrimental. In my works, I want to bring my characters to life, whether they are Asian, Asian American, African American, Caucasian American, or Hispanic. I seek to develop those characters so that readers can relate to them, their plights, their joys, regardless of their race or nationality. Also, by writing for children and young adults, I feel I can help heighten awareness and sensitivity at an earlier age.

I do think there has been a tremendous surge in interest in Asian American topics in recent years. I like to think this is just the beginning. The globalization that has occurred as a result of improved transportation, communication, and international trade has certainly fostered a growing interest in understanding Asian cultures. Also, the growing number of Asian Americans has fueled interest in Asian cultures and in Asian American issues. I am very pleased to see several Asian American authors published in recent years and hope this will be part of a growing trend.

From *Year of Impossible Goodbyes*

Later that morning, Captain Narita came by for a second inspection. He said he wanted to make sure that we were all working as hard as we could to serve "the ever victorious Japanese army and the Heavenly Emperor." Every time he and his lieutenants marched in to inspect our work, chills went through me. He walked by Inchun and me and went into the factory. It was unusual for him to come twice in one morning, and we were relieved when he and his lieutenants left looking fairly satisfied.

But the following morning, Captain Narita came back, and instead of making the routine inspection of the factory, he ordered Aunt Tiger to get Mother. Aunt Tiger rushed inside, and they both came running out.

Captain Narita gazed calmly at Mother as he stroked his mustache that twitched as he formed his icy smile. He spoke very slowly in a hushed tone. We could barely hear him, and even Mother cocked her head slightly to hear. "Your sock girls did not do good work this week. We Imperial soldiers can put them to better use. Our victorious Imperial soldiers need to be rewarded for their heroic achievements on the battlefields. Our great Heavenly Emperor will be pleased to know that your girls volunteered to help our soldiers fight better. Your girls will be honored to bring glory to the Emperor."

I did not know what that meant, but I saw a look of horror come over Mother's face. With a deep bow Mother said, "Most honorable Imperial Captain, it was my fault that productivity went down. I was not able to work fast enough after the loss of my father. Please do not take the sock girls away. . . . " She trembled as she spoke.

Her face was pale and her eyes were filled with tears. I could not believe that she was bowing so humbly and desperately before this cruel little man. She seemed willing to do almost anything to change his mind. "Please let them be . . . give us another chance. I will see to it that the Imperial police are pleased with our sock production. We will please the Heavenly Emperor with more work." I wished I knew what they were talking about. I did not understand why Mother was so frightened. "Most honorable Imperial Captain, please, please. . . . " she said over and over again. With great satisfaction, Captain Narita stroked the edges of his stubby mustache and adjusted his sword belt about his thin waist. He surveyed the yard, lost in his own thoughts. Then he and his lieutenants departed without a word.

We stood listening to the sound of their swords clanking against their guns as they walked away. I was amazed at how this scrawny little man could inspire such fear in my mother with just a few words. I watched Mother's ghostly face as she stared after Captain Narita. She stood motionless and kept looking at the gate as if she were still waiting and praying for him to return with an answer.

I had always had a vague notion that something horrible might happen if the girls did not produce enough socks, but I was never sure what it might be. Aunt Tiger was silently gnawing on her lower lip and furiously tying the socks in bundles. She kept looking over at Mother, who was pacing back and forth.

Mother wrung her hands and trembled. She mumbled under her breath like a crazy person. I knew this was not a time to ask questions. Even Aunt Tiger was silent.

All of a sudden, Okja came running out into the yard. I was surprised to see her, for none of the girls ever left their machines during the day except for lunch. She stared at Mother in silent terror. Whether or not Captain Narita walked into the factory, the girls somehow always knew when he had come by the house.

Mother looked at Okja, but her mind was elsewhere. After what seemed like a long time, she said, "Captain Narita has threatened to take you girls away. He said you did not produce enough socks, but you cannot possibly do any more! I should have been out here with you. What am I going to do, Okja? I better tell the girls . . . I want you to hide. I don't want any of you to come here anymore."

Okja's eyes filled with tears, but she bit her lip to keep from crying. "There is no place for us to hide," she said quietly. "He knows where we live and whom we know, and if he wants to, he'll find us and take us to the front. No matter where we go, we are their prisoners. It'll do no good to hide. He'll only make you suffer more for letting us go. All we can do is work day and night to produce more socks and hope he'll change his mind."

Haiwon came running out into the yard, wiping the sweat from her brow. Squinting in the bright sunlight, she said, "The girls are saying something is terribly wrong. We want to know what's going on. We know the rat was here talking to you. How come he did not inspect the factory? What did he want?" Haiwon looked at Mother and Okja. Suddenly she started wailing, "Oh, no, not that, not that, oh no . . . I wish I were dead, I wish I were dead!" and she fell to her knees crying, pounding on her chest with her fists.

Mother and Okja dropped to the ground and embraced her, steadying her hands and wiping her tears. "Come. Let's go into the sock factory and talk about this and see what we can do," said Mother.

When I got up to follow them, Aunt Tiger grabbed me and kept me with her. I watched as the three of them entered the ugly barrack. I heard the machines go off. There was silence, then violent cries of anguish. It grew quiet again. What were they talking about? I waited. Soon the machines started up again, and I saw Mother come stumbling out. She was drenched with perspiration. She stood listlessly outside the barrack clutching the door handle.

Aunt Tiger rushed to her side and led her to the straw mat where we were sitting. "They are so brave," said Mother to Aunt Tiger. "They want to try to make even more socks in the hope that Narita will change his mind. But I wish they would just try to hide. I don't want them to come back here. I can't bear to see them taken away. I don't care what Narita does to me."

Aunt Tiger looked at Mother in disbelief. "You must be mad with fever! You know Captain Narita better than that by now! Okja is right. They have nowhere to hide. They all know that if even one of them doesn't come to work, they will all suffer for it. We all will. There's no escape for us. We are like mice trapped in a dungeon of wildcats. We are Koreans; we are a cursed race and there is no hope for us as long as the Japanese are around."

Mother didn't seem to be listening. With her fists clenched, she stared at the barrack, praying for a revelation to save her dear sock girls.

Aunt Tiger continued. "They use us, they toy with us, and eventually they'll kill us all, one way or another. Our lives are worth no more than a fly's. 'A voluntary offering for the glory of the Emperor' . . . How skillfully they lie, lie, lie! Those girls would rather die than be 'spirit girls' for the Emperor's soldiers. When I think of how many truckloads of girls they've taken to the front already . . . I heard half of them killed themselves by jumping off the speeding trucks rather than be locked in those latrines and used by those soldiers. Our poor girls!" Aunt Tiger was raving like a mad woman.

Mother suddenly seemed to have realized what Aunt Tiger was saying and whispered harshly, "Please, please stop! The children!" With her fists still clenched, she continued pacing up and down the length of the yard, staring at the sock factory. I wished they would tell me what was happening. What did "spirit girls" mean? Why were they being sent to the front?

I was terribly afraid for the sock girls and yet I didn't even know why. But I was somehow relieved to see Mother up and about. I had been so worried that she would die of grief, crying day after day in her dark room. Within an hour of Captain Narita's visit, she had resumed her duties and was rushing about, overseeing production. Fear and helplessness had been transformed into desperate determination.

The next day Mother got up long before the sun and had Kisa inspect and grease all the machines. The girls came earlier than ever and immediately started working. They had all resolved to do the impossible; they would increase production and make Captain Narita change his mind. For several days, Mother and the girls worked from the crack of dawn until late at night, without even taking a break at mealtimes. Inchun and I busily folded and bundled the socks to keep pace with them.

Mother looked more and more frail. Her face had become flushed with fever. I noticed Aunt Tiger glancing at her with grave concern. One night, as we were finishing up for the day, I heard Aunt Tiger say to her, "You are working like a crazy person. You're making yourself sick, and it won't do any good. The Japanese have been taking our girls for years. We all knew it was only a matter of time." She tried to convince Mother to get some sleep or at least to eat something. I wished Mother would listen to her, but she said nothing and continued to work. Even Inchun and I kept folding socks and mending stitches, working late into the night by candlelight.

Each day Mother waited expectantly for Captain Narita. The Japanese merchants and the police came by to collect the socks and seemed very pleased, but we waited anxiously for Captain Narita's decision. We just kept working, but I could sense that with each passing day, Mother and Aunt Tiger were growing more and more apprehensive. One morning as we worked on in the stagnant heat, Mother said, "I never thought I would say this, but I wish Captain Narita would come by. We need to know if there is any hope. They've been working so hard, and we haven't been paid in weeks now. We'll all go hungry soon. If he doesn't come by tomorrow morning, maybe I'll go to his office and see if those awful guards will let me see him."

Late that night, I watched the dim lights go off in the factory. I didn't go out to the yard to wave good night to the girls. I wanted to be by myself in Grandfather's room. I was tired of working so hard. How long would we have to live like this? When would Grandfather's merciful Buddha or Mother's Catholic God come to help us? As I sat in Grandfather's room trying to recapture his warmth and calm, I looked out and watched the sock girls talking, shaking the day's dust from their hair and clothes, and stretching their weary arms and legs. Some were busily opening and closing their hands to stretch their stiff fingers. Others rubbed their eyes and wiped their tongues with their handkerchiefs to rid themselves of the dust and lint. They exchanged a few words with each other and with Kisa, and then headed toward the gate. "It's starting to rain. Be careful," I heard Mother say. Although exhausted, they all wore a look of liberation as they stared up at the dark rainy sky. They had gotten through another day.

Suddenly, the gate burst open. Everyone froze in horror. Two soldiers stood behind Captain Narita with their guns slung over their shoulders. One of them held a large black umbrella over Captain Narita to protect him from the rain. Through the open gate, I saw a big truck parked outside. I heard Mother moan helplessly, "Oh, Lord, Oh, Lord. Merciful Lord. . . . "

The dark sky broke loose with a crack of thunder and a bolt of lightning. It started to pour. How I wished a huge thunderbolt would strike right where Captain Narita and the soldiers stood. Oblivious of the torrential downpour, the girls started sobbing. "I wish I were dead, I wish I were dead," I heard several of them whimper. They clutched one another in desperation. Huddled together in the pouring rain, they looked like helpless animals. I wished that just this once, I could run out and beat up Captain Narita. But I couldn't move. I sat there watching with tears streaming down my face.

"You should all be very proud and honored that it is now your turn to serve Our Heavenly Emperor. You will give the soldiers the special spirit to fight harder against the White Devils," said Captain Narita cheerfully. "Our Heavenly Emperor will be happy that you volunteered to help the soldiers. Now get into the truck and get out of this rain." The two soldiers began to herd the girls toward the truck. Some screamed and fell to the muddy ground, but were jabbed with guns and forced onto the truck.

"Please do not take them . . . some of them are not even fifteen," Mother implored. "The older ones have babies and old grandparents at home to take care of." Captain Narita smiled for an instant, showing a row of crooked teeth, and then motioned for his lieutenants to hurry as he looked up at the black sky.

I saw Haiwon being pushed toward the truck. I heard her cry just as she had on her birthday. Only this time, her cry was more faint, as though she could not even muster the courage to go on any longer.

I saw Okja spit at the soldier who was jabbing her in the ribs with his gun as he tried to get her onto the truck. The angry soldier lifted his gun to hit her. Like lightning, Kisa shot out from nowhere and kept the soldier from hitting her. The soldier dealt a blow to Kisa instead, who fell to the ground screaming. Okja tried to run to Kisa, but the soldier grabbed Okja and tossed her onto the truck like a dead cat. The other soldier kicked Kisa in the ribs. Kisa lay doubled over in the mud crying out to the girls. Captain Narita looked at him with disgust and shouted to the driver. The truck pulled away and sped off in the darkness of the storm. I knew better than to go outside. From the door of Grandfather's room, I saw my mother standing in the rain, wringing her hands.

Aunt Tiger brought Kisa inside and began bandaging his head. "What made you think you could fight the soldiers with their guns and swords?" Aunt Tiger said. "Haven't you seen enough . . . how they kill us like flies?" I sat down next to them, and I wanted to ask Aunt Tiger where the girls were being taken and what would happen to them. But I felt it was silly to ask. Wherever they were being taken, I could tell it was a fate even worse than death.

Kisa wept uncontrollably, and said, "I will never see those girls again . . . I couldn't save even one of them."

"It was only a matter of time," Aunt Tiger said. "You knew this day would come sooner or later."

"Maybe we will all see each other again. Maybe the war will end soon and they'll return to us," added Mother, as she came inside. When she saw me, she rushed over and held me tightly, as if she wanted to squeeze all the fear out of me and said, "I'm sorry, I'm sorry, I'm sorry. . . . We could truly use one miracle now, just one miracle." Mother's hot tears fell upon my forehead. Her voice was shaking and her body trembled. She was burning up with fever, and she shivered in her wet clothes. I touched her rough hands. All that frantic work had not done any good. It didn't matter how many socks they made. The Japanese could do whatever they wanted and no one could stop them.

From my bed, I heard the Lord's Prayer. I got up and peeked into Mother's room, and there, gathered around a candle and a small crucifix, were Mother, Aunt Tiger, and Kisa. Aunt Tiger was no longer making fun of Mother's Catholic God. I fell asleep as I listened to their devout prayers against the drumming of the rain. Kisa's voice was soothing, and I pretended that his voice was that of my father, three brothers, and my grandfather.

I must have fallen asleep. I felt a hot breeze brush against me, and then strange noises coming from the yard. I lay still in my bed. I could smell the candle that had been burning. I heard whispering in the next room. I got up and saw three figures, peering out at the yard through a crack in the rice-paper paneled doors. They were looking across the yard at the sock factory. I went over and saw that the lights were all on in the sock factory. For a split second I thought Mother's miracle had happened and the soldiers had brought the girls back to make some more socks. "Mother, are the sock girls back?" "Shhh," she replied. "Sit with us and be quiet. The soldiers are taking the machines and loading them onto the truck. They're probably taking them to be made into more weapons."

I rubbed my eyes and looked out. Several uniformed police had dismantled the machines, and were taking them from the sock factory and loading them onto the truck parked outside. "Those are not even theirs to take," said Kisa. "Those are ours. . . . We bought them with our hard-earned money from the Japanese merchants, who probably stole them from other Koreans!"

Mother was quiet. "Since when does ownership matter to the Japanese?" said Aunt Tiger. "They take whatever they need from us. What good are those machines to us now? I had hoped we could trade them in for some rice, but that was silly of me. Let the bastards take them all. What else can we do?"

I was glad to see the machines go. It would be too sad to look at them day after day. Too much had happened today. Soon the rain stopped and there was a cool breeze. I looked out at the stump of the pine tree and the empty sock factory. The front gate was wide open and swinging in the wind. No one bothered to close it. What was the sense? Those gates provided no privacy or security. I wished I had slept through the night. The grown-ups were relieved that we were safe and only prayed that things would not get any worse.

I sat in helpless silence and watched the dawn break. The sun rose like any other day. It shone brightly, as if it knew nothing of our sadness. I felt the bright sun was heartless and cruel to shine so derisively, and I shut my eyes in defiance.

Maxine Hong Kingston

MEMOIRIST AND NOVELIST

With The Woman Warrior: Memoirs of a Girlhood among Ghosts *in 1976, Maxine Hong Kingston opened the space for Asian American literature. Blending personal history, Chinese myths, and imaginative re-creations, she portrayed a Chinese American girl's struggle to balance Old World constraints and New World expectations.* The Woman Warrior *won the National Book Critics Circle Award for the best nonfiction of 1976, has inspired numerous scholarly articles, and was performed as a dramatic play in Berkeley in 1995.* China Men, *Kingston's second book, an American Book Award winner in 1980, focused on three generations of Chinese men, whom she called the building and founding fathers of the United States. In the 1980s on college campuses these* were the most widely read books by any living author, according to journalist Bill Moyers. Kingston's novel* Tripmaster Monkey: His Fake Book *(1989) is about a 1960s Chinese American dramatist and Berkeley graduate searching for his identity and his place in the world.*

Maxine Hong was born in 1940 in Stockton, California. She graduated from University of California, Berkeley, in 1962; married fellow student Earll Kingston; and lived with her husband and son in Honolulu for eighteen years before returning to Oakland. She has received national and international recognition for her work, including, most recently, a Presidential Award in the Humanities from President Bill Clinton.

RESPONSE ⟶
Interview with Maxine Hong Kingston

Q: How do you prefer to be identified?

It's fine with me to be called an Asian American writer, a Chinese American writer, a feminist writer . . . it's fine. I've seen my work studied in English classes, anthropology, African American classes. I like to see the *et cetera, and, and, and.* As we travel here in Taiwan, I see myself being claimed as Chinese. We don't have to choose one thing or another. It's wonderful to be able to cross all sorts of borders, to make that borderland broader. For example, I taught high school for about ten years and had the sense of encountering different cultures in students with different academic abilities. I wanted to be heard by the really bright kids as well as those almost retarded. To be able to communicate through various cultures is really important. My father's comments in the margins of *China Men* were very scholarly, very poetic. He wrote both prose and poetry in classical, traditional Chinese. In [these] marginalia, he gave me the sense that he treated me as an equal and that he was very proud of me. He died at the end of 1991, right before the fire that destroyed our house and all our belongings.

When I finished *The Woman Warrior*, I was thinking about how I could get it published. It was such a peculiar book. My sense of readership was wide—Hong Kong, England, U.S. I think of a universal readership. But in the process of writing, I was writing for myself, putting my own thoughts and emotions down, sorting through them. I think of writing as an artistic transformation of thoughts and feelings. By this I mean finding a use for human experiences, learning meanings common with others so that I can be understood, and I can understand the people/characters I write about. In the United States, people talk about *love* all the time. I think love is *understanding*—myself, my readers, and my characters. When a reader reads, I hope that she understands herself and her place in the world.

I pick different people to address and to be angry at. I don't set out to be working with different genres, but it so happens, when I pursue certain thoughts and ideas, that when they take shape, new genres are also taking shape. I'm pushing boundaries, including generic boundaries. In *The Woman Warrior*, I'm working on what is real and what is not real. It's exciting to play with literary rules and shapes.

Q: I like the variant versions of a story you tell; for example, in "No Name Woman" you give the reader many possibilities for your aunt's pregnancy.

I need to tell stories in that way because that's the way life happens. We need to know what happened before we were born, when we weren't there to witness it. Even classical research gives us different versions. This method I discovered is the most truthful way I can give everyone's view, all the participants. The reader decides what is the truth. The complex and multilayered view, the effects of talk-story—every time you tell a story, it's never the same. I was trying to replicate that in text. I actually found the Fa Mulan chant in the Gutenberg Library.

The beginning is usually a character, a person, sometimes a voice. *Tripmaster Monkey* was very much a voice. My mother, my father, myself—writing begins with a person. Plot comes later. I begin with a portrait and then the picture begins to move, and action and plot come later. I do many literary experiments and work out problems with language and genre, and find the right forms for new stories. The content is always social and political. I am a very political writer. I synthesize these things. It's not possible to separate aesthetics and social conscience. Ethnic Studies at Berkeley reads for politics; the English Department reads for aesthetics. I'd like to see students emerge with both types of education. It bothers me when I see Ethnic Studies categorize politically and think they've done their job.

Q: Will you tell me your thoughts about the recent dramatizations of The Woman Warrior *and* China Men?

For one thing, a dramatic version reaches an audience I haven't had, getting to some non-readers, such as old people who go to the theater, non-Chinese who don't read, and Chinese people who don't read English. In the main, the play captures the spirit of the books, the epic quality. However, teamwork and collaboration changes things. You can't control twenty actors from all over the world, including the Philippines, Hawaii, Singapore, Vietnam, China. There were Chinese, Japanese, and Korean Americans. Sharon Ott did the casting and called it "world theater."

There are nuances I miss. In *China Men* they go tea dancing, which is elegant and civilized. In the play, they go taxi dancing, which is flashy. The play does not present the ambivalences of the text. But wonderful things are being done by the music—a wonderful synthesis of Chinese opera and jazz. And we use mask in an interesting way. All the actors are Asian, and Caucasians are played in white mask over the eyes and cheeks. The biggest difference between theater and writing is that theater is communal activity, while writing is a solitary activity.

I don't have a theory, but there's some kind of miracle that there should be this flowering of Asian American writers and artists now, that out of nowhere—coincidentally—all these people are working at once. In mainstream writing, language poetry, im-age writing, there's a lack of color, of stories. Our parents' lives have been very adventurous. American culture seems very short on story. There's something deep, deep in human nature that needs story, and we Asian Americans are strong in that. In story, there's an ebb and flow that is life moving. It makes sense of the past and carries us into the future. It connects people to people, invents, heartens us, passes information on how to live, helps us see our lives as a wonderful adventure.

Also as Asian Americans, we do participate in aspects of the Eastern mind; this Buddhist, Confucian, Taoist background and way of thinking is very different from the linear West. We bring new ways of seeing. In some ways, it seems as though our world did something way off—the West is yang, the East is yin, and we split apart. The East is bringing yin back to create a roundness, interconnectedness, another way of seeing. The West has always had a romance of the East—Hinduism, Buddhism—we are of the real East—we are the real thing—and we come with a hope, a way to break out of some of the deadlocks that the West has fallen into. We bring a whole new canon, new languages, an entirely different range of rhythms and mind states, a new relationship to language, picture, and music. The poet is a singer, a painter, and a writer in our tradition. In the West, the poet is a writer and that's all.

Q: How do you answer those within the Chinese American community who accuse you of not getting the community's stories right?

I have the stories right. I know when I'm playing around with the stories, and when I'm writing from a true center. I do my homework, my research. I make my choices. Those who complain are not good readers.

Q: Would you talk about that little misunderstanding or rift between you and Frank Chin?

I don't think of it as a misunderstanding or a rift or anything that's between him and me. It's always been him with these attacks, and I usually don't answer at all. He calls me terrible names such as "race traitor." He even wrote me a letter that he's going to beat me up if he sees me. I don't want to honor him with answers. We've never met.

Q: Maybe if you did meet, he would recognize you for the warm-hearted human being you are.

Oh, no, no. I think that in order to recognize a warm-hearted human being, you have to be a warm-hearted human being yourself. Actually, I've stopped reading his work, because I think he does not mean me well. I read for inspiration and life and help, and I don't think he wants to help me.

What are the real important issues at stake? I have identified two. One of them is the racial and cultural myths. Whom do they belong to? Frank would say they belong to *real* Chinese such as himself. And they do not belong to, for example, the Caucasians. My feeling is, if somebody goes to a bookstore and buys my book, then they have bought the myths, and they can have the great myths of China by reading them. The only way that myths stay alive is if we pass them on. He has also been saying that there is a true text, including the chant of the Woman Warrior. Now, I know that myth is not passed on by text; it's mostly passed on by word of mouth, and every time you tell a story and every time you hear it, it's different. So there isn't one frozen authentic version; there are many, many authentic versions, different from person to person.

As a woman, it's absolutely clear to me that we have the freedom of creating alternate myths, and for Frank Chin, as a male, there is a monolith, one monument of a myth. The other difference—I just discovered this recently and am very surprised at this coincidence—I think he just published his translation of *The Art of War*, one of the Chinese books of war. He's brought this into the world at the same time that I am writing my book of peace. You can see the fundamental difference in values.

Terrible stereotyping has been done to us Asian Americans. Our writing has an important task: to show ourselves as real human beings, to show our feminist contributions. It must be terribly hard to be an Asian man growing up in the West. Two of my brothers are very macho in reaction to the stereotype. I'd like to see them be able to relax.

Q: Why did you choose Kuan Yin as narrator for Tripmaster Monkey?

She's compassionate and cares for all her characters. She doesn't want anything bad to happen to them. It's my way of not being a nineteenth-century male God-narrator. I chose a Chinese goddess instead. At my workshops with the veterans, I invoke her before we do our reading. I ring the bell and call her name before we read. Interestingly, Kuan Yin used to be a man. Avolokishvara was his original name in India; he changed sex in the sixth century and became the goddess of compassionate listening. Androgyny plays a large role in my work. Fa Mulan dresses as a man. Tang Ao is turned into a woman. I love Woolf's *Orlando*.

Q: Have you been to Taiwan before?

No, this is my first visit. I visited China, the People's Republic, for the first time after the publication of my first two books and learned a lot about my family. The center of my father's village is the temple. The center of my mother's village is the music hall. Mother's father was a talk-story master. He loved it so much, he didn't charge money. He loved to tell stories about orphans because he wanted to make old ladies cry. If he could do that, he considered himself a success. He did death speeches and farewell speeches. He did many, many things. He made three trips to the New World, including South America and Cuba. He was a fermented bean-curd maker, a wine maker, a judge in the village, and a farmer. Father didn't want to get married. He said he would only marry an educated woman because he didn't think they could find one.

Gu Ching, the name of my mother's village, means "ancient wells." At Sung Mai Wai, my father's village, I saw the well where my aunt drowned. It's right next to the family temple, the ancestral hall. I could've written a scene showing dramatically the sacred versus the profane.

My next project is called *The Fifth Book of Peace*. When I started this book, I thought I was working on an abstract level on philosophies of peace. But I'm finding Chinese-based metaphors and stories. The specific war I'm studying is the Vietnam War. I see the Asian mind so large. Monkey is in Buddha's hand—there's no jumping out of it. The middle section will be about Wittman Ah Sing, who evades the draft by hiding in Hawaii—the center of war operations and home of the City of Refuge. I also want to tell Fa Mulan's homecoming from war and becoming a woman again. I want to counteract *Rambo* and the notion of the impossibility of coming home from war. Our society needs a story of veterans coming home, becoming members of society again, being at peace.

I was just looking through news clippings that I have of that period, and soldiers were still trickling home in the mid-1970s from Vietnam. So it was inconclusive—it wasn't an ending. And I was thinking, I want to make an ending. I want to be able to manipulate reality as easily as I can manipulate fiction. Do we imagine the world? If we imagine characters, can we cause them to appear in the real world? What if I could strongly write peace? I can cause an end to war. The end to the Vietnam War is not just that they stop shooting and we stop shooting. That's not the end. The end has to be something very wonderful. . . . Thich Nhat-Hanh, a Vietnamese monk, has a religious commune in France, and I was thinking how wonderful if I could bring a group of Vietnam veterans to live in community with Vietnamese people. . . . To me, that would be a true ending to the war with Vietnam.

Writing and life have to go together. I want to write about war and peace, so I've gathered a group of war veterans to write with me. I don't want to write about war at a distance. Sometimes in my life as a college professor, I find myself totally surrounded by whites, and young people. Then I call a Chinese friend or relative so I can hear the old language and stories. It's as simple as the aesthetics of the physical self. It's important for me to see people who look like me. In my twenties—as late as that—I picked up a yearbook from a San Francisco high school. There I saw page after page of Asian faces. I thought, oh, look at the variety and the beauty! And it was a book—miraculous rarity, to see these faces in a book. It was a relief from *Seventeen*. I loved looking at them.

Q: You once said you were claiming America in China Men. *When I read* The Woman Warrior, *I felt you were claiming womanhood for all of us. . . . In your* Book of Peace, *what would you be claiming?*

What I would like to do is claim evolution—that we can evolve past being a warring species into a peaceful species so that we are not predators anymore, and that we stop being carnivorous. If only we could stop being cannibals—

Q: Have you any advice for aspiring young writers?

Write every day, even if it's just for a few minutes. Keep alive as a writer. Asian Americans have a very rich heritage. If you can access that, you will have a lot of material. Ever since the beginning of America, there have been fads for Eastern exotica. Regardless of the fad, it's important to write one's own life and the life of all people around you. I've met many people who have lost all the old traditions because they were raised in the suburbs. The task is to find the new stories in the suburbs, and to be very good observers of the life that is there.

EDITOR'S NOTE: With permission of all parties involved, I have interwoven two interviews: one I conducted with Kingston at the Grand Hotel in Taipei on April 7, 1995, and the other by Neila C. Seshachari, published in *Weber Studies* 12, 1 (winter 1995): 7–26.

From *Tripmaster Monkey*

Sky poured pink through the windows. Everyone floated in pink air—spun sugar, spun glass, angel's hair, champagne. The friends moved toward the windows to see where this rose was coming from, and saw everything, the water of the Bay, the glass of houses and buildings, the sky, the dew on the grass, rose-blessed. Is the sun like this every morning if we but wake early enough to catch it? Is it a time of year—a season of rose air? The crew in the lightbooth has flipped on the pink gels, and tinted all the stage and the women's faces. It seemed you could float out the window on the strange atmosphere. There are Chinese people who would explain that Gwan Goong was paying us a visit; the color was emanating from a building in downtown Oakland, where you could have seen Gwan Goong's good red face, or its reflection, upon ten stories of brick wall. You could have asked for any wish, and Gwan Goong would have granted it. You could have been a millionaire. As it turned out, nobody in this gathering of friends was ever again afraid when flying in an airplane. And later one or another of them in danger felt that there was someone protective beside or just ahead of him or her, making a way. They didn't discuss the rose air, didn't compare one's sensing of it with what anyone else was seeing, if anything, until years later when two happened to meet, and somebody said, "Do you remember that morning seeing the air—the air before your eyes and on your hands—pink and rose?" And then they wondered that they had not exclaimed over it at the time. (Could it have been a waft of nuclear testing gone astray from the South Pacific?)

A feeling went through Wittman that nothing wrong could ever happen again—or *had* ever happened. It's very good sitting here, among friends, coffee cup warm in hands, cigarette. Together we fall silent as the sun shows its full face. The new day. Good show, gods. Why don't I, from now on, get up for every dawn? My life would be different. I would no longer be fucked up. I set out on more life's adventure with these companions, the people with whom I have seen dawn. My chosen family. We're about to change the world for the better.

Sunny walked about her house with a brown paper bag picking up paper plates and beer bottles and plastic wineglasses, dumping ashtrays, wiping food up off the floor. "Come on, people, either keep it in your mouth or on your plate," she said. She was a full-time housewife, which she had to be in order to keep the trompes-l'oeil functioning. She was returning what she had put away that needed protection from the party. Half of a round glass table went against one side of the wall, and the other diameter on the other side, the found bottles on top filled to elegant waterlines. Where there had been dancing, she lowered a board hung on chains back down to its height as a table, découpaged with the pages of Beardsley's Savoy book. Salomé's big lips kissing John the Baptist's head, blood looping in designs like her long sleeves. On top of that, pillboxes and a vase of fake lilies, and green bananas ripening to go with the rug. She had painted the gold and black rays of Art Deco shooting out of doorframes. Lance handed out hot towels for faces and hands. O comfort.

"We've only started," said Wittman, out the door and across the porch and down the stairs and through the yard. "This play is immense. Epic. Our story won't fit a one-act on a unit set of crates and burlap bags. I'm going to bring back to theater the long and continuous play that goes on for a week without repeating itself. Because life is long and continuous. The way the theater was in the old days. I mean the old days in *this* country. The audience comes back every night for the continuation. They live with us. The thing will not fit between dinner at the Tivoli and the after-theater snack at Martha Jean, Inc. or the New Shanghai Café." His friends agreed that he should work some more on the play; they would act in it, and they would be on the lookout for more actors and a venue. Then Wittman was again out on the streets, but this time with Taña.

Dew sparked on the lawns and parked cars. A church bell rang a few iambs. Brother Antoninus, are you waking up at St. Albert's? A black-and-white cop car and a black-and-white cab cruised past each other. We're in a good part of Oakland, which used to be restricted. "No person of African or of Japanese, Chinese, or any Mongolian descent will ever be allowed to purchase, own, or even rent a lot in Rockridge or live in any house that may be built there except in the capacity of domestic servants of the occupant thereof." Lance was living there in an integrated marriage, and Wittman was walking there. Oakland Tech ought to be teaching this localest history.

Passing St. Albert's, Taña and Wittman learned that they had something in common. On dates, each with another, they had followed the sound of men's voices chanting, carrying far without electric amplification. Hiding in the bushes outside the gate, they had seen monks in procession around the grass. Breath issued from cowl hoods. Which one of those figures was Brother Antoninus himself? Hands from angel sleeves held and shielded candles. How is it that rows of lit candles stir you so? It's automatic. The candles at the Big Game rally at the Greek Theater the night before the Cal-Stanford game get to you too, religiously. Birthday children become arsonists because if little candles on a cake can make me feel this religious, what if I set fire to a building, why don't I blow up a country? Knowing some Latin from high school, Wittman had felt on the verge of understanding the songs. "Compline," said Taña, "the last prayer at night." The compline had been so wonderful, Wittman admitted that he'd wanted to join up but for his vow against missionary religions. This time of the morning all was still, no people on the grounds, and no lights in the buildings.

Taña had taken off her sandals with the tire treads for a long, barefoot walk around the dog shit of Oakland. She held her shoes in one hand and Wittman's fingers by the other. He sang to her, "Tiptoe through the tulips, through the tulips with me." A bearded man, holding his head with care, climbed some front steps, and before going inside, turned and gave them a wave. Fellow tripper come through the night, come home. Not every last one of us who trips out of a Friday night makes it back home. Across the street, a couple with arms around each other hurried along, then stood to talk, then hurried on. A raven had darted a feather into her hair. He carried a black cape folded over his arm. Yes, all over town, batwings were closing. May the minds that shot off to other planets and dimensions settle gently adown to the ground of our Earth.

A single sheet of newspaper flared up into the air and flew, gliding and opening, and sailed over their heads. *Like a blank piece of paper, I drifted along past the houses, up the boulevard again.* Wittman ran after it, pulling Taña along. Please be the girl that I'm in love with.

Her sandals under her armpits, she held on to his hand with both of hers and dragged him to a stop, and up some side stairs of the California School of Arts and Crafts. She led him to a courtyard, and where she leaned back on a wall soft with moss. He leaned above her, like his elbow against her high-school locker. "Hey, wanta make out?"

She didn't laugh, but looked gravely into his eyes for quite a while. "Yeah. Let's make out."

"Let's swap spit," he said, but giggled his Chinese giggle. He had lost his previous cool. He firmed up his face. Took her face between his hands, blonde hair between his fingers. Gave her a hard kiss. Pulled back to look at her, to see how she liked it.

She looked big eyes back at him. Held his gaze. He loved the way her eyebrows frowned; she was troubled. He was getting to her. He took another kiss, longer. This time when he looked, her eyes were closed.

"Hey, Taña," he said. "Taña. Wake up. Talk to me."

She put her mouth up to his ear, and said, "You want it hot, I'll make it hot for you."

He held her chin, led her mouth away from his ear, back to his own mouth. Lips barely rubbing, he slid past her mouth and attacked her ear. "Hey, tell me. Are you blonde all over? Huh? Are you? Are you blonde everywhere? Blonde body hair? Where else are you blonde?"

"My armpits. My armpit hair comes in blonde. Why? Are you queer for blonde pubic hair?"

Shit. A queer for blondes. If she had brown hair, would he have said, "Are you brown everywhere? Do you have brown pubic hair?" "Blonde chick. White girl," he said, calling her names. "Are you a loose white girl? Where do you live, loose white girl? I want to take you home. And I want you to invite me in."

She ought to have slapped his hands away, and dumped him for acting racist. If you have principles, you do not like him anymore when you find out somebody's a racist or a Green Beret or a Republican or a narc. You ought to be able to sense such a defect, and the obstinacy of it, and run.

"Did you go to 'America Needs Indians'?" Taña asked. Yes, the first multi-media event in the world. There had been movies and slides, color, and black and white, projected against these four walls, the sky with moon and clouds overhead, and music and wise Indian voices chanting like Gregorian, like Sanskrit Buddhist. The crowds turned around and around to see everything, and their juxtapositions. A herd of buffalo charged from one side, and mustangs from the other. Indians riding across Monument Valley, and, simultaneously, close-ups of their faces. The art students had painted one another's faces with Day-Glo. People kept saying, "The tribes are gathering again," which sounded new and old. An airplane or a flying saucer—come for us—would look down and see a square flashing in marvelous light show. Now the walls were dark and no vibes. "Because it wasn't here," said Taña. "It was at the Art Institute." Wittman took her word for it, having been too ripped, and also, Chinese having no sense of direction. (That's why the Long March took so long.) Wittman and Taña might have met each other at "America Needs Indians." "What hours were you there?" "What were you wearing?" "Who were you with?" "Who were you?" "I sort of remember somebody who might have been you. Did you wear braids with a headband?" More and more in common. She can be my continuity- and direction-finder.

They walked out of the school, and he followed her through a gate, be-dighted with rose vines in thorn, then along a footpath with ivy trailing upon it. Her part of the house was in back.

She had wonderful, wonderful digs—flights of mobiles, windchimes, models (bottles and dry sunflowers) for still-lifes on tables and shelves, even the dishes on the drainboard arranged in a composition, cans of brushes, the smells of linseed oil and paint and patchouli, prisms turning in the east windows, madras India Import bedspreads for curtains and bed, spectrums of yellows and oranges, coat-hanger wire webbed with lavender and purple tissue paper over light bulbs, intricate old rugs (whose mazes you could lose yourself in when stoned, a kid again lining up armies of mar-bles). He could live here. He was itching to rummage, and to view life through her kaleidoscopes and prisms and magnifying glasses and scien-tific microscope. He went right over to her industrial-strength easel under the skylight; in its clamps was a sketch of a forest with pairs of points, the eyes of animals. There were smiles in the leaves. "You're a painter," he said. "I wish I were a painter, and always had something to show for it." He spun a land-brown globe—Arabia Deserta, La Terra Inconoscivta, the Great American Desert, Red Cloud's Country, the Unattached Territories, the Badlands, Barbaria, the Abode of Emptiness, the Sea of Darkness, sea ser-pents and mermaids abounding. "Strange beasts be here." Nada ou Nou-vel, whence the four winds blew. And she had a map of the universe—Hy-perspace Barrier, areas of Giants, Supergiants, Dwarfs, Protogalaxies. She's another one who knows how to live on her own, where she belongs in time and space.

She went into the kitchen and boiled water, set up her drip system, ground her beans. Wittman wandered about.

Toulouse-Lautrec's *Divan Japonais* took up one wall; Taña had deco-rated to match that print—the furniture matte black like the man's top hat and the woman's dress, feathered hat, fan and long gloves; the madras picked up the orange hair and the yellow beard and cane. He slid open a box of kitchen matches—a bat, upright, cute face and wings akimbo, not alive. Vampiress? Taña also collected birds' nests with blue and speckled egg-shells, and downy nestling feathers, and a piniony quill. A set of false teeth had a reefer crutched in its grin. Tuning forks and magnets. A cabinet of good paper. A shelf of sketch books. Nudes. A roll of new canvas. Buckets of stretcher bars. He sat at the round table with the crystal ball and apples. There were also a set of brass gramweights as in a lab, a brown velvety cloth bunched around things, collages on boxes. Flows and layers of candle wax relief-mapped the courses of many evenings staying up with friends talking and sculpting. On a postcard of Seal Rock, she had drawn a few lines and dots, and you could see that seals are born out of rocks, and rocks come from seals.

Taña brought over two cups of coffee, sat across from him, smoked. "Wittman," she said, "Darling. I've been thinking: The next time I get it on with a man, I set ground rules."

"Yes? What is it, sweetheart?" She called me a man and a darling, and she wants to get it on. I've never called anyone Sweetheart before, never called anyone anything. "Go on."

"I may not be in love with you. Say, you're the one I'm in love with, I won't let you go. But, say, I meet him tomorrow, I'll leave you. I'm being fair. You don't love me either. We're starting even. There was this guy named Edmund I was in love with when I was seventeen. I know what love feels like. I'm not in love with you. Maybe I cannot love again. But, say, I find him again, or another one like him, I'm going to have to get up and leave you. I don't have an obsession over you, though I do want to make love with you. You don't define my life. I just want you to know how I am before you decide to make it with me. Making love is my idea as well as yours. This isn't just your idea, okay? You're not going to say later that this was all my idea, or your idea. We can each of us cut out whenever we feel like it. If somebody that either of us can love comes along, why, we're going to go, okay? As of yesterday we got along perfectly well without each other. And we're not going to feel destroyed because I'm not in love with you and you're not in love with me. So, tomorrow, if one of us wants to be by himself, nobody's going to phone him up. But we could possibly go on forever not falling in love with somebody on the outside. We may get used to having each other around, and end up growing old together. Do you know Chekhov's concept of dear friends? That's what we can be to each other, dear friend."

Damn. She beat him to it. Outplayed again. He was the tough-eyed one who had been planning to let the next girl know point by point what she would be in for entangling with him. But he'd hesitated, what if she then wouldn't want to be in for it? No girl but the one in his head sat still for a read-out of rules. He'd balked, and she'd taken his lines. Now what?

Taña had been warming and softening wax in her hands and was molding it. Don't go away, Taña. Does she know she looks winsome? Truth and Consequences. He was the loser. Consequences for him. "I think I could love you," he said. "I think I do love you."

Peter Bacho

~~~~~~

NOVELIST

Peter Bacho, born in Seattle in 1950, is a Fil-ipino American writer and teacher. His first novel, Cebu, *won the American Book Award in 1992. His collection of short stories,* Dark Blue Suit, *was published by the University of Wash-ington Press in 1997. He is currently a lecturer in the Liberal Studies Program at the Univer-sity of Washington, Tacoma.*

RESPONSE ⏤

My father was part of that first generation of Filipino immigrants in the 1920s. He worked for a number of years going from fields in California to domestic work and then back, and he did that even after I was born. In 1949, he married my mother and we proceeded into a life of economic insta-

bility and migratory work for a while. Then my mom put a stop to that and said, "Get a regular, twelve-month-a-year type of job in Seattle," which he did. I grew up in a pre-dominantly Filipino and Afro-American neighborhood, which is the setting of *Cebu* and *Dark Blue Suit.* I was educated in both public and Catholic schools. Catholic schools, in my opinion, did a much better job of working with poor minority students. I graduated from a local college in 1971, got a doctorate in 1974, became an attorney for a moment, decided I didn't like it, and shifted over in 1976 to Asian American Studies, a kind of experimental program that was just starting out at the University of Washington. I've been there off and on at different programs or up and down the West Coast ever since.

For a number of years, I was a political writer. Particularly during the 1980s, I was writing for most of the leading important policy journals. I was also pretty much the *Christian Science Monitor*'s expert on the Philippines–U.S. relations during the 1980s. Those were the Ferdinand Marcos years, and I was critical of U.S. policies toward the Philippines. But when the crisis resolved itself with Marcos's death, I moved on to other types of writing.

Dark Blue Suit, my latest collection of short stories, ends with "A Family Gathering." It's autobiographical, to a certain degree. *Cebu,* in contrast, is pretty much a Filipino opera with all the melodrama I could pop in, because Filipino literature tends to be very melodramatic. I did *Cebu* more or less tongue in cheek, but to really understand it, you will have to understand it's from the context of Filipino literature. It's about indefinite redemption within a Filipino Catholic setting. I didn't intend to address a wide audience in this book. It was intended for Filipino Americans. I wanted to say, Let's face the particular problems in our community and see what we can do about them. I think a lot of ethnic writers feel that burden to try first of all to educate their own community. The problem, though, is that the community doesn't really spend a lot of time reading literature. So who picks it up? People outside. A lot of critics liked it. They weren't really sure why. The one who liked it and was sure why was N. V. M. Gonzalez. That's because he's immersed in Filipino literature. He knew what I was trying to do; even more than the American Book Award, it was his review that I treasured.

Dark Blue Suit starts with a dispatch scene, dispatch of IRW Local 37 from Seattle to Alaska for canning in the mid-1950s. It's just like Mardi Gras, if you happen to be a kid. Thousands of Filipinos gathered together in Seattle, and basically they went all around Chinatown. It's like one big party for

about two weeks. And my dad was a part of that because he was a cannery foreman. The collection progresses through different stories in a chronological fashion. My father was a relatively young man at the beginning, and at the end, in "A Family Gathering," he's in the cemetery. So the book tells the stories of a set of characters and a community over a number of years. My primary obligation was to remember the community and my prime readership: the guys I grew up.

Writers do have the responsibility to be spokespersons of their community, but at the same time, they should be free to go off on a tangent. What we owe is fair representation if we are going to deal with an ethnic setting. But at the same time, there are literary flourishes, I guess, that are entirely the problem of the writer. Fae Myenne Ng's book is a wonderful example. I loved her book, *Bone* (1993)—wonderful, wonderful piece of writing. She uses Chinatown as a setting, but there isn't this heavy emphasis on identity or mother-daughter relationship; well, I guess there is some of that, but it's downplayed. It's much more of a universal type of story. I think it's a lovely, lovely story. I suppose some folks might say to her, "Why didn't you write something much more Chinese?" So what? It's a beautiful story. And she was faced with a problem. As a young writer, you don't want to go back over the ground that was so expertly dealt with by someone like Maxine Hong Kingston. Shawn Wong's new stuff is a bit of a diversion. I mean, it goes away from the stuff that other Asian American writers have written about in the past. But I think it's an evolutionary process. As time passes, you can see more ethnic writers feeling free—freer—to talk about other subjects. And I think that's a healthy thing.

In Filipino literature—whether set in the Philippines or here in the United States—there's much less focus on identity and more focus on identifying who the oppressor is and doing something about it. My inspirations were writers like F. Sionil José and Ninotchka Rosca. Rosca's very good—very dramatic and powerful. And there's less focus on identity here. It kind of fits into the way I look at things. I don't spend a whole lot of time thinking about my identity. I already know who I am. If there is a problem with that, I think that's someone else's problem, that's not mine.

On the other hand, this is a receptive moment particularly for Filipino artists and writers because we are talking about centennials here. I mean 1897, 1998, 1999—it all started with war against Spain, and in 1897 there was a temporary truce negotiated between U.S. representatives and General Emilio Aguinaldo. In 1898, the Americans came to Manila Bay. In 1899, Americans started killing Filipinos and Filipinos became Americans. For Asian American artists and writers overall, this is a pretty good moment, but for Filipinos the next couple of years will be particularly noteworthy. We have a huge population here in the United States, almost 2 million people, and we have centennials coming up. For example, I did a presentation at the Smithsonian in April, and they had a big deal in 1998 also sponsored by the Smithsonian. Several of these types of events happened all over the country.

On the subject of writers, Bienvenido Santos, who just died recently, was a wonderful writer. But Leonard Casper, who wrote the introduction to Santos's *The Scent of Apples* (1979), didn't understand him entirely. Casper stressed the longing, the sense of separation and exile in Santos's writing. But one of the things, if you read Santos very carefully, is that he keeps zapping away at these elite sons of bitches who are going to schools on the East Coast and really have something to return to, because their parents are the ones who once exploited poor Filipinos back in the Philippines. They come back with Harvard or Yale degrees and run the enterprises that pay people pennies a day. These are the stories he's telling. Yeah, there's a sense of longing and separation from home and blah, blah, blah, and this is the fiction of different America, or American of difference, that Carlos Bulosan described. Bulosan was on the West Coast, where all the Asian Americans were hated, and on the East Coast, there were few Asian Americans. But just like Bulosan, Santos has suspicions of these elites who accepted him into their midst basically because he is so damn talented. He managed to jump, to a certain degree, the economic and social gap, at the same time remaining very skeptical of the good intentions of his very wealthy peers.

Which role is more important to me, writer or teacher? Teaching. I write when I feel like it, basically. I don't suffer for art. It's more important for me to teach. Teaching is fun. It's the most fun a human being can have as an adult. My goal is to have the students make their own decisions on things. I think the ideal is to present facts and possibly a new way of looking at things, to stimulate discussion, and to have them come to their own conclusions. To make students think—I suppose you can call that a challenge, but that's not really a challenge. I mean, challenge is cutting asparagus in southern California for ten hours a day—that's a challenge. Teaching is fun.

What inspiring words do I have for aspiring writers? That it can be done. If you want to do it, it can be done—as long as you learn the basics of writing and you don't have technical flaws and what have you. You cure up those technical flaws. If you've got imagination, it can be done. I don't think there's anything special about me, to tell you the truth. I suppose critiques, that sort of thing, could discourage people from writing, but everyone's got a story to tell—everybody.

A Family Gathering

As I walk along the edge of the neatly trimmed lawn, I hear (and feel) the opening notes of the annual fall sonata. It's October in Seattle and the rains will come as they always have; I was born here and know the pattern well. And although I've been away, old responses quickly return. I pull down my cap, turn up my collar, and just keep walking as the first few drops touch my neck and face, then stop. I chuckle. It's a feint, an old Seattle trick. The gentle scout drops are a portent of the deluge to come. At the end of the walk, I'll be soaked to the bone.

But I don't mind because it's pretty here—all flowers, grass, and trees. Ringing the far edge, a tall surrounding hedge creates in me a sense of separation and solitude, an appropriate response for a cemetery stroll, but not sorrow because I'm going to a gathering of men that I love.

My father's death surprised me. It shouldn't have; he was 87. But I thought he'd live forever, as would his brothers, cousins, and buddies—my uncles—who came to this land so long ago when racism and violence, migrant poverty, tuberculosis, and despair should have killed them, but didn't. Such forces, the afflictions of the poor, didn't even wrinkle the creases of the zoot suits they wore while standing on corners from Seattle to L.A., where they'd laugh and talk loud, and just wait for the night.

But of course they died just like the rest which, of course, they weren't. At least not like those of us lucky enough to be born here, or a new generation of educated immigrants who came thirty years later from the Philippines and landed on a much softer place. They had truckloads of degrees and well-founded hope, even titles (Dr. Alvarez, Attorney Fernandez, Engineer Rufina) far more impressive than the ones held by their predecessors (Asparagus Cutter Vera Cruz, Fish Sorter Daan, Short Order Cook Cavinta).

The newcomers didn't know what the old men had done and, quite frankly, couldn't care less. They wouldn't see the connections between their comfort and what others had struggled to build. They couldn't see that the old men had heart and did the most with the least, and with a style they could never have and I'll never see again.

It's been sixty years since Dad and his peers arrived, and now they're going one by one. At first, the passings were distant—acquaintances, relatives of friends, other old timers known only by rumor—and now, it's the last rush to the gate. At the start I couldn't see the end, but now I can and mourn their leaving.

Uncle Kikoy was the first. With my father he'd come to this land, toting nothing more than a sack full of hope, soon gone and buried by the dust of migrant jobs. That was his life and, depending on the season, he was planting or cutting asparagus, or canning salmon, a half century cycle broken only by time spent shooting at Japanese soldiers in the Pacific. When he first came to Seattle, he stayed in Chinatown—a place for the poor and the colored—in a one room hot plate walkup. Between jobs, he'd always return to that room; I met him there forty years ago.

"Your uncle," my father said. "He'll watch you."

A few years back when he passed, I swore in a prayer I'd never forget him. It's a promise I've kept. In the time since, whenever I've come home, to Seattle, I've stopped by his grave and said a prayer if I had one, or laid a flower or a coin on his headstone, or just said "hi" and lit a smoke. As rituals go, it's hardly elaborate, nothing profound or eloquent. But then, Kikoy and I didn't talk much in life; his English was bad, my Cebuano was worse. Still, as a kid I just liked hanging around him; I felt safe there in his Chinatown orbit as we strolled by bars and card rooms and pool halls. This preference, formed in childhood, stayed with me through the years. Boy and man, I just like hanging around him. His death didn't change it.

The promise made to Kikoy, I made also to my father who, just this year, was buried not twenty yards away from his cousin. Unlike Kikoy, Dad's English was passable, which allowed him to jump me every time I screwed up a math assignment, and later, marriages and careers. "Your name," he'd hiss and shake his head. "It's who you are, who we are. Don't never shame it."

Of course I ignored him as I gathered shame by the bucket. And of course he was right and I knew it, even as I marched through bogs of weakness and poor judgment, journeys of the young. Of course he was right; he'd earned his name the hard way as a teenage immigrant with nothing to start, but with a church full of mourners to finish. Their hymns of sorrow, impassioned and pure, formed a shroud around my father and lifted him away. I didn't see it, but I felt it. I swear it happened just that way.

Would the same songs be sung for me? I wonder. True enough, I carry his name, but only by accident of birth.

I am now on familiar ground, the northeast corner of the cemetery. I recognize the names; other Filipinos are here as well, like Manong Fabian, twenty years our neighbor, twice that our friend. It's like our old neighborhood, reassembled plot by plot; all that's missing are the sounds—the laughter and the mix of dialects and accents inviting me in, to dinner or just to visit. Friends in life, we've chosen to be together again.

Under the awning of a small brick mausoleum, I light up and sit, waiting for the rain, now windwhipped and horizontal, to pass. It's too strong, even for a Northwest native. I could be here ten minutes or two hours; it doesn't matter. Dad and Kikoy are nearby; I can feel them.

Dad's presence here has made it official, a quorum has convened for a gathering of my family whose full list of members has not yet arrived. Typical of such gatherings, some are stragglers, excused by comparative youth (Mom at seventy) or sheer stubbornness (Uncle Vic at ninety-one). But eventually, they'll be here, all of them who, decades ago, faced a hostile land and didn't even blink. It's another reason to come home. But I can't, at least not yet. There's no work here, maybe in a few years. For now, I'll just have to visit when I can, especially as the roster fills, until my time to join them.

The wind has subsided, allowing the rain to resume its vertical fall. It's a good sign and I start to stir. At my feet lie two cigarette butts, normally an hour's worth of smokes, and I glance at my watch for confirmation. Off by ten. Seventy minutes has passed; it means I'm cutting back, delaying my admission to the gathering. In a way, it comforts me to know that at the end I'll be here and nowhere else. Still, I smile at the postponement, the Surgeon General would be pleased.

I scan the lawn and pinpoint the spot; Kikoy's there. I'll visit him first as I always do, a pattern dictated by order of arrival.

At the gravesite, I hastily cross myself and wonder if I did it right. Is it right to left, or the reverse? It's been so long. Just to be safe, I do one of each then mumble a greeting, tell him I miss him, and hope all goes well. This morning, I have a pot of poinsettias and lay them on the headstone, a small, bare marble plaque. For a year or so after he passed, his girlfriend used to leave flowers, but not a petal since. I can't blame her; she's young, younger than me, and her life goes on. Her time with him was brief; mine went from childhood to middle age. I've assumed the task.

Dad's next, and for him I bring no flowers. Unlike Kikoy, who died an anonymous death, my father was a man of this community; he is mourned and remembered. Flowers from me would be redundant. I slowly approach his gravesite and just as in life, I'm not sure what to say; I'm still searching for a prayer.

I didn't talk much to Kikoy either, but that was never a problem. He barely spoke English, he was an uncle, I had lower expectations. But with Dad I had the impression, dumped by age ten, that fathers and sons are supposed to talk, to hold long heart-to-heart marathons like Ward and the Beaver. It just wasn't his way to talk much to me, other than to warn or scold. What secrets did he own? What fears or hopes? I never knew; he never told me.

Still, I didn't mind because he could have left us—my mother and me, my brother and sister—it would have been so easy. I knew from rumors and examined shards of family history, he'd already left one woman and her family (his too), but the complaints they may have are theirs, not mine. For the survivors (my shadow brothers and sisters), let them come here to howl or to curse him, or to piss on his grave. I won't because even at our poorest, when he drove country roads looking for work, he stayed because he loved us and I knew it.

Childhood poverty strengthens memory, and the strongest images are of Dad covered with dust and later, grease and scabs—blistered and discolored—the signs of accidents, burns from his welder's torch. (Blood money, he called it.) Often I wouldn't see him for days (overtime, he said), maybe a glimpse in the morning or late at night. He did this, I knew, so we could avoid a life of blood money.

Over the years I grew even close to him in an odd, indirect way through intermediaries, like my mother, who told me he stopped smoking the year I was born. Somehow, because of me, he quit cold a twenty year addiction; Salem Menthols were his last brand. Later, she said he carried clippings of the box scores of whatever sport I played; he'd go to Chinatown and show them to his friends. "My boy," he'd say. Sometimes he'd show them to strangers. Still another source claimed Dad cried at my wedding, the first one. We're even, I cried at his funeral.

I am now at his gravesite, and not even the rain, again horizontal, can turn me away. Since the funeral, I've been here two other times; this is the third. During each of those visits I searched for words—eloquent, affectionate, beautiful—that my father had never heard from me. Those words weren't there, at least I couldn't find them. Do they even exist? I try again, then suddenly stop. It isn't necessary. Our bond was wordless; belated eloquence won't change that. A chat with the living, it's the same with the dead.

I smile. I've found my prayer.

"Got in last night," I say softly. "Tired as hell, but I'm glad I'm here." I pause. "Real glad."

PHOTO BY RAMONA SAKIESTEWA

Arthur Sze

POET

Arthur Sze is a second-generation Chinese American who was born in New York City in 1950. He graduated Phi Beta Kappa from the University of California, Berkeley, and is the author of five books of poetry: Archipelago *(1995),* River River *(1987),* Dazzled *(1982),* Two Ravens *(1976; 1984), and* The Willow Wind *(1972; 1981). His poems have appeared in numerous magazines and anthologies, among them* American Poetry Review, Bloomsbury Review, Harvard Magazine, Kenyon Review, Manoa, Mother Jones, New Letters, Paris Review, Seattle Review, America in Poetry, Breaking Silence, *and* Open Boat. *His work has also been translated into Chinese and Italian. He has conducted residencies at Brown University, Bard College, and the Naropa Institute and has given readings at poetry centers and universities throughout the continental United States and Hawaii. He is the recipient of a Lannan Literary Award for Poetry (1995); three Witter Bynner Poetry Fellowships (1980, 1983, 1994); two National Endowment for the Arts Creative Writing Fellowships (1982, 1993); a George A. and Eliza Gardner Howard Fellowship at Brown University (1991); a New Mexico Arts Division Interdisciplinary Grant (1988); and the Eisner Prize, University of California at Berkeley (1971). He lives in Santa Fe, New Mexico, and is currently director of the Creative Writing Program at the Institute of American Indian Arts.*

RESPONSE ⟿

I am a poet. I am also a second-generation Chinese American. My poetry is exemplified by the character *xuan*. This character is etymologically derived from dyeing. The character itself depicts silk dipped below ground level into an indigo vat; the silk hangs from a pole into the dye bath. When the silk is pulled up into the air, it is at first a greenish color. The yarn begins to turn blue because chemicals in the dye oxidize when they come in contact with oxygen in the air. The yarn is then dipped back down into the vat and pulled back up. Each time, the yarn turns darker and richer. Sometimes, the yarn is dipped as many as forty times. The character, *xuan,* is itself polysemous: it means "dark," "profound," "subtle," "mysterious." I believe that poems are polysemous: they have *many* meanings. My poems contain a layering of experience, and they offer a reader a visionary journey. Obviously, my reader is not one who likes to be instantly given the meaning of what he reads. In our consumer society, we are constantly in a hurry to purchase, to consume, and so forth, and we rarely give ourselves the time to slow down and consider the implications and mystery of our existence. My poems ask a reader to read and reread, to experience the layering of our existence, and to embark on a transformational process. I believe there are many readers willing to make this journey, and they are my audience.

I first started writing poetry when I was eighteen. I am now forty-five. I have published five books of poems, and each book has gained a wider audience. My latest book, *Archipelago,* has finally attracted significant attention, though I feel my earlier work—particularly *Dazzled* and *River River*—has deserved closer attention than it has received. Occasionally, reviewers have had an agenda and have reviewed my work according to various preconceptions; they did not look carefully enough at the work itself. Also, I have translated classical Chinese poetry. Critics have praised the translations but not read my own poems with the attention they deserve. *Archipelago* is, for me, a pivotal book, and I am grateful that it has received some serious critical attention. I am also grateful to the Lannan Foundation. When Jeanie Kim called to say that I had been selected for a 1995 Lannan Literary Award for Poetry, I wondered if it was for *Archipelago.* She made it clear that the literary committee had read all my books and had based their decision on my entire body of work.

Is there an "authentic" Asian American sensibility? I'm not sure how Frank Chin defines this "authentic" Asian American sensibility. What is the Asian American sensibility, and how is it "authentic" or "inauthentic"? Is the authenticity derived from experience? I think there *can* be an authentic Asian American sensibility, but the definition needs to "open up" instead of "close down." It needs to incorporate the diversity and complexity of the Asian American experience. When you ask me about the role of the Asian American artist in the larger American society, I question whether it is assumed that the "Asian American artists" mentioned are somehow smaller or lesser in relation to the "larger American society." What is the role of Native American artists or Jewish artists or Irish artists? A role of artists is to provide insight and broaden, deepen, and transform the possibilities of existence. As such, I don't think Asian American artists are a category that is subsumed under or by the "larger American society."

I think Asian American artists need to break stereotypes and stereotypical expectations. I break these expectations by creating poems that are not one-dimensional; they are multidimensional and challenge the reader to stretch and grow.

As an aside that is apropos, there is a famous story where a merchant paid a small fortune to purchase a tea bowl. He invited Sen no Rikyu (the great sixteenth-century Japanese tea master) to a tea ceremony and afterward asked Rikyu for his opinion. Rikyu expressed very little interest in the tea bowl and went on his way. In anger, the merchant threw the tea bowl on the floor and shattered it. A friend later gathered up the shards and glued them back together. Rikyu later encountered this tea bowl and expressed great admiration for it, and it became one of the most famous bowls to conduct the tea ceremony with. By analogy, I think Asian American artists need to shatter expectations and preconceptions of what their art should be, in order to create something new.

The marketing culture we live in exploits people and dehumanizes them. I think the dehumanization of exoticization and commodification exists, and that art needs to humanize. My own poems, though rarely overtly political, embody a politics that seeks to transform, liberate, and renew.

I believe Asian American artists are currently creating extraordinary work. One of the indications of the vitality is the sheer excellence and diversity of work that is being produced. In poetry alone, consider the work of Mei Mei Berssenbrugge, John Yau, Marilyn Chin, Garrett Hongo, Cathy Song, David Mura, Kimiko Hahn, Carolyn Lau, and others. I don't believe their work can be "reduced" to a single political, social, or aesthetic thread. Instead, they are collectively creating a new body of literature that is remarkable for its emotional range and depth, its imaginative complexity, and its visionary courage.

I also believe the current receptivity for Asian American artists is related to the economic boom in the Pacific Rim. As Asian countries have become economic powers, their cultures can no longer be dismissed or reduced to a one-dimensional stereotype.

I believe each multicultural writer/artist must be totally and exclusively answerable to the integrity of his or her vision as an artist. To say a multicultural writer/artist is totally and exclusively answerable to his or her ethnic community, must be the spokesperson of that community, can lead to terribly reductive consequences: for instance, is a Korean American writing only for Korean Americans? Is a Native American writing only for Native Americans? (What if a Native American writer/artist from San Ildefonso Pueblo, population 400, is writing only for that Pueblo?) Is a Black is writing only for Blacks?

I think it is arrogant to assume that a writer can be a spokesperson for a community. I am opposed to this point of view and hope that the writing of a multicultural writer inspires people to tell *their own* stories in *their own* words. Literature is not sociology or polemics, though it can incorporate both. I am excited about Asian American literature because it has broken out beyond boundaries of identity and social concern so that anything is possible. In poetry there is no inherently poetic language: that is, words like *blood* or *moon* often appear in poems, but there is no reason a poet can't incorporate *scissors* or *quark* into a poem as well. Similarly, there is no inherently favorable content for literature: yes, it may concern identity; yes, it may incorporate social concern and politics; but it can also incorporate physics, divination, Zen, calligraphy, mycology, dance, history, ritual, dream, myth.

I believe an ongoing dialogue is essential for insight. I need to say that, in terms of my own evolution as a poet, it has been important for me to translate classical Chinese poets— Li Po, Tu Fu, Wang Wei, T'ao Ch'ien, Li

Ch'ing-chao, Wen I-to, Ma Chih-yuan, Li Shang-yin, Li Ho, among others. When I was a student at Berkeley, I read English translations of these poets and was disappointed by the translations. I was spurred on to read these poems in the original Chinese and also to struggle through the creative process of these poems by making my own translations into English. It was a way for me to claim this poetic lineage. If you look at the field of Chinese translations, Arthur Waley is often lauded, but is his work really that good? On the other hand, the team of translators—C. H. Kwock and Vincent McHugh—I think make excellent translations. Like it or not, we live in a complex world. (I take the word *complex* to be derived from *plex*, "to braid," and *com*, meaning "with" or "together.") We live in a world in which the interactions of different cultures have the possibility of each enriching the other; let us not deny ourselves this opportunity.

There is a tendency to dismiss a priori a writer who has received general acclaim. I think it is important to look at the writer's work. There are instances where a writer has labored with years of neglect and then has suddenly received the recognition she or he deserved. There are also cases where a writer has written a mediocre book, but it has received wild acclaim. The issue of "selling out" needs to be discussed in relation to the issue of "authenticity." It is paramount for a writer/artist to keep his or her artistic integrity. If a writer/artist bends from his or her own integrity, then she or he has "sold out," regardless of whether the work is a popular success or a flop.

I don't think we should place "cause" in opposition with "style," when in fact the writer with an overt cause and a writer with a more intricate style both have their "cause" and their "style." I believe all writing is political: from the choice of words to the images to the metaphors to the form or forms that are employed. In general, work that is more clearly narrative and therefore more clearly accessible has a greater chance of acceptance, regardless of whether the cause be overt or oblique. A writer pursues his or her individual vision but does not necessarily define himself or herself in terms of marginality. I do not believe a writer's identity is determined by how close or how far away she or he is from an endlessly shifting "central canon."

In Your Honor

In your honor, a man presents a sea bass
tied to a black-lacquered dish by green-spun seaweed.

"Ah" is heard throughout the room:
you are unsure what is about to happen.

You might look through a telescope at the full
bright moon against deep black space,

see from the Bay of Dew to the Sea of Nectar,
but, no, this beauty of naming is a subterfuge.

What are the thoughts of hunters driving
home on a Sunday afternoon empty-handed?

Their conception of honor may coincide
with your conception of cruelty? The slant

of light as sun declines is a knife
separating will and act into infinitely thin

and lucid slices. You look at the sea bass's eye,
clear and luminous. The gills appear to move

ever so slightly. The sea bass smells
of dream, but this is no dream. "Ah,

such delicacy" is heard throughout the room,
and the sea bass suddenly flaps. It

bleeds and flaps, bleeds and flaps as
the host slices slice after slice of glistening sashimi.

The Redshifting Web

1.   The dragons on the back of a circular bronze mirror
      swirl without end. I sit and am absorbing form:
      I absorb the outline of a snowy owl on a branch,
      the rigor mortis in a hand. I absorb the crunching sounds
      when you walk across a glacial lake with aquamarine
      ice heaved up here and there twenty feet high.
      I absorb the moment a jeweler pours molten gold
      into a cuttlefish mold and it begins to smoke.
      I absorb the weight of a pause when it tilts
      the conversation in a room. I absorb the moments
      he sleeps holding her right breast in his left hand
      and know it resembles glassy waves in a harbor
      in descending spring light. Is the mind a mirror?
      I see pig carcasses piled up from the floor
      on a boat docked at Wanxian and the cook
      who smokes inadvertently drops ashes into soup.
      I absorb the stench of burning cuttlefish bone,
      and as moments coalesce see to travel far is to return.

2.   A cochineal picker goes blind;

      Mao, swimming across the Yangtze River,
      was buoyed by underwater frogmen;

in the nursing home,
she yelled, "Everyone here has Alzheimer's!"

it blistered his mouth;

they thought the tape of *erhu* solos was a series of spy messages;

finding a bag of piki pushpinned to the door;

shapes of saguaros by starlight;

yogi tries on cowboy boots at a flea market;

a peregrine falcon
shears off a wing;

her niece went through the house and took what she wanted;

"The sooner the better";

like a blindman grinding the bones of a snow leopard;

she knew you had come to cut her hair;

suffering: this and that:

iron 26, gold 79;

they dared him to stare at the annular eclipse;

the yellow pupils of a saw-whet owl.

3.   The gold shimmer at the beginning of summer
     dissolves in a day. A fly mistakes a
     gold spider, the size of a pinhead, at the center
     of a glistening web. A morning mushroom
     knows nothing of twilight and dawn?
     Instead of developing a navy, Ci Xi
     ordered architects to construct a two story
     marble boat that floats on a lotus-covered lake.
     Mistake a death cap for Caesar's amanita
     and in hours a hepatic hole opens into the sky.
     To avoid yelling at his pregnant wife,
     a neighbor installs a boxing bag in a storeroom;
     he periodically goes in, punches, punches,
     reappears and smiles. A hummingbird moth
     hovers and hovers at a woman wearing a
     cochineal-dyed flowery dress. Liu Hansheng

collects hypodermic needles, washes them
under a hand pump, dries them in sunlight,
seals them in Red Cross plastic bags,
resells them as sterilized new ones to hospitals.

4.   Absorb a corpse-like silence and be a brass
cone at the end of a string beginning
to mark the x of stillness. You may puzzle
as to why a meson beam oscillates, or why
galaxies appear to be simultaneously redshifting
in all directions, but do you stop to sense
death pulling and pulling from the center
of the earth to the end of the string?
A mother screams at her son, "You're so stupid,"
but the motion of this anger is a circle.
A teen was going to attend a demonstration,
but his parents, worried about tear gas,
persuaded him to stay home: he was bludgeoned
to death that afternoon by a burglar.
I awake dizzy with a searing headache
thinking what nightmare did I have
that I cannot remember only to discover
the slumlord dusted the floor with roach powder.

5.   Moored off Qingdao, before sunrise,
the pilot of a tanker is selling dismantled bicycles.
Once, a watchmaker coated numbers on the dial

with radioactive paint and periodically
straightened the tip of the brush in his mouth
Our son sights the North Star through a straw

taped to a protractor so that a bolt
dangling from a string marks the latitude.
I remember when he said his first word, "Clock";

his 6:02 is not mine, nor is your 7:03 his.
We visit Aurelia in the nursing home and find
she is sleeping curled in a fetal position.

A chain-smoking acupuncturist burps, curses;
a teen dips his head in paint thinner.
We think, had I *this* then that would,

but subjunctive form is surge and ache.
Yellow tips of chamisa are flaring open.
I drop a jar of mustard, and it shatters in a wave.

6.   The smell of roasted chili;

descending into the epilimnion;

the shape of a datura leaf;

a bank robber superglued his fingertips;

in the lake,
ocean-seal absorption;

a moray snaps up a scorpion fish;

he had to mistake and mistake;

burned popcorn;

he lifted the fly agaric off of blue paper
and saw a white galaxy;

sitting in a cold sweat;

a child drinking Coke out of a formula bottle
has all her teeth capped in gold;

chrysanthemum-shaped fireworks exploding over the water;

red piki passed down a ladder;

laughter;

as a lobster mold transforms a russula into a delicacy;

replicating an Anasazi
yucca fiber and turkey-feather blanket.

7.   He looks at a series of mirrors: Warring States,
Western Han, Eastern Han, Tang, Song,
and notices bits of irregular red corrosion

on the Warring States mirror. On the back,
three dragons swirl in mist and April air.
After sixteen years that first kiss

still has a flaring tail. He looks at the TLV

pattern on the back of the Han mirror:
the mind has diamond points east, south, west, north.

He grimaces and pulls up a pile of potatoes,
notices snow clouds coming in from the west.
She places a sunflower head on the northwest

corner of the fence. He looks at the back
of the Tang mirror: the lion and grape
pattern is so wrought he turns, watches her

pick eggplant, senses the underlying
twist of pleasure and surprise that
in mind they flow and respond endlessly.

8.   I find a rufous hummingbird on the floor
     of a greenhouse, sense a redshifting
     along the radial string of a web.
     You may draw a cloud pattern in cement
     setting in a patio, or wake to
     sparkling ferns melting on a windowpane.
     The struck, plucked, bowed, blown
     sounds of the world come and go.
     As first light enters a telescope
     and one sees light of a star when the star
     has vanished, I see a finch at a feeder,
     beans germinating in darkness;
     a man with a pole pulls yarn out
     of an indigo vat, twists and untwists it;
     I hear a shout as a child finds *Boletus*
     barrowsii under ponderosa pine;
     I see you wearing an onyx and gold pin.
     In curved space, is a line a circle?

9.   Pausing in the motion of a stroke,
     two right hands
     grasping a brush;

          staring through a skylight
          at a lunar eclipse;

     a great blue heron,
     wings flapping,
     landing on the rail of a float house;

near and far:
a continuous warp;

a neighbor wants to tear down this fence;
workman covets it
for a *trastero;*

raccoons on the rooftop
eating apricots;

the character *xuan*—
dark, dyed—
pinned to a wall above a computer;

lovers making
a room glow;

weaving on a vertical loom:
sound of a comb,
baleen;

hiding a world in a world:
1054, a supernova.

Meena Alexander

~~~~~~

POET, NOVELIST, AND MEMOIRIST

Meena Alexander is an award-winning poet, novelist, editor, memoirist, scholar, and teacher. Born in India in 1951, she was raised in India and North Africa and educated there and in Britain. Since 1980, she has lived and worked in New York City. Her books of poetry have been published in India and the United States and include Stone Roots *(1980)*, House of a Thousand Doors *(1988)*, The Storm, a Poem in Five Parts *(1989)*, Night Scene: The Garden *(1992)*, and* River and Bridge *(1995). Her memoir* Faultlines *was selected by* Publishers Weekly *as one of the best books of 1993. The* Shock of Arrival: Post-Colonial Reflections, *her collection of essays and poems, appeared in 1996. She has published two novels:* Nampally Road *(a* Voice Literary Supplement *Editor's Choice in 1991) and* Sandhya Rosenblum

(1996). Her scholarly books include The Poetic Self: Towards a Phenomenology of Romanticism *(1979) and* Women in Romanticism: Mary Wollstonecraft, Dorothy Wordsworth and Mary Shelley *(1989). She is professor of English and Women's Studies at the Graduate Center and at Hunter College, City University of New York, and lecturer in poetry in the Writing Program at Columbia University.*

RESPONSE ⌐

This first question, concerning the genesis of one's work, is a hard one, always. Where does the work come from? From some secret place, I guess, midway between the head and the heart. But I suppose, in another sense, it has to do with trying to make sense of the world into which one is tossed—or should I say "worlds"? Out of this passionate need to make sense, in the rhythms of the available language, comes writing. Of course, there is also always the desire to make words come close to music, or to color; the pure, nonfigurative realm that always lies under. I have in me these worlds that need to be brought together—very crudely, India and America—and sometimes I feel that I keep treading the edges of the fault line in between.

I write for whoever will read. For a writer, it is both a privilege and a necessity—being read. The question of audience is such a tricky one. There is, of course, the part of oneself, formed by the world, its pleasure and brutalities, that one writes for, so writing is a reparation that could not exist without the other self drawn from deep inside. But there is also the actual audience, others like oneself and unlike, women and men. And to deny this would be to deny the historical moment in which one lives and writes, a moment that both crystallizes the words and tries to censure them.

I admire many writers. And from those I admire, I learn. I admire Maxine Hong Kingston for the power of the myth she edges into vision; I admire Anita Desai for fine flowering of detail in which she renders ordinary lives; I admire Wole Soyinka for the resolute embrace of history that his writing gives us.

I see myself in many traditions, and of course, one stream of writing splits open and blossoms into others. Also, I think of the tradition of Indian writers; of women writers; of writers who use English in the postcolonial era. All these have nourished what I do. And there is also the struggle, the exclusion of our lives from the larger canvas here, that writing tries to address. The very

idea of an "authentic" sensibility, however, surely an instrument of exclusion, of aesthetic cleansing if there ever was, makes me very nervous.

The urgencies have to do with giving voice to this burgeoning world, the explosion of energy that comes from multiple sensibilities, all thrusting into and against the previous idea of America. We exist here under the sign of America, and there are multiple ethnicities we need to learn from, as well as racism to contend with.

The challenges to my mind have to do with the enormity of America. Think of this country, this extraordinary continent, built up on the decimation of the native nations that once existed here. And then the push westward, as if all of space were unpeopled and existed purely for the white explorer. I have long been haunted by the fact that Columbus, till the very end, was sure he had reached India; even when considered mad, he was bound in chains and carted away. And of course, he was given fiat, to take whatever lands he touched for the king and queen of Spain and for Christendom. To work this land, slavery came in, that terrible human transport. Now all this, as well as the exuberance and energy of America that comes from its immigrant traditions, needs to be considered.

Asian cultures exoticized? Yes, there is truth in this, something that started with the colonial era. Asia was seen as the "Other," as a spiritual continent—distant, exotic, and as such, pure counterpart to the more powerful forces of the West. By rendering a culture exotic, you marginalize it, think of it as far less relevant to the day-to-day comportment of life, than something that is middle-of-the-road. And of course, the exotic can be written off, seen as disposable, when the crunch comes. In these circumstances, to render an Asian woman's life—in my case, an Indian woman's life—in, say, East Brunswick, New Jersey, in its ordinary and not so ordinary lineaments might be a useful, even a creative task.

I think this is an exciting moment for Asian American writers. The "canon" of American literature is hotly debated, and in the imaginative sense, the territories are opening up. For me, it is the challenge of bringing together the postcolonial world of my upbringing with the new multiculturalism in America that is so compelling. I am grateful for the sense I get from readers that what I write, in some way, illuminates their world. After all, writing is such a lonely business; one sits alone and does it, but there is always the underlying, if fragile, hope that words can play back into the world. It is interesting to me how in India, different sorts of details or issues in my writing will be cast into relief than in the United States.

I enjoyed my visit to Wisconsin very much, meeting with students, reading poetry and prose, answering questions. I was deeply moved by the ways in which you are building up an Asian community, questioning oneself, others, what "identity" might mean, right in the heartland of America. In fact, in a fiction I am working on, I have set a scene right by Lake Mendota—directly inspired by my visit.

Imagining Dora

She sat in the sunlight on a bench in Union Square, imagining Dora. Somehow this was necessary to her. She took long walks alone, feeling the wind blow on her cheek, feeling her great distance from Stephen. Though they lived in the same apartment, they did not have very much to do with each other.

Sometimes images, torn loose, flowed through her. Past and present and future, all mingled, as leaves fallen from a tree, odors grown moldy together, a rare pungency. Or the music of the tanpura mixed with zither and lute. She considered this state a newness she was entering into and if people left her alone, she felt she might be able to live better.

So it was, one summer, while Dora was away with her grandmother, traveling in Wisconsin, Sandhya found herself sitting on a park bench, right by Harlem Meer. There were the young mothers all about her, with their tiny infants popping out of slings and sacks, feeding bottles tied onto strollers. She watched gulls circle the air, heard a dog barking, sharply.

Then Sandhya saw her own Dora, grown now, way in the indistinct future. She was oddly comforted by this vision. The child was still as skinny as ever, but she had survived, survived her own mother. And there she was in a bright yellow dress racing past Café Lalo, past the Empire State Building, past the Gandhi statue in Union Square. The wind blew her hair clear away from her face. Her features shone in the sunlight. She approached a park and halted for a minute under a tree.

Where had Sandhya seen that tree before? Its leaves were a yellowish color. Not autumn colors, but hard, as if sculpted from gold. There was a slight rise, by the tree, and the sky was spotted a gentle pink. Dora was sitting down by the tree, her feet almost touching water. There was water by her child, a stream of water or perhaps a lake? Sandhya wasn't sure. She could see a book Dora was opening up.

She shivered suddenly. How could the child have found her journal? It was the one with crude green covers she had stitched together all by herself. Then she heard Dora's voice. Dora was no longer by a tree. She was in a white room with a balcony. There was something about the room Sandhya recognized, but quite what, she couldn't tell. The rug perhaps, on the floor? How had Dora found her way in there? Someone else was in the room with her. A young man, but his head and shoulders were a dark blur. She heard Dora's voice, a young woman's voice, filling her. Why was Dora's voice coming to her?

I read the words in mama's hand:
Went and sat with him by the water's edge.
As I read those words, a curious disturbance filled me. As if sweet water on the surface of Lake Mendota had poured into me, filling me up like a jug. And someone had taken the jug, shook it so harshly, grey water churned.

A dark girl stood over me, her hair tight in two braids. She was shaking the jug, shaking me so hard, I wept to be let go.

"It's me," I cried.

I dropped the book on a flat stone by the tree. I got up. I strained my eyes so that I was looking as far away as possible. As far away from my body and her book, as I could get. Across grey water, the color of goose feathers, the sky tilted.

When I was able to wipe my eyes free of wind and water, I turned to the stone where I had set her notebook. Quickly I found the page. It looked a little different.

I read the sentence again:
She went and sat with him by the water's edge.
And then the next sentence:
I wish I had a high window.
Both sentences were written in her crabbed, sloping hand, as if the wind had brushed a clump of water reeds too roughly, knocked over a few stalks so they sprawled over the stouter ones that still were held up by their own effort. I was sure the rest of the book was empty. The ink was dark blue, the color she always used. Often the plastic bottle stood at the edge

of the refrigerator, squat, irregular. As if she needed to see the ink bottle in the kitchen, somewhere out of the corner of her eye. Mama dressed in her pale green sari with the reeds painted on the border, leaning over the stove. She had neglected to set the kettle right and the flames were naked, almost in her belly. But she was staring out, her torso slightly twisted, to the right, out of the small window that gave onto the apartment court-yard. The blackened walls were visible, and above the flat roof, the pallor of the city sky. She stared and stared at the sky as if searching for some sign there.

"Mama, mama," I cried, tugging at her sari.

When she didn't respond, I picked up the outer edge of the wafting green sari and crept down low so I was the size of a small animal. I loved the warmth of her, loved hovering inside my mother's clothing. Slowly, her hand came down and groped for my head. Stroked it through soft silk.

I can feel her fingers now, muffled with silk, in my hair.

So she sat with him at the water's edge. I thought to myself.

The Hudson's edge. Where else could they have gone?

Perhaps they walked when the plum blossoms came out in Riverside Park. Twilight already. They held hands, saw the twisted trunks of small trees, bark turned indigo in the half light, the showy pink petals.

But how could they have walked alone at twilight?

I was so young and could not be left alone. Dinner had to be cooked, before papa returned. Perhaps someone stayed with me, grandma, or Dominique who sometimes babysat for me.

Perhaps it was broad daylight, and they rubbed shoulders with young mothers, lovers, grandmothers.

They made their way, carefully, to the river.

But how could she have gotten as close to water as I am now? There is no openness there, to the Hudson River. The river is fenced off, with metal and wire. Waves grow rough as the wind beats off the condominiums of New Jersey, off the scarred edges of the Palisades.

What did his hand feel like as she held it? Did she clasp it tight, or let it fall free? He had a mole on his right thumb. I know that from a letter she wrote.

So he was her secret life.

Mama's other life all those years I was growing up. They were sitting side by side on a wooden bench. The leaves were delicate green, clenched. She was pressed up close to him. His hair was all grey. I think he was shorter than she. I did not see his face.

When I told Eric about it, he said:

"Are you sure it was your mother and him you saw?"

I had shied away, not wanting to go closer. Not wanting to see her face, her expression.

This morning I said to Eric:

"I am coming to sit by the side of the lake and read mama's notebook."

He had nodded, as if he took it for granted. But then he ran his fingers through his hair, staring at me, till Yasunari called him away.

Yasu used to be a tramp in Gingee, upstate New York, he told me so himself. "What else can an Asian do," he asked me, "what else?"

"See you tonight," I called to Eric as I stood in the street, looking in. Yasu waved back at me.

"Not waving, but drowning."

Where does that line come from? Why does it come to me?

It must be the letter to Aunt Sosa. Still it's not the kind of line mama would write. Writing came to her with great difficulty. There were whole months, whole portions of years, when she couldn't write a single letter home.

"As if a single syllable home would tear me apart. There must be others like me, no Dora? Think of the thousands of miles the flimsy letter must fly, the hazards of that crossing, an airplane that escapes bomb threats, then the postman with his torn bag, monsoon rain splashing down."

Actually mama said very little. It was more like: "Dora, I can't write home to my own mother." She said this as she stood there with a kitchen knife, peeling potatoes, running cold water over the thick brown skins. French fries and spaghetti and meat balls were the only American foods she was comfortable with.

"Will you draw a picture, Dora, I can send your grandmother in India?"

When I said nothing, she went on: "Please."

I shook my head till my two braids flew into my eyes, blinding me. Not that I wanted to be cruel or anything, but I had no interest in my Tiruvella grandparents. A week later, after feeding my guinea pig with some raw cabbage I got from the salad mama was cutting up, I opened my new book of crayons and made a picture. I checked with her first.

"A lady getting into an airplane. Is that OK?"

She perked up at that. "Of course darling."

"I'll make the sky blue. OK?"

"Blue."

She repeated the word. She seemed happy as she saw the picture I made in the new drawing book grandma Muriel had bought me. The picture was of a lady in a sari with a big black bag in one hand. In the other, she held onto a little girl with two long braids. They were going up the steps of an airplane. The steps were outlined in black. Around the plane, there was blue sky. Bright blue crayola in stripes. And stars. She liked that. Stars in a blue sky. I think I made the sun too. So the sun and the stars both shone on that lady holding the little girl by the hand as the two of them got into the shiny airplane.

Later, angry with her for tearing me away from Rosie and Jennie and Wanda, away from summer camp and hot dogs and pizzas, streets full of girls jumping rope by their stoops, I made myself a dream: that the shiny clocks and clothes and chocolates, tubes of saffron and skin cream and shampoo that she had bought so carefully to take back to India, had all changed, changed utterly.

When she stepped out of the plane and opened up her bag, it was full of rotten tomatoes, shriveled cabbages, blackened onions. They oozed a stench liquid. She screamed. In the dream I heard mama screaming as I just stood in the airport lobby, staring at my shoes, saying nothing. Nothing at all.

"Why don't you draw any more?" Eric asked me. "We could get pencils, paper." He seemed so eager.

I could feel my heart beating as he looked at me. Thump, thump, like a fish flapping its tail against a flat stone in the lake.

"We could get charcoal, Dora, you might like that. Look!" And he held up a stick he had got out of Yasunari's backpack.

But I shook my head, quite adamant.

Yasunari was there too. "Why? Why?" He asked quite delicately. All around us in the café were Yasunari's charcoal drawings, the latest exhibit of them in the only gallery he could find.

"What were you doing in that picture?"

I wanted to move them away from Eric's question.

"Yasunari, it's you, isn't it, in that picture you made? What are you doing?"

"There?"

I nodded.

For some reason Eric was tapping his foot hard, as if he didn't want me to ask.

"That's me with grandma rooting for coal."

"Rooting?"

"Sure. Internment camp, during the war years in Southern Idaho. The men would throw a whole pile of coal in the middle of the yard and make everyone jump for it. We got very little. It was bitterly cold in the nights. Grandma felt it most of all. She made us children huddle by her, to warm her blood, but still her body shivered. In the morning, before the others woke up, she took me out, made me walk by her.

" 'You have good eyes Yasunari,' she'd say, 'good eyes, my child.' I scraped the ground with my eyes for bits of coal others had missed. I can still see those black glittering bits. Like your eyes, Dora. They're from your mother right? Where is she now, your mother? She's Indian, no?"

I nodded.

"Where then?"

"New York."

"And your dad?"

"He's moved to Connecticut."

"Ah, the green fields, green dollars. See him ever?"

"Yasu, here's some tea."

Eric was pouring out half of his own green tea into Yasunari's mug, which was always empty. Empty mug man Yasunari called himself in jest. He was on unemployment, on disability too for damages sustained by the soul, long term damages from internment camp—that's how we thought of it. Eric was his nephew in a roundabout way. Eric's mother is part Japanese, and Yasunari is Eric's mother's second cousin, third generation from the Seattle area.

"That's why I made the golden eagle. We know things Columbus never knew. Look."

Yasunari pointed, a thin trembling finger.

"I first saw it when I was a child in the internment camp in Southern Idaho. Desert, Dora. Dry, cracked, nothing gold there. Don't get me wrong, Dora. I saw that plane, coming down on me. With bombs in its belly. Tracking out into the desert wasteland. I was seven in '41. My sister said we couldn't use the bathrooms till ten thirty in the morning. Why not? Because mom says they have to take out the hanging bodies. It was damp in the bathrooms—Suicide? Yes, yes, my people keep these things quiet. Camp, my dear child, was no Hayakawa picnic."

"A waterfall there, you have?" I pointed to another picture. I wanted him to keep moving with his voice, keep on going.

"Yes, I went to its head as a child. I bobbed up and down for hours hoping I would be washed off and I wasn't. I wasn't. O God, why, why not?"

"And that other?" I asked.

Now he was looking straight at me, picking up courage:

"That other is a picture of the great tree with golden leaves that is spoken of in Revelations. Next to it I have drawn the salmon. I make it a symbol for the Asian landlocked in the mid-west, a loneliness in his soul. The salmon brought from the west coast doesn't breed well here."

How slow and sad his voice was as he hunched over his tea cup. I held onto Eric's hand, listening as Yasunari went on:

"The foremothers and fathers of ours, following the salmon, the buffalo, the llama and the camel, founded this continent, the two Americas as well as Europe, Pakistan, India, and this eagle swooped down on the arms of a young god. I shall call him Krishna in honor of your Indian mother. Yes, Krishna coming to gather up our lost tribes, the tribes of Asia and America."

Suddenly I shivered. I pulled the thin black cardigan about me. It was the cardigan Eric had given me for my birthday. I wanted black so I could work in it, and the scrapings of charcoal, or the dark inks I favored, wouldn't show. It came to me out of the blue, when I heard Yasunari's voice. That I was to be the burial ground for the rage, the horror that his people, our people had suffered. And of out my body, the whispers would grow: snip, snap, hot blast, glass cut, souls aghast.

Later, I think it was a day later, we met, all three of us, right by the waters of Lake Mendota. As Yasunari watched me, I stooped low to the grass blades, bent my body so I became a curved thing, a bonsai tree with a load of brilliant black blossoms, Yasu was always talking of, a crooked thing the wind blows through.

And in my head I thought, I will not die of rage, I will not let us all be consumed by hate, we must live. I was fearful he would begin again with the internment camps, with the bombardment of the Mekong Delta during the Vietnam War. I did not want that. I did not want any of that. Why did it have to be my history? As if he heard my thoughts, he said:

"Dora, Dora, I saw your aunt Draupadi once, in Gingee, and scared her. Tell her that sometime. Dora, Dora, promise me we'll all live by the water, as we did in exile once, in Babylon."

And Yasunari of the coal blackened eyes started singing ever so softly, and took a piece of metal where it lay by his shoe and he made a music that Eric and I holding hands, moving closer to the waters, danced to.

After hearing her child's voice in that way, Sandhya felt utterly worn out. She trembled as if she had lost a skin. As if those dancing feet were within her, pounding her old life down. She stood by the bench and leant her whole body against a tree. It was an oak tree she thought. She could feel the tree taking her weight. Her back against the tree, she looked out. In the distance she saw the glistening streets of the city. Through the mistiness in her eyes they seemed whorled, as a snail's shell might be, cast into flatness. She heard other voices now, voices of young men and women, a pack of them, approaching her. For a little longer she would stand, with her back to the oak tree, feeling the sunlight on her face. Then she would walk into the massive, nervous city, quickly.

EDITOR'S NOTE: Yasunari in this story is based on the artist Munio Makuuchi, whose poems appear in Part II of this book.

Darrell Lum

FICTION WRITER AND PLAYWRIGHT

Author and playwright Darrell Lum was born in 1950 in Honolulu, Hawaii. With Eric Chock in 1978, he founded Bamboo Ridge Press, a small literary press devoted to publishing work that reflects Hawaii's multicultural people. Lum's own work draws on the humor and heartbreak of growing up in Hawaii speaking pidgin English (Hawaiian creole English). It explores the formation of a "local" identity, one formed by grandmothers who arrived in Hawaii as children at the end of the nineteenth century and of whom he was ashamed as a child, longing to be "all-American"; by a grandfather who wrote classical Chinese poetry in an outdoor gazebo he called "Lum's Pavilion of Filial Piety Inspirations"; and by all the stories that continue to weave in and out of his life. He has published several works for children and two collections of short stories, Sun: Short Stories and Drama *(1980)* and Pass On, No Pass Back *(1990), which received the 1992 Outstanding Book Award in Fiction from the Association for Asian American Studies and the 1991 Cades Award in Literature. He has received a fellowship in literature from the National Endowment for the Arts and playwriting commissions from Honolulu Theater for Youth, funded by the Rockefeller Foundation, and from the Kumu Kahua Theatre. "Paint," which follows his response, is from* Pass On, No Pass Back. *The reader will discover, as with Mark Twain's* Huckleberry Finn, *that reading aloud will help cross the barrier erected by the unfamiliar spelling of pidgin English, and an interesting character and situation emerge.*

RESPONSE ⟿

The difficulty with trying to define *Asian American* is, of course, the difficulty in trying to pin down a single definition to encompass a multiplicity of identities. I actually like the idea of the possibility of confusion and of mistaken identity: Asian Americans misidentified as Mexican . . . as Native American . . . as recent immigrants. "Is your English from Jamaica?" It's a reminder to me that we must acknowledge our connection to other third world or marginalized people. Even if we see ourselves as completely mainstream Americans, when we are mistaken for someone else, we are, at least for the moment, reminded of how much we are still outsiders to mainstream American culture.

I'm a local (loco?) writer. *Loco moco* is an island dish invented on the Big Island in the 1950s: a couple of scoops of rice topped with a hamburger patty, an egg cooked sunny-side up and runny and smothered with brown gravy. Real aficionados add tabasco, salt, pepper, and ketchup. An acquired taste. Locals and local writing are definitely an acquired taste. Like *loco moco,* familiar food is put together differently; my background and upbringing might well be characterized as familiar influences put together in a different way. Same but different.

Every writer needs to feel a part of a community of writers and readers who can provide him or her with feedback and response that is honest and supportive. He or she needs to feel safe enough to take risks, to make mistakes, to experiment and still have the support of his peers. He also needs to have his community provide the intense scrutiny that only other writers and critical readers can give. I am fortunate to belong to such a group of writers and readers. We have met monthly for eighteen years now, for a potluck dinner and a three- or four-hour writing workshop. This is where you can show your goofiest pieces of writing and still get a careful and thoughtful reading and not feel too embarrassed if it bombs. The audience that I create for, then, is very much like myself or the members of this community. One of the things I look forward to every month is reading through the stack of xeroxed manuscripts. It's like Christmas— exciting and full of promise and surprise. Reading the work of the others gives me energy and helps me in my own struggle to write. Over the years, I've come to realize that the notion of writing as a solitary enterprise may well be yet another American myth—the writer as the rugged American individualist. My writing is very much formed and influenced by my membership in a writing community. Yet I think we all have distinct and diverse voices and take care to preserve and respect them. The group reads critically, and we depend on each other to point out when we use clichés or a stereotypical depiction of a character or ethnic group. For island writers this is especially important because our literary history of oppression and denial and a popular image based on the fictions of James Michener's Hawaii and Elvis movies makes us particularly vulnerable to attitudes and beliefs based on what others have told us about ourselves rather than real, lived experiences.

Q: Frank Chin claims there's an "authentic" Asian American sensibility. Is he right? If so, how would you define it?

Funny you should ask, because Chin once accused me of failing to present the heroic in local pidgin, since all the pidgin speakers I depicted were misfits and retards. Again, if one starts from the premise that there can be only one "authentic" voice, then he's right. But I think we need to allow for more than one voice and a wider range of authenticity. He's right in reminding us that we *should* know our heroes, our history and that of our ancestors. But the cultural knowledge of our ancestors may be as muddled as our own. I don't think Chin is saying there ought to be a kind of "cultural police" to dictate what we are to write, nor am I saying "anything goes," that the Asian American writer does not have to write responsibly about his/her community. As in most things, I think the answer lies somewhere in between. Further, Hawaii writers have to always be vigilant about reinforcing colonial or paternalistic attitudes and beliefs that might have become so ingrained in our thinking that we fail to question them or we accept them as truth. I think that if we are to succeed as an artistic community, we need to admit into our literary world the *possibility* of acts of heroism from retards and misfits. We need to acknowledge a larger and wider range of voices that speak to us and for us.

The Asian American artist has a more difficult time "disappearing" behind his or her work by virtue of physical appearance, or surname, or details that suggest a non-White culture. I don't think we have a choice about our Asian American identity. Regardless if ethnicity is an element in his work or not, the Asian American artist needs to consider stereotypes, the history of Asian Americans in this country, and past literary and media depictions.

We embarked on a cover-art and artist portfolio series with Bamboo Ridge to feature the wave of Hawaii visual artists who trained and made their reputation in New York shortly after World War II. Isami Doi is generally their mentor and center of a community of artists who used the GI bill to attend art school. These old-timers had significant careers, numerous one-man shows, and national reputations, only to return home to relative obscurity. How was it

that I never learned about these guys in school . . . Satoru Abe, Harry Tsuchidana, Tadashi Sato, Bob Ochikubo, Jerry Okimoto, Ralph Iwamoto . . . artist and poet Reuben Tam . . . even as a college art major in Hawaii? We need to be aware of who has come before us. We need to be aware that some of this information has been suppressed and that some of the barriers to our knowledge of Asian American artists have been put up by ourselves. There may be a good measure of self-loathing, self-deprecation in our ignorance: the plantation ethic saying that whatever we do will never be good enough . . . we'll never be as good as haoles (Whites) from the mainland; that success must be validated by measures outside of ourselves, mainland standards. And even when these artists "make it" on the mainland, they return to relative obscurity on Hawaii. Thus the local Asian American artist has an added burden to shoulder, the responsibility to know a history that may not be easily known. One that may be hidden or suppressed. This, too, is part of who we are.

I once saw a porno film that featured an Asian stud surrounded by a bevy of Asian women . . . there was *Asian* in the title somewhere, presumably so that prospective viewers could figure out what the film depicted. The trouble with this one (I suppose it's dangerous to be admitting that I even watched this stuff) was that this was the first one that I had seen that starred an Asian male (quite remarkable in itself). The trouble was that when he got his pants off, his penis was ludicrously long (perhaps two feet, knocking around his knees somewhere) and obviously rubber. This Asian stud, then, wasn't really a stud but an Asian male who needed a prosthesis. Indeed, we haven't come very far from Charlie Chan movies. (There's something satisfying about comparing Charlie Chan to pornography though.)

The depictions of Asians, Hawaiians, and pidgin speakers on television have been similarly "pornographic." If one were to judge the islands by the stories on *Marker, One West Waikiki, Jake and the Fatman, Magnum P.I.,* and the granddaddy of them all, *Hawaii Five-O,* you could only conclude that the islands are occupied by sinister Asians who speak "fortune cookie" talk or stupid Hawaiians and locals in nonthinking roles who can barely speak. The plantation still exists in the television and film industry, with the producers thinking, "You people ought to be grateful that we decided to film in the islands and bring money into the economy," while the locals have characterized most shows as the "stupid haole" bossing around people of color. The short-lived network show *Byrds of Paradise* (the only non-cops-and-robbers show of the bunch) at least attempted to depict some of the complexities of living on an island in a multicultural setting. Its demise due to poor ratings was the cause for a groundswell of support: picketing and letter writing to the network protesting its cancellation. Yet what were these supporters advocating? Have we become so used to being the flunkeys and the housekeepers that we actually like these roles, these depictions? Curiously, there was no picketing or letter writing to demand that Asians and Hawaiians become the center of a few episodes or to demand that the network solicit scripts from local writers, depicting stories from the inside. In other words, we're still depending on outsiders to tell our stories; to tell us about ourselves.

While there has been increasing recognition of my work in the schools, there still exists particularly at the college level, the resistance to embrace local literature wholeheartedly. This has been manifested by the fact that although students respond very positively to work in pidgin and are able to give detailed, insightful analyses, the examination of local literature tends to be peripheral to the literature course, i.e., is placed at the end of the semester, is used via xeroxing or optional texts. There appears to be a relaxing of the rigor and expectations that professors have of local literature pieces, and this may be consciously or subconsciously saying that these works are less than important as works of literature. Alternately, they may be resistant to venturing into "unknown" territory, literature where the student might have greater cultural knowledge than the teacher.

I'm probably most pleased and grateful when readers recognize themselves in a story I have written. Or are moved to tell me about a situation in their own lives that my story has caused them to remember. The sense of connection that occurs when reader and author come together because of the common experience of the story. It's magic. Truly magical. Or when they discover something about a story, an interpretation, that I hadn't thought about before. Or when they use it with an audience that I would ordinarily think too young or not sophisticated enough to make sense of it. When that connection happens, author to reader, reader to author, reader to some other person, reader to himself . . . I'd like to think that I had a part in causing some kind of dialogue to occur. And that we've been enhanced by it.

Q: If Asian Americans write about subjects other than their identity and our common cause—justice and equality—can they still be called Asian American writers?

Nah, call em haoles.

It seems to me that writing about identity and the cause of justice and equality are noble goals for all writers. And of course, all writers can write outside of these areas . . . does writing outside of these areas change the identity of White mainstream writers? Does

Laureen Kwock's identity change when she writes romances as Clarice Peters? In the case of romances, does it matter if the author/editor/publisher opts for a more generic romance author's name? Do we respond differently? I think we do, and when we (or our publishers) try to make us invisible, we cheat ourselves of the opportunity to further demonstrate the diversity of Asian American voices.

If you accept that you can never separate one's identity from the work, then each piece defines and redefines what it is to be Asian American. What would a romance with an Asian American sensibility be?

Q: Should we claim exclusive rights to our history and culture . . . assert that non-Asians cannot truly understand or interpret our material, our work?

It's an open field for anyone, really, but unless we tell our stories the way we know them to be, someone else will tell them for us . . . probably wrong. Hawaii's story was appropriated (stolen, according to some) by Michener and others who led us to believe that we had no literature. I can't see how we could ever claim "exclusive" rights to stories about Asian Americans, and even the notion of trying to tell the story of an entire people boggles my mind. (It seems almost arrogant to even try; perhaps it's because we know of too many exceptions, too many particulars, to be able to write the epic.) I think the more stories we tell, the greater likelihood we will be able to combat the stereotypes and help readers discern the difference between the real and the fake. And every now and then a story comes along by someone (sometimes Asian, sometimes haole) that is just so blatantly inauthentic that it just pisses me off . . . and it serves as a reminder that if we don't continue to make efforts to get things right, no one else will.

So the Asian American immigration story can and should still be told, even if it seems like it already has been told. There are many more stories to tell. The collective stories of all of us will then speak for all of us. No *one* story will fix the experience for us. We and others will see that Asian Americans are indeed a multiplicity of voices, a complex web of influences. The Asian American epic would, for me, most likely be a compilation of these individual stories and how they contribute to a larger Asian American community.

Q: Has the Asian American writer who attracts a wide non-Asian audience "sold out?"

The crabs-in-the-bucket theory (the crab that is about to escape the bucket is pulled back by its own) . . . success in the White world must mean that you sold out, is what the other jealous crabs might say. This argument, of course, is overly simplistic but cannot be just dismissed. We need to always be on guard to figure out where and when we have been co-opted. For locals, we need to be constantly on guard for vestiges of colonial attitudes creeping back into our belief systems. It is truly a constant battle. Part of our responsibility is to check with our communities . . . to be self-critical. . . . Are we too quick to criticize? Have we been "good soldiers" and closed ranks and endorsed anything by a Hawaii writer? Are we overly modest about our accomplishments? The crab pulling us back is often ourselves . . . just as the crabs helping us out of the bucket are also each other. Regardless, in my view, "selling out" is sometimes a perception brought on by the notion of rejecting your community once you've "arrived." Hawaii's governor Ben Cayetano, a Filipino American who grew up in a poor section of [Honolulu] and attended Farrington High School, a tough inner-city school, has said that pidgin has no place in the school (despite being a pidgin speaker himself) and that he was the only attorney in his graduating class of five hundred students. He seems to forget that legions of pidgin speakers helped get him elected, as did many, many blue-collar and white-collar workers. His classmates, all nonattorneys apparently, are the backbone of the islands' workforce. His story, that he had to "overcome" his pidgin and his socioeconomic background, seems to be a denial of his community.

The distinction between writers (or writings) with a "cause" versus those with "style" is a troubling one, because it assumes that one precludes the other. The most successful pieces of writing, I think, integrate the two . . . have that combination of passion and craft that makes good literature. I don't set out aspiring to break into the "canon," and the canon discussion dangerously plays into the perception that someone has to act as the gatekeeper, selecting some, omitting others.

What is exciting to me are the prospects of new Asian American writers who have been empowered to experiment with their poetry and fiction. I'm seeing more and more pieces being published that might disturb the majority. Some pidgin pieces by Lois-Ann Yamanaka and some by Zamora Linmark, centered on sexual orientation and physical and mental abuse, have been first published outside of Hawaii, and by presses that don't necessarily have an Asian American focus.

Scholars of Asian American literature have begun to muster the courage to consider more noncanonical works, and I am gratified that they have chosen to do so. I think the discovery that these scholars are making is that Asian American literature is not necessarily a literature in its infancy . . . it is a literature full and diverse and complex enough to withstand critical scrutiny using many of the traditional critical standards. What re-mains is for scholars to employ critical theory as well as their own understanding of what it means to be Asian American to examine those noncanonical pieces of literature that the mainstream might otherwise ignore or misread. It means making a new canon based on a new critical standard, perhaps more reflective, more inclusive, more accepting of diversity, of family ties or myth. Scholars need to "sink their critical teeth" into examination of pieces that might be imperfect by some standards but serve to advance the community of Asian American writers and literature. Admittedly, it's difficult to walk the fine line between advocacy and scholarly "objective" analysis, but scholars are in a position to change the canon, and the pieces with the "meat" (content) are more likely the pieces that prod, provoke, and incite readers. Sometimes these are the pieces with more passion, perhaps, than craft. Perhaps this, too, is a characteristic of Asian American literature: its themes and human relationships are more deeply felt, often attributable to a real-life incident or a meaningful personal experience, versus the focus of a story being simply a demonstration of the author's craft.

I have no real desire to replace the study of "dead White guys" with "dead Asian guys." Local lit will probably always be marginal, on the periphery. And Asian American lit, as it becomes more central, may appear to lose its identity as the obvious Asian American themes and references become less visible. But taken as a whole, the body of Asian American lit will remain, I think, distinctly Asian American, as new immigrants tell their stories. Imagine my excitement when a Vietnamese student told me, matter-of-factly, of her family's story of immigration . . . ending up in Texas as a shrimp boat fisherman . . . the Forrest Gump story . . . only hers was real. Her story will join others as we continue to define Asian American literature.

Still, even from a position of centrality, the struggles are hardly reduced. Look at politics in Hawaii. Here, Asian Americans have held political power and have been central in government and labor for nearly fifty years. Yet the story of the election of our Filipino American governor and his Japanese American running mate is typical of the stories of a struggling immigrant family, the single-parent family, the struggle of poverty and race. Theirs has not been an easy task, even when the political arena in the islands has been dominated by Asian Americans.

This question is also interesting because Bamboo Ridge was accused at a recent forum of being the new canon and neocolonial. We had apparently appropriated the term *local literature* to mean primarily Chinese and Japanese American, to the exclusion of Filipino and Native Hawaiians. Perhaps this is how canonization occurs . . . marginal for eighteen years, then bingo, we're the canon. Local literature that has become more "central" still acknowledges the struggles of an immigrant past or that of disenfranchised people . . . hardly canonical or neocolonial.

Paint

Sometimes I feel mean. I like go bust someting. Some guys like bust car antennas but I only like go spray paint. I donno, I feel mean and I feel good at da same time, you know. It bad, but still yet I like spray paint. I donno why. Make me feel mean when I stay painting but feel like I stay doing someting. Someting big you know, so dat I stay big, too. I no paint swear words la dat. I paint my name and make um fancy wit curlicues undahneat. Sometimes I paint my babe's name but I no like do dat too much, bumbye everybody know, you know. Sometimes I paint one surf pickcha. One real tubular wave wit one guy jes making it . . . cranking through, you know.

When you paint on one new wall, j'like you stay da first one in da world fo spray paint. Even if you know get someting undahneat dat you went paint before, when da wall stay new, I mean, when dey jes paint up da wall fo cover da old spray paint, j'like stay da first time you painting. You can feel da spray paint, cool on your hand. You can smell da spray, sting your nose but sweet, j'like. I no sniff, you stupid if you sniff, bumbye you come all stoned and you no can spray good. But j'like it make you feel big. Make you feel good dat your name stay ovah dere big. Like you stay *somebody*.

Coco. Ass my name. "Coco '84" is what I write. I no write um plain, I make um nice, you know. Fat lettahs. Outline um. Wit sparkles. Da kine dat you can make wit white or silvah paint, like one cross or one star. From far, j'like your name stay shiny. I stay undah da freeway aftah school fo watch my wall. I watch um from across da street by da school parking lot. Everybody who pass look at my wall everyday. I try put someting new everytime so get someting new fo everybody to see. Only little bit at a time, like some more lines on da wave or one diffrent color outline on my name, stuff la dat. Jes about everybody look at my wall, even if dey pass um everyday, dey look. Sometimes when get some other guys by me aftah school I no can paint new stuff but da people dat pass still yet try look fo figgah out what stay new.

Aftah school I gotta wait fo my mahdah pau work pick me up. Sometimes I stay by da guys when dey no mo baseball practice la dat but most times I stay by myself. Everyday gotta plan how you going paint. When you paint, you gotta plan um good. You gotta be fast. You gotta know what you going do. And you cannot get nabbed. How many times I almost got nabbed, man.

One time somebody went put "Rockerz Rule" on my wall. Was anykine way. Wasn't nice. Had some guys hanging around da wall and I went ask dem, "'You went make dat?' "So what if we did?" one of da guys went tell me. I told dem, "Eh, I know da guy Coco, and he going bust your head if he find out you went spray on his wall. He big you know, Coco." Dey went look around first fo see if I had backers. Since nevah have nobody, dey went ack like dey was tough. But finally dey went go away. Dey nevah spray nutting else except fo dis one punk kid went spray and walk. Had one crooked black line all da way across my wall. I would've beefed um but I nevah like. I would've given um lickins. I could've taken um.

Nobody know I spray paint. Nobody even know I stay Coco. If they knew, they would say, "Naht, dass not you. I heard Coco stay one big guy. You too runt fo be Coco." Funny yeah, but dass me. Ass me, Coco. One time I going paint one big mural and everybody going know ass me. Would be good if you no need paint fast and hide when somebody come. Could make um nice and people would even buy da paint fo me. I would make da whole wall wit spray. I would paint faces, my face ovah and ovah and I would make um look mean and tough. And I would look *bad* and I would be feeling good. I would make sparkles and you could see dem shining in my eyes. I would use silvah and some black paint. People would tink, "Who did dat nice one?" Dey wouldn't paint um ovah. Dey would buy me paint. Dey would gimme money fo paint da walls all ovah da place. Wouldn't need to do work in school. Da teacha would gimme one spray can, not brush and paypah, la dat. Junk, when you paint in school. Gotta do certain tings, certain way. No can be big. No mo feeling. Ass why spray paint mo bettah. Make you feel mean. And bad. And good.

One time had one lady came by da wall. She wasn't one teacha or nutting cause she had long hair and had jeans and tee-shirt la dat. I had to hide my spray can when I seen her coming. I nevah like her bust me. But you know what, she had her own spray can and went look right at me den she went spray on my wall:

REVOLUTION FOR THE 80's

MAY DAY.

Den she went little mo down and went spray out my "Coco '84," and went put "WORLD WITHOUT IMPERIALISM, NO IMPERIALIST WARS" right ovah my surf pickcha. When she was pau she went look at me and say, "You know what dat means?"

"No," I told her.

"Dat means we gotta tell people to fight da government. Gotta get da people together and tell da governments not to have wars. Gotta give da poor people money and food and power la dat."

"Oh," I said. "But lady, why you went spray um ovah da wall? You nevah have to spray um ovah Coco's stuff. You could've put um on da top or on da side or write smaller. Look how you went jam up my pickcha. I mean Coco's pickcha."

"Sorry," she went tell kinda sassy.

"Why you gotta paint da kine stuff?"

"Cause I like. So what, kid." She was coming little bit piss off. So aftah she event go away, I went try fix my wall up. But she went use red. Hard fo cover, red. She nevah have to put um right ovah my writing. I wanted dem fo come paint da whole wall awready, erase um so dat could start ovah. I jes went get my can spray and I went stand in front da lady's words. I was feeling mean. Not good kine, jes mean. I went write "LADY—HATE YOU" not nice wit fat lettahs or sparkles but jes anykine way. I nevah care. Was ugly, jes like her's one.

When my mahdah came pick me up, I seen her reading da wall. "Who went do dat?" she went ask me. I told her one lady wit long hair and tee-shirt. I went ask her who dat kine lady was and she went say, "Dat Commanists dat. Not Americans. Hippies." She told me, "Dey good fo nuttings." I was looking out da window when we went drive away. Couldn't even see "Coco" anymore.

I couldn't tink about anyting except what I was going paint ovah da hippie lady's words. First I thought I could paint some more surf pictures but I went check my colors and I figgahed would be too hard fo cover da words. Da lady, she went write big. I thought I could do "Coco '84" mo big but still couldn't cover da lady's words. Would use up all my paint.

Aftah school da next day, I went to my wall. Could see da lady's words from far away. I jes went look at her spray paint words. Ass all was, jes words. Ugly words dat nobody like read. Not like mines, not nice wit sparkles la dat or curlicues or one pickcha of one surfah in da tube. Jes words . . . anykine words. Everybody going say, "Hoo da ugly. Who did dat?"

What if dey tink was me? Betchu da painter guys going come paint da wall fast. J'like the time somebody else went write "Sakai Sucks" and everybody knew dey was talking about Mr. Sakai, da principal. Dey came right away fo paint da wall dat time.

Nevah feel good anymore fo look at my wall. Wasn't mine anymore. Wasn't Coco's. Wasn't even da hippie lady's cause she no care. Was nobody's.

And den da next day had posters pasted up on da wall. Was some more stuff about May Day and had one pickcha of one guy holding up his fist. Dey nevah only put one, but dey went line um up. Had maybe six or seven or eight all line up. Cover everyting: My surf pickcha, my name, even my "hate you" words. And dey went paste um on good. Dey went use someting dat stick real good to da cement and den dey even put da paste on da top so dat da ting was stuck extra good. No can peel um off. Hardly can scrape um even. Only little bit. I seen da hippie lady aftah school looking at da posters.

"You went do dat?"

"What you tink?" she went tell me.

"I donno. You went do um, eh?"

"So."

"You shouldn't have done dat. Coco going come piss off, you know. Dis his wall. Maybe he might even call da cops or someting."

"Who's dat, Coco? Dat you? Betchu da guy no stay. If he so big, how come he no come talk to me himself? From now on dis is everybody's wall. Not only Coco can paint on dis wall. Anybody can paint. Me. You. Anybody."

She jes went keep on talking, "Eh, you no need be scared of Coco. He ain't so tough. What he going do to you?"

"Yeah but, not supposed to be writing on da walls . . ."

"Who said? Da government? Coco? Coco went paint first. He went liberate dis wall first time. But now he no can hog um. Dis wall is fo everybody I tell you. Uddahwise he stay making up anykine rules. J'like one nudda government."

"Hah?"

"How come you gotta watch dis wall to Coco? You jes being Coco's stooge, you know. You shouldn't have to be scared of Coco. Dat's jes like da people who scared of the government. I mean you no need be oppressed by somebody else. . . ."

Couldn't tell what she was saying cause one truck was going on da freeway and from far could hear one police siren. Da lady went stop talking and we went look up at da freeway listen to da siren coming closer. Went pass.

I jes told her, "No paint on top Coco's wall, eh. Or else you going be in trouble. Coco, he big, you know. He *somebody,* you know." She nevah say nutting. She jes went walk away but I was still yet telling her anykine stuff, "You no can jes cover up my wall la dat. Was *my* surfah. Was *my* wave. Was *my* name! I hate you hippie lady!"

I went get my can spray and I jes started fo paint one face right ovah her words. I donno whose face. Jes one face. Was black and red. Had plenny lines in da face. Was one mean and sad face. I jes went keep on adding lines to da face and came mo black and mo black until was almost like one popolo but wasn't. Jes was one face wit plenny lines on um. Da paint went run out when I was fixing up da cheek. Went drip. I couldn't finish um. I went cross da street and watch my face.

Had some guys in one truck, regular fix-da-road guys, went come and look at da posters. Dey took out anykine scrapers and some real strong kine paint thinner fo take da posters off.

"Awright," I went tell dem.

"Damn kids do anykine yeah," one guy went tell me.

"Naht, wasn't kids. Was da hippie lady," I went tell him.

"You know who was?"

"Yeah, da hippie lady who come around here sometimes."

"You not da one, eh?" da man went ask me.

"Nah, but da guy Coco spray."

"Coco spray dis kine words?" Da man was pointing to da word "hate" between da posters. Could only see "lady" and "hate" left.

"Nah, he make nice kine Stuff. He no paint ugly stuff."

Dey went clean off all da posters and started to paint da wall.

"What fo you paint da wall awready? Da hippie lady only going paint um again. What fo?"

"At least going look nice fo little while," da boss guy told me.

"Eh, try look dis face," one of da guys went point to my pickcha wit his roller. "Not bad yeah? Look almost like somebody crying wit dis red drip ovah here. You know who went do dis one? Pretty good artist. Too bad gotta cover um up."

I jes went turn around. I started fo cry. I donno how come.

Garrett Hongo

POET

Born in 1951 in Volcano, Hawaii, Garrett Hongo grew up in Gardena, in South Los Angeles. After graduation from Pomona College in Claremont, California, he had a traveling fellowship to Japan and then attended the University of Michigan, where he won the Hopwood Prize for Poetry. He has a master of fine arts degree from the University of California, Irvine. From 1976 to 1978, he founded and directed a theater group, the Asian Exclusion Act, in Seattle. He has published two poetry collections: Yellow Light *(1982) and* The River of Heaven *(1988); the latter was awarded the Lamont Poetry Prize by the Academy of American Poets. A recipient of fellowships from the Guggenheim Foundation and the National Endowment for the Arts (NEA), he has edited* Under Western Eyes: Personal Essays from Asian America *(1995),* Songs My Mother Taught Me: Stories, Memoir, and Plays by Wakako Yamauchi *(1994), and* The Open Boat: Poems from Asian America *(1993). His latest book is* Volcano: A Memoir of Hawai'i *(1995). He is currently professor of English and creative writing at the University of Oregon.*

RESPONSE

I was born in Volcano, Hawaii, but my parents left with me when I was six or eight months old, and I didn't go back until 1982, when I went to give poetry readings. Then I felt, suddenly, that I'd been returned to what I'd always loved. The landscape was

103

magnificent: the rainforest, the fogs, the mists, so thick with growth, the different kinds of birds, the *hapu'u,* the *ohi'a* trees. It was a little concerto of vegetation, all different flowers. It was just great to me. We'd cross the summit of Kilauea and get into the volcano itself, and the volcanic surface is so stark, like ocean that had been drained of water. That contrast, that blankness and then that lush vegetation not one and a half miles away, stayed in my soul. It really went down deep. From then on, I tried to create a language that would be adequate to the feelings and inspiration and sublimity that I felt in that dramatic landscape, which stayed in my body. Since 1982, everything has been dedicated to getting the language to the level of what I found in the landscape.

I think I got this language in *Volcano,* my memoir, a sort of "forgetoir," stuff that everyone wanted to forget and that I dug up—family history and landscape back in Hawaii. I think it's a repose of the soul—a language that would be adequate to the spectacular landscape, to the needs of my own mind, and to the stories of my family. The small yearnings of heart as well, I think I got that. I'm pretty happy with what I was able to do with the language of the heart. That's my favorite, the current book.

Of the anthologies, my favorite is Wakako Yamauchi's book, *Songs My Mother Taught Me.* She was a mentor of mine, and it was her seventieth birthday. I was powerfully motivated to do the right thing. I wanted to speak for an entire life lived with letters, which is what Wakako did, and introduce her to the wider Asian American audience and the audience in general, make an accounting, a tribute to her work, to her whole life. Wakako is one of the first Japanese American short story writers. She has given us a legacy. It was special to me.

My interest in poetry goes back a long way. Poets seemed to me emotional and direct, and their language was always so beautiful. They seem poised up there like really wonderful classical musicians with music in their bodies and their minds. They spoke so well, not just their poetry but in between reading the poetry. They felt like the most articulate, noble people. I hadn't met a lot of fiction writers. In college, I heard the poets like Philip Levine and Galway Kinnell. I had a great poet as a teacher, Bert Meyers, who knew so much about literature, and having grown up with Japanese Americans during World War II, he also knew about the internment. He seemed very open to my discussions about race, too. So I was lucky I found a mentor and an inspiration.

I began by writing love poems when I was in high school, for a girl who sat in front of me in creative writing class. I wanted to impress her. Then I wrote out of loneliness. I found Chinese poetry and its regulation fairly early on. That gave me a way in, in terms of the poise of emotion that was always present in Chinese poetry. I think that's how I started.

I always liked theater as well. We had great theater when I was at Pomona College, but the parts were always for White people or Black people, and Asians were never thought of—except for the guy who did Kabuki, but then he exoticized us. I refused all things like that. But when I was a graduate student at the University of Michigan in 1974, I saw Frank Chin's *The Year of the Dragon* on PBS, and it really was powerful. I hated the acting, but I loved the writing—what he was able to say about Chinese people. Then I met Momoko Iko, who wrote *The Gold Watch* (1974), who encouraged me. In Los Angeles in 1975, I dropped out of school and I went to meet Wakako Yamauchi and hung out with her and Momoko. They were filming *The Gold Watch* that summer. I tried to absorb as much as I could. When I was in Seattle in 1976, I got involved with a theater group called the Asian Exclusion Act, and I staged all those plays, starting with *The Year of the Dragon,* by Frank Chin. The second play was Wakako Yamauchi's *And the Soul Shall Dance,* and then we did a play of mine, *Nisei Bar and Grill,* and *The Gold Watch,* by Momoko Iko.

I wouldn't call myself a playwright, however. I am a poet who tried playwriting. I think the art itself, once you get a script, is fascinating and exciting. Directing a play was like playing a team sport, like football or basketball. You had to know where people would be going, feel their energy and channel it toward a result that fit an idea you wanted to produce. The technique was fascinating and the world of theater was fascinating. In Asian American theater, you're up against certain biases already set in people's minds: the idea that we're a sideshow to the main show, and a lot of Asian Americans are uncomfortable seeing portrayals of themselves on the stage. So there's a complicated and powerful moment. That theaters have sprung up in numbers since the 1970s is a very interesting fact.

When did I first realize I was an Asian American? I never really thought I *wasn't* an Asian American. I don't think I went through that kind of thing, like a lot of people. David Mura talked about how he tried to be a White writer, just a writer. At some point, he sort of snapped and then realized that he was an Asian American. He now says that he is a Sansei (third-generation Japanese American) writer. I didn't have that kind of demarcation. Back in college, I was always writing poems about Gardena in Los Angeles, the Japanese American community where I lived; about my grandfather

who was imprisoned during World War II. In fact, the first poem I published was called "Issei," dedicated to my grandfather. It's about how he turns to me at one point during my childhood and insists that I'm Japanese. He was very concerned that I know the history, that I knew what was done to us and how we were treated during World War II. That was my strongest loyalty, I guess, from the beginning. So my very first moment might have been when I was seven, when my grandfather said that, and I had no choice thereafter.

There have been times when I've struggled with the idea of what an Asian American writer was. I remember being taunted once at an MLA convention in 1980 or in 1979. I'd just published a poem in the *New Yorker* called "Yellow Light" about my old neighborhood in Los Angeles, which is Korean Town now. A bunch of writers—we called ourselves minorities then—were going out for drinks. But I had not slept enough and just wanted to go back to my hotel room to sleep. There was a Chicano writer and a lot of Asian American writers. One of the writers was telling me, "Oh, Garrett, now that you're published in the *New Yorker,* you can't hang out with us anymore." That really hurt me. That was mostly about me and my own fears of leaving the community and accepting White standards, I suppose, of beauty and literature. I don't know. There was a moment of conflict there. I did go back to my hotel room, but I didn't sleep.

It's been hard for me that way. Every time you write a poem or publish a book, somebody accuses you being disloyal to what you were before. That's pretty much always happened to me. Somebody out there says you are a sellout every time that you try to write something.

I don't write with a lot of audience in mind. I write with a feeling, or a style, or an aesthetic dimension in mind. I don't really work very well if I think in terms of audience that directly. I'm not that kind of writer.

What audiences do I hope for? I would like to believe that my work is acceptable to any audience. But I know it's not. The work is about the common experience of people who are not of the elite. Yet my language is quite dense. A friend who works for *Reader's Digest* says that my work is extremely literary, and every time I commit words to a page, I have a high style. And I would say that is the case.

I write for intelligent, sensitive people who are searching. I write for those who believe in the beauty of the land, the nobility of all peoples, who are willing to acknowledge their own history. I don't think in terms of market or audience share. That doesn't work for me.

I have had my share of recognition, I'd say. I think we all are going to be given at least a little of what we deserve. I think I've certainly been given that. I've been given time to write, time to develop, although that's been challenging at several moments in my life. For me, there are distinctly three audiences, in a way. First, there's the audience for poetry, which is the general audience of poetry in America, and I seem to be very well received there; the second book was well received by readers and by my fellow poets. And then, the Bill Moyers book (*The Language of Life,* 1995) has begun to put my work out there. Second, there's the Asian American audience, which is a bit distinct from that more general audience for poetry. I think I've developed that audience mostly out of my anthology work—and the intellectual interest, or disagreement, has emerged from that. A lot of people feel challenged by what I've written. The young people at universities are now responding to that challenge. They are not necessarily the people who would read

the poetry. Third, there's an audience I've been getting through *Volcano,* my memoir—people who are interested in the literature of landscape, people who love Hawaii—and these audiences seem to be a little separate right now. Maybe it's just because I've moved around so much in terms of genre.

What's lacking? I would say what's lacking from *me* is more work. I need to write more. I wish I could. I just don't seem to be very fast.

Several things have shaped this present moment. One is the emergence of Asians as Asian Americans, which is great. We constitute an American people in a very powerful way. The culture has awakened to our presence in a way that's not as paranoid as it has been in the past—the yellow peril and all that. And we're no longer labor, plantation workers to be exploited. We've emerged into consciousness, asserted ourselves into arenas of culture.

Two, there have been breakthroughs; for example, in Maxine Hong Kingston, who wrote *The Woman Warrior,* we have a genius who introduced the idea of Asian Americans to the largest possible audience. She was followed up by Amy Tan, who had huge popular acceptance, and David Henry Hwang. I think all these figures/presences (*The Woman Warrior, The Joy Luck Club,* and *M. Butterfly*) have really changed things.

Commercially, economically, I think that New York publishers have seen that movies and Asian American writing can sell. The reasons for that are complicated, and they are not pure. They are not the reasons that young Asian American writers would necessarily like, not the reasons that I necessarily would subscribe to. There's the appeal of exoticism. There's the idea of being a voyeur of a foreign culture that's promulgating a stereotype, and then there's what we do with it. It's complicated, very complicated.

Beyond these things, there's the presence of writers such as Robert Olen Butler, who has written *A Good Scent from a Strange Mountain* (1993), which is about Vietnamese Americans and which has become very popular. It portrays Vietnamese Americans although it was written by a Caucasian. That becomes complicated. A book just arrived at my desk at school, with the bare back of Asian woman with long, glossy, black hair flowing over her shoulders, sheets wrapped around her hips, and some kind of highlighted chopstick writing. It seems to be directed toward an exotic market. But there's also *Native Speaker,* by Chang-rae Lee (1995); *The Colors of Desire,* by David Mura (1995); and *The Phoenix Gone, the Terrace Empty,* by Marilyn Chin (1994). For every book like the former, there are books like the latter. This is a rich moment. When I was younger, I could think of only a half dozen Asian American writers. Now, name-dropping from the top of my head, I probably couldn't stop at sixty. There are also Kazuo Ishiguro and Timothy Mo in England. There are Bharati Mukherjee and Anita Desai. There's lots of diversity now. I think it's pretty good, pretty interesting.

I think criticism of successful Asian American writers is quite backward, frankly. There are people like Frank Chin who out-and-out attack people. That's just asinine. It's jealousy, fear of diversity; it's megalomania, as far as I can see. Behind him, there are complainers. I guess you're always going to have them. I think what they fail to separate, what they are angry about, and what they're sensitive to is the stereotype, and how literature—all forms of cultural representation—engages stereotypes in one way or another, either directly to explode it completely, the way Frank Chin's work does, or indirectly. You are always working with symbolic distance. I think their analysis is frankly incomplete. The critique of Kingston, say, or Tan or Hwang depends on a misunderstanding of the idea of the way culture functions and the way language is disseminated.

The writer, the artist, is not in control of reception. We don't own those systems. Those are systems of power that exist along with the idea of knowledge, the *episteme. No* individual controls that. How you are perceived is out of your control. You produce the work. It goes into a mechanism of entering into the culture, and then there's cultural reception. The mechanism for cultural reception itself is imbued with incredibly stereotypical, racist symbols, attitudes, and notions. Insofar as you engage the issue of race at all, you are also going to engage the problematic of having that engagement distorted in the system of reception and dissemination. That distortion is what people are critical of and is the problem.

You cannot censor the work, you cannot control the voices of the artists, heaven forbid. But what we can do is critique the system of reception, which then portrays what you have said or have written. For example, you can be tried for crimes that you have not committed if the system says you have committed those crimes, as in the 1931 case of the Scottsboro Boys. Take that incident—nine young Black men in a train car with a White woman—obviously she was raped by these Black boys, and they are going to be lynched. Why? Because that is the operative stereotype in the culture about Black men and White women; number one, because of the reversal of the actual historical fact, which is the White slave owner taking pleasures from Black women in slave quarters. No matter what the truth about that incident, no matter what was or was not committed, the story that is operative is the story of rape. Therefore, the Black men will be lynched. That story is so powerful in the cul-

ture that it doesn't matter what kind of testimony anybody gives or what really happened. It's already existing as a narrative in
the culture. Is it the fault of the Black person
to have been inside that story at a certain moment? Of course not. This is at the top of the
issues in the Clarence Thomas hearing. In
Hawaii, there is the Massie case—another
instance of trial by stereotyping and political
domination.

It is very difficult for people to understand that the artist is not in control of these
notions embedded in culture and society.
What we artists can do is to enter into those
projections and adjust them, destroy them—
or attempt to—or manipulate them to get
people to think differently. That's the artist's
responsibility. I think the best artists all do
that. I think Maxine Hong Kingston does it;
I think they all do it. Oftentimes, however,
readers project onto David Henry Hwang or
Maxine Hong Kingston and Amy Tan the
racist stereotypes that are already out there.
But if you look at the works very closely,
they in fact are engaging the stereotype in
order to take it apart. They channel different
emotions.

David Henry Hwang makes fun of the
stereotypes, pointing out how ridiculous they
are. An enjoyment of the danger of sexuality
is embedded in David Hwang's works. Maxine has this powerful wish to mythologize—
not to borrow from a prior mythology but to
remythologize the mundane moment, those
moments which have been thought of as
mundane. In *China Men,* the Chinese guys
in Stockton (California) reminisce about
working on the railroad or in the gold
mine—she mythologizes those men and
turns them into the gods of luck today. If it
were not for her, those moments would be
out of history, out of mythology; they
wouldn't exist in fact. She can mythologize
the moment when women are ironing

clothes, rather than rigidly reproducing the
story of Monkey. That's what she's doing.

I very much disagree with a narrowing,
jealous, mean-spirited approach to the critique of Asian American writers. If you really
want to look at cultures, you need to look at
the operations of culture from afar. You can
see how systemically culture (insofar as
American culture is racist) reproduces itself
in cultural mechanisms. But to try to hang an
individual artist—that's asinine.

Media representation of Asians? I think
Asians are more fully dimensional these
days. My children get to see Asians being
regular people. They are not so exotic or
stereotypical anymore. So that's better. I
think those of us who are older—and I'm
kind of in the middle these days—are more
sensitive to things like *Flower Drum Song*
and *The Mask of Fu Manchu* than the younger
people, who have enjoyed not only more lib-
erties and opportunities in some ways but
also portrayals that are more humane. I'm
not saying that we should be complacent, but
things have changed.

I don't write about stereotyping much in
my poetry or memoir, but I face it in my essays, in my three anthology introductions. I
talk about the operative stereotype in the introduction to *Under Western Eyes.* I talk
about reproduction of the Other and the tendency of culture to sensualize and to co-opt
the idea of separate races and to present race,
as you say, "to commodify the female and ex-
oticize the race itself"—that's a strong tendency of our culture. That's definitely the
case. And also to sexualize race in a way: the
Black male and the Asian female are highly
sexualized in terms of popular representations in our culture. Those are areas of high
problematic and high cultural power, which
we play into socially and politically just in the
way we live our lives. Some artists are more
conscious of these things than others. Take

Chang-rae Lee—he creates a Korean American male who's very complicated and extraordinarily sensitive and guilty for having left the immigrant culture and, perhaps, for having entered into a disappointing personal relationship with a White woman. It's interesting and powerful. I think those kinds of portraits are going to be emerging; perhaps not as magnificently done as Chang-rae's, but people are going to be awakening to that kind of consciousness.

David Mura has said that people who are not of color can live in such a realm of privilege that they very infrequently meet with the issue of race in America. And that keeps things the way they are. And then, if it's introduced to them, it's an intrusion, and there are only certain kinds of rote responses: one is hostility/belligerence, and the other is condescension. Either way, they want to get rid of it as soon as possible so that they can go back to their lives of privilege, their country clubs. I would say that is definitely the case in universities, in my experience. At the same time, I worry about creating separate educational states along lines of color. That's a concern of mine as well.

Poetry seems to be a way that I can get everybody going in a direction that seems to please people. As I teach poetry, the issues of race come up, because frequently there'll be people of color in my classes. In the graduate program, we attract not only people of color but international people. I've got a Nepali, a Turk, a Thai, and a Singaporean, and a Pakistani. And issues of language, race, and culture come up all the time. I had a Chicano student from California who wrote lines with occasional Spanish words, and some of the White students took offense at not finding that language accessible. We then got into a discussion of how one should write and of audience, and the Chicano student would say, "I ain't writing for you honkies. I'm writing for people back home in the barrio. I'm writing for La Raza: their body." Then all the students will have been exposed to that kind of thinking, and there might emerge some way to manage their refusal to accept each other. Both sides have to engage the issue and start thinking. That happens a lot in my workshop, particularly, at the graduate level. It's been interesting.

The Nepali student once brought in a very gorgeous poem, a lush poem with a lot of references to the history of Nepal, to the partitioning, also to the language and the plight of women in Nepal. Some of the poem was difficult for most of us, particularly the vocabulary. One solution is to have a glossary, I suppose, but another solution is not to have one. Why shouldn't English be open to new emergences, new ways of using the language? English is an international language now. It's not simply written by Anglo-Americans or Brits. It's being written by people born in Nepal, by South Africans. That's interesting. That, I'd say, is the most interesting thing I've done in teaching, working with people like that. At the undergraduate level, it's a much less volatile atmosphere simply because most of the students at Oregon, where I teach, are White.

I think I'm more open to international writers in English and writers of color than a lot of my colleagues. I feel more comfortable with them. So they end up on my syllabi more. I do have a bit of edge, more than an edge, about the recognition of English as a international language than I do simply about writers of color. So I teach Chinua Achebe, Salman Rushdie; I taught Rushdie's book of essays *Imaginary Homelands* (1992) along with Kazuo Ishiguro's *The Remains of the Day* (1989). We look at the issue of geographic, cultural, and racial identity. I would like to contrast *The Remains of the Day* and Gunter Grass's *The Tin Drum* (1964), even though the latter's in German. I don't think I am pigeonholed in terms of time period. I don't focus that way. Neither do I want to be too narrow in category.

Inspiring words for aspiring writers? There are a lot of different ways that writers develop. One way is to seek a community and to emerge from it. And you become a certain kind of writer. You can emerge from a milieu around a kind of lifestyle and culture and be a purveyor of that kind of spontaneity. You are young and you're coming from a group of people; you're having fun. You are of those people. You know you can write about that. You don't need to pretend to be something else. On the other hand, if you are a loner, your work is not always involved so much with an ensemble of people; so it's more of a lonely vigil of consciousness. That's fine too. I think that good works emerge from both kinds of life. Terry McMillan has written a very wonderful popular novel. She's sort of the homegirl novelist of Black women's experience. She goes around. She has fun. She's real sassy, and she enjoys herself. She writes what she writes. Someone who comes from the lonely vigil of consciousness goes and writes her way. Either way is fine. Just accept yourself and be open to your enthusiasms and gifts, whether sparky, spontaneous, and hilarious or serene, sedate, and contemplative. The most important thing is to respect the gift that you have been given—whatever it is.

Find a good teacher, someone who's been around the block and who's not very interested in reproducing an agenda, in collecting acolytes. My own teachers—in the community and in the MFA program at the University of California, Irvine (Charles Wright and C. K. Williams)—were very important for me.

Finally, focus. I've worked in a lot of different areas—poetry, theater, editing—they require a lot of commitment and they're all important, too, but I wouldn't ask it of everyone to cover that much territory. It's probably more fun to write just one kind of thing.

Ministry: Homage to Kilauea

Thinking about volcanoes gives me hope—
      all the pure of it.
When my two boys were babies, to help them fall asleep in the
      afternoons,
I liked driving them out from the house we always rented in
      Mauna Loa Estates,
up the highway a mile or so through the park entrance,
then plunging down past all the micro-climates and botanical
      realities
until I got to the swing in the road just before the turnout to
      Kilauea Observatory at Uwekahuna,
where I could pull over into a little gravel slot by the roadside
    and let all the air-conditioned tour buses
      and shining red rental cars
      and USGS Cherokees and geologists' Broncos swoosh by

while I took a long view
over the saddle towards the veldt-like lower slopes of Mauna Loa,
      my boys already asleep in the back seat.

    What I liked was the swoop of land,
the way it rolled out from under my beach-sandaled feet,
    and the swimming air,
          freighted with clouds
    that seemed the land's vision rising over it.

I could have been the land's own dream then,
and I liked thinking of myself that way,
as offspring come to pay it the tribute of my own thoughts,
      little brainy cyclones
that touched down in the lava channels
      or drained back into rivulets of wind.
"Cloud and Man differ not," I joked to myself,
"All is One under Heaven." And why not?

    What if we were to recast ourselves as descendants
all gathered at the foot of our heresiarch mountains,
drawn by a love like primitive magnetisms and convection currents
    calling all things back to their incarnate sources? Our
lives might be ordered by a conscious abstinence,
a year of giving up to save for a trip home.
We would sacrifice for an earthbound commitment—
      homage to birthplace,
source rock come up from a star's living depth.

What would be the point other than to step into the sulfuric
      cleansing of volcanic clouds?
Our dithyrambs of dream-mountains not quite earth's equal
but more vague than that—like clouds around Mauna Loa,
drifting continents of vapor and dust
riding the gyreing wind-gusts over Halemaumau and Iki,
mantling of evanescence on the tropical shoulders of an angel?

    Aren't we the earth become known to itself,
we celebrants of a sublime not completely dreadful,
but companionable too, its presence like two sleeping children,
innocent dragons
      fogging the car's rear window with a visible breath?

David Mura

POET, MEMOIRIST, AND PERFORMANCE ARTIST

David Mura is a poet, creative nonfiction writer, critic, playwright, and performance artist. A Sansei, or third-generation Japanese American, born in 1952 in Great Lakes, Illinois, he grew up in Chicago. Mura is the author of two memoirs— Turning Japanese: Memoirs of a Sansei *(1991 Josephine Miles Book Award and a* New York Times *1991 Notable Book of Year) and* Where the Body Meets Memory: An Odyssey of Race, Sexuality and Identity *(1996)—and two books of poetry:* After We Lost Our Way *(1989 National Poetry Series Contest winner) and* The Colors of Desire *(1995, winner of the Carl Sandburg Literary Award). He is the author of* A Male Grief: Notes on Pornography and Addiction *(1987), and he adapted Li-Young Lee's memoir* The Winged Seed *(1995) as a play, performed in 1997 at Pangea World Theater in Minneapolis.*

Mura's own multimedia performance pieces include Relocations: Images from a Sansei, Silence and Desire, After Hours *(in collaboration with pianist Jon Jang and actor Kelvin Han Yee), and* The Colors of Desire *(with African American writer Alexs D. Pate). A film version of the last of these,* Slowly, This, *was broadcast on PBS in 1995. Mura was featured on the Bill Moyers series* The Language of Life *(1995).*

A recipient of numerous writing fellowships and grants, Mura has also published essays about race and multiculturalism and was a founder and artistic director (1991–1997) of the Asian American Renaissance Company (AARC), an Asian American arts organization in Minnesota.

RESPONSE ⬲

The origins for my work come out of being Japanese American at this time, this place, in this country. My writing also comes out of a long journey—an investigation—that I've been undergoing about my identity—what it means to be a Japanese American, a person of color, and a man in this country. I really grew up—as I've written about—in a middle-class, White suburb, where as an adolescent I thought it was a compliment when a White friend would say, "I think of you, David, just like a White person." And my journey has been from that consciousness—where I wanted to be thought of as a White person—to a realization that I wasn't White, that I was a Japanese American, and what in hell did that mean?

That sort of journey of consciousness in terms of identity also has been reflected in my literary influences. When I went through my English major in Grinnell College (Iowa) and five years of graduate school in English at the University of Minnesota, from 1970 to 1979, I think I read a group of poems by Amiri Baraka, and that was it. I read no other writers of color. My education was very heavy in the dominant, European American tradition: virtually all White authors, most of them male. I did take one course in feminism, Shakespeare, and psychoanalysis in grad school, for which I was thankful. After graduate school, I took a course in French criticism, which introduced me to structuralism, Marxism, and Freud—and all of those offered me a very different way of looking at literature, one in which the issues of power, economic politics, and historical context suddenly became legitimate questions to ask when you read and create literature. So it was only after graduate school that I began to ask questions about the canon and about identity. I was struck by Walter Benjamin's "history is the tale of the victors," especially since people like me were not written about in the history books.

Then I ran into Frantz Fanon, and that set my head ablaze. Fanon wrote about the young Black schoolchildren in the French West Indies reading about "our ancestors, the Gauls," and about the Great White Hunter going in to civilize the savages in Africa. Fanon said what this Black schoolchild is learning is self-hatred and self-neglect.

All of this is also deeply tied into issues of race and sex. Fanon wrote about how certain Black men, over and over again, slept with White women, and he examined their psychology and talked about how that drive was fueled by a belief that if I sleep with a White woman, then I'll be as good as a White man. When I read that, I again went, "Hmm. That really applies to the way I've been thinking about sexuality, and I really need to question that."

Right now, a lot of my writing has to do with the issues of what it means to be Japanese American in the context of a pan-Asian vision and to see Japanese American/Asian American identity in relation to other people of color. For a long time, a lot of people of color have tended to think only of either their own community or their community in relationship to the White majority, and not so much in relationship to other communities of color and the identities of other people of color.

I first wrote *Turning Japanese* because I felt there was a gap in my bookshelf, a book of somebody like myself. Beyond that, I've come to realize that I write for a Japanese American audience, an Asian American audience, then an audience of people of color, then an audience beyond that. At the same time, with each piece I write, my sense of audience shifts, depending on the occasion and the kind of piece I'm writing. There are certain times when I am addressing the dominant culture about issues I think the dominant culture needs to address. There are other times when I'm writing to an Asian American audience or an audience of color.

When I write poetry for the page, I'm writing to a certain literate audience of poets of color, first and foremost—an audience in which I presume some knowledge of contemporary poetry. But in my performance pieces, I don't presume that sort of knowledge. Also, of course, if you're writing for theater and the audience doesn't get it the first time, you're in trouble. Writing for the page, I assume people will read the poem over and over again. In a performance I'm doing with a Black friend of mine about our relationship and African American–Asian American relations, any time I say something on that stage, I think about how the Asian American audience will interpret it and how the Black audience will interpret it. One of the changes in my own writing in the last few years is that I understand to a much better degree what it means to be an African American in this country, and therefore I think a have a better sense of how a Black audience will react to my work. That was something not at all on the table in my creative writing workshops. That's a question I also don't think is on the table for a number of Asian American writers. And that question has come more and more to provide a context for the way in which I think about my work. I believe that my Japanese American identity is also formed in relation to African Americans. An example I use in the show (and it's in the poem that follows this response) is when Father got on a segregated bus in the South. Bill Hosokawa writes that the Whites, in suspecting the Nisei of disloyalty to the nation, urged them sit in front.

And the Blacks embarrassed many Nisei by saying, "Us colored folks got to stick together." Hosokawa goes on to say that if the Nisei could not live in the racially polarized South unnoticed as a yellow-skinned American, elsewhere in the country, after the war, he found it was not too difficult to be accepted in the White man's world.

What's obvious here is that Hosokawa sees the Nisei as embarrassed by the solidarity the Blacks are offering him; he's not interested in being accepted in the Black world—he's interested in being accepted in the White world. And that's understandable: you sit where the power is. My father said, "Yeah, we sat at the front of the bus. When we went to lunch counters, we always sat with the White people. If we went to the movies, we sat below the balcony." But the way I talk about this issue in the show and in public is that I think America was offering Japanese Americans a bargain: you will get to sit in the front half of the bus, but you will never get to sit in the very front, and you will *absolutely not* be able to drive the bus. Also, you must not pay attention to what's happening to the people in the back of the bus. And you must claim no relationship to the people in the back of the bus. And if you do all this, we will let you be an honorary White, and that's a political choice, a choice of how you constitute your identity. If you begin to say, "I have a relationship to the people in the back of the bus; I'm not going to sit in the front of the bus unless everyone else is able to sit in the front," that's a very different choice. White people look at you differently if you say that, and Black people look at you differently. And African Americans know when Asian Americans are playing the honorary White game. And when that happens, there's really no reason for them to trust us.

The mistake we make is trying to make identity unitary—trying to create an essentialist identity. In other words, my identity is something that is fluid, constantly changing, and that has many facets. If I'm sitting in a room with Sansei, that feels different to me from when I'm sitting in a room with Nisei and Issei, because they talk about different things. And that feels different to me from when I'm sitting in a room with Asian Americans, or a room of people of color, or a room with mixed people, or if I'm the only person of color in a room with White people. Similarly, I feel different sitting in a room with men from when I sit with women. In all those situations, different facets of my identity are heightened; the conversation is conducted in a very different way; the type of things I feel safe saying are different—my identity shifts slightly. And if I, as a writer, am going to depict the complexity of my existence, I need to be able to describe and understand all of those different types of experiences. If I'm sitting in a room with working-class Asian Americans, then with middle-class Asian Americans, those differences are highlighted along class lines. For me, class comes to be an issue that's been buried, under the table.

Is there an "authentic" Asian American sensibility, and how to define it? It is the sum of the experience of all Asian Americans. If I am an Asian American, and I have an experience, that is an authentic Asian American experience. I can interpret that experience in a number of different ways. But it seems absurd to me to say that if, instead of sitting on the lawn with my daughter, I'm sitting in J-town in Los Angeles with my daughter, it's somehow a more authentic Asian American experience. Rather than starting from a prescriptive or idealized notion of identity, I'm saying that identity comes out of what exists. You will be able to understand the nature of your experience only by acknowledging what actually exists in that experience, including the

contradictions within it. If you base a political agenda on idealization, it is bound to fall.

Let me make it clear that I'm not saying that being against idealized or essential notions of identity means that I'm against political action. In fact, I'm saying that that sort of identity mitigates against effective political action.

As Asian Americans, I think that we have to do justice to the true complexity of American history, American society at present and in the future. This means, again, that we have to understand the multiplicity and complexity of our own identities and situations. We have to make a number of different connections, both globally and within this country. We cannot afford to narrow our vision.

I feel people have political responsibilities, but for me, to talk about it as dictating particular duties puts upon it a puritanical vision I don't quite agree with. I've done a lot of work locally helping to start up an Asian American arts organization, and frankly, it's been a lot of fun. It's interesting because the deeper we get into the issues of community and art, the more complicated they become. For me, my involvement in that comes out of a sense of moral obligation, but it also comes out of a curiosity about the world, which is part of what it means to be an artist. I feel like I have a better understanding of issues around who I am and around my community than I would have if I didn't do what I've been doing.

We are at a place of building infrastructure in our communities. Our generation is the first in which we had Asian American Studies departments, and those were the first institutionalized manifestations of an Asian American consciousness. But if you get down to the local level, the sort of coalition building that needs to happen is still a long way from happening. Here in the Twin Cities, there are vast differences among different Asian American groups. How do you begin to bridge those gaps? How do you organize people to get them to see the common interests in banding together, to get them to understand their own diversity and their difference from each other? I think that the microcosm of pan-Asian ethnicity and organization reflects the macrocosm issue that America faces: finding a unity within this diversity. And that's incredibly difficult. You're often dealing with Asian enmities—between the Vietnamese and the Hmong, between Chinese and Japanese, Japanese and Korean. You're dealing with people who oftentimes are working very hard to survive, to support their own community. And it's hard to get people to see beyond the horizon of their own groups to the benefit of forming coalitions. All community organizing work brings experiences that are valuable for me and others, but it does take away time from actually sitting at a typewriter or standing on a stage creating artwork. There's a constant back and forth. One of the things I can compare it to is the experience of what happens in postcolonial or in smaller countries, where artists end up becoming a part of not just the cultural but the political and social life of the country, as in Poland, Mexico, or Chile. The art is, in the end, larger because of that, particularly in comparison to a lot of American art.

Q: At its inception, was Asian American Renaissance conceived primarily as an arts institution, or was there always a political goal?

It's interesting, because I've always thought of art as being involved with politics, but I just wanted to see Asian American artists presented in the Twin Cities. I'd been to the West Coast, and I'd seen certain artists, but the Midwest is not like San Francisco. My impetus to help start the AARC came then

out of just wanting to *see* Asian American artists. One of the key people in the group, Valerie Lee, was coming out of social services, and she perceived it as a tool for social organizing. She and I had a lot of long, fruitful discussions, and the more I thought about these issues, the more I saw how my position as an artist really is tied up with community building. My own personal explorations of identity really were fostered by the work that I was doing: if there is no Asian American audience, then a big part of the audience for my work is gone. If the Asian Americans decide to adopt White models of identity and assimilate, then this is something for me to worry about—will anyone be interested in what I write about?

Valerie came from this social science–Maslow hierarchy of needs: you feed the people, house them, and then you worry about the other stuff. Gradually she began to think, that's very Western, this compartmentalization. And we began to feel that for the community to articulate its own needs to formulate a political and social agenda, we need to come to terms with who we are, in terms of both their past and our present. The obvious necessities in that are culture and art. On another level, I wanted younger Asian American artists to have an opportunity to find each other, work together, support each other, and have institutions supporting them, in a way that I didn't have when I was growing up.

Q: Speaking of engendering audiences—through your writing and through the Arts Renaissance—how would you characterize the reception of your work? What is most lacking, and for what are you most grateful?

In *Turning Japanese*, I was pleased with the way the book spoke to Japanese Americans of my parents' generation, not just of my generation. I was pleased that it seemed to speak to people on the West Coast, not just in the Midwest. I've been pleased with the way it's spoken to some young Korean Americans who have gone back to Korea and felt that it explored some of the issues they were dealing with.

What was curious about the reaction to my book was that every Asian American reviewer started with my identity as the center of the book, while many White reviewers wanted to jettison that as subjective and less universal; they wanted to say that the meat of the book was the writing about Japan. The implication is that writing about Japan is universal and that writing as a Sansei is subjective, not universal. But that misses the whole point: because one point of my book is that anybody's experience with another culture is subjective, and unless you examine that subjectivity and understand how it is formed, you're going to be *more* blind than if you assume you possess prejudices and a subjectivity that need to be questioned and examined. I think what I would change is White reviewers, their understanding of these issues, and that's going to take a long time.

I feel I'm moving further and further away from the White Mandarin literary structures and thinking in this country. In certain ways, those are the people who still hold a great deal of power in the culture; it gets less and less every year, but it's there.

Q: Is this a particularly receptive time for Asian American writers? Is acceptance by the dominant society evidence of assimilation?

Society will constantly try to turn it into assimilation—into a flattening of difference. One of the ways they do that is by presenting multiculturalism under the rubric of a universal humanity. So that teaching or reading multiculturalism means that Asian American women have problems with their moth-ers, and that African American couples have troubles in their marriages, and that Native American people deal with old people dying, et cetera, et cetera. But such an approach ignores the deeper questions which the works are asking about American history and what it means to be American, and about our political structures, how power and wealth are distributed in this country. There's a way in which multiculturalism can be eviscerated of the deeper political questions it asks.

The reason why I don't think that will happen is that these questions are not simply being asked by the literature but through the ballot box, through the economy, indeed, in all aspects of society. And these questions will be asked more and more vociferously as the proportion of people of color in this country grows. And we will come to a time of reckoning about this issue. If we know that this country, in the middle of the next century, will no longer have a White majority, what does that mean for the majority which holds power now? How are they going to give up power, or are they going to give up power? What does it mean for people of color in their relationship to each other? Asian Americans will be something like 12 percent of the population in 2050; Blacks will be 22 percent; Hispanics and Latinos, 26 percent. That's a very different country, and if people are going to expect a culture that reflects them, the culture had better change. Otherwise, you run the risk of something like South Africa.

Q: Do you feel Asian American women writers have been more readily accepted than Asian American male writers? If so, why?

I think there are reasons—aside from issues of quality—that have to do with issues of racism in this culture, and the way racism relates to issues of sexism and sexuality. A White feminist is going to be interested in a book about being an Asian American woman in a way that she's not going to be with a book about being an Asian American man, because the work of an Asian American woman relates to her own experience as a woman. But White *men* aren't going to look at my book, necessarily—or at least, at this stage of our political development today—and think, "Ah! Here's another brother writing about what it means to be male in this society!" The range of readership is probably less for me as an Asian American male than it is for an Asian American woman. I'm talking here about outside the community, as opposed to those inside the community. The same case could be made, I think, for African American authors. There, again, I think you see more successful (in terms of sales) African American women authors.

Why? The reasons for that are incredibly complex. Why would it be any different in literature? Beyond that, I think about the issue of interracial dating. There was an article in the Bay Area about this, and all the people [in these relationships] in the article said, "Love transcends race, love is color-blind, et cetera, et cetera." *But,* none of those Asian Americans were dating somebody who was Black, Latino, or Native American. They were all dating White people. Also, these Asian American women were outdating, at a rate of three to one, . . . Asian American men. Why is that? I would venture to say that it is because Asian American women are more attractive to Caucasians than Asian American men. One could ask: Does this have any sort of effect on the perception of work about Asian American women and Asian American men by the dominant culture? Obviously, when you deal with that question of physical attractiveness, it has nothing to do with the quality of the person—it has to do with the way that racial stereotypes and power imbal-

ances filter themselves through sexual differences in communities of color.

This does not say that I'm not thrilled by the success of Asian American women authors. Still, I once read a reply by Hisaye Yamamoto on this issue that just did not examine the question in very much depth. She said, basically, that Asian American women writers are simply better. But she would preface this by saying in the past, women had been discriminated against. And I wondered, if women were discriminated against in the past though they could actually write well, how it is that now that women are doing better, it's simply because they're writing better? These questions are much more complicated than people want to make them. I think you can ask these questions about this issue without succumbing to a Frank Chin sort of attack on women writers.

Q: A common belief is that the dominant society has emasculated the Asian male, commodified the Asian female, and exoticized Asian culture in general. Do you agree?

I don't know if I want to sign on the dotted line to that statement. I do feel that the culture—and even our own Asian American community—has very few images of anything that resembles me. I oftentimes feel that I'm speaking into a cultural vacuum. When I am doing performance work, what's so nice is that I can throw up stereotypical images onto a video screen and then just simply present myself on the stage and let the audience deal with the differences. The dialectic to free oneself of stereotypes is paralleled by a dialectic to free yourself from essentialist notions within the community, too, about who you ought to be. I know this one well-known Asian American male writer who said [of my work], "Ohh, the sex in that book is very creepy," implying that I was talking about things that shouldn't be talked about in terms of issues of sexuality, and I really resist that.

In terms of interracial sexuality: I don't believe the notion that "love transcends race." I'm in an interracial relationship, but I cannot say that when I look at my wife, the way I look at her is still not conditioned by notions from the White dominant culture of what beauty is. Nor can I say that her condition as a White person in this society and my experience as an Asian American do not come up over and over again in our relationship in issues which we often argue about. The point of our being in a relationship is not for us to ignore the differences in our experiences. We have to deal with them. . . . We can't be blind to the fact that my life has been different from hers in part because of issues of race. If you do that, you do not have intimacy in the relationship and you do not have trust. If you have trust, then you can talk about those issues.

Q: Have you become more conscious of this through being a father?

Yes, in many different ways. I think the biggest way is just seeing how much you don't control. Your children are barraged by aspects of the culture that you have no control over. And half the time, you have no notion of how you are affecting your children, particularly with regard to the future. I think parenthood is one long lesson in your own fallibility and limitations and your ability to control anything. You try to teach your children, to help them learn about the world and about themselves, but there's only so much you can control.

Q: You've written of poets who have necessarily evolved into cultural hybrids, having seen center after center dissolve before them, trying to keep up with global expansion. Do you still enjoy and cherish that disequilibrium, and do you consider cultural hybridization as limbo, homelessness, rootlessness, or something else?

I used to think of it as some sort of limbo, but now I think of it as a condition which characterizes more and more people's experiences across the globe, and which is an interesting place to speak from. Rather than limbo, it's an advantage.

Q: In the AWP Chronicle, *you wrote that the novel was the only literary form truly born in and equipped for treating the modern era. Would you elaborate on how form or genre affects what and how you write?*

I was paraphrasing Bakhtin. There are works of fiction and nonfiction which are like those optical illusions where you look at a thing one way and it looks like a vase, and then you look at it another way and it looks like a face. I like working in many different forms: each of them allows me to do a different thing. I learn different things which I take back to each form: when I do performance poetry, it teaches me things about poetry for the page; when I write for the stage, it teaches me things about dialogue for when I go back to memoir writing.

Philip Gotanda and I were talking recently about this. There are opportunities now for artists of color to become larger than we thought we could and to explore more possibilities than we thought we'd be able to. And in fact, there are certain demands that we do that. In that way, this is a very exciting time to be an artist of color. Another way of looking at this—Garrett Hongo and I have talked about this—is that his [Hongo's] memoir, Li-Young Lee's memoir, and my memoir are large, long glosses of how to read our poetry. We have had to provide a cultural context for people to read our poetry since it's not there in the culture. So there was a necessity for us to write the memoirs, almost as an *ars poetica* and at the same time a creation of a critical cultural tradition out of which our work comes.

Q: What are your thoughts about Asian American Studies in the Midwest?

Asian American Studies departments are crucial, more so in the Midwest. For young, Midwestern Asian Americans, there's so much pressure from the dominant culture to forget who they are, to deny who they are—to stop any investigation of questions that come out of their experience, which is different from the White culture. Unlike on the West Coast, there's much less around them that would help, support, and force them to ask those questions. I think you can get along with this identity in the Midwest, denying the questions that come up as people of color, especially when you're one person of color among many White faces. The problem is, every single experience that does relate to that, you have to stuff—you have no way to talk about it. That means that certain experiences you may have with your parents, or in dating, or on the street, or when you go see movies like *Breakfast at Tiffany's,* or *Sweet Sixteen,* or *Rambo,* or *Rising Sun* . . . you won't be able to talk about; what happens when someone calls you "gook" on the street, or you ask somebody out and you don't know how they're responding to you, and if that has something to do with race; or the ways you feel about your parents or their culture. If you have no place to talk about that, you build up this fund of experiences and emotions that you are trying to deny, black out, compartmentalize. If you do that long enough, your identity will become skewered, and the pressure on your psyche can become extremely intense.

~~~~~~

The Colors of Desire

1 *Photograph of a Lynching (circa 193–)*

These men? In their dented felt hats,
in the way their fingers tug their suspenders or vests,
with faces a bit puffy or too lean, eyes narrow and close together,
they seem too like our image of the South,
the Thirties. Of course they are white;
who then could create this cardboard figure, face
flat and grey, eyes oversized, bulging like
an ancient totem this gang has dug up? At the far right,
in a small browed cap, a boy of twelve smiles,
as if responding to what's most familiar here:
the camera's click. And though directly above them,
a branch ropes the dead negro in the air,
the men too focus their blank beam
on the unseen eye. Which is, at this moment, us.

Or, more precisely, me. Who cannot but recall
how my father, as a teenager, clutched his weekend pass,

passed through the rifle towers and gates
of the Jerome, Arkansas camp, and, in 1942,
stepped on a bus to find white riders
motioning, "Sit here, son," and, in the rows beyond,
a half dozen black faces, waving him back,
"Us colored folks got to stick together."
How did he know where to sit? And how is it,

thirty-five years later, I found myself sitting
in a dark theatre, watching *Behind the Green Door*
with a dozen anonymous men? On the screen
a woman sprawls on a table, stripped, the same one
on the Ivory Snow soap box, a baby on her shoulder,
smiling her blond, practically pure white smile.
Now, after being prepared and serviced slowly
by a handful of women, as one of them
kneels, buries her face in her crotch,
she is ready: And now he walks in—

Lean, naked, black, streaks of white paint on his chest
and face, a necklace of teeth, it's almost comical,
this fake garb of the jungle, Africa and All-America,
black and blond, almost a joke but for the surge
of what these lynchers regarded as the ultimate crime
against nature: the black man kneeling to this kidnapped
body, slipping himself in, the screen showing it all, down
to her head shaking in a seizure, the final scream
before he lifts himself off her quivering body . . .

I left that theater, bolted from a dream into a dream.
I stared at the cars whizzing by, watched the light change,
red, yellow, green, and the haze in my head from the hash,
and the haze in my head from the image, melded together, reverberating.
I don't know what I did afterwards. Only, night after night,
I will see those bodies, black and white (and where am I,
the missing third?), like a talisman, a rageful, unrelenting release.

2 *1957*

Cut to Chicago, June. A boy of six.
Next year my hero will be Mickey Mantle,
but this noon, as father eases the Bel-Air past Wilson,
with cowboy hat black, cocked at an angle,

my skin dark from the sun, I'm Paladin,
and my six guns point at cars whizzing past,
blast after blast ricocheting the glass.
Like all boys in such moments, my face
attempts a look of what—toughness? bravado? ease?—
until, impatient, my father's arm wails
across the seat, and I sit back, silent at last.

Later, as we step from IGA with our sacks,
a man in a serge suit—stained with ink?—
steps forward, shouts, "Hey, you a Jap?
You from Tokyo? You a Jap? A Chink?"
I stop, look up, I don't know him,
my arm yanks forward, and suddenly,
the sidewalk's rolling, buckling, like lava melting,
and I know father will explode,
shouts, fists, I know his temper.
And then,
I'm in that dream where nothing happens—
The ignition grinds, the man's face presses
the windshield, and father stares ahead,
fingers rigid on the wheel . . .

That night in my bedroom, moths,
like fingertips, peck the screen;
from the living room, the muffled t.v.
As I imagine Shane stepping into the dusty street,
in the next bed, my younger brother starts
to taunt—*you can't hurt me, you can't hurt me . . .*—
Who can explain where this chant began?
Or why, when father throws the door open,
shouts stalking chaos erupted in his house,
he swoops on his son with the same swift motion
that the son, like an animal, like a scared and angry little boy,
fell on his brother, beating him in the dark?

3 *Miss June 1964*

I'm twelve, home from school
with a slight fever. I slide back the door
of my parents' closet—my mother's out shopping—
rummage among pumps, flats, lined in a rack,

unzip the garment bags, one by one.
It slides like a sigh from the folded sweaters.
I flip through ads for cologne, L.P.'s, a man
in a trench coat, lugging a panda-sized Fleischmann's fifth.
Somewhere past the photo of Schweitzer
in his pith helmet, and the cartoon nude man
perched as a gargoyle, I spill the photo
millions of men, white, black, yellow, have seen,
though the body before me is white, eighteen:
Her breasts are enormous, almost frightening
—the aureoles seem large as my fist.
As the three glossy pages sprawl before me,
I start to touch myself, and there is
some terror, my mother will come home,
some delight I've never felt before,
and I do not cry out, I make no sound . . .

How did I know that photo was there?
Or mother know I knew?
Two nights later, at her request,
father lectures me on burning out too early.
Beneath the cone of light at the kitchen table,
we're caught, like the shiest of lovers.
He points at the booklet from the AMA
—he writes their P.R.—"Read it," he says,
"and, if you have any questions . . ."

Thirty years later, these questions remain.
And his answers, too, are still the same:
Really, David, it was just a magazine.
And the camps, my father's lost nursery,
the way he chased me round the yard in L.A.,
even the two by four he swung—why connect them
with years you wandered those theaters?
Is nothing in your life your own volition?
The past isn't just a box full of horrors.
What of those mornings in the surf
near Venice, all of us casting line after line,
arcing over breakers all the way from Japan,
or plopping down beside my mother,
a plateful of mochi, *pulling it like taffy*

with our teeth, shoyu *dribbling*
down our chins. Think of it, David.
There were days like that. We were happy . . .

4

Who hears the rain churning the forest to mud,
or the unraveling rope snap, the negro
plummet to rest at last? And what flooded my father's eyes
in the Little Rock theatre, sitting beneath the balcony
in that third year of war? Where is 1944,
its snows sweeping down Heart Mountain,
to vanish on my mother's black bobbing head,
as she scurries towards the cramped cracked barracks
where her mother's throat coughs through the night,
and her father sits beside her on the bed?
The dim bulb flickers as my mother enters.
Her face is flushed, her cheeks cold. She
bows, unwraps her scarf, pours the steaming
kettle in the tea pot; offers her mother a sip.
And none of them knows she will never
talk of this moment, that, years later,
I will have to imagine it, again and again,
just as I have tried to imagine the lives
of all those who have entered these lines . . .

Tonight snow drifts below my window,
and lamps puff ghostly aureoles
over walks and lawns. Father, mother,
I married a woman not of my color.
Tell me: What is it I want to escape?
These nights in our bed, my head
on her belly, I can hear these thumps,
and later, when she falls asleep,
I stand in our daughter's room,
so bare yet but for a simple wooden crib
(on the bulletin board I've pinned the sonogram
with black and white swirls like a galaxy
spinning about the fetal body),
and something plummets inside me,
out of proportion to the time
I've been portioned on this earth.

And if what is granted erases nothing,
if history remains, untouched, implacable,
as darkness flows up our hemisphere,
her hollow still moves moonward,
small hill on the horizon, swelling,
floating with child, white, yellow,
who knows, who can tell her,

oh why must it matter?

Karen Tei Yamashita

NOVELIST

Karen Tei Yamashita is a Japanese American born in California in the 1950s; her mother was a teacher and her father the pastor of a Japanese American church in Los Angeles. After graduation from Carleton College in Minnesota, Yamashita received a Thomas J. Watson Fellowship to study Japanese immigration in Brazil. For three years she gathered stories from the Japanese Brazilian community, which became the basis for Brazil-Maru, *named by the* Village Voice *as one of the twenty-five best books of 1992. She married architect and artist Ronaldo Lopes de Oliveira, and after nine years in Brazil, she immigrated back to the United States with her husband and their two small children. Her novel* Through the Arc of the Rain Forest *won the 1991 American Book Award and the 1992 Janet Heidinger Kafka*

Award. A third novel, Tropic of Orange, *was published in 1997. Yamashita has written several theatrical performance pieces with themes relating to Asian American life:* Hannah Kusoh: An American Butoh *(1989),* Tokyo Carmen vs. L.A. Carmen *(1990),* Noh Bozos *(1993), and a musical formerly named* Godzilla Comes to Little Tokyo *and sometimes renamed* GiLAwrecks, *written with composer Vicki Abe. Yamashita currently teaches creative writing and literature at the University of California, Santa Cruz. She has incorporated her response to my questions in the following academic parody, which was written for this volume but appeared in* DisOrient Journalzine *(Los Angeles, 1996) and in Japanese translation in* The Enigma of Myself, *edited by Ryuta Imafuku in Tokyo in 1997.*

Siamese Twins and Mongoloids: Cultural Appropriation and the Deconstruction of Stereotype via the Absurdity of Metaphor

In her latest novel, *Siamese Twins and Mongoloids,* Yamashita draws from the true story of Chang and Eng Bunker, the original Siamese twins, born in 1811 in a river houseboat in Meklong, sixty miles west of Bangkok in the country then known as Siam. Chang and Eng were attached from birth to each other slightly below the chest by a fleshy extension much like an arm, about six inches in length and eight inches in circumference. Brought to the West by Americans interested in exploiting the novelty of the attached Siamese, Chang and Eng initially made their way across America and Europe as a circus attraction, working briefly for P. T. Barnum. Eventually, however, they became American citizens, settled in North Carolina as landowners, farmers, and slave owners. They married Southern sisters, Sarah and Adelaide Yates, and between them fathered twenty-one children. They were considered pillars of their community in Mount Airy, North Carolina, and saw their sons fight and die for the Confederacy. Both died on January 17, 1874, and are buried together in White Plains, North Carolina.[1]

From the true story, Yamashita extrapolates a present-day L.A. Asian American satire, hurtling the reader headfirst into the messiest regions of this curious American subculture. Throughout the text, it will be seen that Yamashita uses Asian metaphors in a typically Sanseiesque manner, erroneously appropriating these traditions for her own subcultural purposes. These purposes are ostensibly to deconstruct stereotypes into metaphors of the absurd and thus render them impotent.[2]

In the mid-sixties two healthy twin baby boys were born to a Sansei couple in Gardena, California. The couple—known Asian American movement radicals—had made a conscientious decision to live and work in the community and chose Gardena, a small working-class city on the great metropolitan skirts of L.A., where an Asian American enclave continued to thrive. With faith in the power of the people, the Sansei couple raised and educated their boys to epitomize mentally and physically the very perfection of Asian America. Indeed, the two boys grew to be men unlike any others—mentally astute, politically correct, sensitive, visionary, artistic, and physically exquisite. The only imperfection—a word denied by the boys and their parents—was the inconvenience of being bound to each

---

[1] Irving Wallace and Amy Wallace, *The Two* (New York: Simon & Schuster, 1978).
[2] See B. Huang, *Absurdity and Impotence* (University of California at Irvine Archives, 1993).

other near the hip by a thick fleshy ligament much like an arm, five to six inches long and about eight inches in circumference. Since words like Oriental *and* Siam *were considered passé, the boys were simply referred to as Asian American twins.*

Thus Yamashita abandons the Old World word, *Siam,* and embraces its politically correct equivalent, *Asian American.*

The boys are given heroic names. The boy to the left is named Heco, after the thirteen-year-old Japanese boy Hikozo Hamada (later Joseph Heco) who—rescued from a storm by an American ship and taken to San Francisco in 1850—became the first Japanese to become an American citizen. The boy to the right is named Okada, after John Okada, author of the great Asian American novel *No-No Boy* [1957]. Heco has an extremely pragmatic and logical mind, while Okada's is fluid and highly imaginative. Despite the analytical nature of his mind, Heco seems motivated in his actions by his brother's imagination. Thus Heco is the artist of the two. Likewise, the artistically minded Okada seems influenced by his brother's rational intelligence in his uncanny ability to perform mathematic calculations with acrobatic skill. Throughout the novel, Yamashita plays with the infinite confusions of right-[3] and left-brain qualities between the twins. Furthermore, the twins are given a sort of red-diaper[4] upbringing, à la sixties Asian America.[5]

Unlike most Asian Americans who were merely bright, the twins were indeed brilliant, teaching each other to read and write by the age of four. By the time they were ten, they had both discovered and devoured the dusty abandoned texts of Marx and Mao, replete with pencil marks and yellow highlighter. They read Malcolm X, *old issues of* Gidra *and the* Amerasia Journal; *a variety of Asian American studies texts;* Aiiieeeee!; *books and articles on postcolonialism, corporate structure, and world economics; communal experiments; issues of* Mother Jones *and* The Nation, *old KPFK newsletters—anything and everything within their reach. Their minds were like great sponges sucking up the life and times of their immediate environment and then moving outward in an ever-growing spiral, forging forth from Gardena as the center and into the universe.*

Yamashita twists the accepted stereotype of the straight-A Asian student[6] and further boggles the imagination by endowing the twins with a kind of exceptional perfection and completeness.

[3]L. Uba, "Right Brain Attributes in Asian Americans," *Journal of Psychology* 38,3 (1987).
[4]See Marx.
[5]*Gidra* (1967).
[6]See *White Paper: Grade Point Averages and Asians* (UTLA, Sept. 1966).

In this imbibing of life, the two boys grew to find their talents in all arenas of human intelligence. While Heco took up the taiko *and* shakuhachi, *Okada preferred jazz fusion; thus the saxophone and the keyboard. While Okada took up* sumi-e, *Heco was occupied in painting great canvases in oil with colorful abstractions. Heco was a great talker, a person of verbal wit and humor and social charm and political persuasion. Okada was more introspective, intuitive, a gifted psychoanalyst. A social animal, Heco enjoyed team sports: baseball, basketball, volleyball, football, soccer; he was a team player, a tactician, the captain of any team. Okada took up the sports of the individualist: running, swimming, archery, scuba diving, weight lifting, judo, and karate. Both were consummate athletes. Heco was known to have pitched a season of no-hitters, and Okada won the decathlon. Indeed, these were not only the Asian American Twins, they were young men of a new era, the twins of an Asian American Renaissance.*

As if to add offense to injury, Yamashita further inserts, "Heco drove a 400 HP Twin Turbo Supra, while Okada preferred the Mazda RX7."[7]

If you don't remember this Renaissance[8] having occurred, it is because, as Yamashita contends, "it was rather short in duration." This is not surprising. Just as "stews are no longer simmered over the stove for several hours but rather nuked into shape in a matter of minutes," life's cultural and historical moments, once cast over a period of years, have been compressed to media sound bytes. The idea that anything should last a decade (as in the sixties, the seventies, etc.) becomes patently absurd.

The Asian American Renaissance was a small, exciting blip funded in part by fiscal tightwaddedness of the former generation (sacrifice) and redress checks, and despite the continuing recession of the times. Its disappearance was heralded in part by the age of the personal computer, when so many fine Asian American minds went cyber. Never having developed Heco's incredible facility with verbal expression or oratorical persuasion, thousands of Asian Americans found solace of expression through the invisibility of E-mail and the ultimate democracy of a network where your physical being—the color of your skin, the size of your genitals, or the approximation of your features to a soap opera star—made no difference whatsoever. Perhaps what this proved was that the tremendous inroads made by the twins to obliterate old perceptions of Asian masculinity had made no difference at all; or on the other hand, perhaps the questions posed in former days of an emasculated Asian male, or for that matter, a commodified Asian female, were no longer of any consequence.

---

[7]B. Huang, *The Stereotype of the Asian Driver and Its Sources* (unpublished, private collection).
[8]B. Huang, *The Asian American Renaissance* (private papers, ca. 1994).

Yet, for one, small moment in time because of these exceptional twins,

Asian men were considered tall enough to play for the NBA, attractive enough to be leading men and box office sellouts, sexy enough for full frontal nudity, masculine enough to perform martial arts and sex, shrewd enough to run corporate structures, politically savvy enough to move into Washington, White enough to move to Beverly Hills, Black enough to play the sax, sensitive enough to marry Asian American women, and wise enough to be men.

The twins' story is woven into the fabric of Asian American life. Here a kind of circus, with its particular circles of hell, exists to house Yamashita's romp. In so doing, Yamashita proposes a special place in this purgatory for what she signifies as the non-*prophet*, where institutions like the JACL (Japanese American Citizens League) and the National Japanese American Museum forever recalculate their overhead.[9] Another circle is reserved for an academic bureaucracy where academics shred into little pieces eternal mountains of textbooks by Takaki, Hosokawa, Ichioka, and Kitano. In the background, hundreds of middle-aged movement radicals pound *mochi* into the literal shapes of the moon to the deafening sound of a thousand *taikos*. Everywhere "the exotic and the haiku reside together."

In one arena of combat—Asian American Gladiators—Asian women stomp on Asian men, and Asian men stomp on Asian women.[10] In the end, Asian grandmothers win the day and are hailed as pioneers.[11] In Yamashita's tale, Asian pioneers are somehow always old, no matter what year—1906 or 1966—it is. This has the uncanny and paradoxical effect of making the first generation of immigrants surreally ageless or aged. In the meantime, the second generation goes to camp or war.[12] While the first generation is forever "trapped in wrinkles," this interminably middle-aged generation listens to swing music. Curiously, however, the sound of the *shakuhachi* always accompanies the scenery, whether it's camp, Little Tokyo, or a family album.[13] "There's something about an Asian face that wants a *shakuhachi*," says one filmmaker, "however, Chinese opera will also do."

Despite the incredible array of occupational possibilities for two men whose talents should enable them to draw the very map of their destinies,

[9]See Kafka.
[10]See *Rafu Shimpo* (May 1992).
[11]See *Tozai Times* (June 1990).
[12]Ibid.
[13]"Sites and Smells of Asian America," *Los Angeles Times*, Travel Section, May 5, 1982.

Yamashita casts Heco and Okada as a dentist and an optometrist.[14] "Mind you," justifies Yamashita, "this was a conscientious decision based on a shared philosophy of usefulness to community, a striving for independence, the continuation of a cultural tradition, obvious practical considerations, and the possibility of having Wednesdays off."

Heco goes on to receive his degree from USC, and Okada receives his from UCLA. Again, the stereotypes blossom into extracultural improbabilities. "Head, shoulders, eyes, and teeth, eyes and teeth . . .," chant the cute Yonsei children in the park.

Immediately after graduation, Heco and Okada take a year off to circumnavigate the earth. They do so on foot, bicycle, motorcycle, bus, sailboat, and train. This is the most intimate and engaging portion of the novel—an unforgettable journey described by Okada in his journals and charted by Heco in his watercolors.[15] Heco has an interest in archaeology and musicology, while Okada focuses on geography, ecology, and political economic structures. Okada finds that he has a good facility with languages. Heco, because of his great charm, can always make himself understood. For a moment, one might believe that Yamashita had achieved a new stratum in her own detailing of the Asian American literary purgatory.

Throughout this journey, Yamashita dabbles in descriptions of Disney films made on location wherever the twins happen to be. These films always seem to be about White people having adventures with animals and exotic ethnic people. As time goes on, things change a little. The White people still have their adventures, except that they now occasionally sit in the audience. In this world, Asians come in and out of the media. As Heco points out,

Sometimes we are Chinese on boats smuggling ourselves into the gold mountain; sometimes we are Thai adolescents selling our bodies and spreading AIDS; sometimes we are Vietnamese gangs in Cerritos; sometimes we are Tritia Toyota or Connie Chung; sometimes we are the Rising Sun; sometimes we are Korean 7-Eleven store owners; sometimes we are Kristi Yamaguchi; sometimes we are Amy Tan. Occasionally we sell hamburgers, shop at Vons, or drink Coke. We hold hands across the world, hold hands with Africa and China and Russia. The world drinks Coke. What have we got to do with this?

---

[14]See B. Huang, "Tinker, Tailor . . . Asian Americans in the Professions," *Amerasia Journal* 3,30 (1970).

[15]Heco's whimsical watercolor of the twins struggling together to ride a camel at the foot of the Sphinx, for example.

What, indeed.

Alas for the reader, the world is vast and fascinating, but at the end of their peregrinations, the two young men still return to Gardena,[16] eager to begin the business of their lives. They open their double offices in one of many conveniently located minimalls. Predictably, their businesses grow and thrive. After all, "Who could resist being treated by such demigods? And you could get a reduced fee for a double appointment: have your teeth cleaned and your vision checked all at once." Certainly this is a boon to so many people on a tight work schedule.

Here Yamashita betrays her essentially utopian vision.

It was not just the quality of the service, the honesty and competence of the doctors, or their social responsibility, enunciated by an easy system of credit; something about the twins' place of work radiated Asian American life at its best. Unlike any formal center—be it the YMCA, the JCI, the Buddhist Church, the Baptist Church, the Asian American Studies Center, the JACCC, or the Nisei Vets—the offices of Heco and Okada seemed to be bustling with social activity and service.

For example, at any time, you can get a meal in the twins' offices. This is because of an ongoing potluck of food brought in by patients, often in lieu of payment but mostly because "eating has always been a highly important means of social interaction. No food; no culture."[17]

And unlike most doctors' offices, where the magazines are generally *Time, Newsweek, Sunset,* and *People,* Okada and Heco offer a wealth of printed materials from the *Rafu Shimpo* to books of Asian American literature. Dog-eared copies of Frank's *Donald Duk* and Maxine's *Tripmaster Monkey* are side by side for easy reference. Videos of *Who Killed Vincent Chin?* and *Hitohata* are also available. As time goes on, more books and videos are brought in, borrowed, and exchanged. Shelves are added, and the offices are known to have such an eclectic library that often scholars call in, inquiring about rare or out-of-print books.

A table with flyers and a bulletin board with notices meet the eye as clients make their next appointment. If the receptionist is free, "she might even assist you in that urgent rape or drug hotline call."[18] A revolving game of *goh* goes on in one corner of the waiting room, and a personal computer is available to access the network and talk to the world while contemplating a root canal. Even without an appointment, you can at any hour find stim-

---

[16]See *1986 Thomas Guide,* 63.
[17]Karen Tei Yamashita, *Noh Bozos* (1993).
[18]1-800-hot-line.

ulating conversation in the waiting room or parking lot. Heco, who thrives on talk, can always be persuaded to join in and make insightful and discerning comments. Okada, as mentioned, is a quieter breed; he prefers an occasional game of *goh.*

As suggested, the activities of the Heco-Okada offices spill out of the offices themselves. On weekends, a basketball court is set up in the lot, and the corner reserved for landscaping is increased to include a community garden. Soon Heco and Okada find themselves in a position to lease the space next door; they need a bigger waiting room, preferably "with space for a ping-pong table, a sound system, kitchen, child care, gallery space, and a small stage." As time goes on and things expand, only the smallest space is actually reserved for the dental-optometry practice itself. Heco and Okada become an institution. All of it somehow gets run by itself, by, chortles Yamashita, "the generosity of the community that supported itself, by the enthusiasm of people who need each other."

One day, the IRS[19] comes around and wants to know

what in hell's name Heco and Okada were doing. Was this a for-profit or non-profit venture? Looking at the books, many of the clients had never paid up, but none of this was taken as a loss. Was this social welfare? Someone had a Spam musubi *concession in the waiting room; what was that? What was this bill for basketballs and yellow paint? And this one for a composting bin? What was this "waiting room account," anyhow?*

This is how Heco and Okada get into the business of nonprofit.[20] Pretty soon, they get an administrative manager and a development officer, set these people up in their own offices, and let them create their "burgeoning bureaucracies complete with faxes, files, committee meetings, and grant proposals." As the development officer suggests from the beginning, her work will pay for itself, meaning that "if she went after a grant for thirty-thou, she'd better get another one to pay her salary."[21] This all makes good sense. After all, Yamashita asserts, the Heco-Okada Works are providing a "critically needed aspect of community. Attracted by affordable health care, the community could also find time to be a community." Of course, the development officer never puts it quite this way; she instead refers to the "public readings given by community writers, the Keep Asian American Youth off the Streets Program and the Lunch for Seniors Program."

[19]Form A2734-C.
[20]*The IRS and Non-Profit Corporations* (pamphlet, 1967).
[21]B. Huang, "The Development Nightmare," in *An Anthology of Development Stories* (New York: Houghton-Mifflin, 1998).

Funders wanted to see tangible programs, not philosophical perspectives. Never mind that the writers did their readings for free, the youth program was run by volunteers, and the lunches were donated by homemakers and restaurants; any grant support went to critical support and overhead. Once again, the Asian American community showed itself to be a model minority for other communities to copy.

Eventually, Heco and Okada get married. This is after a long period of continuing speculation about their love lives and their sexuality, further fueled by the tremendous excitement fostered, ironically, by a book and calendar of nude poses[22] featuring the Asian American Twins. They have a brief brush with Hollywood (Doublemint gum, Nike commercials, and ninja features, among other gigs), stirring national and international sensation. They get on *Arsenio,* and an offer is pending for a dentist-optometrist sitcom—a sort of "Asian American *Cosby Show* with double the pleasure." Producers approach "the two Amys—Tan and Hill—" to do the scripts, but the executive producers say, "What do we need Asian writers for? A joke's a joke." Still, fan mail floods in from everywhere. New clients are on waiting lists that stretch out to several years. Everyone—male and female—wants an appointment with "the most desirable optometrist-dentist team in the world."

So Yamashita's gross tale engrosses until finally, Heco and Okada marry two sisters.[23]

The sisters were not twins or even biological sisters, which accounted for completely different physical features. One sister was the result of artificial insemination; the other was adopted. Heco married a strangely beautiful Eurasian with green eyes and perfect hair, who did the nightly news for Fox Television. Okada's sister was one-quarter Cherokee, one-quarter African, and one-eighth Palestinian and three-eighths Micronesian. She was an artist and spiritual healer and specialized in native linguistics.

The wedding takes place on the parking lot under the hoops. "A great multicolored rainbow coalition multicultural tent" is extended to house the guests. Spam *musubi*[24] is served along with sushi, dim sum, teriyaki tacos, and Filipino spring rolls. Chili is the main dish. The list of performers is endless, short of being tedious; everyone from Dan Kwong to Cold Tofu and from Great Leap to Hiroshima is there to regale the nuptials. To the delight

[22]*The Asian Male Revealed* (Little Tokyo: Asian Persuasion Press, 1996).
[23]*Sistahs.*
[24]M. Marquardt, *101 Ways to Eat Spam* (Honolulu: Cooks Nook, 1988).

of everyone, Philip Gotanda comes dressed in a Godzilla costume, and David Henry Hwang as Madama Butterfly. Mako comes as Mako. Warren Furutani and Mike Woo make "politically moving speeches." George Takei autographs plastic replicas of the *Enterprise* with a red Sharpie, and Pat Morita does a karate demonstration in which he introduces his double, who proceeds to break bricks with his bare hands. It's noted, "If you missed this event, not to worry. VC captured every moment on video (copies available for 19.99 plus tax and shipping),"[25] and everyone who attended came away with a souvenir T-shirt to commemorate the occasion, a silkscreen *Design by Oris* with the suggestive contours of the Asian American Twins themselves."

But the festivities, as grand as they are, are incomparable to that night of nuptial bliss. Throughout the novel, the obvious question of Heco and Okada's sexual possibilities strains and tenses the imagination.[26] Finally and mercifully, Yamashita describes in torpid detail a titillating sexual encounter of passionate dimensions yet untold in Asian American romance literature.

Whatever speculations you may have about that incredible night and nights to come pale when one reflects on the reality and the mathematic possibilities of position, sexuality, culture, race, politics, genetics, DNA. Bodies entangled upon bodies, the great union of Asian America with all women, with all America—mind, body, and spirit—the great gift. Amen.

Thus ends the novel, messaging its way through the Southland's Asian American subculture to its absurd climax, full of surreal and bizarre matter—at most, a futile ejaculation. Ultimately, whether Yamashita succeeds in deconstructing stereotypes with her pen of absurdity is dependent on the reader's ability to grasp a varied and often confused text of cultural appropriations and innuendo in order to laugh.

[25]213-680-4462.
[26]Telephone interview, October 1997.

Chitra Banerjee Divakaruni

~~~~~~

POET AND FICTION WRITER

*Chitra Banerjee Divakaruni was born in India and came to the United States at age nineteen to continue her studies, getting a master's degree from Wright State University in Dayton, Ohio, and a Ph.D. from the University of California, Berkeley, both in English. She has published three books of poetry—*Dark Like the River *(1987),* The Reason for Nasturtiums *(1990), and* Black Candle *(1991)—and has edited* Multitude: A Cross-Cultural Anthology *(1993). Her collection of short stories,* Arranged Marriage *(1995), won the Oakland PEN Award, and her novel,* Mistress of Spices, *appeared in 1996. Concerned about the welfare of women, she has worked with Afghani women refugees, battered women, and women from dysfunctional families. She helped found and since 1991 has been president of MAITRI, a South Asian women's service for victims of domestic violence. She lives in the San Francisco area with her husband and two children and teaches creative writing at Foothill College.*

RESPONSE ⤺
For Whom I Write

Dear Amy,

You have asked for whom I write. Audience.

When I think that word I see an image, circles within circles and at the center a tiny dot, the writer, myself. That is where I begin: writing for myself. What I write comes first from my own concerns, my own perplexities with the world, my own angers and joys. What I write must move me, must satisfy me, must make me feel at once a sense of having discovered—and having uncovered—a truth. If not, it must go no further.

At this point in creation I cannot think of audience; to imagine the responses of others—positive or negative—would freeze me. At this point I must focus on the writing only, to try and make it the very best it can be, diction and drama, compassion and character, climax and catharsis. Only the writing counts.

But my truths are a part of other people's truths, just as the dot exists within, and is part of, each concentric circle. I acknowledge this. And so—I am most aware of this as I work on revision—I *am* writing for others. Unless I reach them, my writing will have failed.

First, yes, I write for my community—the Indians in America, telling our common experience, our language, our foods, our festivals. And yes, some of our secrets.

And simultaneously, for that larger group, the Asian Americans, with whom I share a vision of the world: of family, of virtue, of being marginalized, of being in exile.

Also—but now the circles are blurring—I am writing for the women. Women of color, yes, but my other sisters too, for haven't we all been mothers and daughters and sisters and wives? Haven't we all faced oppression (I know this from the various shelters I have worked in) one way or another?

And at this point I discover suddenly that I am writing for everyone, every reader in America, in the world (is that perhaps what the final, comprehensive circle is emblematic of?), who is willing to sit down with my book and consider what I am trying to say.

I want two things of them.

I want them to know me and my people as we are. I want to break the stereotypes that they might hold in their heads. I want them never to be able to stare at us the same way, never to Madame-Butterfly or Indiana-Jones us again.

But also—and I want this equally—I want them to come away saying, "My God, these people are people just like me." At some moment in the story—different for each reader—I want the boundaries of race and culture to dissolve in the heat of the human heart. I want them to say, "Ah yes, I *understand* why this character acted this way. If I were in his or her place, could I have done any different?" I want them to be shaken by the commonness of the experience the book is offering. I want them to identify, and be sea-changed forever by that identification.

Writing must come out of what we know, what we feel, the stories we are told as children, the inequities we live our lives trying to avenge. It must be rooted in a people and a place, whatever we choose that to be. It must smell of the earth: monsoon rain, a crowded Calcutta bus, warm *chapatis,* the loved one's hennaed hands. But ultimately it must transcend all that to reach across time and space and memory to touch those who have never—and who will never—live as we have lived. What else is literature for? Because if it is only the specifics of a culture we want to record, surely a sociologist or an anthropologist could do it better.

And so: yes, I want my writing to reach non–Asian Americans. Non-Asians. Not just here in America but all over the world. And here's something else: I want to reach nonliterary readers who would generally hesitate to pick up a story by a writer with a name that sounds like mine.

When one of the stories from my book *Arranged Marriage* was excerpted in *Good*

Housekeeping (July 1995), several of my writer friends responded disdainfully. "*Good Housekeeping!*" they said, in a tone that implied "Good grief! At least if she'd sold out to the *New Yorker* that would have been something!" But the same reasons that made them disdainful made me happy. I *wanted* the general reader to be exposed to my work. I hoped the story—about an Indian woman whose in-laws want her to abort her baby when they find out it's a girl—would make the reader think of things she normally would not. I was the writer with a sociocultural mission, all set to educate.

But here's the surprise, at least for me. I was amazed and moved and humbled by the letters I received in response to the story—mostly from non-Asians. They were warm and concerned and eager to learn more. Several asked me to recommend other books for them to read. Several told me of books by Asian writers they had enjoyed (some of which I myself had not read). Several went on to share traumatic incidents from their own lives.

This experience has made me eager to try and reach greater numbers of such readers. I want to make it easy for them to understand me. I want—to use a metaphor borrowed from computerese—to be Reader Friendly. I want to cut elitism (which can be cultural as well as literary) out of my work. If I can structure a sentence in a way that is simpler and still says what I want it to say, I will do so. If I can set up the context to clarify the meaning of a word from my language, I will do so. Both *Arranged Marriage* and *Black Candle* have glossaries and notes at the end. I chose to include them.

I don't believe any of this means compromising my art. Clarity and simplicity are virtues I believe in. So are inclusiveness and tolerance. They are, in some ways, quintessentially Asian virtues.

Each Asian American writer must, of course, choose his or her own writing path. But this is my hope: if enough boundaries are crossed through writing and reading, ultimately boundaries will become less important. If understanding and interest and knowledge is created among different ethnic groups (include White America, which is after all a conglomerate of ethnic groups), ultimately distinctions such as "mainstream" and "minority" will become less meaningful. The marginalized will move to the center of the page. I think the time is right for it.

Is this selling out, Amy? I don't think so. To tell a writer she should write only for her own community is like telling her she should read only writers from her own community (which is far different from saying we should support our own Asian American writers). Who among us would agree to such censorship?

There are two quotations I remember often. I think they deal with the notion of audience and community and a writer's purpose, all the issues we have been grappling with. One is by Kafka: "A book should be an axe to shatter the frozen sea inside us." The other is by Donne: "Because I am involved in mankind." Dead White males, yes. But their writing has transcended, for me, all those three characteristics: has reached across time and race to give me something of enduring value. Something to aim for as I write, as I live.

I hope my writing will do the same for someone else. Someone not necessarily Asian American.

If this is selling out, I guess I'll just have to keep doing it. Again and again and again.

Yours,

Chitra Banerjee Divakaruni

Clothes

The water of the women's lake laps against my breasts, cool, calming. I can feel it beginning to wash the hot nervousness away from my body. The little waves tickle my armpits, make my sari float up around me, wet and yellow, like a sunflower after rain. I close my eyes and smell the sweet brown odor of the *ritha* pulp my friends Deepali and Radha are working into my hair so it will glisten with little lights this evening. They scrub with more vigor than usual and wash it out more carefully, because today is a special day. It is the day of my bride-viewing.

"Ei, Sumita! Mita! Are you deaf?" Radha says. "This is the third time I've asked you the same question."

"Look at her, already dreaming about her husband, and she hasn't even seen him yet!" Deepali jokes. Then she adds, the envy in her voice only half hidden, "Who cares about friends from a little Indian village when you're about to go live in America?"

I want to deny it, to say that I will always love them and all the things we did together through my growing-up years—visiting the *charak* fair where we always ate too many sweets, raiding the neighbor's guava tree summer afternoons while the grown-ups slept, telling fairy tales while we braided each other's hair in elaborate patterns we'd invented. *And she married the handsome prince who took her to his kingdom beyond the seven seas.* But already the activities of our girlhood seem to be far in my past, the colors leached out of them, like old sepia photographs.

His name is Somesh Sen, the man who is coming to our house with his parents today and who will be my husband "if I'm lucky enough to be chosen," as my aunt says. He is coming all the way from California. Father showed it to me yesterday, on the metal globe that sits on his desk, a chunky pink wedge on the side of a multicolored slab marked *Untd. Sts. Of America.* I touched it and felt the excitement leap all the way up my arm like an electric shock. Then it died away, leaving only a beaten-metal coldness against my fingertips.

For the first time it occurred to me that if things worked out the way everyone was hoping, I'd be going halfway around the world to live with a man I hadn't even met. Would I ever see my parents again? *Don't send me so far away,* I wanted to cry, but of course I didn't. It would be ungrateful. Father had worked so hard to find this match for me. Besides, wasn't it every woman's destiny, as Mother was always telling me, to leave the known for the unknown? She had done it, and her mother before her. *A married woman belongs to her husband, her in-laws.* Hot seeds of tears pricked my eyelids at the unfairness of it.

"Mita Moni, little jewel," Father said, calling me by my childhood name. He put out his hand as though he wanted to touch my face, then let it fall to his side. "He's a good man. Comes from a fine family. He will be kind to you." He was silent for a while. Finally he said, "Come, let me show you the special sari I bought in Calcutta for you to wear at the bride-viewing."

"Are you nervous?" Radha asks as she wraps my hair in a soft cotton towel. Her parents are also trying to arrange a marriage for her. So far three families have come to see her, but no one has chosen her because her skin-color is considered too dark. "Isn't it terrible, not knowing what's going to happen?"

I nod because I don't want to disagree, don't want to make her feel bad by saying that sometimes it's worse when you know what's coming, like I do. I knew it as soon as Father unlocked his mahogany *almirah* and took out the sari.

It was the most expensive sari I had ever seen, and surely the most beautiful. Its body was a pale pink, like the dawn sky over the women's lake. The color of transition. Embroidered all over it were tiny stars made out of real gold *zari* thread.

"Here, hold it," said Father.

The sari was unexpectedly heavy in my hands, silk-slippery, a sari to walk carefully in. A sari that could change one's life. I stood there holding it, wanting to weep. I knew that when I wore it, it would hang in perfect pleats to my feet and shimmer in the light of the evening lamps. It would dazzle Somesh and his parents and they would choose me to be his bride.

When the plane takes off, I try to stay calm, to take deep, slow breaths like Father does when he practices yoga. But my hands clench themselves on to the folds of my sari and when I force them open, after the *fasten seat belt* and *no smoking* signs have blinked off, I see they have left damp blotches on the delicate crushed fabric.

We had some arguments about this sari. I wanted a blue one for the journey, because blue is the color of possibility, the color of the sky through which I would be traveling. But Mother said there must be red in it because red is the color of luck for married women. Finally, Father found one to satisfy us both: midnight-blue with a thin red border the same color as the marriage mark I'm wearing on my forehead.

It is hard for me to think of myself as a married woman. I whisper my new name to myself, Mrs. Sumita Sen, but the syllables rustle uneasily in my mouth like a stiff satin that's never been worn.

Somesh had to leave for America just a week after the wedding. He had to get back to the store, he explained to me. He had promised his partner.

The store. It seems more real to me than Somesh—perhaps because I know more about it. It was what we had mostly talked about the night after the wedding, the first night we were together alone. It stayed open twenty-four hours, yes, all night, every night, not like the Indian stores which closed at dinnertime and sometimes in the hottest part of the afternoon. That's why his partner needed him back.

The store was called 7-*Eleven.* I thought it a strange name, exotic, risky. All the stores I knew were piously named after gods and goddesses—*Ganesh Sweet House, Lakshmi Vastralaya for Fine Saris*—to bring the owners luck.

The store sold all kinds of amazing things—apple juice in cardboard cartons that never leaked; American bread that came in cellophane packages, already cut up; canisters of potato chips, each large grainy flake curved exactly like the next. The large refrigerator with see-through glass doors held beer and wine, which Somesh said were the most popular items.

"That's where the money comes from, especially in the neighborhood where our store is," said Somesh, smiling at the shocked look on my face. (The only places I knew of that sold alcohol were the village toddy shops, "dark, stinking dens of vice," Father called them.) "A lot of Americans drink, you know. It's a part of their culture, not considered immoral, like it is here. And really, there's nothing wrong with it." He touched my lips lightly with his finger. "When you come to California, I'll get you some sweet white wine and you'll see how good it makes you feel. . . . " Now his fingers were stroking my cheeks, my throat, moving downward. I closed my eyes and tried not to jerk away because after all it was my wifely duty.

"It helps if you can think about something else," my friend Madhavi had said when she warned me about what most husbands demanded on the very first night. Two years married, she already had one child and was pregnant with a second one.

I tried to think of the women's lake, the dark cloudy green of the *shapla* leaves that float on the water, but his lips were hot against my skin, his fingers fumbling with buttons, pulling at the cotton night-sari I wore. I couldn't breathe.

"Bite hard on your tongue," Madhavi had advised. "The pain will keep your mind off what's going on down there."

But when I bit down, it hurt so much that I cried out. I couldn't help it although I was ashamed. Somesh lifted his head. I don't know what he saw on my face, but he stopped right away. "Shhh," he said, although I had made myself silent already. "It's OK, we'll wait until you feel like it." I tried to apologize but he smiled it away and started telling me some more about the store.

And that's how it was the rest of the week until he left. We would lie side by side on the big white bridal pillow I had embroidered with a pair of doves for married harmony, and Somesh would describe how the store's front windows were decorated with a flashing neon Dewar's sign and a lighted Budweiser waterfall *this big*. I would watch his hands moving excitedly through the dim air of the bedroom and think that Father had been right, he was a good man, my husband, a kind, patient man. And so handsome, too, I would add, stealing a quick look at the strong curve of his jaw, feeling luckier than I had any right to be.

The night before he left, Somesh confessed that the store wasn't making much money yet. "I'm not worried, I'm sure it soon will," he added, his fingers pleating the edge of my sari. "But I just don't want to give you the wrong impression, don't want you to be disappointed."

In the half dark I could see he had turned toward me. His face, with two vertical lines between the brows, looked young, apprehensive, in need of protection. I'd never seen that on a man's face before. Something rose in me like a wave.

"It's all right," I said, as though to a child, and pulled his head down to my breast. His hair smelled faintly of the American cigarettes he smoked. "I won't be disappointed. I'll help you." And a sudden happiness filled me.

That night I dreamed I was at the store. Soft American music floated in the background as I moved between shelves stocked high with brightly colored cans and elegant-necked bottles, turning their labels carefully to the front, polishing them until they shone.

Now, sitting inside this metal shell that is hurtling through emptiness, I try to remember other things about my husband: how gentle his hands had been, and his lips, surprisingly soft, like a woman's. How I've longed for them through those drawn-out nights while I waited for my visa to arrive. He will be standing at the customs gate, and when I reach him, he will lower his face to mine. We will kiss in front of everyone, not caring, like Americans, then pull back, look each other in the eye, and smile.

But suddenly, as I am thinking this, I realize I cannot recall Somesh's face. I try and try until my head hurts, but I can only visualize the black air swirling outside the plane, too thin for breathing. My own breath grows ragged with panic as I think of it and my mouth fills with sour fluid the way it does just before I throw up.

I grope for something to hold on to, something beautiful and talismanic from my old life. And then I remember. Somewhere down under me, low in the belly of the plane, inside my new brown case which is stacked in the dark with a hundred others, are my saris. Thick Kanjeepuram silks in solid purples and golden yellows, the thin hand-woven cottons of the Bengal countryside, green as a young banana plant, gray as the women's lake on a monsoon morning. Already I can feel my shoulders loosening up, my breath steadying. My wedding Benarasi, flame-orange, with a wide *palloo* of gold-embroidered dancing peacocks. Fold upon fold of Dhakais so fine they can be pulled through a ring. Into each fold my mother has tucked a small sachet of sandalwood powder to protect the saris from the unknown insects of America. Little silk sachets, made from her old saris—I can smell their calm fragrance as I watch the American air hostess wheeling the dinner cart toward my seat. It is the smell of my mother's hands.

I know then that everything will be all right. And when the air hostess bends her curly golden head to ask me what I would like to eat, I understand every word in spite of her strange accent and answer her without stumbling even once over the unfamiliar English phrases.

Late at night I stand in front of our bedroom mirror trying on the clothes Somesh has bought for me and smuggled in past his parents. I model each one for him, walking back and forth, clasping my hands behind my head, lips pouted, left hip thrust out just like the models on TV, while he whispers applause. I'm breathless with suppressed laughter (Father and Mother Sen must not hear us) and my cheeks are hot with the delicious excitement of conspiracy. We've stuffed a towel at the bottom of the door so no light will shine through.

I'm wearing a pair of jeans now, marveling at the curves of my hips and thighs, which have always been hidden under the flowing lines of my saris. I love the color, the same pale blue as the nayantara flowers that grow in my parents' garden. The solid comforting weight. The jeans come with a close-fitting T-shirt which outlines my breasts.

I scold Somesh to hide my embarrassed pleasure. He shouldn't have been so extravagant. We can't afford it. He just smiles.

The T-shirt is sunrise-orange—the color, I decide, of joy, of my new American life. Across its middle, in large black letters, is written *Great America*. I was sure the letters referred to the country, but Somesh told me it is the name of an amusement park, a place where people go to have fun. I think it a wonderful concept, novel. Above the letters is the picture of a train. Only it's not a train, Somesh tells me, it's a roller coaster. He tries to explain how it moves, the insane speed, the dizzy ground falling away, then gives up. "I'll take you there, Mita sweetheart," he says, "as soon as we move into our own place."

That's our dream (mine more than his, I suspect)—moving out of this two-room apartment where it seems to me if we all breathed in at once, there would be no air left. Where I must cover my head with the edge of my Japan nylon sari (my expensive Indian ones are to be saved for special occasions—trips to the temple, Bengali New Year) and serve tea to the old women that come to visit Mother Sen, where like a good Indian wife I must never address my husband by his name. Where even in our bed we kiss guiltily, uneasily, listening for the giveaway creak of springs. Sometimes I laugh to myself, thinking how ironic it is that after all my fears about America, my life has turned out to be no different from Deepali's or Radha's. But at other times I feel caught in a world where everything is frozen in place, like a scene inside a glass paperweight. It is a world so small that if I were to stretch out my arms, I would touch its cold unyielding edges. I stand inside this glass world, watching helplessly as America rushes by, wanting to scream. Then I'm ashamed. Mita, I tell myself, you're growing westernized. Back home you'd never have felt this way.

We must be patient. I know that. Tactful, loving children. That is the Indian way. "I'm their life," Somesh tells me as we lie beside each other, lazy from lovemaking. He's not boasting, merely stating a fact. "They've always been there when I needed them. I could never abandon them at some old people's home." For a moment I feel rage. You're constantly thinking of them, I want to scream. But what about me? Then I remember my own parents, Mother's hands cool on my sweat-drenched body through nights of fever, Father teaching me to read, his finger moving along the crisp black angles of the alphabet, transforming them magically into things I knew, water, dog, mango tree. I beat back my unreasonable desire and nod agreement.

Somesh has bought me a cream blouse with a long brown skirt. They match beautifully, like the inside and outside of an almond. "For when you begin working," he says. But first he wants me to start college. Get a degree, perhaps in teaching. I picture myself in front of a classroom of girls with blond pigtails and blue uniforms, like a scene out of an English movie I saw long ago in Calcutta. They raise their hands respectfully when I ask a question. "Do you really think I can?" I ask. "Of course," he replies.

I am gratified he has such confidence in me. But I have another plan, a secret that I will divulge to him once we move. What I really want is to work in the store. I want to stand behind the counter in the cream-and-brown skirt set (color of earth, color of seeds) and ring up purchases. The register drawer will glide open. Confident, I will count out green dollars and silver quarters. Gleaming copper pennies. I will dust the jars of gilt-wrapped chocolates on the counter. Will straighten, on the far wall, posters of smiling young men raising their beer mugs to toast scantily clad redheads with huge spiky eyelashes. (I have never visited the store—my in-laws don't consider it proper for a wife—but of course I know exactly what it looks like.) I will charm the customers with my smile, so that they will return again and again just to hear me telling them to have a nice day.

Meanwhile, I will the store to make money for us. Quickly. Because when we move, we'll be paying for two households. But so far it hasn't worked. They're running at a loss, Somesh tells me. They had to let the hired help go. This means most nights Somesh has to take the graveyard shift (that horrible word, like a cold hand up my spine) because his partner refuses to.

"The bastard!" Somesh spat out once. "Just because he put in more money he thinks he can order me around. I'll show him!" I was frightened by the vicious twist of his mouth. Somehow I'd never imagined that he could be angry.

Often Somesh leaves as soon as he has dinner and doesn't get back till after I've made morning tea for Father and Mother Sen. I lie mostly awake those nights, picturing masked intruders crouching in the shadowed back of the store, like I've seen on the police shows that Father Sen sometimes watches. But Somesh insists there's nothing to worry about, they have bars on the windows and a burglar alarm. "And remember," he says, "the extra cash will help us move out that much quicker."

I'm wearing a nightie now, my very first one. It's black and lacy, with a bit of a shine to it, and it glides over my hips to stop outrageously at mid-thigh. My mouth is an O of surprise in the mirror, my legs long and pale and sleek from the hair remover I asked Somesh to buy me last week. The legs of a movie star. Somesh laughs at the look on my face, then says, "You're beautiful." His voice starts a flutter low in my belly.

"Do you really think so," I ask, mostly because I want to hear him say it again. No one has called me beautiful before. My father would have thought it inappropriate, my mother that it would make me vain.

Somesh draws me close. "Very beautiful," he whispers. "The most beautiful woman in the whole world." His eyes are not joking as they usually are. I want to turn off the light, but "Please," he says, "I want to keep seeing your face." His fingers are taking pins from my hair, undoing my braids. The escaped strands fall on his face like dark rain. We have already decided where we will hide my new American clothes—the jeans and T-shirt camouflaged on a hanger among Somesh's pants, the skirt set and nightie at the bottom of my suitcase, a sandalwood sachet tucked between them, waiting.

I stand in the middle of our empty bedroom, my hair still wet from the purification bath, my back to the stripped bed I can't bear to look at. I hold in my hands the plain white sari I'm supposed to wear. I must hurry. Any minute now there'll be a knock at the door. They are afraid to leave me alone too long, afraid I might do something to myself.

The sari, a thick voile that will bunch around the waist when worn, is borrowed. White. Widow's color, color of endings. I try to tuck it into the top of the petticoat, but my fingers are numb, disobedient. It spills through them and there are waves and waves of white around my feet. I kick out in sudden rage, but the sari is too soft, it gives too easily. I grab up an edge, clamp down with my teeth and pull, feeling a fierce, bitter satisfaction when I hear it rip.

There's a cut, still stinging, on the side of my right arm, halfway to the elbow. It is from the bangle-breaking ceremony. Old Mrs. Ghosh performed the ritual, since she's a widow, too. She took my hands in hers and brought them down hard on the bedpost, so that the glass bangles I was wearing shattered and multicolored shards flew out in every direction. Some landed on the body that was on the bed, covered with a sheet. I can't call it Somesh. He was gone already. She took an edge of the sheet and rubbed the red marriage mark off my forehead. She was crying. All the women in the room were crying except me. I watched them as though from the far end of a tunnel. Their flared nostrils, their red-veined eyes, the runnels of tears, salt-corrosive, down their cheeks.

It happened last night. He was at the store. "It isn't too bad," he would tell me on the days when he was in a good mood. "Not too many customers. I can put up my feet and watch MTV all night. I can sing along with Michael Jackson as loud as I want." He had a good voice, Somesh. Sometimes he would sing softly at night, lying in bed, holding me. Hindi songs of love, *Mere Sapnon Ki Rani,* queen of my dreams. (He would not sing American songs at home out of respect for his parents, who thought they were decadent.) I would feel his warm breath on my hair as I fell asleep.

Someone came into the store last night. He took all the money, even the little rolls of pennies I had helped Somesh make up. Before he left he emptied the bullets from his gun into my husband's chest.

"Only thing is," Somesh would say about the night shifts, "I really miss you. I sit there and think of you asleep in bed. Do you know that when you sleep you make your hands into fists, like a baby? When we move out, will you come along some nights to keep me company?"

My in-laws are good people, kind. They made sure the body was covered before they let me into the room. When someone asked if my hair should be cut off, as they sometimes do with widows back home, they said no. They said I could stay at the apartment with Mrs. Ghosh if I didn't want to go to the crematorium. They asked Dr. Das to give me something to calm me down when I couldn't stop shivering. They didn't say, even once, as people would surely have in the village, that it was my bad luck that brought death to their son so soon after his marriage.

They will probably go back to India now. There's nothing here for them anymore. They will want me to go with them. You're like our daughter, they will say. Your home is with us, for as long as you want. For the rest of your life. *The rest of my life.* I can't think about that yet. It makes me dizzy. Fragments are flying about my head, multicolored and piercing sharp like bits of bangle glass.

I want you to go to college. Choose a career. I stand in front of a classroom of smiling children who love me in my cream-and-brown American dress. A faceless parade straggles across my eyelids: all those customers at the store that I will never meet. The lace nightie, fragrant with sandalwood, waiting in its blackness inside my suitcase. The savings book where we have $3,605.33. *Four thousand and we can move out, maybe next month.* The name of the panty hose I'd asked him to buy me for my birthday: sheer golden-beige. His lips, unexpectedly soft, woman-smooth. Elegant-necked wine bottles swept off shelves, shattering on the floor.

I know Somesh would not have tried to stop the gunman. I can picture his silhouette against the lighted Dewar's sign, hands raised. He is trying to find the right expression to put on his face, calm, reassuring, reasonable. *OK, take the money. No, I won't call the police.* His hands tremble just a little. His eyes darken with disbelief as his fingers touch his chest and come away wet.

I yanked away the cover. I had to see. *Great America, a place where people go to have fun.* My breath roller-coasting through my body, my unlived life gathering itself into a scream. I'd expected blood, a lot of blood, the deep red-black of it crusting his chest. But they must have cleaned him up at the hospital. He was dressed in his silk wedding kurta. Against its warm ivory his face appeared remote, stern. The musky aroma of his aftershave lotion that someone must have sprinkled on the body. It didn't quite hide that other smell, thin, sour, metallic. The smell of death. The floor shifted under me, tilting like a wave.

I'm lying on the floor now, on the spilled white sari. I feel sleepy. Or perhaps it is some other feeling I don't have a word for. The sari is seductive-soft, drawing me into its folds.

Sometimes, bathing at the lake, I would move away from my friends, their endless chatter. I'd swim toward the middle of the water with a lazy backstroke, gazing at the sky, its enormous blueness drawing me up until I felt weightless and dizzy. Once in a while there would be a plane, a small silver needle drawn through the clouds, in and out, until it disappeared. Sometimes the thought came to me, as I floated in the middle of the lake with the sun beating down on my closed eyelids, that it would be so easy to let go, to drop into the dim brown world of mud, of water weeds fine as hair.

Once I almost did it. I curled my body inward, tight as a fist, and felt it start to sink. The sun grew pale and shapeless; the water, suddenly cold, licked at the insides of my ears in welcome. But in the end I couldn't.

They are knocking on the door now, calling my name. I push myself off the floor, my body almost too heavy to lift up, as when one climbs out after a long swim. I'm surprised at how vividly it comes to me, this memory I haven't called up in years: the desperate flailing of arms and legs as I fought my way upward; the press of the water on me, heavy as terror; the wild animal trapped inside my chest, clawing at my lungs. The day returning to me as searing air, the way I drew it in, in, in, as though I would never have enough of it.

That's when I know I cannot go back. I don't know yet how I'll manage, here in this new, dangerous land. I only know I must. Because all over India, at this very moment, widows in white saris are bowing their veiled heads, serving tea to in-laws. Doves with cut-off wings.

I am standing in front of the mirror now, gathering up the sari. I tuck in the ripped end so it lies next to my skin, my secret. I make myself think of the store, although it hurts. Inside the refrigerated unit, blue milk cartons neatly lined up by Somesh's hands. The exotic smell of Hills Brothers coffee brewed black and strong, the glisten of sugar-glazed donuts nestled in tissue. The neon Budweiser emblem winking on and off like a risky invitation.

I straighten my shoulders and stand taller, take a deep breath. Air fills me—the same air that traveled through Somesh's lungs a little while ago. The thought is like an unexpected, intimate gift. I tilt my chin, readying myself for the arguments of the coming weeks, the remonstrations. In the mirror a woman holds my gaze, her eyes apprehensive yet steady. She wears a blouse and skirt the color of almonds.

Kirin Narayan

ANTHROPOLOGIST AND NOVELIST

Writer, anthropologist, and folklorist Kirin Narayan was born in Bombay in 1959 to an American mother and Indian father. She came to the United States at age sixteen and has a doctorate from the University of California, Berkeley. She is currently associate professor of anthropology and South Asian Studies at the University of Wisconsin–Madison. In addition to her novel, Love, Stars, and All That *(1994), she is author of two books on Indian storytelling traditions:* Storytellers, Saints and Scoundrels: Folk Narrative in Hindu Religious Teaching *(1989), which won the 1990 Victor Turner Prize for Ethnography and shared the Elsie Clews Parsons Prize for Folklore, and* Mondays on the Dark Night of the Moon: Himalayan Foothill Folktales *(1997), an experiment in collaboration with a wise vil-* *lage woman, Urmila Devi Sood. The National Endowment for the Humanities and the John Simon Guggenheim Foundation are among the many granting agencies that have supported Narayan's work. Currently, Narayan is at work on a new novel titled* Husbands as Foreigners.

RESPONSE

Reading/Listening

Gripping the pencil down close to the point, as soon as I learned how to write, I began journeying into stories. A few of my notebooks are saved in plastic from monsoon mold at my mother's house. Every few years I look through these stories during visits home. There is one story I particularly like that I wrote when I was about five. Fairy Al-

149

ice is sunning in a lotus. She hears a noise behind her and "knows no more." When she comes to, she is locked in a dungeon. A captured prince is her companion. She promises to rescue him, and—I forget how—finds the way out of the dungeon. Then she marries him and they live happily ever after. "Nani," my American grandmother from Grand Rapids, Michigan, was named Alice. "Ba," my Indian grandmother, born in the Kathiawar forest during a plague, was named Kamala. In Sanskrit, Kamala means "lotus" and is associated with Lakshmi, the goddess of good fortune, who typically sits or stands in a lotus. With Fairy Alice resting in the lotus, I seem to have been bringing together my two backgrounds. At the same time, I was drawing on the motifs swirling through the many volumes of fairy tales from around the world that were lined up on our crowded household shelves.

English was the language in which I was first literate, and ironically, it was in English translation and as written texts that I believe I first encountered Indian fairy tales with occasional valiant heroines of the sort that this early story drew on. But then, too, my grandmother Ba, speaking a nasal Gujarati-accented Hindi, liked to hold forth about the times different gods had personally granted her audience. Eyes widening, tattooed wrists flinging in the air, she dramatically reenacted events, such as how the whiskered albino cobra (definitely guarding buried treasure!) had led her to Shivji Bhagavan, who stood shining, calf deep in our fields, raising one enormous benevolent hand. In my grandmother's oral tales, she was always the fearless heroine rounding up blessings for the family.

Nani, my other grandmother, taught me to write and read. Even now, my handwriting bears tilts and flourishes from her turn-of-the-century script. Among the many books that Nani offered me was Louisa May Alcott's *Little Women*. Poring through this book under our corrugated aluminum roof with bougainvillea blooming through the window bars, the flap of the fan, and the distant rush of the sea, I was immediately transported from Bombay to Massachusetts's falling snow. I don't know how many girls around the world Jo March has inspired to recognize themselves as writers, but I was certainly one of them. Though adults directed the question "What will you be when you grow up?" more to my brothers than to me, I was always ready with the declaration that I would be a Writer. I had grandiose plans to publish my first novel by the time I was ten, but as it happened, I was more than twenty years overdue.

Our Bombay household in the 1960s and 1970s stood at the confluence of many cultural influences. Indian artists, musicians, scientists, maharajas, and journalists would come out for a day at the beach, loaded down with stories of independent India's place in the world that my father's beer would help unloosen. We also gave refuge to a steady stream of beatniks, Western academics, hippies, and seekers of enlightenment (what my father called "Urugs," from "Guru" spelled backward), whose tales spanned their own childhoods, their love affairs, the hashish trail, and the quirks of assorted religious teachers. I learned early on that if a child appeared to be occupied—especially if she was ostensibly reading—adults would assume they had their own privacy. I listened in on many of these tales and then happily listened again as my mother retold the choicest tales brought in by one wave of visitors to the visitors who came next.

Perhaps most writers' inspiration arises from the confluence of written and oral stories. In my case, going to graduate school in anthropology with an emphasis on folklore has underscored the ways in which my writing Muse rides the tiger of orality. Learning to listen, to transcribe with a sense of rhythm and intonation, to re-create gestures as performance, to locate stories within larger cultural settings and look for wider transcultural motifs has been invaluable for me as a writer. My two academic books about storytelling in India have enriched the scope and style of what I address in my fiction.

Multiple Identities

Since I came to college at sixteen I have been based in the United States, though I often return to India for visits ranging from a few weeks to a whole year. Positioned between India and America through ancestry, I continue to live in a fluid space between the two places in both geographic and imaginative terms. In this sense, the label "Asian American writer" would seem to hold. At the same time, it is one label among many.

A few years ago, I wrote an essay called "How Native Is a Native Anthropologist?" In that essay, I struggled with issues of insiders and authenticity in terms of anthropology, a discipline founded on the notion of cultural difference. I argued that instead of thinking in dichotomous terms, such as "insider/outsider" or "native/foreigner," it is more useful to acknowledge that we all carry multiple identities that are evoked in different contexts, positioning us in a panoply of ways. Race, class, nationality, ethnicity, gender, profession, sexual orientation are only a few of these tangled threads of identity that can be tugged into view depending on where one is and with whom one is interacting.

Along these lines, while I might be an Asian American writer, I am also, in different contexts, a South Asian American writer, an Indian American writer, an Indian writer, an American writer, a writer in English, a woman writer, a feminist writer, a heterosexual writer, an anthropologist writer, a writer of academe, a younger writer, an older writer, and so on and so forth. To my great surprise, the Library of Congress headings for my first novel, *Love, Stars and All That*, begin with "Women graduate students—California—Berkeley—fiction." I do not think that whoever doled out subjects for the book could have read very far, for though much of the novel is set in India and in Vermont, there is a mantra-like repetition to the "California—Berkeley and Berkeley (Calif.)" subject headers. "East Indians—California—Berkeley—fiction" comes in almost as an afterthought, as the third attempt at definition. It would seem that according to the Library of Congress, I—who was raised in Bombay and now live in Madison—am first and foremost a California writer!

Choosing a label is a strategic act, and sometimes others choose for you or exclude you. Labeling is a way of forming alliances, even as it is a way of delineating boundaries to keep outsiders squarely outside. I do not think that any single label can possibly locate or contain all the sources of inspiration or possible audiences for a writer.

I write for myself: because I feel compelled to, and because the beauty of words and the mysterious unfolding of plots make the dense givenness of life more bearable. But when I write, I hope that the people to whom I feel close will enjoy this, too. My primary imagined audience is a circle of friends from a wide range of ethnic backgrounds and experiences. I am aware that some of my friends are more attuned to certain nuances in my fiction than others: the academics might not get the allusions to Bombay life, even as the friends I grew up with may not get the in-jokes shared with fellow academics, and so on. All the same, I hope to write accessibly enough that no one picking up any of my books would feel altogether excluded.

In keeping with the issue of multiple identities, there are so many permutations of Asian American experience that the notion of an "authentic" Asian American voice can be constraining. For fiction to have any force, I believe it must emerge from familiar experience. Simply sharing a trait such as "Asian American" does not mean that one can write with any conviction across differences such as class, and so, when an upper-class person of South Asian origin attempts to write from the perspective of a poor peasant immigrant in an effort to get at an authentic voice, to me this ends up being far more inauthentic than if the writer had remained within the parameters of his or her own familiar world. I also do not think that fiction writers need be responsible for accurately representing the Community, for not only does this confuse the boundary between factual ethnography and imagined fiction, but it suppresses the existence of multiple, overlapping, and discordant communities. Perhaps it is to explore these issues of shifting identities and multiple communities that in the novel I'm now trying to write, one of the main characters is Indian American while the other is an American raised in India.

Reception

As I just mentioned, my first audience is usually a cross section of close friends: Indian American, Japanese American, Jewish American, European American, and "plain" American; academics, lawyers, scientists, artists; women, men; straight or gay. These forbearing friends are often my readers as a manuscript is still emerging, and their comments often influence what happens next. For example, my friend Manuela Albuquerque (of Goan Indian ancestry and now settled in Berkeley, proving that the Library of Congress may be onto something) has not only demanded entire scenes but has told me

in no uncertain terms when twists in the plot are unconvincing: she is among my best and toughest readers. The finished text ends up being not entirely mine but also a collective product, wrought from the generosity and affection, and alas, sometimes the displeasure, of those who've given me their time.

Once a piece is published, I have found the most enjoyable part of published work to be the way it goes out as one's envoy, rekindling long-lost acquaintances and making new friends. *Love, Stars and All That* has brought me letters, E-mails, and office-hour visits from people I may not otherwise have met. Many of these are young South Asian Americans or South Asians living in America. Many of these are women. But I have only to look in my file marked "Letters, V * and all . . ." to be reminded of the young Jewish American woman who sees herself in Gita's late romantic start, the Hmong American student who identified with Gita's studiousness, the retired professor who laughed at the depictions of academia, the young Indian American man who buoyantly announced that Saroj Aunty has inspired him and his aunt to name all her saris. Reviewers in major newspapers were mostly kind, with the painful exception of a fellow South Asian American writer. But long after reviewers have moved on to more recent books, the human connections emerging from the novel have been an ongoing and enormous gift.

A particularly important new set of connections has been to fellow Asian Americans, particularly writers. More than any other way, I have found myself as an Asian American writer by being graciously included by others who share this label. To chase about Madison looking for *tzung dze* in May, to talk about parallel legacies of female virtue encoding family honor, to celebrate not writing like John Updike, and to stay up late at conferences reveling in the different storytelling traditions that surface in our writing—all this has been a rich and unfolding legacy of joining in the emergent category "Asian American writer."

A guiding axiom for me has been the advice that J. D. Salinger's character Seymour Glass gave to his brother Buddy: "Write what you'd most love to read." This may take one away from mainstream literature and preexisting models of successful writing. But I do believe that in being true to oneself—to one's peculiar amalgam of sensibilities, insights, aesthetics—a writer can most effectively speak to and for all the multiple communities in which she or he claims fellowship.

Firoze Ganjifrockwala (from *Love, Stars, and All That*)

Here we sit in the latest Indian food disaster on Telegraph Avenue. Bapuji no Bistro is the name of this one. I don't give it more than a few months. The food is hopeless, just some generic spices thrown around in oil. There are misshapen batik *apsaras* on the wall, empty Kingfisher and Taj Lager beer bottles lined up along the windows, and plastic roses in plastic vases on the tables. Gita is on one edge of her chair as though she's expecting a cockroach to creep up from the side. And of course coming to this place was my idea.

I'm trying to get Gita into a conversation about Simone de Beauvoir. I think that de Beauvoir is fantastic, even if everything she says doesn't hold up cross-culturally. She really gets to the heart of the phoniness involved in this whole virginity business and inequality between the sexes. I mean, genders. OK, gender, whatever. Not that I would use words like *virginity* or *sex* with Gita. It would only make her stiffen her back: the sacred is tabooed with interdictions, just like Durkheim said. I have just been outlining the general principle of Woman as Other for her.

She sits there fidgeting with the pita bread that is supposed to be a *chappati,* soaking it up in that awful lentil soup they've sprinkled with curry powder and passed off as *dal.* Those big, haunted eyes, those delicate veined hands, that hair hanging over one shoulder, and her mind definitely somewhere else. It makes me feel like a bastard to be talking at her. I think that at this point neither of us is paying much attention to what I have to say, but I can't seem to stop the lecture.

She's weird. The way she keeps a distance—in the clipped conversation, in the averted eyes, the body held taut across the table—I tell you, man, it makes me feel bad. It makes me feel as though I've got some sort of hidden criminal tendencies and if she doesn't watch out I'll be pouncing in a flash. This kind of attitude is really a problem with Indian women. OK, I don't mean to essentialize, let's say some Indian women. It's the whole cult of virginity. The quest for the perfect hero, to whom they will finally surrender themselves. Women end up being too bloody paranoid. They're afraid that if they loosen up a little it means they'll completely let go. When they get to America, there's so much damn sex in the air that if they're the uptight sort they go into deep freeze.

OK, so I know that men back in India can be awful when a woman gets into a crowded train compartment or a bus. Delhi buses are apparently the worst—if you're a woman you get completely fingered. In the crush, men take the opportunity to grab at buttocks and squish breasts. She went to college in Delhi—no wonder she's so anxious about this sort of thing. But it's not just her, though, it's just about every second *deshi* woman you meet out here, whether she's from Bombay or Calcutta or Madras. And the ones who aren't uptight end up getting involved with foreign guys. I swear it: foreign. It's the difference that adds mystery and erases any residue of fear or guilt. For example, Najma. We're in the same feminist theory class. She's the sort who will smile right at you and laugh at double meanings in words. The kind of girl—well, woman—who can really be your friend. And who's she involved with? Guess. Some American scientist type. When I was an undergrad out at Boston it was the same thing. Either they're nervous and dart off or they're already taken by some foreign bugger.

Dinaz said, "Look after Gita. She's damn brainy but she's a mouse who keeps to herself." So I call up Gita at least once a month and we go out to eat together. What I don't understand is, if she's so brainy, why the hell is she so insecure about what she thinks? You try to start an intellectual conversation, and she mostly agrees, looking at a spot just beside your left ear. If she says anything, it comes out apologetic. I mean, what's wrong with the Indian educational system if intelligent women can feel inadequate just because they're intelligent? Because it disqualifies them to be wives who listen sweetly as their husbands pontificate? What does it do to you if nothing you ever say is challenged? We talk about the oppression of women, but we need to also think about the psychological effects on men.

A month or two ago I was trying to explain to her about us all being products of colonialism. She was more with me that day, a mind like a whip, cracking out dates. What year the East India Company got to India, what year the Battle of Plassey made British power dominant over the French, what year the first War of Indian Independence was, when Gandhi started his agitations. I can't remember all the dates now, even if I tried. But the thing is, she doesn't see that this all relates to her, that all the impact of all those dates is inscribed in every elite Indian's mentality. I don't know what sort of Indian she *is—Das* is probably something from the north. But look at the weirdness of it all: me originally from Iran but settled in Gujarat, then Bombay, for God knows how many generations. That's at least on my

Indian side. Her from somewhere in north India. Both of us eating fake Indian food in Berkeley, California, and we're not speaking Farsi or Gujarati or Bengali or Punjabi or Hindi but *English* to each other. I mean, just think about it for a minute. If she's so smart, why is she just applying her mind to those books and not out to actual life? Insecurity? Could be. As though she has to have some corner of the world in which she's stable before she starts questioning anything else. It's probably those goddamn nuns. You should hear Dinaz on the subject of that convent they all went to. I know it was the nuns who drove Dinaz to her big revolt of taking up modeling. What's so depressing about it all is that Dinaz thinks that showing up in a bikini is revolt. How can the inequalities in Indian society ever be overturned if women are wasting their energies on these petty revolts? I bet that Gita thinks that going out for a walk alone with that professor fellow is something so scandalous it's titillating. I saw how flustered she was when I met them getting into his car near the marina. And all it is is a walk. Big bloody deal. All I can say is that I wish the professor good luck. Even if he has some strange ideas about being reincarnated as a Parsi. There's something about her that . . . oh hell, to melt her primness even a big important man like him is not only going to need luck but supernatural intervention.

So my thoughts are running one way and my speech is still carrying on. Gita is still watching me with this distracted, weary look.

"So that's de Beauvoir," I say. "You might not agree that it's all universal—in fact, anthropologists are looking into whether there are any societies where the genders are equal. But you have to acknowledge that for our backgrounds, at least, it sort of fits."

You know what Gita says to me after this whole long monologue? She focuses right on my face and she asks, "Firoze, do you think there's a postal strike on in Bombay?"

Now what the hell sort of response is that?

Katherine Min

POET AND FICTION WRITER

Katherine Min is Korean and American and Korean American. Born in Urbana, Illinois, in 1959 to parents who came to America after the Korean War, Min grew up in Charlottesville, Virginia, and lived in Seoul for one year as a teenager. She completed a bachelor's degree in English literature from Amherst College in Massachusetts (1980) and a master's in journalism from Columbia University (1981). In 1982, she returned to Korea and worked for the Korea Herald *for a year. In 1985, she was back in the United States, working first at Dartmouth College, later at the University of Virginia, and currently in the News Services Office of Plymouth State College in New Hampshire. Min's stories have appeared in* Prairie Schooner, Triquarterly 89, Beloit Fiction Journal, Chattahoochee Review, *and* Ploughshares, *among other publications. She won an NEA Fellowship in 1992, a New Hampshire Council Grant in 1995, and two McDowell Fellowships in 1995 and 1996. Her story "Courting a Monk" won the Pushcart Prize in 1998.*

RESPONSE
Of Anger and Ambivalence

Most of the time I am angry. Pissed off about small things: stockings marked "nude" that are four shades too pale for my legs; strangers who congratulate me on my excellent command of the English language, never assuming I could be a native speaker. Pissed off about big things: that my beautiful half-Korean daughter gets called a "Chinese alien" by playground bullies; that Asian Americans are not running major American publishing companies and paying lip service to multiculturalism by taking on one or two White writers a year.

Anger fuels my work and drives me wildly through an imperfect life. It is, strangely, empowering, though it is grounded in impotence. It is valuable to me because without it I would be merely depressed. What am I angry about? What aren't I angry about? But then I am ambivalent. Did I mention my ambivalence? When anger and ambivalence get together, you get the kind of psyche that stalls and starts like an old car, backfiring and stuttering, stuck in reverse, unable to locate neutral.

I am angry that no one would ever ask John Updike if there is an "authentic" White sensibility. Who would think to lump *Rabbit, Run* with John Gardner's *Grendel* or John Irving's *The World According to Garp*? Why is it that when you belong to the mainstream, to the "ground zero" of American experience, you are afforded your individuality—while ethnic writers are somehow pigeonholed, marginalized, lumped in all together, as though we weren't all also as individual and varied in our experience with the world as to be—each one of us—separate beings?

But then I feel conflicted. Asian American writers do share similar territory. Sort of like writers from Baltimore. Certain landmarks will be recognizable, the streets might feel familiar. Presupposing that Asian American writers are writing about being Asian American, which they are wont to do, it stands to reason that they will be dealing with some of the same issues—issues of growing up in two cultures, of racism and self-hatred, of uneasiness and assimilation. Isn't it only fair to see them as a natural group?

Yes and no. I think of the stunning musculature of Maxine Hong Kingston's prose, the humor of Frank Chin, the storytelling of Amy Tan, and I find more there that is different, that is defining, than there is to compare. The fact that they are all Asian Americans and write from their own experiences as such is a "duh," a given. What they do with it—and isn't this true of all writers?—is everything.

When it comes to literature, I am pretty much blind to gender or ethnicity. I loved Woolf, Twain, Flaubert, and Dostoyevsky long before I discovered Louise Erdrich, James Baldwin, and Maxine Hong Kingston, and now I love them all. I admire Amy Tan but don't like her prose; I was disappointed with Fae Myenne Ng's *Bone* (1993) and Gish Jen's *Typical American* (1991). I liked David Wong Louie's *Pangs of Love* (1992) and Gus Lee's *China Boy* (1991). My favorite novel is, embarrassingly enough, *The Great Gatsby*. What can one possibly make of that? Except that I want open possibilities, free rein—to read what I like, to write what I like. I do not like the expectations put on me as an Asian American writer. I want to feel free to write about Whites, Blacks, Jews, Icelanders. Would anyone publish a book by Amy Tan that had no Chinese characters? Is our only authority in our skin color, our ethnic origin? If that is true, then we have a long way to go, indeed.

I even get angry about the label "Asian American." It's absurd that the mainstream publishing world, priding themselves on "discovering" ethnic writing, thinks of us as a monolithic product to be peddled like an exotic novelty, some new cultural knickknack for a curious White audience. I am Korean American. Being Korean American is a little like being the fourth daughter in a traditional Asian family. No one cares at that point.

You're sort of in the shadows, a smaller, slightly faded copy of an original design. "Oh, you're *Korean,*" people say, usually disappointed that they cannot then share with me their passion for *ikebana,* their recent photographs of a trip to Beijing. "Do they speak Chinese over there? Wasn't there a war?" At least people have heard of China and Japan! I look at the Chinese in this country with envy and wonder: they are visible, a power block, with huge communities and a largely intact culture. I look at the Japanese Americans and have to overcome prejudice instilled in me by stories I grew up listening to, told by my parents and other relatives, of the brutal colonization of Korea and other Asian countries. We are not a unified front. Why should we be? Who would link German, Irish, and French American writers? Because we share a race does not mean we share a sensibility.

Which isn't to say Asian American writers should all have to fend for themselves in their separate soups. (See what I mean about ambivalence?) I am not grateful to be the "flavor of the month," to have such a fuss made about multicultural literature and the result be a recommended daily allowance of diversity; Amy Tan and Oscar Hijuelos eked out of the mainstream presses like commemorative coins. But if it is true that the demographics are really changing, that multiculturalism is not a fad but the economic and political reality of the future, then I am sincerely glad to be alive and writing now, in among all the other voices that have not been listened to before, that were not heard. As resistant as I am to being pigeonholed, I am genuinely interested in what other Asian American artists are doing, what they make of their experience, how they have dealt with certain common issues.

I am uncomfortable, however, with insulating ourselves inside cozy Asian American Studies programs and small specialty presses, taking all our marbles and going home, forming our own cliques, our own "old-boy networks." Having been forced to assimilate into a predominantly White culture (growing up in suburban WASP neighborhoods in Virginia and upstate New York), I am uneasy in a majority. Hell, I'm uneasy in Korea, where my looks fit just right, but my whole cultural orientation, my ineptness with the language and general intolerance for traditional sexist and racist notions, keep getting me into trouble. My Americanness makes me a minority among my own tribe.

My brother, who is young and given to sweeping statements of utter certainty, accused me once of being co-opted by White society—by which he meant that I married a White man; that I live in New Hampshire, where ethnic diversity is as unthinkable as a snowless winter; that I simply expect to be the only non-White face in any given room or gathering; that in my surface life I dwell in a kind of Norman Rockwell ether. When I was a child, I wanted to be blond; as a young woman, I married one. And I see the self-hatred in that, the rejection of my own identity. But what did you expect, raised as I was on peanut butter and jelly sandwiches and *The Brady Bunch,* on Barbie dolls and Dick and Jane, tartan skirts with oversized safety pins, Shirley Temple and Marilyn Monroe?

My earliest embrace of the only culture I inhabited was all-encompassing; I invented fantasies for myself about literally shedding my own skin. Later, I grew to hate myself for all that fawning self-hatred, piling shame on top of shame, atoning by going to Asian student gatherings and playing with my food as others chattered happily in their native languages. But I was still attracted to sandy-haired boys in button-down oxfords and docksiders, boys I met in abundance at Amherst College, who drove VW bugs and had summer houses on Nantucket. After a while, I simply grew tired of chastising myself for the incongruities, the unease. The contradictions were who I was; they were my identity, my true heritage.

And this is the bottom line. I belong to neither place. I am not completely comfortable in the society I grew up in, nor the one with which I am linked by race and ancestry. I feel uneasy always, apart. And that is, perhaps, the defining characteristic of every writer's consciousness—that feeling of being the outsider, the observer, the one for whom the world is watchable. This is the source, perhaps, of my feeling of constant conflict, of being able to see both sides.

I write, as most of us do, from the presumption of individuality, of unique vision. Being Asian American, like being Catholic or being a survivor of Auschwitz, is a circumstance, something someone happens to be. For an artist, it is a point of departure, not a destination, not the summing up. How we react to the accidents of our births and lives is the subject of our work. That is universal.

Anger and ambivalence are a hell of a combination. My husband says I get most angry about the things I cannot change—and he is right. My anger is the impotent rage of the small and powerless, and my ambivalence is a straddler's stance, the constant self-questioning position of the hybrid.

Anger may drive me to write, give me subject matter, infuse me with purpose, but the act of writing moves me beyond anger, to a place where literature lives and breathes— a place that is truly color blind, meritocratic. There is no affirmative action here, no quotas or white-hooded gatekeepers. It is a place apart from the publishing world, unfortunately. But it exists. It is a place to grapple with what one makes of oneself and the universe, honorably and without restraint, where words are the only enemy and boon; where the only thing that can defeat you is the limits of your own vision, and the fact that it is not possible to say what is most deeply felt.

~~~~~~

The Brick

My father's dentures sat in a cup full of water by the bathroom sink, each tooth eerily elongated, pink gums gleaming. I hated and feared them. They seemed to watch me, regarding my habits of hygiene in permanent, gnashing judgment. I began to drape them with toilet paper whenever I went in.

My father found them uncomfortable. When in the house, sitting in the orange armchair reading his magazines, he always left them out. His mouth without them was puckered and concave, giving his narrow face the appearance of a skull.

He took them out at the dinner table despite my mother's objections. Immediately upon gobbling the last of the rice in his bowl, or sucking the last noodle, he would slip his dentures out and put them on his napkin. Click, click would go his tongue as he cleared the food from beneath where the dentures had been. He would turn on the news and continue to move his tongue around in his mouth, gesturing for me to turn the volume up. It was the time of the counts—how many of them, how many of us—and of the pictures of the muddy dead; strange still photographs from a restless medium. And my father was riveted.

"Kevin, Jane, you are excused now," my mother would tell us as we all sat and watched. My father shook his head at the TV screen and muttered. "Communists," he'd say. "Viet Cong, the worst. Look at that, look at that! Oh my God!"

Words occurred to me, arguments rehearsed themselves eloquently inside my head, but I said nothing. In matters of rebellion, I, like the Viet Cong, preferred guerrilla war.

My father wore an American flag pin on the lapel of his coat, but still the boys who hung around the corner liquor store called names as he walked past. In the pharmacy, the salesclerk looked pained as my father asked her questions. Her pale mouth would go slack, her nose crease. "What?" she'd ask, insolently, until I'd want to slap the color into her cheeks. My father would patiently repeat himself and get angry if I tried to intervene.

"I can speak myself," he'd say.

"But she just kept pretending she didn't understand you."

"It's the accent." He would shrug. "She's not used to it."

My brother came home crying one day because some boys at school had called him gook. "They said American boys were dying because of me," he said. "They said I wasn't worth it." His small, serious eyes looked red behind the black-rimmed fortress of his glasses.

My father frowned. "You tell them you're Korean," he said.

"Oh, Dad," I protested. "They don't understand the difference."

My father turned his attention to me. His eyes had no centers. "This is your fault, Jane," he said. "You brought this on."

I felt heat on my face, as though I'd stooped to open an oven door. "My fault?" I said.

"You're American girl because I make you American girl, but you're not grateful. You think America's wrong, bad country. Stupid! You think you like communism? What do you know about it?"

"Yubo," my mother said, putting a hand on my father's elbow, "*kujima.*"

"Stupid girl," my father grumbled and turned away. "Stop crying," he said, cuffing my brother on the ear. "Show dignity."

Other pictures came into our living room. Of campus protest: antiwar demonstrators burning draft cards, going limp as they were dragged to the police vans. This got my father going. His tongue would click madly against his gums. "Stupid people," my father would shout, lisping slightly. "Idiots! Send them to North Korea, to Soviet Union. See how they like it!"

I was secretly impressed by the images. I saw a Vietnamese monk immolate himself in protest. His loosely fitting robes tucked beneath him, he burned; the flames flared across his body with the wind. In my room, I held my hand over a candle until the heat made my head tight with pain. I wrote poems about the senselessness of war, with chess metaphors and images of dead men's eyes. A few got published in the high school literary magazine.

Amy Zimmerman and I organized a school walk-out in support of peace. About 70 kids participated. Some of them just wanted to skip gym class or to smoke a cigarette outside in the parking lot, but we held defiant peace signs up at the principal, a large man with a small head who turned red to the roots of his hair yelling at us to get back inside. Amy and I held a brown paper sign we'd stolen from the cafeteria and written on the back of: PEACE NOW. U.S. OUT OF VIETNAM. The other side said, "Go Trojans. Crush Schuylerville High." It got an inch or two in the local paper. I was quoted as saying I thought high school students needed to get more involved in the movement.

"Chink, chink," the boy on the street called after me. "VC spy. Why don't you go home where you belong?"

"I feel shame for you," my father said, jabbing at the newspaper with a pointed finger. "Stupid girl think she knows anything about war? Better stick to your study. Maybe you get better grades."

My father had a passion for skiing. He threw himself into it with customary intensity. In the summers he would study maps of ski areas, smoothing them across his lap, tracing new trails with his finger. We'd take day trips to mountains. We rode the chairlifts up and hiked down a trail, my brother and I windmilling through the steep grass. And in the winters, we'd go skiing every weekend, waking up in the dark to get there by the time the lifts opened.

My mother wasn't very athletic and she didn't like the cold. She took my brother out on the bunny slope for an hour and spent the rest of the time in the lodge with a book. I liked to go fast. My father tried to teach me a snowplow turn, exaggerating the shift of weight as he slid in wide arcs from one side of the trail to the other. But I preferred to barrel down straight, stopping at the end by falling over.

"Dangerous!" my father hissed, yanking me up with a gloved hand. "Learn to steer."

I broke a ski pole at Killington, bent it in a fall. I tried skiing without it, but it was hard to keep my balance. My father took me to the shop in the base lodge and we looked at poles. The prices were high there, and the salesclerk looked at us skeptically.

"Where you folks from?" he asked.

"Schenectady," my father said.

"Oh, no," the man said, laughing, "I mean originally. You know, what country?'

"Ah," my father nodded. "Korea."

I gripped a pair of sky blue ski poles and bent my knees. They felt heavy; the rubber grips were hard against the palms of my hands.

"Korea, huh?" The man's eyes narrowed. He seemed to consider something. "I was over there. Inchon," he said. "Coldest damn country I ever seen." He grinned. "That *kim chi* keeps you people warm, though, doesn't it?"

My father nodded, bobbed his head.

"Couldn't stomach the stuff, myself," the man said. "Course, it's been a few years since I was there, but it was like a desert then, just rubble and dirt and little kids by the sides of the roads. You done well to come over here."

Inside my thermal underwear, turtleneck, ski sweater and parka, I was starting to sweat. "Come on, Dad," I urged him. "Let's get this pair."

But he continued to listen to the man, smiling politely and bowing his head.

It filled me with rage, this bowing and scraping of my father's, his coolie servitude. I could barely stand to look at him. That he was my father made me ashamed.

"Yeah, you're lucky to get over here, I guess." The man frowned. "What line of work you say you're in?"

"I'm an engineer," said my father. "At GE."

He looked impressed. His eyes widened under a thick brow. "An engineer! Well, I guess you've done well for yourself so far from home. Your English is pretty good, too. *Anyoung-hush-a-mi-ka.* How about my Korean, huh?" He laughed and my father joined in.

"Good! You speak very well," my father said.

"Come on, Dad. Let's get these."

My father turned to look at me and the recognition came back into his face. He nodded and took the ski poles from my hand.

"You folks have a nice day now," the man said as we left. His gaze lingered on us as we walked away.

"Couldn't you see he was making fun of you?" I said when we were outside. "He hates us, can't you see that?"

My father blinked me. He sucked in the cold air. "You look for hate, you find it," he said. "Why look?"

On television the Tet offensive unfolded, setting my father on the edge of his chair. The Viet Cong attacked Saigon and Hue and 30 other provincial capitals. The communists controlled the entire western half of South Vietnam.

My father shook his head at the images of combat—men in helmets lined with leaves firing rifles into jungles, dead soldiers with dog tags, Vietnamese people in straw hats. "Viet Cong made big mistake," he said. "Now they see what Americans do." He looked at me. "Jane, you think Americans should go home, leave country to communists," he said mockingly. "You want communists win."

"Of course not, Dad. You don't know what I want," I said and left the table.

I wasn't home when it happened, but when I came back, there was a police car parked in the driveway. Someone had thrown a brick through the living room window. Written on the side of the brick in white chalk was the word "gook."

My mother sat in the chair furthest from the window, crying. My brother stood in back of her, picking with his fingers at the nap of the fabric. Standing in the middle of the room, his foot a few inches from the broken glass, my father conferred with the policeman. He seemed calm. He looked up as I came in.

"Oh, Jane," he said. "You're home. We worried about you."

"Who did it?" I asked. "Do they know who did it?"

"That's what we're trying to find out," the policeman said. "Got any ideas?" His notebook was open.

I looked at my father. "Well, what about the boys who hang around outside Pattersons? Rick Leszczynski and that crowd?"

My father shook his head. "No, no, I don't care who did it," he told the policeman. "Let's just forget about it."

"But, Dad," I protested, "those guys are always hassling us, calling us names. I'm sure one of them must have done it."

The policeman wrote something down.

"I don't believe it," my father said.

But after the policeman left, my father sat in the orange armchair for a long time. He'd covered the hole as best he could with a piece of cardboard from the basement, taped across it with masking tape. My mother and I had cleaned up the glass, vacuuming the rug to get the smallest slivers. The brick had been left on the coffee table, its message smudged so it looked like "cook."

"Who would do such a thing?" my mother muttered as she tidied up. "Aiee, Yubo, maybe we should just go back home."

My father gave her a severe look. "This is our home, Mi Young," he said. "We are American citizens." He didn't have his dentures in and his words came out strangely slurred, as though he'd been drinking. He stared out the bandaged window, puckering his lips thoughtfully. His eyes were opaque.

"Dad?" I said.

He looked at me and I saw he was angry. He stood up. "Stay here," he commanded. He grabbed the brick and made for the door.

"Yubo!" my mother shouted. She pushed my shoulder. "Jane, go get your father!"

I followed my father's shadow down the street, past the close brick houses separated by chain-link fences and newly-tarred driveways, to the commercial end where the boys hung out in front of the liquor store.

There were only three of them out there, Rick Leszczynski, Tim Patterson and another guy. They were big compared to my father, with the dense solidity of youth. I knew them from high school. My father was screaming at them, waving the brick in the air as though he meant to heave it.

"You stupid boys, what do you know about me? . . . Nothing, you don't know . . . I fought with Americans during Korean War, side by side with American soldiers . . . I get Ph.D. from SUNY Albany . . . I am American citizen . . . My children born here . . . "

I watched from a distance as my father sputtered. Toothless, with a heavy accent, he was almost inarticulate, but the boys seemed to listen attentively.

" . . . you threaten my family? You destroy my property? Why don't you fight for your country, you're so patriotic? Why don't you helping U.S.A. against communists? Aiee! *Keh-saki-ya!*"

As his English broke down, my father switched to Korean, his voice rising in a hysteria of curses. The three boys stood motionless, leaning against the wall. They appeared stunned by my father's tirade. Rick glanced quickly in my direction, then looked down. Finally, my father threw the brick against the ground and a few chips flew off. He spat and muttered and turned away.

"Crazy old man," one of the boys said, softly.

I followed my father back to the house. His shoulders stooped as he walked, his hands hung loosely at his sides. He looked tired, exhausted, as though he'd been walking all night.

"Dad," I said, "it's okay."

My father wheeled around. His expression was incredulous. "You tell me it's okay," he said. "I don't think so." He stared at me. His whole face seemed to be collapsing, from his cheeks to his jaw; his skin hung slack on sharply angled bones.

When we got to the house, my father went in, but I stayed outside on the front step, forcing my breath in the dark. Grey clouds obscured the stars.

"You look for hate, you find it," my father had said. But what if it searched you out, dogging you everywhere you went, until you heard it like the pulse beat of your own heart, always? I had thrown the brick to make him see the truth, but he had only seen the lie—had seen the hate in them and not in me. I felt a bitter triumph, like a sudden blooming, and I wept for my own despising.

Stewart David Ikeda

NOVELIST

Stewart David Ikeda is a hapa Yonsei (part-White fourth-generation Japanese American) born in suburban Philadelphia in 1966 to families who, somewhere down the line, started out elsewhere—in Europe and Asia. His novel, What the Scarecrow Said *(1996), received multiple awards and was named a finalist for the Barnes & Noble Discover Great New Writers Award. He earned his bachelor's degree from New York University, where he studied dance, theater, and writing, and his master of fine arts degree from the University of Michigan, where he was awarded a full fellowship and two Avery and Julie Hopwood Awards. His story "Roughie" first appeared in* Glimmer Train *and in* Voices of the Xiled: A Generation Speaks for Itself *(1994) and follows his "Response." Ikeda taught creative writing and Asian American Studies at the University of Wisconsin–Madison for three years and now lives in Cambridge, Massachusetts. He is currently editing the internet magazine* Asian American Village.

RESPONSE ⤿

Inspiration for my writing comes from revelations of malice, absurdity, tenderness, heroism, terror—in myself and in my world, family, and friends. And I have a powerful impulse to role-playing; if I hadn't majored in theater at the Performing Arts School in Philadelphia, I'd have been one of those fellows I used to hassle in the lunchroom, their eyeglasses held together by Band-Aids, huddled over a heated game of Dungeons and

Dragons. My research is Stanislavskian: I'll tour pathology wards to write as a physician, donning rubber gloves and literally delving into the messy details; I'll wander the red-light districts; in a pinch, I'm not above dressing in character. Writing of the internment, I baked for hours in the desert ruins of Gila River and planted myself in the mock barrack in the Smithsonian—became part of the exhibit. I'm attracted to the experiential aspect of writing, which can help expand voice and identity.

Story origins are random or untraceable, but how one tells stories is easier to pin down. Always conscious of myself as a "mixed" writer—literally and metaphorically—I remain keenly aware of the distinction between mixed race and "mixed up." Some would have us believe these are synonymous. (I often see this in students and critics.) I am also conscious, then, of myself as existentially, emotionally, and politically mixed: as a man, heterosexual, American, artist, agnostic, Japanese American, WASP, East Coaster— simultaneously and in concert, and that's a rush. Equally conscious of and curious about what I am not (a woman, Japanese), I feel fortunate that my palette is so broad. Teaching Asian American Studies brought this all into focus for me—observing the polarized relationships between students as they enter the class, their alliances shifting back and forth across the workshop table as in an ongoing game of Hot Potato, and then their slightly dazed expressions as they leave the class better writers, with more interest in other lives and cultures.

Q: For whom do you write?

Well, my mom wants an apartment in the Dakota on Central Park West; my partner is an academic; I write every day for the IRS and landlord first, then for everyone else. That is, that the writing is first well crafted, com-

pelling, and clear is my job; I imagine my first-grade teachers reading it, and MBAs, house painters, everyone. The notable exception is when I write about Japanese American history and WWII, where I increasingly find myself writing for my grandparents' generation and to my own. It's a game of catch-up, where I argue multiple points of view, try to set a few records straight and mostly to stake a claim—to tell what early Nikkei [people of Japanese ancestry living outside Japan] did, rather than rehash what was done to them.

I always hope to engage with people who don't already or necessarily agree with me. One of my most gratifying public readings was at a library in the teeny-tiny town of Clinton, Michigan. As co-organizer for the series, I initially felt compelled to censor myself and others to what I assumed were community standards—no sex, no swearing, no academic jargon, *definitely* no sex—until left with one poem about fly-fishing and a few unwilling readers. Of course, I was wrong. Not at all provincial, the audience wore its critical hats to the first reading, where I served up a satirical piece about corporate incursions into the Girl Scouts. Afterward, over cookies and bubbling green punch, I enjoyed a stern, honest, line-by-line exposé of my inadequate research ("We have Troop Leaders, not Den Mothers!"). The second reading, featuring an Asian American bill and (gasp) lots of sex, was a smash. Then, I risked a short-short about waste and violence in an old East Coast "inner-city" neighborhood of mine, attacking the experiential distance between the story and the TVs of a town like . . . well, Clinton, Michigan. I reached a crescendo, hit the end—boom! I waited. In the ensuing silence, I thought, "They hated it." Later, sheepishly nibbling a cookie, an audience member admitted that she hadn't known the story was over. Then, more forcefully, she prescribed cutting the final paragraph (which I did, to the story's improvement) and went on: "You know, it really got me to thinking . . ."

Q: Which writers do you most admire?

I'm always surprised when people can answer this question. I cannot. There are too many writers I admire, respect, envy—some I am indebted to, and even some I love. What these artists share is that they're writers first and foremost, who work with their sleeves up and whose writings are parts of their life processes, hands extending beyond the page into the macrocosm. Studying with the Israeli poet Yehuda Amichai changed my young worldview: For him, poetry lives in every daily detail—the world is one gigantic poem waiting to be tapped. It's easier to say which writers are to be feared. I distrust people who can be miserly with their words and stories—who make writing a secret, exclusive, members-only, or wholly private endeavor. This includes Asian American writers and scholars who would make our young literature an alternate old-boy's club and who presume to speak for "us." There are too many stories yet to be told, especially in "ethnic literature"—this vast naked city. I've recently come to appreciate younger fictioneers such as David Wong Louie (and later, Gish Jen), who exhibits a dizzying variety of styles, voices, and stories. In *Pangs of Love* (1992), his characters attain that rarest of roles: they give voice to his dreams of Chinese America without ever seeming simplified, boiled down to cultural tokens—and he exoticizes nothing. That book strays so far from expressing "the Chinese American experience," but it expresses *a few* such experiences with exquisite precision.

Q: Do you see yourself in a tradition of American writers, Asian American writers, or writers of color—or are these distinctions even meaningful?

Now, with established As. Am. programs, I can point to sundry models of Asian Americana and say: "Not me." I've always enjoyed and identified with John Irving's work, the messy, action-packed lives of his WASP characters; to read David Mura's painful, intimate poems has been like viewing a mirror. In the kinds of stories I want to tell, I may have more in common with Irving than with Mura. But I have something Irving doesn't have: He can write of his puritanical, New England physician grandfather who served in the army and of characters fighting the Japanese in Burma; I can write of *my* Protestant, Anglo, middle-states physician maternal grandfather, who spent WWII bombing the Japanese in Burma *while* my paternal grandparents, also American-born landowners, were ousted from their California home as Japanese themselves (we couldn't bomb Pasadena, after all). Ultimately, neither of us can "own" these stories, but we can spin versions of them in more engaging, instructive, memorable, and complex ways than our grandfathers could.

No, the distinctions cannot be meaningful; to me, they smack of marketing-speak. They render bodies of individuals into market segments and are sometimes wielded in ways that reinforce separatism, which I take personally. I choose to consider myself the vanguard of our culture, a sign of blessed mongrelization to come. I see this in my students, too; those individualists drawn to writing inevitably balk at restraints, simplification, categorization, stereotyping. I do not tell them, "Write what you know," as the cliché goes, but "Know what you write and know your limitations." Ours is a lonely job: We work in solitude, at an often-thankless task resulting in poverty, alcoholism, ridicule, or isolation. (I think of Rushdie's continuing exile as our collective symbol and our point of shame.) It can be extremely lonely when the writer realizes that *she will* never *write* the *Great American Novel.* It seems obvious, but it is a rude awakening. The best—or at least, the most prolific—writers may then realize they can write one or even a few great American novels (though in our global mongrelization, we may find even this insufficient). And this gives way to relief: otherwise, we'd be out of a job.

Q: Is there an "authentic" Asian American sensibility?

Of course: We are a short, sallow folk from California or Hawaii who always migrate in groups. We avoid meeting people's eyes because we don't want to embarrass them with our good looks (our fine-boned frames, enviable almond eyes; many women have said they'd kill to have my strong, thick hair) or frighten them because our hands and feet are registered deadly weapons. There are fine distinctions to be made, though: We Japanese share a penchant for suicide and self-mutilation not shared by our more placid Chinese compadres. The pioneer anthology *Aiiieeeee!* correctly told us that Asian America evolved from Japan, China, and the Philippines—despite the current hullabaloo, I believe that admitting any more nationalities would be too messy. Hmmmm . . . while we're at it, define American.

Here's a Japanese American experience: A young WASP-Japanese Yonsei writer grows up in Philadelphia, wholly White-identified until "discovering" WWII, the upheaval and dislocation of his family. He enters an As. Am. lit course to aid his metamorphosis into a Japanese American. He reads Hisaye Yamamoto: "Any extensive literary treatment of the Japanese in this country would be incomplete without some acknowledgment of the camp experience." Accepting this, believing that his story must lie in the desert camp of Gila River, he enlists his grandfather's help to write a histori-

cal novel. It is about a Nisei man like his grandfather, forced to relocate to the East Coast where—newly bereft of home and family—he builds a new "family" or community among White New England farmers. A West Coast friend reads the manuscript and is unsettled, deciding, "You know, this is an atypical story." The writer spends many years believing that experiences like his family's were not authentic. He wonders if the story is worth telling.

Here's another experience: The writer's grandfather did not go to camp but was released to attend the University of Wisconsin on a Ph.D. fellowship. His pregnant wife waits in Gila River for him to get settled and send for her, but arriving in Madison, he is told that the university was just declared off-limits to people of Japanese ancestry because of a new military program. He is sent off homeless and wandering. Fifty years later, his grandson—who has been told none of this—is hired to teach young people about writing "the Asian American experience" at the same university's Asian American Studies program. The grandson decides both experiences are worth the telling.

The irony of my appointment at Madison almost made me take up religion; only some divine hand could have devised it—whether as some perverse practical joke or else as some righteous spiritual victory. But I'm not very religious, and finally it's my grandfather's victory, not mine. Some could question my "authority" or "authenticity" as an Asian American author or teacher. But you know, I can live with that. Authority or not, I do know the historical issues of our literature; I take care to state my terms and to acknowledge my limitations within the text, through point of view or through choosing "fiction" over autobiography, confession, memoir, et cetera. It saddens me when writers I admire take exclusive (racist, essentialist) stances; it is my natural and naive bigotry to believe that *writers* know better. It is what poets instinctively knew long before physicists: that the universe is relative; that the more precisely you measure one aspect of a thing, the less truly you can measure another, *and that's what forces us to write our second book, poem, or song.* "The Asian American Experience" is fool's gold. Muttness is the sign of the times. I advise people to watch me. I am open to donations and film contracts.

Q: What are the most pressing burdens/responsibilities/challenges facing Asian American writers today?

First, we should beware of being swept up in what a big-brass editor described to me as "the flavor of the month" in mainstream publishing. It will pass. When it does, let us keep those bookstore "Asian American" shelves in flux, growing and emptying. We must ensure that our books are accessible—not only clear, engaging, provocative, and communicative but also cross-listed in bookstores, offered through Book-of-the-Month Club, and not misshelved (as I recently found Hisaye Yamamoto's *Seventeen Syllables* in "Japanese Literature"). Rushdie is our responsibility, and the NEA, our students, and the Asian American Writers Workshop, too.

Our primary collective responsibility is to write well and truly. To leave a trace, and one that will be read. To give voice to those individuals prevented from speaking for themselves. To be of use. This means being generous with our experiences, which can help shape a blueprint for a new, truly multicultural global village. For writers, the melting pot and the mosaic alike are shackles, at odds with the extraordinary possibilities of a vital literature, insufficient to capture our shared muttness in the world. Let us devise a new model. I suggest that a Pointillist model (I may not be the first to put it this way) is most *useful* to the writer—that is, the writer who does not write caricature. This may sound old-fashioned, corny, politically naive, and practically impossible, but the specters of individualism—precision, complexity, specificity, independence—are nonetheless the burdens and powerful tools of the art.

Finally, let us realize where we are standing and that we are standing somewhere, and from that vantage point dare to be "atypical" and to make waves. Our field sometimes seems so obsessed with recapturing/redefining a long-suppressed/misinterpreted history that it becomes a closed boat, like old Noah's ark. How easily the excluded become exclusive. Let's hope our editor-writers, such as Jessica Hagedorn and Garrett Hongo, remain the mercenary, freelance ombudsmen for our field, opening the boat, navigating uncharted frontiers. It is our duty to participate in resolving our current American identity crisis. That means that as voices for America and parts of its culture, we cannot forget that the soul of the *dreaded* White American male is among our charges, too. We bear some responsibility for making White a color again and helping it find its place in the new canvas we're all painting.

This brings me to a note about the relationship between writing and ethnic studies. Being of a generation lucky enough to have benefited from Asian American Studies programs, I feel I owe it to those teachers who helped me to exert myself similarly on my students' and readers' behalf and to use my skills to communicate ideas arising from the academy that it does not always communicate very clearly itself. When the "safe space" that engenders these ideas becomes a closed space, I feel I also owe them an occasional tweaking, to say, "It is 1998, not 1978, and we who have learned in As. Am. programs still have a few questions for you." For example: A few years ago, I attended a conference at which a well-intentioned panel of "nontraditional" teachers sought to distinguish between "P.C." and multiculturalism. The panel detailed various paradigms and perspectives that would create a revolutionary, college-wide "multicultural" curriculum using, I think, the alternate reading of "Columbus's discovery" as an example. But even revolutionaries are not immune from cronyism, and when one deeply distressed, "traditional" student protested, "B-b-but, what about the truth? I've always been told that the purpose of higher education is a pursuit of Truth," the safe space prevailed. The panel failed to recognize that what may be obvious to a middle-aged scholar can have devastating implications for a freshman's worldview and most cherished beliefs. Neither engaging with his challenge nor inviting him to attend their classes nor quite censoring him, they turned instead to each other and *they laughed.* Rolled their eyes, grinned at the child. Beyond disappointed, I was angry; not only did they lose an opportunity to perform their important intellectual mission, but worse, they may even have alienated a *book buyer.* There are too few of these around already!

Overall, I'm pleased to see the messy state of this field, its pressing questions of inclusiveness. I am pleased to see more Indians, Pakistanis, Vietnamese, Burmese, Hmong, Koreans and their descendants and other adventurers pushing the "boundaries" in my classes, at conferences, in anthologies. I am pleased to hear young, unscruffy voices within the JACL [Japanese American Citizens League] planning postredress, broad-based civil rights activities without forsaking history. Asian American literature—and to some degree, all "ethnic literatures"—is mostly defined by history, which grows dim

and just plain grows. I'm interested in seeing how Asian Americans can also be defined by the futures they project. I do this personally by trying to "know what I write"; and as a teacher, by scanning periodicals for new works by young Asian Americans; by trying to listen to my students—rather than argue them down—when they care more for MTV than history; and by trying to understand what's happening to us now, here, today.

Q: A common belief is that the dominant society has emasculated the Asian male, commodified the Asian female, and exoticized Asian culture in general. Do you agree?

I'm not sure I can answer this, except to say that in the interplay between writer and reader, you can't avoid entering the realm of *type,* but you can counter stereotype by refusing to be reduced to wholly sociological, psychological, political, et cetera, readings. Type is the jaw trap between entirely surrendering and entirely hoarding the ability to define oneself. Writers may defy being stereotyped as essentially exotic, but damned if we'll give up the right to be as individually exotic as we please. It rankles many, but I do try to people my stories with characters "who just happen to be Asian American" as the story allows it; this, in lieu of constructing another default White character just out of habit or imaginative laziness. I will do this even if they're cretins, assholes, sexists, sluts, and wimps; this, in lieu of propping up another dehumanized, stereotyped Yellow victim-hero-saint in the name of "positive representation." Bharati Mukherjee often plays with type, flirts with stereotype, braves "negative portrayals" of morally ambiguous characters, both Asian and non-Asian; once locked into class, caste, and gender, at odds with experiencing diversity, she gets off on the rainbow, and I view her as one of our more optimistic and celebratory writers.

Q: Is this a particularly receptive time for Asian American writers? What circumstances have shaped this moment?

Yes, it's certainly a time for art focusing on ethnicity, but it's more certainly a time to develop new *readers* in meaningful, lasting ways. As the world grows smaller and book buyers seek fresh voices and new perspectives, publishers and Asian American artists are serving up more varied work to wider audiences than ever before. Unfortunately, this means it's also a time for backlashing by some scholars, critics, and various literary conservationists who fear an "assault" on their sundry canons; I've met academic folk who have actually jibed, not lightly enough, that we have *enough* books already, so there's no point to writing more. Unhappily, this includes some Asian Americanists; in erecting an alternate, ostensibly "nontraditional canon," some carry over old critical tools and expectations and thus can tend to a traditional caution and rigidity, devaluing the new. Yet the whole notion of a "canon" is ultimately inappropriate for a field whose pioneer figures are not dead White males, or even dead Yellow males, but include many folk still around to drink beer with. Whatever literary conservationists may say, people who cherish literature will both value past works and seek out the new, fresh, unusual, oddball. If my student—attracted to our living, breathing, dynamic, evolving literature—opts to spend her time with Amy Tan rather than *Hard Copy*, it is a substantial victory for *all* American literature.

Q: How would you characterize the reception of your work? What is most lacking? For what do you feel most grateful?

General reviews of *What the Scarecrow Said* have ranged from sufficient to gratifying to terrific but inevitably tend to be less concerned with *my book* than with the phenom-enon of internment itself and whether or not I represented "The Japanese American Experience." (One good review faulted my inability, as a Japanese American, to make an *imaginative leap* to write about White characters.) My favorite review was a pan. In the archconservative *Weekly Standard*'s "Are Asian Americans the New Jews?" I held a proud place within a random pool of Yellows that included Tan, Jen, Mura, and other fine company. Running us through a bizarre Ethnic Lit 101 litmus test to measure our *new-jewness* against the good-ol'-days of Philip Roth, Saul Bellow, et al., the author uncovered evidence that, in fact, Asian Americans' contribution to American letters was so much "ethnic whining" and a subversive fifth column campaign in the culture wars to replace the Holocaust(!) as the moral center of the literary universe(!) with U.S. internment camps(!). *Oy vey.* I'm pleased to say that in his conclusion, at the very rock bottom of this multiculti takeover of American Lit—possibly *all* of Western civilization—is little old moi. Though it hurt to learn I was not a new Jew (after Nisei, Jewish groups make up my most supportive audiences), I loved this review.

In general, I was surprised how many people remained, in 1996, both ignorant of and hungry to learn about this chapter of our history. Thus, Q & As on my tour often became history lectures. It's not exactly "writerly" work, but it's needed, and I take it seriously. Around the same time, two other "internment novels" topped the paper- and hardback best-seller lists. That David Guterson (who's a good writer) and Danielle Steele (who's, um, a popular writer) are White and write with that sensibility is not problematic in itself; however, that they are held up by some as authoritative (pioneering, unique, the *only*) literary sources on the fact and meaning of the internment *is* very troubling to me. Similarly, *Come See the Paradise* (1990), the only mainstream film to focus on internment, is a hatchet job, a whitewash, re-casting Dennis Quaid as the moral center in what NPR likened to a Costneresque noble savage drama: *Dances with Japanese*. Meanwhile, the "atypical" *Scarecrow* curiously, if not surprisingly, attracted the least attention (not "support" or "favor" but actual attention) from Asian American critics. These overall have responded with a great, gaping silence.

Among the Hmong there are shamans who dispense stories not merely for education, entertainment, or enlightenment but as a healing art. That's finally what writing and sharing *What the Scarecrow Said* was like for me. Most literally, it led to a meaningful exchange with my grandfather just in time to hear his long-silenced stories, as he lay on his deathbed with a progressive terminal illness. It similarly brought me together with his whole Nisei generation—also tight-lipped, also dying. Culturally, Nisei are gift givers, and they responded with overwhelming gen-erosity: sending letters, E-mails, handicrafts; bringing homemade *manju* and their moth-bally camp IDs to signings. At readings, nervous grandmas commandeer the Q & A, rise to tell their own camp anecdotes for the first time to an audience of strangers and the awestruck grandkids seated beside them. Nisei are *not* touchers, but we have hugged and kissed, wept and laughed with each other. They don't say, "I loved your book," but "Thank you for telling this story." While it's gratifying that the book sells well, that it's taught both in history and English classes, et cetera, I'm finally most grateful to those readers who have engaged with me, encouraged me, corrected or argued with me—who have shared their own stories. They remind me that I've only added a little spice to the mix, that there are still so many complex tales out there yet to be told, that historical shame and the shameful things we've yet to do comprise a smog we're all generating, but that these are always leavened by moments in the sun, too.

Roughie

It's a TV voice replaying in your mind saying a life don't matter, as you watch Little Man hiding from a service revolver. And what's one more or less dog's life anyway?

Little Man bent over behind a reeking Dumpster, crying. Just home from school—still wearing his knapsack, his Turtles bag, still holding the clay candlestick holder he made in Pottery—to find his father in the pen out back with Roughie, pistol in one hand, other trying to lock the gate behind with an old, tied-up electric cord. And Little Man's stepsisters crying too, faces pressed up against the storm fence like at the zoo.

Sound of backfire on the street. His father usually says, That's just a car backfiring, Little Man. Maybe firecrackers. Just take the girls down the basement and finish your homework. But now, Little Man hears the boom and jumps anyway.

Get back! his father tells the girls, in his big bullhorn cop's voice. GET BACK NOW!

They just go on. He slaps the fence, knocks them on their butts. Tama staying down, holding her head, but crying on and on, not missing a beat. Singing out, don't do it, don't do it—and Maddy as usual saying nothing.

Little Man collects himself, breathing trash, old chicken from the Dumpster, mourning Roughie. 'Til he can't stand it. 'Til best thing's to get it done, fast, clean, over and out. Makes him leave his cave, to watch, maybe help—but swearing aloud he won't shoot her himself.

Roughie looking electrocuted, shaking like an old dying woman. Growling, like she knows a magnum got a bead on her. Glazey-eyed, drooling, like Little Man seen on that old junkie booting on the stoop yesterday. Only, old junkie felt no pain. Roughie, she'd beg for it herself if she could speak. She'd be brave, say, Right between the eyes, and hold her breath to make an easier target. But here she's not in her right mind, hurting with rat fever.

Do it, Daddy, Little Man says, hopping the fence. He's a rare boy that way—so sharp and stubborn—just views a situation and right off knows what time it is, makes the decision, sticks to it like Krazy Glue. 'S why he's in that school gifted program—got that hard-headed sticking power, like now, with his little heart breaking, he sticks solid with his father. Says, I'll get the gate—she won't get out. Make the pain stop, Daddy.

Little Man's father eyeballs the boy. Red-eyed, clear as day he's been chugging a few hard ones. Feeling painless himself, or anyways won't remember it. Stink-breath and wobbly, his gun hand waves up and down in slo-mo like a palm tree on *Hawaii Five-O*. Tells Little Man, Fuck off outta here now, boy. Take your sisters in the house.

I gotta stay with Roughie. She'll be scared if I ain't with her.

When his father whops him, Little Man's nose starts spilling over his white shirt, but he don't back off one milli-inch. Just standing, not even crying. In this miserable, man-sized voice too big for his small body, he says, You heard Daddy, you girls get in the house now, quick. Roughie won't stop hurting 'til you go. Please.

Like she's been possessed all sudden, Tama stops bawling, blinks her big eyes, and gets up off the ground, still holding her head. Maddy follows—scared to be two feet away from Tama. Door slams behind, and you hear Tama shout inside, He ain't *our* daddy. And Little Man's father, dark as a storm, shouts, You just wait, you little bitch! You're in my goddamned house now! But Little Man digs in next to his father and waits, just waiting like Buddha. Soft as a park pigeon, he says, Roughie—Daddy, please.

His father looks at the gun stupidly, then raises it at Roughie, zombie-like, like since he don't know what to do he decides better just shoot something. But then, Daddy's all shaky, got the quivers, and there's a click, then a pop, just like that. Flame from around the barrel, just like when you first stick a match in the oven pilot that's been off for a while. Shot's not so loud itself, but keeps going and going on, bouncing like a Super Ball up and down the backs of the yards and houses.

You wait for it to stop and all to quiet down, but then hear a terrible, terrible whine, like a sick baby crying at night, but it's Roughie. See her caved down in front, ass hung high in the air, shivering like she's in Alaska without an igloo. The most beautiful dog ever. Makes you wanna cry yourself, seeing her chest, all sexy and hairy white and gold, with a big red chunk out of it, and she down begging on her front paws with the side of her face and nose in the dirt. That son of a bitch . . . old, drunk, shaky son of a bitch missed from no feet, only took a fat piece outta her heart, but didn't finish the job. You wonder how this sorry shot, always strutting around big Mister John Wayne policeman, ever killed a man before.

Little Man and his father froze-stiff, locked-up, like before they wasn't scared of no rabid dog, but a half-dead, miserable pile of bloody hair scare them into mummies. Hear Tama just inside the screen door, wailing louder than ever. Look around and notice heads popping out of neighbors' houses, the two Johnson boys opening and closing the blinds at their rear window, ducking back. See that giant, Octavius, bolt out into his yard, shirtless, rippling like Arnold Schwarzenegger, carrying his own piece and looking dizzy and blinded like he just woke up.

Oh shit, shit, he shot her. Devil shot Roughie. Po-lice bru-tal-i-ty!

Everybody buzzing and hushing each other and clucking their tongues, even weeping, because near everyone loved Roughie. They knew her, remember her hounding the grocer, stalking the subway, trucking after the Good Humor van, summertime, playing with kids in the sprinkler. Lotta folks think more of her than Little Man's father. Now he's scanning around looking trapped, shouting, Mind your own nosy businesses; there's nothing for you to see here. He starts swinging 'round with the pistol, pointed down a little, and you see the heads pop back into their houses like squirrels in a tree, except for Octavius. He just spits and yells, Yessir, Officer, and starts back in slow. But even Octavius loved that Roughie. Yells, She worth twenty of you, before disappearing.

Roughie's ass comes down finally, crumples over into the dirt in a heap. If anything on this earth worse than readying yourself to die, then getting only *half*-killed, only Jesus can tell you what that is.

Little Man's the first one of them to snap to. All four-foot-something of him jerks awake, and with those tiny brown hands he tries to take the pistol from his daddy. That wakes up Senior. Says, Get back, damn you, you'll get hurt, don't . . .

And Little Man: We can't leave her like that, Daddy. It's okay, I'll do it, I know you don't want to do it, I can do it.

See, a special boy—Little Man's no coward. He adjusts. He floats.

There's a blur and scuffle, and old Roughie lifts up her eyes like she'll pull the trigger herself with just willpower, then POP! and this time you wait for the bouncing to stop, Pop, pop, down the block, and it's all quiet and you hold your breath and pray for Roughie. 'Til she starts whimpering again.

Then you see Little Man. His expression all squirming brown pain; looking old, used, in his white button shirt and leather belt that wraps near twice around his skinny body, *strangling* that pistol. Got that bulging knapsack, half as big as he is, piled on him, like a midget soldier in a Vietnam movie. And camouflage eyes to match—frosty, into the North Pole, gone. You see his fingers start squeezing again.

It's the voice in your mind and on the TV that says a life don't matter. But a life's not nothin'. You're pissed. But you're outta there, fast as feet will take you. And you don't know how things ended up for Roughie.

Images, the Spoken Word, Dance, and Music

Flo Oy Wong

ARTIST

A contemporary mixed-media installation artist, Flo Oy Wong was born and raised in Oakland, California's Chinatown. She has shown her work extensively at local and national levels, most recently at the Smithsonian Institution in Washington, D.C., for the inaugural National African American Museum Project exhibition. Her numerous awards for her work include the 1995 President's Award for the Women's Caucus for Art. Wong is cofounder of the Northern California–based Asian American Women Artists Association and has served on the national board of the Women's Caucus for Art (WCA) since 1991. In 1995 she was the WCA representative at the NGO (Nongovernmental Organization) Forum on Women in Beijing, and she has hosted art administrators and artists from the People's Republic of China as well as visiting Indonesian women artists. Essays about her work have appeared in Doug E. Blanchy's Pluralistic Approaches to Art Criticism *(1992),* Women Art Educators III *(ed. Kristin J. Congdon and Enid Zimmerman, 1993), and the journal* M/E/A/N/I/N/G *(May 1990). Her painting* Square Gone Haywire *graces the cover of* A Gathering of Voices on the Asian American Experience *(ed. Annette White Parks, 1994). Her painting* House of Light *may be found on the cover of this book.*

RESPONSE

I'm a narrative artist, and I focus on personal stories—my family's and my husband's family's. I didn't set out to do this in a conscious way. It came about in a serendipitous search for my voice as a visual artist. I started my search more than twenty years ago. In my late thirties, I went to the local community college to take some art classes in order to become a professional artist. I took life drawing and liked it. After I completed the classes, I formed an organization with some women called the Green Wagon. We maintained our drawing sessions in our own homes, and we hired nude models to pose for us. We rotated these sessions among our houses. One day it was my turn to host the drawing sessions. Normally the sessions ended at three o'clock, at which time my son came home from high school. What I didn't know was that Brad was coming home early that day. He happened upon the studio time while the model was still posing. She was embarrassed and Brad was embarrassed. Later, the other artists could no longer afford to pay for the drawing sessions with the model. I was in a quandary because I still wanted to work from live models. I began searching for alternatives. One day, I flipped through my family album, and I saw these photographs of my family when we were running our restaurant in Oakland's Chinatown during the 1940s and the 1950s—and I thought, well here are some bodies and some figures, not necessarily nude but they're bodies. I started to draw them and discovered that the drawings worked. That was in 1983.

I was thrilled that happened because I could do the drawings at low cost, but I was also satisfying another need—to explore images from my own family and my own culture.

How would I identify myself? In an ideal world I would be an American artist of Chinese descent. I call myself that way, too, sometimes in my statements. But I don't hesitate to call myself a Chinese American artist. I say first-generation and I identify that I was born in Chinatown, because racial and cultural components are very important to me. Again, in an ideal world, we wouldn't identify ourselves in this way. We would just be artists and the other parts wouldn't matter, but even when I don't categorize myself, I'm categorized by others anyway. And so I decided to adopt the categories and the identities and make them positive for myself.

My recent installation work has to do with rice and rice sacks, in which I talk about, from a narrative point of view, culture and gender and other kinds of explorations connected with those issues. My Asian Rice Sack Series is growing. I started in 1978 when I was a student at De Anza Junior College in Cupertino, California. I was inspired by Lee Tacang, a Filipino art instructor. In an exhibition he used rice sacks in an installation about his Filipino migrant youth. At that point, I didn't understand what he was doing, because I had been Eurocentrically trained. I didn't realize that as artists, we could use iconography from our cultures, from sources other than a White or Western culture. At first when I saw his installation, I was very disrespectful. I didn't understand it. I couldn't believe he had asked us to come see what he had created. Then, when he started talking, I was absolutely overwhelmed with what he had to say about being a young Filipino migrant worker. Lee taught me that we could draw from our own histories. Once I understood that, I started with an experimental rice-sack piece in 1978 and submitted it to the student art show. The juror didn't accept it. The critique was that my piece was not as well thought out as it should be. I was a novice artist, and I was very hurt by the rejection. I then put rice sacks away.

In 1986, I regained courage after I met Ruth Asawa, who is a Japanese American sculptor from San Francisco. She crochets wire with crochet hooks. I thought, gosh, this woman is crazy; if she can do that, then I can certainly sew my rice sacks together. I was already exhibiting as a working artist and was much more confident than in 1978. I began to use the rice sacks as a canvas to tell my stories. In my first major piece, *Eye of the Rice: Yu Mai Gee Fon,* which I began in 1986, I cut rice sacks into pieces and fragments and reconfigured them. I sewed them into a new pattern and design. I added sequins and lace and found objects. For four years I sewed the sacks together without any embellishment. I didn't realize that I was actually in the throes of retrieving a very personal story about my family. In 1990, an older sister, Li Keng, asked me to critique an unpublished autobiography. In it was the story of my father's shooting when I was an infant.

I was absolutely floored when I read her manuscript and focused on the story of my father's shooting. I realized then that I didn't want to admit, on a conscious level, the story I was retrieving. As I sewed the rice sacks together, I heard my mother's voice. I didn't want to hear whatever she had to say, but her voice came to me from the piecing together of the rice-sack fragments. When I finished critiquing my sister's manuscript, I realized that I was retrieving that terrifying story of my father's shooting.

I'm conjecturing that I was about eight months old at the time. I was in the house when my father was shot. Nellie and our late sister Leslie were home. Our three older sisters were at school. My dad was shot by a relative because our family belonged to our village association lottery. Our family was very poor, and my dad was accused of embezzling money from the lottery to buy food for us. I had just been born. There were six of us children; I was the sixth daughter. My dad took money from lottery treasury to buy us food.

According to the family legend about the shooting, the lottery board of directors met without my father after he was unable return the money, and a relative was assigned to kill our father. This relative made an appointment to see my dad. My mother managed to put together a decent lunch, chicken, rice, and a bottle of whiskey. No matter how poor you were, you always managed to put something on the table when a relative came. My mom cooked the lunch, and afterward, as she cleared the dishes in the kitchen, she heard a shot. This was at our house on Harrison Street. My mother ran out of the kitchen and saw my father bleeding on the floor. She realized that someone would call the doctor and the police. She ran out of the house in her slippers and caught the assailant. Nellie writes about this in a poem.

Eye of the Rice: Yu Mai Gee Fon is about three things: my personal feelings about this tragedy, my mother's courage to hold the family together, and my father's courage to live. He didn't die. Four bullets were fired at his body. The fourth bullet was stopped by a watch. On *Eye of the Rice,* I've created an eye shedding tears. From the eye (located in the upper right-hand corner of the piece) there are seven rows of tears, made from sequins and stars. As the tears cascade, they link with the spirals—which are stars inspired by Vincent van Gogh's *Starry Night.* In van Gogh's painting, where the stars are swirling in the sky, he is discussing impending death. In my work, I use the stars to talk about my father's near death. There are three major spirals. The first is mine. In the center is my Chinese name, Oy, which means "to love." My star is connected to my mother's, which looks like a ganglion, a nerve center. These sequins spread out, and our spirals are connected to our father's. There is an antique watch hanging by his spiral. The watch refers to the actual one that saved his life.

I tell the verbal part of the story with English and Chinese text superimposed on the commercial text printed on the rice sacks. In 1992, I was scheduled to show *Eye of the Rice* at Capp Street AVT in San Francisco. I was terrified because I was telling a family secret in public. In traditional Chinese families and other families, you don't reveal family secrets. With my nondominant hand, I wrote brief narrative text. I was frightened. To relieve my anxieties, I asked my friends to come to my studio to bless the piece.

When a friend saw the narrative text written in pencil she said, "Flo, you need to be bolder with this." I then sequined the emerging narrative text. I tell the story mysteriously through phrases that are scattered throughout the whole piece. One phrase reads "Pop, cousin shot you." Others are "Brave poppa, you live" and "Ma, you ran and caught the killer." I don't really mean "killer," because my father didn't die. I use "killer" because our relative intended to murder my father. Three years ago, I added a phrase, "My tongue speaks," influenced by Marlon Riggs, the videographer who created *Tongues Untied* (1990), a video about African American gay men. He reluctantly became a storyteller about African American gays because no one was telling their story. I, too, was a reluctant storyteller about my father's near tragedy.

I recently returned from Bemis Center for Contemporary Arts in Omaha, Nebraska, where I had a three-month residency. It was a nurturing place to make art, and I felt so safe that I was finally able to add, "They said you embezzled funds." For the nine years prior to that, I didn't have the courage to include that statement. *Eye of the Rice* is now fourteen feet by twenty-five feet. The last five feet comprise the heartland section. It's made of rice sacks that I took to the heartland to work on or those that I collected from Chinese restaurants in Omaha. Ree Schonlau, the director of Bemis, gave me some longer beads, which are three or four inches long. I used them to

write the word *heartland*. The word *heart* refers to my own heart, as well as the heart of the America. I play on words in both the Chinese and the English text.

Is my artwork also therapy, self-examination and self-realization? It is definitely a catharsis. It acts as a work of healing for me. A lot of artists don't want to admit that those issues exist in their work. In Western art history, particularly in the contemporary period, we are supposed to do artwork for art's sake. What I have done is admit that these issues are true and then do them. Making *Eye of the Rice* has allowed me to deal with unanswered questions that I had. A question that I added to the piece in 1993, when I was a resident at Headlands Center for the Arts in Sausalito, California, is the phrase "Where was I? All I know is that I was there." My sisters Nellie and Leslie were at home. My other three sisters were in school, and I was a baby. I want to know where I was when my father was gunned down. What I really need to do, ironically, is use *Oakland Tribune* microfilm to look up the story and the date of my father's shooting. I am not sure if I want to do that after our brother Bill's firing from that paper. I am interested in the emotional aspect of this resonating narrative in my life.

How does my work communicate and what do I hope other people will get out of it? Several things: the innovative use of material, the combination of sources from Chinese culture and Western culture, the erasing of the boundary between high and low art. I am really innovative with this piece. While I was charging ahead with courage, I was also insecure about making it. But I had to do it. I didn't have a choice. It was as if I was the vehicle for making it, but someone else was directing me. The work just came through my hands. I opened myself to that, I was receptive to that. It is now getting quite a bit of recognition. It is going to be shown at

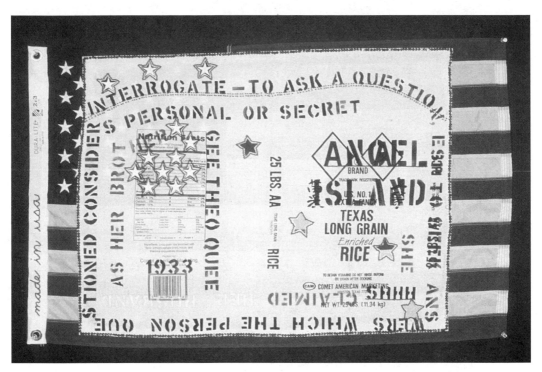

Flo Oy Wong, Made in USA: Angel Island Shhh. *1998. Approx. 2' × 3'. Sack, flag, sequins, beads.*

University of California, Santa Cruz. It has been and continues to be well received.

I was very surprised that even though the story is particular to my family and to my own healing and struggles, there are people who identify with it on many levels. I showed it in 1993 in Headlands, and a man came to me said, "Thank you. I had a wonderful father; we should do more stories about our fathers." So he identified with it with as a father story. Somebody once claimed I was discriminating against him. He was from Arkansas, where rice is grown. Most of my rice sacks were from Texas. So he identified with geographic location. Somebody else commented that a photo of my family should be added. This was when I exhibited *Eye of the Rice* without having worked into the piece the personal story of the shooting. There was nothing explicit about my family—it was just a bunch of rice sacks sewn together—but she

understood it. In Nebraska, many people came to see it. I was amazed because I didn't realize I was tapping into the history of quilt making in the heartland. It does look like a quilt. In fact, it looks like a map. People read it as a map of the United States. It does look like paths and boundaries of states because of the way I sew the sequins. There is so much going on in the piece—the commercial text, the facts themselves, the bilingual text, and the sequins and beads.

It's not linear at all. I didn't decide ten years ago that the piece would be forty feet wide and draw it out. It is definitely organic—in the same way the story of my father's shooting has been organic in our family. *Eye of the Rice* is the first of my Asian rice-sack pieces. The second is the childhood story of my husband, called the *Baby Jack Rice Story*.

Baby Jack records the memories of my husband, who grew up during segregation in

Flo Oy Wong, My Mother's Baggage. *1996. Suitcase—pages 1 and 2. 20³/₈″ high × 3″ deep × 30½″ wide. Mixed media—suitcase, scanned photos.*

Augusta, Georgia, in a tricultural environment. *Baby Jack* explores and pays respect to his endearing friendship with two African American brothers, one of whom is still alive. Chinese have lived in the South since the 1870s. The installation is titled *Baby Jack* because my mother-in-law called my husband *be be jai* (baby son), which his friends transformed into "Baby Jack." I use photographic silk-screen images from my husband's family, his childhood best friend's family. I use red because it is the good-luck color for the Chinese, and I use brown for African Americans. The photographs are randomly silk-screened onto the sacks. Each sack is approximately eighteen by twenty-three inches or twenty-six by thirty-nine. Around the edge of the sack, I use thread to sew the text. I talk about Ed's friendship within the context of his family in Augusta, Georgia. We also produced an accompanying videotape called *To Bay Min,* which means "to give face." My husband, my son, and I went to Georgia to conduct interviews and to shoot scenes.

Baby Jack has received a lot of attention because, in a historical way and a sociopolitical way, I am telling about a time when African American men provided leadership. In the 1870s, when the Chinese moved to the South, it was African Americans who helped

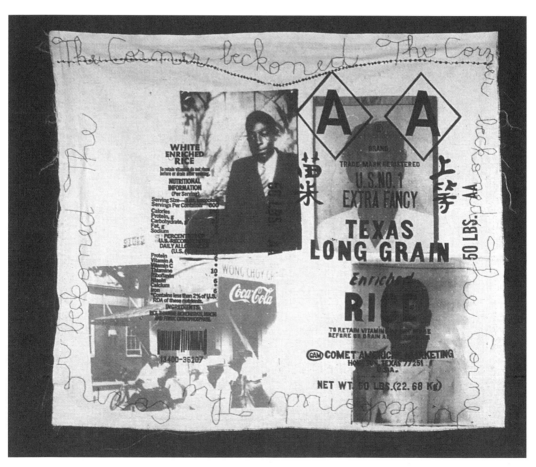

Flo Oy Wong, Baby Jack Rice Story: The Corner Beckoned. *1993. Approx. 20″ high × 36″ wide. Mixed media—sacks, sequins.*

them acclimate to their neighborhoods. During segregation in the 1940s, the city fathers designated the Chinese as "honorary Whites." As such, they attended White schools, but they had to live and work with the Blacks. The economy that held society together was made up of grocery stores. My father-in-law located his grocery store on a corner because he wanted business from both sides of the street. He continued the practice, brought from southern China, of making the front of the building a store and the back living quarters.

My father-in-law went to Augusta because members of his village from China settled there. The early Chinese pioneers built the railroad across the continental United States in the 1870s. When the job was completed, these men were abandoned by the railroad companies. Left behind, they started Chinese communities. In the 1870s, the canals in Georgia needed to be reconstructed. The freed slave labor moved north, and Southern cities lost sources of labor. The Chinese became the new source of labor. They helped reconstruct the canals. In the 1870s, a Chinese man opened a tea shop on Broad Street in downtown Augusta. Because segregation was not the law at that time, the Chinese had stores throughout the city. Later, Chinese stores were relocated in the African American neighborhoods.

This installation is an homage to the late Boykin Cade and his brother, Cush, who lived around the corner on Hunter Street, near my father-in-law's store. Ed met them when he was seven years old. Both the African American and the Chinese American houses in Augusta were very small. There was little electricity and no indoor plumbing. Because the houses were hot and stuffy on summer days, people would leave their houses and congregate around the front of my father-in-law's store. This was in the 1940s. There was a bench for people to sit on. There, people played checkers. They teased each other. Magicians came to entertain them. A hypnotist came around. Traveling preachers came. It was a gathering place for men only. I am talking about and celebrating this in the work.

Ed met Boykin and Cush and he idolized them. They were older, wiser, more experienced. Boykin was quite charismatic. He was the leader. He got them into all sorts of trouble and would leave them holding the bag. He took them fishing. They did all kinds of things. They knew about a bootleg whiskey operation. They watched as the bootlegger hid his booty in the field. They stole bottles of the bootlegged whiskey and sold it to local folks. A woman saw them and tapped their conscience by warning them. The bootlegger, she claimed, put lye in the whiskey. "You will have killed the people who buy the whiskey," she said. So Ed and his friends, seven to twelve years old, retrieved all the bottles. They gathered and burned them in a big bonfire. Ed still talks about that today.

There are three components to the installation. One is the forty rice sacks that hang floor to ceiling in a quiltlike fashion. There is a video section. And if there is enough exhibition funding, I am invited as a visiting artist to tell the stories on site. So they get the story from me, and they also get to hear the story on the video from Ed. Ed helped with the video, our son Bradley helped write the script, and my sister Nellie is the narrator. Jon Jang and Anthony Brown, who do Asian-Black music, provided the music. It's quite an experience.

Q: How do you account for your extraordinarily creative and productive family? Your sister Nellie is a poet; your brother Bill is a journalist who has appeared on the MacNeil/Lehrer News Hour.

Well, as children, we were told that we should be seen and not heard. Everything was *heung gao*—you have to listen, be a good kid, and listen to the strict Chinese teachings. We were pretty much squelched. But we were growing up with all this richness in our lives. Once we had a chance and gave ourselves permission, we opened the floodgates. Our other sister Li Keng, who is now seventy-one, is writing stories. The lid was put on me in so many ways that when it became time for me to explode, I really did. But I was fearful of explosion. Next year I will have been an artist for twenty years, and I am only now getting comfortable. I can talk about these things without the emotional weight because now I realize that people identify with the stories. While the stories are very particular, they are also universal. They are talking about what we are as people and who we are.

I credit several movements and individuals for this moment, which is favorable to Asian American artists. I credit the Civil Rights movement. I credit the feminist movement. I also credit the leadership provided by Frank Chin. I call him the "godfather" of Chinese American literature. He is very controversial, and not everybody agrees with him. Some of my friends call him a misogynist. But at the same time, he had enough courage to tell our stories in public, to not just accept a Western, Eurocentric cultural framework. Now there are lots of Asian American writers. By each of us doing what we do, we gain courage from one another. I feel like the writers have been more well known than the visual artists. Now the visual artists are getting recognition. There is a Chinese artist from China named Hung Liu. In the fifteen years she has been in the United States as an immigrant artist, she has really become very famous because of her immense talent and the stories she tells. There

are others like myself who are very public, participating in the cultural fabric of America. We are now standing up and saying, "Hey, we want to be visible. Our stories are important." It is part of a self-empowering movement that I think may have come anyway, but clearly the Civil Rights and feminist movements acted as mentoring political events. They gave us strength and courage to move forward culturally.

I love the courage of writers like Sky Lee. Do you know the book *Disappearing Moon Cafe?* Lee's story is from the gut, from the heart. It's an insider story that comes from the heart of historical Chinese immigrant experience, of tough Chinese women experiences. It's not written for a White audience exclusively, just a universal audience. I happen to agree with Frank about the emasculation of males. That's why I liked *The Great Wall,* the movie by Peter Wang. It shows really handsome Asian men, men we could call "studs." They have a feeling of sexuality and aren't afraid to express it. Our past media portrayal is so stereotypical and limiting. We need to get beyond the Charlie Chans, and beyond these hatchet-men mentalities. Those stereotypes hang on, but with us empowering ourselves as writers and playwrights, et cetera, we are really moving forward. I'm just glad to be contributing in visual arts. I realize that a writer reaches a wider audience than a visual artist. The important thing is that we are doing it.

We Asian American artists can give this society a sense of culture, from the inside. I just read an interview with the woman who made the movie *Salaam Bombay* [Mira Nair, 1988]. She was tired of the "White man look at the native" kind of movie. I read that and I thought, that's exactly it. I'm tired of White people presenting other cultures and sometimes co-opting us and our cultural iconography and symbols, using them from a dominant point of view. I like the idea of us telling our stories from the inside. We tell them so elegantly and so beautifully. Our voices are really needed. We add to the enrichment of America. America is not only rich just because of European settlers. It is that political view that really drives me, that keeps me going. I don't want people like you and me to be shut down anymore. We have the skills and the techniques to get our messages out. We have learned to be players in the cultural game.

Q: Do you think Frank Chin is right in insisting on a certain authentic Asian American sensibility?

Well, that's where I differ from him. I have my strong point of view as to what authenticity is, but if I don't happen to agree with other people, I don't see it as my place to condemn. I might question and wonder why that person is coming from that point of view. I think that the cultural context is big enough to accept all points of view, whether we agree with them or not. I don't believe in censorship in that kind of way. I don't know if Frank is meaning censorship. He has his own point of view, and he is entitled to it. I think he knows by now that not everybody agrees with him. I'm sure he has received lots of feedback.

Frank was Bill's best friend in high school. Nellie used to type his poetry for him when he was getting started. Frank asked me to critique his poetry. He was so sophisticated. I didn't know what he was talking about when he asked me to critique his work. I applaud him for his courage and for being out there. He had a lot of issues to work out, and he still does. I don't necessarily care for all the content of his writings, but at the same time, I celebrate that he writes. We all need that mentor out there. There is room for all of us. Wouldn't it be boring if we had all the same kind of writers, all the same kind of artists, all the same kind of poets and playwrights? We would be saying that Asian America is monolithic. But you and I know that we are not. We're so diverse. There are so many stories to tell. I love the fact that the stories get funnier, or more exciting, or more bizarre, eccentric and eclectic.

We are not responsible as artists to be spokesmen for a community. That's the way we are viewed. Sometimes it gets confused, and we assume that role in an incorrect way. But that is not our responsibility. I make my art because I make it for me. I've been very fortunate that it has gone beyond me and that people understand what I have to say. Not only do I do rice-sack work; I draw and I paint. I just did a suitcase book, with scanned photographs. I am finding all kinds of ways to tell my story. There is even diversity within me as an artist. The important thing for me is to get the story out. I can do art for art's sake—I'm capable of doing that—but it lacks passion and compassion. My art is strongest when it comes from my personal sources. I am actually reluctant to use my personal sources. Every time I run from doing something, I end up doing what I run from. I ran from doing *Eye of the Rice*. I didn't want to tell the story. But my mother's voice was such a positive nag in my head that it just exploded. The only story that I didn't have that kind of running from was Ed's story, because I am not emotionally related to it in the same way as the stories about my siblings and parents.

I am now trying to do more stories about my mom. I want to tell my mother's story, because she was an illegal immigrant. I have already done an installation on her using rice and bricks and some of my drawings from the Oakland Chinatown Series about her illegal immigrant status. I was talking back to [California] Governor [Pete] Wilson and his anti-immigration, anti-affirmative action stance. That installation is called *Paper Sister: Instructed to Tell the Truth.* My mom came as an illegal immigrant in 1933 because of the 1882 Chinese Exclusion Act. She had to take on an identity as my father's sister in order to enter the U.S. because, broadly interpreted by the Supreme Court, the 1924 National Origins Act said that Chinese wives of U.S. citizens could not enter the U.S. My dad was a U.S. citizen and my mother was a Chinese wife. I tell that story, but I want to tell it again, either in a rice-sack form or a suitcase form. I am going to do another suitcase book.

The suitcase book is called *My Mother's Baggage: Lucky Daughter.* I put the story into an old American Tourister suitcase. I beaded two pairs of gloves. The left glove says "lucky" and the right glove says "daughter." People who read my book wear the gloves to flip the pages. This is old-style luggage; when you open the suitcase, there is a flap to prevent your clothes from spilling out all over the place. I use all parts of the suitcase as pages of the book. It is a very personal story. I retrieved it about a year ago. It is about me being the lucky daughter in our family. Traditionally in Chinese American families, the lucky daughter is the female who preceded the birth of a son. Judy Yung of UC, Santa Cruz, in her research on Chinese American women of San Francisco Chinatown, has explored the concept of "lucky daughters." She herself is a lucky daughter. I am a lucky daughter. In my case, I wasn't wanted by my mother because I was the sixth daughter. She and my father had no value as parents because they gave birth to five girls. The desire for sons is so strong in traditional Chinese American culture. My mom cried for a month after I was born. I tell this story. I didn't find out that my mom cried when I was born until I was fifteen. I was a teenager coming home from Oakland High School to Chinatown on a bus when a friend said to me, "Hey, you know what? When you were born, your mother didn't want you." Can you believe this? In a public place, too. Shocked, I cried. When I got off the bus, I ran the few blocks to our restaurant in Chinatown. I found my sister and asked her if it was true. She said it was true. She didn't lie.

These are the pages of the book. I tell the story with photographs and text cut out from magazines. The text is similar to text in a ransom note. I just thought of doing it that way within the texture of the deteriorating suitcase. I tell how my mom didn't want me and that she gave me a Chinese name different from my sisters to change her luck. Changing her luck, she thought, would allow her to bear a son. My mom was superstitious and incorporated her superstitions into her daily life. Back to my siblings' names—the middle ideogram in all my sisters' Chinese names is *li,* "beautiful." My Chinese name doesn't mean "beautiful." At first I thought my name meant "to get people to love." But just recently, in Lincoln, Nebraska, I learned its real meaning. After a Chinese New Year dinner in Lincoln where I was asked to be the guest speaker, some people in the audience, without knowing my history, heard my name and said, "If your mom named you that it means that she didn't want you." This was said in a public venue. I wasn't hurt or shocked because I had already dealt with the issue and had already accepted it. They said, "The way she named you meant that she saw you as the daughter of another family." So I wasn't the prize. I end my *Lucky Daughter* book by saying that by the time I was married and the mother of a daughter myself, my mother said to me, "You know, I love you because you brought my son to me." What I didn't put in the book was that I had answered my mother, "No, I want you to love me for myself." When I said that, my mom couldn't understand. She couldn't get that into her head because she was a victim of good old Chinese sexism. We are still suffering today from this gender-based philosophy Confucius imposed on our culture.

In a second book that I want to do now, I am going to use scanned photographs and the ransom-note technique. I am going to tell the story of how my name is different. I am going to use the very same first page of the first book to continue it. I will have a different page for each sister. First, my siblings' names, all including the word *beautiful.* Then I will have a page for me, the only one whose name doesn't include *beautiful.*

I'm also in the midst of a new project. I received a Nebraska Arts Council Multicultural Awareness Grant to create an installation with two African American women artists from Omaha—Pam J. Berry and Reece Crawford Tocho. When I met them, while at Bemis, we discovered that we had a Chinese-Black connection. Pam has a Chinese great-grandfather. Reece has an adopted Chinese uncle. Her grandmother adopted a young Chinese boy when they were living in New York. This uncle is now grown and owns a grocery store in the inner city in Houston. Reece still goes to see him and stays with him. She calls him "uncle," and he speaks Spanish and Ebonics. When Pam, Reece, and I met, we were blown away that we had all these connections beyond our surface skin. With our installation we're presenting photographs, sculpture, and textiles. My job is to sew Kente cloth and rice sacks together to make a skirt for the throne. Pam is taking photographs. Reece is sculpting the frames and the throne. The throne is large enough for the three of us; it's a huge one, which will have three heads to represent us,

and it will have two arms, one which will form a teacup. That's because I served them tea when they visited me at Bemis. Under the huge skirt, which should billow onto the gallery floor, will be our six feet. The installation will be called the "Kente Rice Women: Talking Our Connections." I am ready to explore cross-cultural work and collaborations. I really believe it is artists who can make things happen, not politicians. I am really a blessed person, because in making my art, I am enriched.

Q: Would you speak about the painting I hope to use for the cover of this book?

When I created the cover painting, I was in a blue funk. I was looking for the light in my life, but I didn't know where it was. I started this painting just letting my brush go wherever it wanted. Pretty soon this house appeared. Actually, I didn't like the painting and threw it in the trash. Then I retrieved it and studied it and found that the light was in my own house. The painting was a validation of the light that came from me. All along I was looking for light outside of my house, while the light is in me.

And it's a yellow light. In the past, I was always so obedient to authority. Now, as an older person, I can say no and find that the world doesn't open up to swallow me. That is what being an artist has done for me. It has allowed me to assume my own power, to take it back, and to acknowledge it. Before, I gave it away—to my parents, to males, to the dominant culture. I like taking it back. I don't mind sharing power. There's enough for everybody. I'm not saying that you are the only source of power or that I'm the only source of power. There's multiple power, and when we sit at the table, it becomes quite a feast because we share. I love that concept of sharing.

Munio Makuuchi

ARTIST AND POET

Born Howard Takahashi in Seattle in 1934, Munio Makuuchi is a Japanese American artist, word- and papersmith, creator of what he calls "aerogami" (elaborate folded and cut paper constructions of birds and fabulous animals that fly). From ages seven to eleven, he was incarcerated with his family in the relocation camp at Minidoka, Idaho. At twenty, he took his mother's maiden name in protest against his father's "macho Hemingway samurai" negativity. He earned a bachelor's degree from the University of Colorado at Boulder, a master of arts degree from the University of Iowa in Iowa City, and a master of fine arts degree from the University of Wisconsin–Madison. He has taught fine arts at the University of Wiscon-sin–Janesville and spent seven years teaching at the University of Ife, Nigeria. He has had numerous group and solo exhibitions in Europe and Japan as well as in the United States, and his works have been presented in the Madison Civic Art Museum, the Resenwall Collection in Pennsylvania, the Grunwald Graphic Center at the University of California, Los Angeles, the Campbell/Steele Gallery in Iowa, among many other galleries and museums. He also published a book of poetry and prints, From Lake Minidoka to Lake Mendota, *in 1994, and four other books contain his prints and designs. Although primarily a graphic artist, Makuuchi has asked that his poems be his response to the questions.*

From Lake Minidoka to Lake Mendota

The Restitution

The Reconstitution of the Constitution
restimulated my childhood memories—
POW—7 to 11 years old—
and so with middle perception
'returned' with—
      prose/poems and
      aqua forte drawings—
      yet hoping not to
          wimp/limp
          into/your consciousness
          on crutches of self pity
but to emphatically shade experiences
      (a sacred act in and of itself)
for are not most of us prisoners
      of our own skins
      yearning to be free?

Lake Minidoka

The only re-settling
      "pond in town"
my rafting and ice skating sledding place:
While testing the early fresh
ice with its creak, crack,
frozen thunder/lightning sounds
I fell through . . . and
      emerged through carp/crap
      a paper draped proto-Godzilla
      Mifune energized—
      baptized
      immune to anything
      to survive everything—
Where today the largest and sweetest
melons grow yet a tainted taste—
remembered.

Ah, to reach the state of enuf shit
Lift up my head to sunshine and fresh air
and "come up smelling roses"
thorny though they may be.

Dry Land Eel

The main sport of camp
was rattlesnake hunting
whole gunny sacks full
They skinned them alive . . . naked
and threw them into the "can"—shit pits
red, green, blue, purple
varicose-veined
the colors of the
Grunewald painting
hung in a mad house—
a Jackson Pollack ala rotunda
of silent slimy slithering
snakes—entwined—
snakes in pits of shit—

Primary School Cat House to "Dog House"

For the first couple years my shy sister (then)
never said a word in grade school.
When she finally spoke was asked "Why the silence?"
"I'm angry at those people with all those cats
    that kicked us out of our home."

Black Diamonds

Grandma T. was always too cold there
—it wasn't always "fair" weather—
We would go "coal picken"
after the big pile was plucked . . .
Grandma and I with sticks
would pig em out of the ground.
Even then I was aware of the powerful awing
    primal act—
        going on—
An old hunched woman and a child:
    "Rooting" the ground.

The Knothole Gang

At the fairground horse stables we were herded into
we useta pop out the knotholes and
peek into the private parts of other lives . . .
Later on we polished those knots like precious stones
    a remembrance . . .
Today I'm an artist and legal window peeker.

Religiopolitical Military

Father said grandpa was postman and mayor of a village
and cared not for the religiopolitical-military buildup
and left for America . . .
Mom said Grandma T. had servants back home
and gave gramps a hard time as he struggled in the New Land.
He was a photographer.
Introduced Kodak to Japan
and perhaps too genteel a Buddhist
to survive well in this frontier country.
I was told a story that he would walk around the block
the other way to avoid stepping on ants crossing his path.

Aftermath . . . Bathroom

My sister
    overheard mom talking—
"You can't go to the bathroom
    before 10:30 a.m.
    because they had to take out the
    H
    a
    n
    g
    i
    n
    g
    B
    o
    d
    i
    e
    s
    !"

These images still hang in our memories.

P.S. I wiped this out of my memory bank until my
sister reminded me 45 years later.
Funny, I always wanted to do drawings of a couple
holding hands while hanging . . .

The Golden Eagle

Is my Spirit Bird
from the Valley of the Golden Eagle
[in the Snake River Canyons]
    near our
        "Campground" . . .
With the Golden Eagle
I soar from the incense smoke
uplift of the tar shelter's red
glowing pot bellied stoves
    of
        cold bitter winters
    further
        higher
           and with
                silent grace—

Blue Spotted Golden Eagle

We of the "Original Tribe"
don't want to hear about Erickson-Columbus.
It was my forefathers and four
Great-grand-god-Mothers*
who found and founded this continent, etc. etc.
following the Eagle
Salmon
Caribou
Bison
and
Llamas, Camels
and
the stars

*Incas, Mayas, Aztecs, Mexicans and Native Americans are traced to the four grandmothers.

And under the wings of the Blue Spotted
Golden Eagle—
Wings gathering the "Lost Tribes."

This Eagle flew down the Steppes
Through Northern/Eastern Europe,
India/Pakistan, to land on the
Arms of a Turkoman Kahn . . .
and those of the gods of Teotihuacan.

"Shake and awake and remember
where you come from . . .
I found you naked and clothed you,
I found you hungry and fed you—
Follow the grey wolf under
. . . the Full Blue moon out of the Valley"*

While Black, Bald, Red, White and
Golden Eagles
claw clutched tumble through
rainbow-harmonized skies.
Shake and awake and remember . . .

(Dedicated to the late Seyfettin Manisaligil)

Be Tofu-like

And so like tofu
    we enriched and
enhanced
      our surroundings.
We even brought up the
      real estate values
        with our
        real values.

Lucky/Unlucky 13?

Years later
Pa and Ma came to Iowa City
to visit with newborn son, Jamie.
I caught a 13-pound walleye

*Found carved in stone by a returning Kahn from Turkey in China.

below the dam in the Iowa River.
She filed for divorce
as soon as my parents left.
Above Sun Valley in the Salmon River at Sunbeam Dam
where I dreamed of fishing for 32 years,
I finally caught a salmon—13 pounds (again)
It swam 1,000 miles in and upland from the sea . . .

The experience saddened me.

Go Fish

Create and communicate
whether to
>   cut bait
>   fish
>   or even
>   be bait
Go fish:
create and communicate.

Wild Watermelon Fields

There are blacks who
refuse to eat watermelons
and asians who refuse rice . . .
Anyhow, once in camp they
brought in truckloads of us
kids and unleashed us in
the watermelon fields
we went wild—
eating our hearts out
eating only the hearts out.

Lest We Forget the Homeless

Attempting to record my father and
my Japanese American art and poems of Remembrance
my soul tracks,
two J/A historical institutes in California indicated
they had
neither the time nor interest.
"After all the camp experience was

a duration of only four years of our history
and we are not here to advertise your art."
In my "home town"
a local museum man sez,
"We've done enuf J/A camp shows."
& a brutally frank desktop
publisher who deals with camp issues
sez, "I've not the time or interest in your poems or prints of camp."
She was never in camp even!!
Such "class" arrogance . . .
The little tokyo museum sez,
"You can't show here since you didn't
do 'em in camp," tells me to contact a
Long Beach show.
They sez, "You can't show here cuz
this is a show of camp done by people
who were not in camp."
"Yellow Balled" again!!

Within the image: *Rooting for Coal —*   PCP   Munio Makuuchi (aka Howard Takeshoshi)

Munio Makuuchi, Black Diamond, Rooting for Coal. *Drypoint intaglio.*

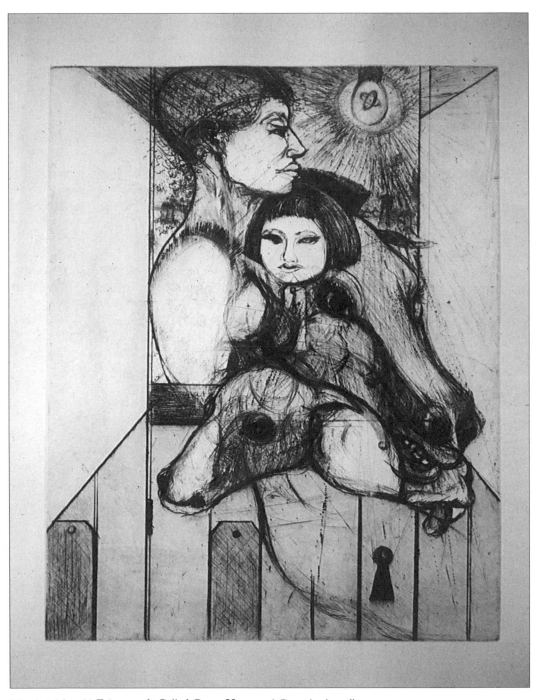

Munio Makuuchi, Fairgrounds Called Camp Harmony? *Drypoint intaglio.*

Munio Makuuchi, Gathering the Lost Tribes under Blue-Spot-Tailed Golden Eagle Wings. *Drypoint intaglio.*

Munio Makuuchi, Diane as Victory Garden—Even 1/16 "Japanese" Blood. *Drypoint intaglio.*

Ping Chong

PLAYWRIGHT

Ping Chong is a theater director, playwright, choreographer, video and installation artist. He was born in Toronto in 1946 and grew up in New York City's Chinatown. He is the recipient of an Obie Award, six National Endowment for the Arts Fellowships, a Guggenheim Fellowship, two McKnight Playwrights Fellowships, a Trust National Theatre Artist Residency Award, a National Institute for Music Theatre Award, and a 1992 New York Theatre and Dance ("Bessie") Award for Sustained Achievement. His works for the stage include The Games *(with Meredith Monk, 1983),* Nosferatu *(1985),* Angels of Swedenborg *(1985),* Kind Ness *(1986),* Undesirable Elements *(a series, 1992–), and his East/West Trilogy, which includes* Deshima *(1990),* Chinoiserie *(1995), and* After Sorrow *(1997). His work has been presented at major museums, festivals, and theaters throughout the Americas, Europe, and Asia. His* Kwaidan, *a puppet theater work based on the Japanese ghost stories of Lafcadio Hearn, toured nationally throughout 1998 and will be performed in Japan in 1999.*

RESPONSE

Q: What is the origin/genesis of your work?

A sense of wonder. The need to express that fundamental sense of wonder.

Q: For what audience do you create your work?

An audience that is interested and curious about the extraordinary nature of human existence and the diversity of human culture.

Q: Do you identify yourself as an American artist, an Asian American artist, or an artist of color? Are these categories separable?

I detest exclusivity.

Q: Some claim there's an "authentic" Asian American sensibility. Do you agree?

I detest exclusivity.

Q: What is the role of the Asian American artist in the larger American society?

The role of Asian American artists is as varied as American society itself.

Q: Are there risks and challenges peculiar to Asian American artists? If so, what are they, and how do you meet them?

The challenge for Asian American artists is the same as it is for Asian Americans in general. To alter the perception of Western culture as the inevitable culture for all peoples, to recognize it for what it is: cultural imperialism. To create solidarity among ourselves despite our differences, to create solidarity with other people of color, to create a united political voice so that we are empowered in politics, in the arts, and in the media—which remains the most powerful and insidious tool of the status quo to perpetuate ignorance, misconceptions, and to keep people of color in a state of negative self-regard as second class citizens.

Q: A common belief is that the dominant society has emasculated the Asian male, commodified the Asian female, and exoticized Asian culture in general. Do you agree? Please explain, and if you agree, how do you confront these in your work?

Yes, I agree. It's a long haul.

Q: Do you think this is a particularly receptive moment for Asian American artists? If so, what circumstances (historical, political, social, or other) have shaped this moment?

Economics.

Q: How would you characterize the reception of your work? What do you feel has been most lacking in this reception? For what are you most grateful?

I characterize the reception to my work as varied. As to what is lacking in the reception of my work, who are we talking about? How can one generalize a response? I am most grateful that I have been able to do my work on my own terms.

Q: Should the multicultural writer/artist be the voice of his/her ethnic community, or can s/he express an individual vision and personal concerns?

I detest policing what artists should or should not do. I think ideologues should be shot point-blank.

Q: If Asian Americans write about subjects other than identity and community concerns, can they still be called Asian American writers? In other words, how do we define an "Asian American" work—by the racial ancestry of its producer or by its subject matter?

Only a bigot would say an artist can't express themselves any way they want. He or she should be dunked in concrete.

Q: Should we, as Asian Americans, claim exclusive rights to our "personal property" (our histories, our cultures), asserting that non-Asians cannot truly understand or interpret "our" materials?

In general and at this historical moment, yes. But I would not deny anyone who is sincere the right to interpret anything, whatever his or her origins are. Friends come in all colors, as do enemies, who may come in our own color as well. Let's not forget that.

98.6—A Convergence in 15 Minutes

The things they share,
The full mystery of an Other

Eyes, ears, nose, mouth,
the ability to breathe, breath.
You know, the givens:
billions of cells working in unison
to create a walking, prancing, dancing
likely to function
likely to not,
full fledged, miraculous being,
him, her, us, them, you, me.

The full mystery of an Other
The things they share.

She's 5′ ½″ tall, dark eyes, short hair
What one would describe as petite,
seeming to need protection,
seeming to not,
seeming to be assured
and seeming to not,
hesitating and seeming to not,
not to be that is.
One thing's for sure:
she moves with a buttery grace.

The things they share.

He's 5′ 9″ tall, dark eyes, very short hair,
blind as a bat,
leaning toward aging like the rest of the world,
150 lbs. at the last encounter with a scale
which he passes every day on the way
to confronting himself in the mirror mornings.

The things they share.

She is Chinese (*the word* Chinese *is spoken in Chinese*)
He is Chinese (*the word* Chinese *is spoken in Chinese*)
People of the Central Kingdom (*spoken in Chinese*)

In another age or in another language,
they would have been:
the folks from Cathay
or la chinois, or chino
or gaijin which means foreigner in Nippon,
take a slow boat to China, amen.

The things they share.

The full mystery of an Other.
A familiarity with dry, salted fish,
slabs of roast suckling pig,
fermented shrimp paste,
steaming bowls of white rice,
chopsticks rising and rising
again and again,
the likely, unlikely pleasures of fresh killed poisson
gleaming with peanut oil, speckled with soy sauce,
dressed in an aromatic mess of curling ginger and scallion,
tossed with sesame oil.

Slapping across a kitchen floor
I once ran after a fish with my uncle
when it jumped out of a Chinese newspaper
off a chunky, chopping block.
When we caught up with it
he gave the fish a good whack
on the side of its head and
led it to its fate and our stomachs, amen.

The things they share.

Neurons, one thousand billion of them,
sending messages in languages
we could never hope to understand.
Neither rain, nor sleet, nor snow, nor hail
will stay the neurons from their appointed rounds
chattering away in an everlasting cacophony
fierce with life.

The things they share.

Siblings. He has five. (*Names five siblings in Chinese.*)
She has 2. (*Names two siblings in Chinese.*)

The older brother (*names him in Chinese*),
the brother 2nd to none,
the brother of brothers, she adored.
They were an alliance at the altar of art.
They were a shelter for one another
in a world of parental storms.

The full mystery of an Other.

He was my idol. He was my guru. He was always adventurous and daring. When he was 10 years old he held a lit firecracker in his fingers on a dare and blew off the top of his thumb. At 16, he was already a gourmand. One of the dishes he created was called Sole Picasso. He had an incredible appetite for life. He taught me that there was a bigger world out there and it was there for the taking.

When we went to classical concerts he would show me when to turn the pages of the program so as not to disturb the other audience members. He was a snob, an aesthete, an intellectual, a spoiled rotten, first born, number one Chinese son. The pearl in the oyster. The world should worship at his feet. He was impossible, but I loved him. He was my brother.

The full mystery of an Other.

In 1978, he decided to be a self-appointed cultural ambassador of China. He dressed appropriately by donning the classic Mao suit and had his picture taken in it, all over the world as a conceptual work of art. In 1978, when my parents came to visit us, they took us to Windows on the World in the World Trade Center. My brother didn't have a suit and "Windows" had a dress code so he wore his Mao suit instead. When we arrived at "Windows" the Maitre d' took one look at him and treated him like a VIP, a gentleman from the East, an emissary from Cathay. My parents were not amused. "We escaped from China because of this. How could you do this to us?"

The full mystery of an Other.
The things they share.

Downy breath in the wintry cold,
a likelihood of feeling pain when pierced,
ever beholden to gravity, gravity,
susceptible to the vagaries of existence & colds,
warm to the touch,
a constant temperature of 98.6.

The full mystery of an Other.
The things they share.

Mother, mama, ma mere, her . . .

My mother was part of the 1st generation of women admitted to St. John's University in Shanghai. She majored in English literature. My mother would say, "People, are still reading Shakespeare because it's all true: People are, mean, violent, cruel and vindictive to one another." My mother drilled me in Wordsworth, Coleridge, Shelley and all those other 19th century wordsmiths.

The things they share.

My mother joined the Chinese Opera when she was 13 years old. She couldn't read or write so she learned the libretto by rote. One day while on the road with an opera company she learned that her mother had died. The proprietaire in the opera company refused to let her go home to mourn her mother. She cried and cried until she couldn't cry anymore but it was to no avail. I can still hear her wailing now. On her knees before the proprietaire.

The things they share.

He met her & she met him. He met her & she met him for the 1st time to discuss what would become this performance. She wanted a solo exactly 15 minutes long, quinze minutes, exactement. He asked himself: What is a solo? A person alone? Unaccompanied? Is it a cello piece performed by Yo Yo Ma or Charles Lindbergh's flight across the Atlantic to a crescendo of praise in Paris? Solitary, isolated, insular, separated, alone, single-handed. Solo, the longest river in Java. Solo, a city in Java.

What if a solo is actually a duet that's actually a solo? What if our interaction as 2 artists and 2 people who barely know each other is splayed open like a cadaver on a morgue table, like the messiness and chaos that making art really is, like the exercise in humility that making art really is?

The things they share.

2 opposable thumbs, 4 digits,
a pair of hearts pounding furiously away
keeping both of them alive
and well,
flexible joints,
eyes, ears, nose, mouth,
the ability to breathe, breath.
Have I said this before already?
Homo sapiens, amen.

The things they share.
The full mystery of an Other.

I visited my grandmother on my father's side in 1979 in Vancouver, Canada where she had settled. She was born in 1888. She was 90 years old. She used to store her groceries in her dishwasher because she was a very short woman and it was easier for her to reach things there. I remember she never said much, but she liked having me sit on her lap and she would very softly stroke my hand and smile her Bodhisattva smile, her sourire sympathetique. On her 70th birthday she had a huge banquet thrown for her. We had to kowtow to her, while she sat, very proud and erect dripping jade and diamonds on a throne. Grandmother had all her bases covered. Although she was born Buddhist she also converted to Christianity so that she would be sure to get to heaven.

The full mystery of an Other.

A year before my mother's 81st birthday she announced to my sister (*her Chinese name spoken in Chinese*) that she wanted the banquet of banquets, the repas of repas. She wanted all the relatives there in whatever shape or size, and she wanted a shark's fin to be served to one and all. When the August day came we had to kowtow to her as she sat, very proud and erect, the matriarch of matriarchs, dripping jade and gold on a throne. Then she fell asleep at the dinner table surrounded by her children.

The things they share.

She is here this very evening
before your very eyes, dancing.
He is here too as an after glow,
a digital hop, skip and jump,
a voice in a room tapping
against the thin membrane of
your collective eardrum
rippling across the room
as undulating sound waves,
dancing with her dancing
as a voice would and might
and is doing here and now.
He is a dancing voice against
her dancing body together and apart
and this very moment,
this exact moment,
will never be the same again.
It is that fragile.

The things they share.

I remember it very well. I was 8 or 9 years old. I was hovering over my plaster dinosaurs and woolly mammoths in a world of my own even then when I heard my sisters and my mother come in.

I remember it very well. My mother was wearing very, very red lipstick, there was a dainty curl of hair symmetrically placed on each side of her forehead. She was wearing a heavy, dark mink coat that was cold to the touch. It must have been winter.

I remember it very well. My mother was wailing inconsolably. She was drunk and she was reeling and she was not to be comforted. She was wailing for the son she had to give away in Vancouver, Canada so very many years ago. She was wailing for her son, my immediate brother whom I have never met.

I remember it very well. It was then that I understood why I was never close to my older brother (*names brother in Chinese*). It was then that my hands grew cold.

The full mystery of an Other.

The things they share.

On March 10th, 1990, in his apartment at 14 Maiden Lane at 4 A.M. my brother died of AIDS. The Police woke me up in the middle of the night and took me to my brother's apartment to identify the body. They did not give me a chance to be alone with him one last time. I had been there the day before visiting him. He was full of energy. He was bright and alert. He wanted to eat dim sum and I got it for him. I gave him a shiatsu massage. I didn't expect him to leave me so soon. I said to my mother, "But he seemed so well. How could he fade so fast?" My mother said, " He died between 2 and 4 A.M. The sun could not rise at the darkest hour." "But he seemed so well." "It's like a mirror reflecting the light one last time, flipping over to catch the light, before giving it back to the void." This is what my mother said.

The things they share.

A solo exactly 15 minutes long, quinze minutes exactement. What is a solo? Her brother dying in the middle of the night on Maiden Lane? My mother's grief over the loss of her son so many years ago? Her grandmother's proud recognition of her matriarchal majesty on her 70th birthday? Being the only Chinese girl with a rice bowl cut, round plastic glasses in ankle socks from the crown colony of Hong Kong who said things like," Hello, how do you do? My name is Susan Tseng. Would you like to take afternoon tea with me? It gives me great pleasure to play in the orchestra." What is a solo? A fish dashing across the kitchen floor for dear, dear life? Recalling the brother I lost and never had?

The things they share.

The solace in art as a refuge from pain.

The things we share.

The certainty that we enter this world alone.
and exit it alone. Holy mortality. Amen.

Photo by Bob Hsiang

Genny Lim

~~~~~~

POET AND PLAYWRIGHT

Genny Lim is a Chinese American poet and playwright, born in 1946 in San Francisco and reared there. Lim received a Goldie from the San Francisco Bay Guardian *and an ImprovisAsians! Award from Asian ImprovArts for her work as a performance poet. Her frequent music and poetry collaborations have included concerts with musicians Max Roach, James Newton, Herbie Lewis, Jon Jang, and Francis Wong. Lim's plays,* Paper Angels *(1978) and* Bitter Cane *(1989)—anthologized in two recent volumes,* The Politics of Life *(ed. Velina Hasu Houston, 1993) and* Unbroken Thread *(ed. Roberta Uno, 1993)—have been performed both here and abroad in China.* Paper Angels *was broadcast on PBS in 1985. She is also the coeditor (with Him Mark Lai and Judy Yung) of the American Book Award–winning* Island: Poetry and History of Chinese Immigrants on Angel Island, 1910–1940 *and author of a collection of poems,* Winter Place *(1988). Lim teaches and cochairs the Humanities Program at New College of California in San Francisco and serves on the San Francisco Art Commission.*

RESPONSE ↩
Word Up

My writing is an extension of who I am— a Toisan American baby boomer, single mother, poet, educator, performer, Buddhist, woman, and teacher. I write in the English language because that is the only language I was taught to write in. My ideal would be to sing all my stories in the old *Muk*

213

Yi tradition, accompanied by a wooden fish clapper, wandering from place to place; or in meditative pose, like the great Tibetan yogi Milarepa. Unfortunately, I am too dependent on the written text and on English as my primary means of articulation. The constant tension between my words and my underlying meanings manifests in a kind of *Chinglish,* which conforms neither to literary English nor to the idiom of my native Toisanese. Embodying a language with the soul of another one poses a constant dilemma, because language, by virtue of its linguistic structure and syntax, mediates cultural sensibility and how one sees reality. It can, as we have seen with many people of color, undermine the cultural voice by hemming it in an artificial construct that impedes, rather than facilitates, honest expression. Value becomes placed, then, on one's imitative skill, rather than on one's individual truth.

Ngugi Wa Thiong'o said in his farewell to the English language as the chosen vehicle of his writing, "The effect of a cultural bomb is to annihilate a people's belief in their names, in their languages, in their environment, in their heritage of struggle, in their unity, in their capacities and ultimately in themselves; for instance, with other peoples' languages rather than their own. . . . The intended results are despair, despondency and a collective death-wish" (*Decolonising the Mind: The Politics of Language in African Literature* [London: James Curry Ltd., 1981], 3).

One dramatic outcome of Western assimilation is the loss of the oral tradition. In southern rural China, where my family spoke a peasant dialect called *Sze-Yap* and sang *Muk Yi,* storytelling was a folk art. Today that tradition is virtually extinct, and the songs are remembered only by the very old, who mourn the fact that the young are no longer interested in the old traditions. My own mother, who is ninety, sang some of these songs as a child. I remember snatches of songs, which were protection chants to ward off evil spirits.

When I first heard the recordings of Southern rural blues musicians such as Howlin' Wolf, Leadbelly, and Mississippi John Hurt, I immediately responded with familiarity. The clarity of the struggle, the pain and joys of simple living recounted in soulful rhythms and dissonant scales of the working poor, enabled me to see the link between two cultures, Black and Yellow. I knew nothing about ethnomusicology or cultural anthropology at the time, but I had a gut feeling that the music was key to exploring the connection between the African and Asian cultures.

While it is too late for me to become literate in the mother tongue of my ancestors, I am saddled with English to use on my own terms. The transformation of language is a minefield of dangers and frustration. One falters with moral insecurity when leaping over boundaries and knocking sensibilities with the czars of aesthetics and style. Content inevitably becomes penalized for lack of form, and form, too often, becomes a façade for content. Whatever is uttered is a political act, be it a bomb or a sedative.

Of late, the writers who resonate most for me are the poets and mystics like Tu Fu and Lao Tzu, the Rishis of the Upanishads, the Sufis like Rumi, the Buddhists like Milarepa, the Dalai Lama, Chogyam Trungpa, and Thich Nhat Hahn. Their universe is expansive, not solipsistic. Their message is transcending, not transitory. Far be it for me to advocate religiosity as a literary goal or to proselytize my readers, as did the colonizing missionaries throughout our oppressed histories; I simply am bored with nihilistic angst.

The writers who pioneered the field by launching their souls into the heat of debate, such as Federico Garcia Lorca, Pablo Neruda, Gabriel García Márquez, Langston Hughes, James Baldwin, Ralph Ellison, Amiri Baraka, and Toni Morrison, to name a few, cut through verbiage and complacency. The crackling thunder of their courageous voices, the urgency of their moral visions, the seething humanity that their works embrace, teach us how, as writers, to bear witness to the times we live in.

I am happy to come along after them, and I am happier for others to come after me, but it is not for me to speculate on the future of Asian American literature. The field is wide open and healthy in the respect that more diverse voices are being heard today than ever before. I don't think we need to be too self-congratulatory about our newfound presence in the media, however. We have to keep in mind that it's not an accident of nature but the historical culmination of over a century of struggle in America.

Writers are less afraid to explore their histories, both personal and collective, than in the old days, when a subtle disclosure could spell ruin for a family. The first and second generations, due I believe, to the damaging effects of immigration exclusion and wartime relocation, practiced self-censorship to an extreme. We were safe if invisible and better off if we were assimilable. The price we paid for invisibility and accommodation, of course, was loss of identity and self-determinism.

When we finally rediscovered our voices in the 1960s, Asian American pride and identity were the big issues. Authenticity of the Asian American experience and, following that, the Asian American sensibility were the standards for political correctness. Who determined what those standards would be was open to debate. One could be Asian and very assimilated in speech and language. Did that mean, then, that the person did not have an "authentic" sensibility? Whose sensibility were we measuring "Asian American" against? "Asian American" as derivative of immigrant stock? working-class or professional? urban or suburban? Cantonese, Southeast Asian, Indian, or Mandarin? Cultural assumptions of what was Asian American proliferated on college campuses like loaded dice.

There is no one style, no one cultural voice, that characterizes Asian American writing. We are as diverse as any ethnic group can be. We do, however, share a common history in this country. Just as African Americans have a shared legacy of slavery, oppression, and struggle in the Americas, Asians, too, have a long background of discrimination against us. To deny this history is to ignore, in a sense, one's cultural identity. That is inauthenticity. Denial of self is the inability to contextualize one's condition in the larger sociohistorical analysis. Because one doesn't encounter racism in one's own life doesn't mean that it doesn't exist or that those who experience it are paranoid.

The model minority myth that so many middle-class Asians mistakenly aspire to is a naive survival strategy, perpetuated by the American dream. It promises that if Chinamen and Japs keep our noses clean and don't make trouble like the incorrigible Blacks and Latinos, we'll get what Whites have. This modern version of the "house nigger" not only damages one's self-image, it conspires against viable collective avenues for addressing social change. The model minority is the house nigger of America. They show how oppression can be rewarded and how seductive second-class citizenship can really be. Model minorities persisted in ignorance, until they hit their heads on the glass ceilings of America's corporate skyscrapers. Then the reality that a "houseboy" could never become master shattered the dream that violence was neither systemic nor random. Asian hate crimes don't happen accidentally.

Krishnamurti talks about attentiveness. How important it is to be fully conscious, or mindful, as the Buddhists say, cannot be underestimated. Asian men can be emasculated only if they are afraid. Asian women can be commodified only if they allow themselves to be. The process of transformation requires total surrender and immersion in whatever experience one is afraid of. Confrontation allows for greater understanding and, ultimately, release. As a writer, as an Asian American, I must witness in totality, the negative along with the positive dimensions of who I am. Not to do so would be irresponsible. According to the Upanishads, it is better to tell a shameful truth than a decent lie.

That's not to say we shouldn't be proud of our achievements, but we should keep in mind that the larger goal is our collective struggle for social justice. The fact that there are an average of three mass-murder killings a month occurring in this country and that at this very moment a woman or child is being raped is very sobering.

As a writer, I am a witness to all that I know to be true. I'm the product of an urban environment. I'm a lover of nature and freedom. I need to be near a body of water in order to feel peaceful, but I also thrive on the heartbeat of the city as inspiration for the music, rhythm, dissonance, and passions of life. Music gives sway to my senses and I am inspired by legendary artists such as John Coltrane, Duke Ellington, Charles Mingus, Thelonious Monk, Dizzy Gillespie, Miles Davis, Lady Day (Billie Holiday), Dinah Washington, Sarah Vaughan, and Carmen McRae, for their blues investigations into life. They are in tune with what's inside. Check them out if you want to learn about texture, rhythm, phrasing, or style.

I have been fortunate to have been able to perform my poetry with some of the finest musicians in the business—Max Roach, Herbie Lewis, James Newton, Jon Jang, Francis Wong, Cash Killion, and Anthony Brown, to name some. For me, the magic of the living word is healing gospel and the spontaneous power of the human voice can never be replaced by a computer. By comparison, the written or electronic word will always be a ghost of the living being it struggles to incarnate.

From *La China Poblana*

La China Poblana may be called a dramatic poem or a poetic drama because its form is nontraditional and expressionistic. It does not develop in chronological narrative, nor does it fully depict the historical events of its main character's life. It is, rather, an exploration into the psychological and spiritual journey of a Chinese woman who lived in the 1600s to become a great healer and saint in Mexico.

She was kidnaped by pirates at around age twelve and brought to Mexico on a Manila galleon. Sold to a wealthy couple in Puebla, she acquired the nickname La China Poblana for her piety and healing powers. Several books written during her lifetime by two confessors, documenting her visions, ecstasies, loquations, hallucinations, astral journeys, and miracles of healing, were destroyed during the Spanish Inquisition.

In the end, the only tangible legacy and testament to her existence was the dress she left behind, *la china poblana,* which survived to become the national costume of Mexico. It is worn during *El jarabe tapitio,* the Mexican hat dance. The following is an excerpt, scenes 5 and 7 of *La China Poblana.*

SCENE 5

Mirra is sewing the China Poblana skirt, with dazzling sequins and embroidery. Doña enters with a tray of food.

DOÑA MARINA: Mirra, you have been sewing for days. When are you going to stop?

MIRRA: When I die.

DOÑA: Oh, Mirra! Do you think all your sewing can free all the Chinese and Indians? I tell you, Mirra, your boundless compassion cannot change men's lustful hearts. The heat of the sun burns with the blood of Mexico's slaves. It has always been so. Profit begets profit. There is nothing a God-fearing Christian woman can do. You will get sick if you don't stop to eat. The only time you stop is when you hear the church bells. Then you go off to pray!

MIRRA: Will it be possible to get me more thread today?

DOÑA: (*Sighs*) You talked again last night.

MIRRA: I was saying my prayers.

DOÑA: No this was different. Your eyes were burning bright in the candle-light. You were speaking as if possessed. Speaking as if to the divine himself. But in another tongue! I was too frightened to disturb you. You were overcome! Oh Dio, tell me child, what ails you, Mirra? (*She touches Mirra's forehead*)

MIRRA: Doña Marina. Don't be afraid. I am a woman of God. I am a woman born of God. It was the Lord himself whom I visited last night. Please don't tell a soul! No one would believe you. It is a miracle. Ah Jesus! Jesus! Jesus! Sometimes I can feel my spirit leaving my very form! I fly straight into the light!

DOÑA: Oh hush, please don't talk so! It makes my flesh positively freeze!

MIRRA: There is nothing to fear, Doña! It is our Holy Father! He talks to me.

DOÑA: Oh Child, that's blasphemy!

MIRRA: He does!

DOÑA: What does he say to you?

MIRRA: He tells me I am his child.

DOÑA: Indeed.

MIRRA: He tells me how to look into the insides of things. How to touch things!

DOÑA: In so many words?

MIRRA: I can't explain. He speaks through me.

DOÑA: Then it's you who are speaking, not him!

MIRRA: No I can feel him. His presence fills me like a river of light!

DOÑA: Dear, dear, your conversations with God are beyond me! I'm too old and ordinary to be swept by holy flames. (*Thoughtfully*) My poor child, do you ever think about the past? Can you remember anything of your childhood?

MIRRA: (*Reminiscing*) I remember a song my mother once sang:

> "How yee gaw suey sin far,
>
> Howyee gaw suey sin far,
>
> Sin far law gaw jai,
>
> Ngaw de gar . . . "

DOÑA: Oh Mirra, that's lovely. What does it mean?

MIRRA: It's a traditional new year's song in celebration of the blossoming lily flower.

DOÑA: (*A knock on the door. Doña goes and opens the door*) Who are you?

JUAN: (*From outside*) My name is Juan Pablo. I've come to see Mirra.

DOÑA: Come in.

JUAN: (*He sees Mirra sewing and bows to her on his knees*) I came to thank you in person for my freedom.

MIRRA: (*Beaming, she extends him her hand*) It's so good to see you free!

JUAN: (*He takes it and kisses it*) I can't tell you how touched I am by your kindness. You resemble the Virgin in every manner. (*Almost in tears*) I came to see you because I wanted to see what an angel looked like in person.

MIRRA: (*Laughs*) You won't be disappointed if I don't don my halo and wings?

JUAN: You are more than an apparition, kind Mirra. They say you have great healing powers! They say the farmer Rogelio was lying as if dead on the *petate*, and you raised him up by merely chanting and touching him! You are a divine being in the flesh! I owe you my life. Because of you I can now have a life. Because of you I no longer have to haul stones or sleep among mules.

MIRRA: You shouldn't believe every rumor you hear. What will you do now, sir?

JUAN: I will work at the livery for board and a decent wage!

MIRRA: That sounds wonderful. I am happy for you.

JUAN: If you should ever need anything, anything at all, dear lady, please don't hesitate to let me know. I will be your servant for life!

MIRRA: (*Laughs*) I thought we were through with that! Good luck with your new life, Juan Pablo. May God bless you with everlasting faith and devotion!

JUAN: Gracias, Gracias, my good señorita. (*Exits*)

DOÑA: He is not bad looking, Mirra.

MIRRA: Oh Doña Marina, when will you ever quit trying to marry me off? Don't you know there is more to life than two people falling in love? The love I have is greater than two people's. Oh Doña Marina, how can I explain? It is greater than you or I! It transcends the sky!

This love I have fills me daily with wonder.

This love I feel blossoms, blossoms . . .

Its fragrance permeates, its petals enshrine.

Untouched by man's hands, like the sun's rays

whose rays burn without devouring,

like the sky, which lifts, without holding.

Oh bliss, oh source, untied, like the wind

that rests, but never dies.

You elude the eye, like the swallow!

(*Fadeout*)

SCENE 7

A priest's quarters, fifty years later. The priest is in deep thought. He has spent the night carefully pondering several volumes of books in front of him. Outside, there is a loud din of huge crowds gathering outside the cathedral. He appears oblivious to the noise. A loud knock on the door. Father removes his spectacles and goes to the door. A breathless middle-aged woman enters.

FATHER: Ah Gloria, what brings you? Do you have a confession to make?

GLORIA: Oh Father, it is not the confession box I have need of. Do you not hear? The crowds are growing by the moments. Thousands! Thousands of peasants from the countrysides, noblemen and women from as far as Acapulco and even Mexico City! Listen, to them, father!

(*We can hear them shouting, "Saint Catarina! Holy Saint Catarina! Holy Virgin Catarina de San Juan!"*)

Do you hear them? They are calling her Saint Catarina de San Juan!

FATHER: (*Angrily*) That is ridiculous! That is heresy! Mob heresy I tell you!

GLORIA: (*Shocked*) What do you mean, Father? You knew Catarina! You knew her miracles! How can you say it is heresy?

FATHER: Unless the Vatican officially recognizes Catarina as a saint, she is nothing more or less than Catarina de San Juan. These decisions are of a holy order. It is not for hysterical peasants to determine otherwise. Do you understand?

GLORIA: Then I fail to see the wisdom of a church which denies the obvious! Father Confessor, you have heard with your own ears countless stories of Catarina's miraculous powers of healing! Why I would not be standing here before you a free woman, if she had not freed my father from indenturehood fifty years ago!

FATHER: Gloria, dear, you do not understand the seriousness of what you are proposing. If every favored individual were to be recognized for a good deed or two, then the saints canon would be littered with countless ordinary beings. A saint is a supreme being! It is for God, not for me to decide, who, what and when a person shall be canonized.

GLORIA: But you can counsel the Vatican, Father! You can tell them of Catarina's supernatural powers! We can all bear witness to the accounts!

FATHER: That's exactly what I am afraid of.

GLORIA: I don't understand, Father.

FATHER: There is a fine line between sorcery and divine power.

GLORIA: But she was a devout Catholic! And what difference does it make if it all results in good? (*No answer*) May I ask you a question, Father? Did you or did you not ever yourself witness Catarina's holy visitations? (*She glances at his books*) Tell me, Father, did you?

FATHER: Catarina had described her hallucinations to me.

GLORIA: Hallucinations?

FATHER: I believe that is what one would call them. Visions, ecstasies, loquations, astral journeys, characteristic of those adept in the arts of ritual magic. (*Indicating the volumes of books*) Do you know how many come to me by the numbers each year, holding vigils with stupendous accounts of the Virgin weeping and shedding blood through the streets? Do you have any idea what it would be to verify each one of them?

(*The noise of the crowd now grows thunderous. Gloria goes to the window.*)

GLORIA: The crowds grow unruly. They want a last glimpse of their saint. They are locking the cathedral doors to keep them out!

FATHER: Gloria, I must prepare for the funeral, if you'll excuse me.

GLORIA: (*Downcast*) Yes, forgive me, Father. How rude of me to intrude on your Holiness. I will not trouble you further. (*Exits*)

(*The crowd noise is becoming riotous. The priest gathers the books and prepares to incinerate them.*)

FATHER: (*Crossing himself*) May God forgive me for vouchsafing these heretical documents. I hereby disavow any claim to the authenticity of these miracles. May they burn in the memory of Catarina de San Juan, a child of God, plucked from the heathens of China.

(*He crosses himself, then places each volume in the flames.*)

(*Fadeout*)

David Henry Hwang

~~~~~~

PLAYWRIGHT

David Henry Hwang is best known for his hit Broadway play M. Butterfly *(1989), which was awarded the Tony, Drama Desk, Outer Critics Circle, John Gassner, and L.A. Drama Critics Circle Awards and has since been staged in over three dozen countries. His nine other plays produced in New York include* FOB, *for which he won the 1981 Obie Award, and* The Dance and the Railroad, *first performed in 1981. For composer Philip Glass, he wrote the librettos for* The Voyage *(1992), which premiered at the Metropolitan Opera House, and* 1000 Airplanes on the Roof *(1989). As a screenwriter, he penned the feature films* M. Butterfly *(1993) and* Golden Gate *(1993) and has also done adaptations for directors Sydney Pollack, Martin Scorsese, and Jean-Jacques Annaud. He has just completed a new play and* is currently working on a second screenplay for Scorsese. He also cowrote the song "Solo" on the 1994 album Come, by the Artist Formerly Known as Prince. Hwang was born in Los Angeles in 1957 and attended Stanford University and the Yale School of Drama. In 1994, he was appointed by President Bill Clinton to the President's Committee on the Arts and Humanities.*

RESPONSE ⟿

Definitions

The fundamental definition of Asian America is a good starting point for my conviction that virtually every aspect of Asian American life is currently in flux, part of a continual evolution. Terms that were adopted twenty-five years ago to characterize common experiences may be rapidly passing from relevance.

Take, for instance, *Asian American* itself. I've always loved the term because it is so profoundly *American.* Chinese nationals rarely, if ever, consider themselves "Asians." In America, however, my life experience is closer to, say, that of a Japanese American like Philip Kan Gotanda than to a citizen of the People's Republic like director Chen Kaige. By calling myself "Asian," I affirm the supremacy of culture over biological ethnicity. Though Gotanda and I may hail genetically from different ethnic groups, in America we come from a similar culture.

Asian, however, has its sloppy side as well. Movement leaders recruited it in the 1960s and 1970s to replace *Oriental,* which was identified as colonialist and ridiculed as geographically unspecific; "Where is the Orient?" I remember an Asian radical asking rhetorically. Yet his definition of *Asian* was equally vague. To use the term accurately, we must include Arabs, Turks, Kazakhs, and the vast majority of Russians east of the Ural Mountains. Instead, we have tended to limit our definition to East Asia (the former "Orient") and only recently to include the Indian subcontinent and Pacific Islands. How can we resolve these inconsistencies?

Furthermore, with increasing intermarriage by Asian Americans, defining ourselves by ethnic origin may soon become a questionable exercise in racial purity. Dean Cain, star of the television series *Lois and Clark,* was recently featured in several Asian American periodicals, though the public is largely unaware that he descends from an Asian grandfather. From a purely genetic standpoint, what distinguishes Cain from Phoebe Cates, Eddie Van Halen, Keanu Reeves, Meg Tilly, and other stars with one Asian grandparent who are not customarily acknowledged to be Asian American? Do we define ourselves by ancestry, visual appearance, or some other factor?

Finally, traditional definitions of Asian America are further challenged by the commonality of experience. Does, for instance, a fifth-generation Chinese American Harvard graduate from a wealthy family really have more in common with a Hmong newcomer than, say, an Ivy Leaguer of Latino or Jewish ancestry? How do we maintain our perceived unity in the face of increasing community diversity?

The answer, it seems to me, lies in the fact that categories exist to serve people, not the other way around. More important than race, national origin, or genetic heritage are those groups and individuals that define *themselves* in response to shared experiences, frustrations, and needs. The factor of self-definition becomes the key. Dean Cain is an Asian American because he chooses to identify with the community. Similarly, immigrants become Americans when and if they choose to define themselves as such.

The idea that Asian America includes any individuals who define themselves as its members opens at least two potential cans of worms. First, can individuals who lack any Asian ancestry at all define themselves as Asian American? Conversely, are Americans of Asian descent who reject community affiliation therefore no longer Asian Americans? I propose a radical answer for the future: to both these questions, yes. I refuse to echo centuries of racism by defining my experience through a narrow set of genetic parameters that contain virtually no other implications for human behavior. I recently met a "White" woman in Seattle who was adopted as an infant by Nisei parents. If she wants to consider herself "Asian American," who am I to exclude her?

I would extend this concept of self-definition to the arts as well. A work defined by its creator as Asian American, I would argue, should be accepted as such, then criticized and judged like any other piece from the community. Many Asian Americans, myself included, identified with the movie *Dragon: The Bruce Lee Story* (1993), though neither the writer nor the director was of Asian ancestry. (The film was produced, however, under the banner of Oliver Stone's Ixtlan Productions, whose president is an Asian American.) If the director of *Dragon* were to call it an Asian American movie, I would be proud to accept it as such. I'm sure there are people who consider *Dragon* more Asian American than the movie version of *M. Butterfly,* though the screenplay of the latter is credited to an Asian (myself)! Conversely, the filmmaker Gregg Araki appears to identify with the gay community more readily than with other Asian Americans; I feel no compulsion to contest his right of self-definition. Asian Americans who write about subjects other than identity, justice, or equality should have the option of determining whether or not they consider these works Asian American. In this sense work is defined neither by the racial ancestry of its producer nor by its subject matter but by the intention of its creator. Personally, I define all my work as Asian American, because I define *myself* as such; it is simplistic to infer from this, however, that all my writing would include Asian characters.

Only time will tell if the term *Asian America* will remain relevant in categorizing the common experiences of one group of people. I believe if the term itself does not pass from usage, surely our perceptions of it will evolve. We are fond of thinking that the changing demographic face of America will bring great changes to White men. But we cannot afford to be so smug. The future will bring great change to us all, and every day

may cause us to consider and redefine our terms.

Responsibility, Criticism, and the Problem with Chin

Those of us who identify our work as "Asian American" are, in effect, inviting members of the community to judge whether or not our vision reflects their *own* experience. When evaluating works of art, I believe some critics misrepresent the community by speaking or writing as if it were a unified monolith. When such critics say a particular artist's vision does or does not accurately portray the community, they are actually evaluating whether the work reflects the *critic's* vision of the community. By ignoring this fact, they attempt to deny their own subjectivity.

Consider any prominent work of art by an Asian American, and the community's diversity becomes undeniable. For every Asian who considers Maxine Hong Kingston's *The Woman Warrior* or my *FOB* a breakthrough work, someone else has labeled them White racist propaganda. This is precisely the function of art—to provoke, to inspire discussion and passionate disagreement in content as in form. In this way, art serves as one tool by which members of the community *define themselves*, through accepting or rejecting part or all of an artist's vision. I doubt it is the goal of any community leader to impose a common mind onto all Asian Americans. Presumably, we who believe in the "movement" seek to expand human dignity, justice, and the range of personal choice. That is why no single artist can speak for the community; only the *community* of artists can serve such a function.

The most heated debates among Asian Americans center on cultural authenticity; the most common criticism any Asian American artist hears is that his or her work "reinforces stereotypes." I criticized *Miss Saigon* for reinforcing the stereotype of Asian women as submissive. *M. Butterfly* was criticized for reinforcing the stereotype of Asian men as effeminate. *The Joy Luck Club* was criticized for reinforcing the stereotype that Asian men are undesirable. *The Woman Warrior, The Kitchen God's Wife,* and *FOB* were all criticized for inauthentic uses of Chinese mythology. *The Chickencoop Chinaman,* when first staged in Seattle, was picketed by Asian Americans for reinforcing stereotypes of broken English–speaking Chinatown tour guides.

This is all as it should be, for authenticity must be constantly debated and redefined as our real experiences evolve. Twenty-five years ago, when the movement was founded amid Third World Solidarity, could we have anticipated our current dilemma, when a poll reveals that African Americans consider Asians to be the most racist of all ethnic groups? Certainly there exist historical similarities across time, such as the persistence of the "Yellow peril" mythology. Yet we cannot ignore new developments in our definitions of authenticity. I recently heard an Asian American academic propose to write a paper on "The Sexual Objectification of the Asian Male," as a response to the recent proliferation of Asian man–White woman couplings on television and movie screens. This is certainly something few of us would have predicted in the 1970s!

In this context, Frank Chin's oft-cited claim of an "authentic" Asian American sensibility unwisely ignores community diversity and denies the right of individual Asian Americans to decide what reflects their own experience. In my opinion, Chin is the ayatollah of Asian America. His quest to set himself up as the arbiter of the "real" and the "fake" strikes me as hypocritical. Like Khomeini issuing a *fatwa* against Salman

Rushdie for violating the Koran, Chin presents himself as a defender of truth against blasphemy; in fact, Chin's working definition of "fake" appears to be any Chinese American artist who receives more attention than himself.

The issue of inaccuracy in cultural portrayals is an important one and should not be reduced to "Yellower than thou" self-promotion. Though he criticizes authors such as Kingston, Tan, and myself for drawing on Chinese folklore inaccurately, Frank Chin and other fundamentalists fail to recognize that living art transforms, re-creates, even violates old archetypes and legends in order to reinterpret them for changing realities. Shakespeare's *Richard III,* for instance, is inconsistent with the historical record. Similarly, both the "Monkey King" legends and the "Romance of the Three Kingdoms" are artists' transformations of historical fact into epic myth. In his own work, Chin allows himself the freedom to be inaccurate; "Gee, Pop," for example, brilliantly reimagines Gwan Gung, though in terms few historians would recognize. If we acknowledge, therefore, that deviation from root culture sources is not ipso facto "fake," then such determination falls into the realm of subjectivity. Though I acknowledge him as a major positive influence on my own decision to become a writer, Chin's sexism and homophobia, in my opinion, undermine his credibility as a critic.

A similar set of erroneous assumptions exists among some Asian Americans: The fact that a work attracts a wide mainstream audience is taken as evidence that the artist has "sold out." If only life were so simple! Just as the commercial reception accorded a work cannot tell us whether the artist is a "good" or "bad" person, it is similarly absurd to take popular response as a shortcut guide to his or her political character. Consider *M. Butter-*

fly: the play was a great success, the movie a terrible flop. Some might therefore conclude that the movie was more "threatening" to mainstream audiences, the play more "assimilated." Asian American critics of the film, however, also argue that it was "depoliticized"; for example, the play's speeches about White men seeing the East as submissive and exotic were deleted from the big-screen version. Are we to conclude that director David Cronenberg, by cutting these speeches, made the project so much more "authentic" that it was rejected by the American public? Clearly, the notion that cultural inauthenticity promotes commercial success disintegrates into a complicated series of political contortions.

I find it also simplistic to equate admission into the general literary "canon" with abandonment of a political "cause." On the contrary, certain writers come to the attention of the establishment precisely because they embody an issue that may be present in the Zeitgeist. It would be difficult, for example, to find a writer more identified with both Marxist theory and the radical gay community than Tony Kushner, yet his *Angels in America* made it into even Harold Bloom's quite conservative canon.

In summary, on questions of responsibility, I believe the multicultural artist is no different from any other, in that she or he is finally answerable not to an ethnic community, nor to an artistic community, nor to the nation at large, but only to his or her own artistic conscience. For we must strive to tell the truth *as we see it,* with as much skill as we can muster. We then expose our work to the public, for any interested person to accept or reject on his or her own terms. This does not mean we close our ears to criticism; on the contrary, our work demands critique and judgment. We hear the voices of our critics, however, as other opinions, not as some monolithic "voice of the community." And we know that our art will change only if our vision of the world does so first. For the only sin the artist can commit is knowingly to lie.

The Current State of Asian American Art

The current time appears to be a rather productive one for Asian American artists, particularly writers and filmmakers. Undoubtedly, the stereotypical Western fascination with Asian femininity and its perceived exoticism plays some role in the popular success of certain works by and about women. Also significant is the pragmatic reality that works by Asian women enjoy two natural markets—Asian Americans as well as mainstream women—whereas White men are not similarly predisposed to identify with works by Asian men. Nonetheless, the success of writers like Tan and Kingston has paved the way for men as well, and the critical acclaim accorded such male authors as Chang-rae Lee and Li-Young Lee speaks positively to this trend.

I also find notable the relative willingness of Hollywood to liberate Asian American filmmakers from ethnic pigeonholing. Wayne Wang directing *Smoke,* Ang Lee directing Jane Austen's *Sense and Sensibility,* myself adapting such mainstream properties as Caleb Carr's *The Alienist* or Isaac Asimov's *Foundation Trilogy*—all these contrast strikingly with the experience of African American directors, who are still largely rejected as incompetent to deal with anything but the Black experience.

The reasons for this relative acceptance are complicated. The West has always had an ambivalent relationship to the East, dating back to the days of Marco Polo, when Europe learned it was technologically inferior to China. The stereotypes of "Oriental wisdom" and "ancient secrets" create an opening whereby the conflicted Western mind may more readily accept Asians as capable of creating universal art. Demographically, the current wave of Asian American art reflects a population boom in our community, coinciding with the emergence of a generation of American-born, college-educated Asians conversant in ethnic politics as well as mainstream aesthetics and relatively familiar with the dominant power structures.

Though I believe that the artist's responsibility is primarily to his or her own aesthetic, I also feel compelled to infiltrate and "mongrelize" the larger American society. A century ago, a dominant American population descended largely from Northern and Western Europeans was invaded, with much fear and resistance, by "undesirables" from Eastern and Southern Europe. One hundred years later, who can deny that, say, Italian Americans have both transformed this culture and been transformed by it. Though hysterical xenophobes such as the author of *Alien Nation* may find this difficult to accept, today's cultural revolution is no less natural, no more dangerous. Americans of African, Asian, Latino, and Native origin are beginning to exert influence in truly significant numbers; my personal goal is to help bring to life within these shores the next world culture. This would be by no means, incidentally, a historical first. Multicultural civilizations have flourished in many empires, including medieval Venice and the ancient Chinese capital of Xian. But the world is bigger now than those societies knew, and the mission of breaking down old boundaries and discovering new cultural fusions is a task that each day excites me and makes me proud anew to be an Asian American artist.

Trying to Find Chinatown

CHARACTERS

BENJAMIN (Caucasian male, early 20s)

RONNIE (Asian-American male, mid 20s)

SETTING

A street corner on the Lower East Side, New York City. Present.

NOTE ON MUSIC

Obviously, it would be foolish to require that the actor portraying "Ronnie" perform the specified violin music live. The score of this play can be played on tape over the house speakers, and the actor can feign playing the violin using a bow treated with soap. However, in order to effect a convincing illusion, it is desirable that the actor possess some familiarity with the violin, or at least another stringed instrument.

Darkness. Over the house speakers, FADE IN Hendrix-like virtuoso rock 'n' roll riffs—heavy feedback, distortion, phase shifting, wah-wah—amplified over a tiny Fender pug-nose.

Lights FADE UP to reveal that the music's being played over a solid-body electric violin by RONNIE, a Chinese-American male in his mid 20s, dressed in retro-60s clothing, with a few requisite 90s body mutilations. He's playing on a sidewalk for money, his violin case open before him, change and a few stray bills having been left by previous passers-by.

Enter BENJAMIN, early 20s, blonde, blue-eyed, looking like a Midwestern tourist in the big city. He holds a scrap of paper in his hands, scanning street signs for an address. He pauses before Ronnie, listens for a while. With a truly bravura run, Ronnie concludes the number, falls to his knees, gasping. Benjamin applauds.

BENJAMIN: Good. That was really great. (*Pause.*) I didn't . . . I mean, a fiddle . . . I mean, I'd heard them at square dances, on country stations and all, but I never . . . wow, this must really be New York City! (*He applauds, starts to walk on. Still on his knees, Ronnie clears his throat loudly.*) Oh, I . . . you're not just doing this for your health, right? (*He reaches in his pocket, pulls out a couple of coins. Ronnie clears his throat again.*) Look, I'm not a millionaire, I'm just . . . (*He pulls out his wallet, removes a dollar bill. Ronnie nods his head, gestures towards the violin case, as he takes out a pack of cigarettes, lights one.*)

RONNIE: And don't call it a "fiddle," OK?

BENJAMIN: Oh. Well, I didn't mean to—

RONNIE: You sound like a wuss. A hick. A dipshit.

BENJAMIN: It just slipped out. I didn't really—

RONNIE: If this was a fiddle, I'd be sitting here with a cob pipe, stomping my cowboy boots and kicking up hay. Then I'd go home and fuck my cousin.

BENJAMIN: Oh! Well, I don't really think—

RONNIE: Do you see a cob pipe? Am I fucking my cousin?

BENJAMIN: Well, no, not at the moment, but—

RONNIE: All right. Then this is a violin, now you give me your money, and I ignore the insult. Herein endeth the lesson. (*Pause.*)

BENJAMIN: Look, a dollar's more than I've ever given to a . . . to someone asking for money.

RONNIE: Yeah, well, this is New York. Welcome to the cost of living.

BENJAMIN: What I mean is, maybe in exchange, you could help me—?

RONNIE: Jesus Christ! Do you see a sign around my neck reading, "Big Apple Fucking Tourist Bureau?"

BENJAMIN: I'm just looking for an address, I don't think it's far from here, maybe you could . . . ? (*Ronnie snatches the scrap of paper from Benjamin.*)

RONNIE: You're lucky I'm such a goddamn softy. (*He looks at the paper.*) Oh, fuck you. Just suck my dick, you and the cousin you rode in on.

BENJAMIN: I don't get it! What are you—?

RONNIE: Eat me. You know exactly what I—

BENJAMIN: I'm just asking for a little—

RONNIE: "13 Doyers St.?" Like you don't know where that is?

BENJAMIN: Of course I don't know! That's why I'm asking—

RONNIE: C'mon, you trailer-park refugee. You don't know that's Chinatown?

BENJAMIN: Sure I know that's Chinatown.

RONNIE: I know you know that's Chinatown.

BENJAMIN: So? That doesn't mean I know where Chinatown—

RONNIE: So why is it that you picked *me*, of all the street musicians in the City—to point you in the direction of Chinatown? Lemme guess—is it the earring? No, I don't think so. The Hendrix riffs? Guess again, you fucking moron.

BENJAMIN: Now, wait a minute. I see what you're—

RONNIE: What are you gonna ask me next? Where you can find the best dim sum in the City? Whether I can direct you to a genuine opium den? Or do I happen to know how you can meet Miss Saigon for a night of nookie-nookie followed by a good old-fashioned ritual suicide? (*He picks up his violin.*) Now, get your white ass off my sidewalk. One dollar doesn't even begin to make up for all this aggravation. Why don't you go back home and race bullfrogs, or whatever it is you do for—?

BENJAMIN: Brother, I can absolutely relate to your anger. Righteous rage, I suppose, would be a more appropriate term. To be marginalized, as we are, by a white racist patriarchy, to the point where the accomplishments of our people are obliterated from the history books, this is cultural genocide of the first order, leading to the fact that you must do battle with all of Euro-America's emasculating and brutal stereotypes of Asians—the opium den, the sexual objectification of the Asian female, the exoticized image of a tourist's Chinatown which ignores the exploitation of workers, the failure to unionize, the high rate of mental illness and tuberculosis—against these, each day, you rage, no, not as a victim, but as a survivor, yes, brother, a glorious warrior survivor! (*Silence.*)

RONNIE: Say what?

BENJAMIN: So, I hope you can see that my request is not—

RONNIE: Wait, wait.

BENJAMIN:—motivated by the sorts of racist assumptions—

RONNIE: But, but where . . . how did you learn all that?

BENJAMIN: All what?

RONNIE: All that—you know—oppression stuff—tuberculosis . . .

BENJAMIN: It's statistically irrefutable. TB occurs in the community at a rate—

RONNIE: Where did *you* learn it?

BENJAMIN: I took Asian American studies. In college.

RONNIE: Where did you go to college?

BENJAMIN: University of Wisconsin. Madison.

RONNIE: Madison, Wisconsin?

BENJAMIN: That's not where the bridges are, by the way.

RONNIE: Huh? Oh, right . . .

BENJAMIN: You wouldn't believe the number of people who—

RONNIE: They have Asian American studies in Madison, Wisconsin? Since when?

BENJAMIN: Since the last Third World Unity hunger strike. (*Pause.*) Why do you look so surprised? We're down.

RONNIE: I dunno. It just never occurred to me, the idea of Asian students in the Midwest going on a hunger strike.

BENJAMIN: Well, a lot of them had midterms that week, so they fasted in shifts. (*Pause.*) The Administration never figured it out. The Asian students put that "They all look alike" stereotype to good use.

RONNIE: OK, so they got Asian American studies. That still doesn't explain—

BENJAMIN: What?

RONNIE: Well . . . what *you* were doing taking it?

BENJAMIN: Just like everyone else. I wanted to explore my roots. And, you know, the history of oppression which is my legacy. After a lifetime of assimilation, I wanted to find out who I really am. (*Pause.*)

RONNIE: And did you?

BENJAMIN: Sure. I learned to take pride in my ancestors who built the railroads, my Popo who would make me a hot bowl of jok with thousand day-old eggs when the white kids chased me home yelling, "Gook! Chink! Slant-eyes!"

RONNIE: OK, OK, that's enough!

BENJAMIN: Painful to listen to, isn't it?

RONNIE: I don't know what kind of bullshit ethnic studies program they're running over in Wuss-consin, but did they bother to teach you that in order to find your Asian "roots," it's a good idea to first be Asian? (*Pause.*)

BENJAMIN: Are you speaking metaphorically?

RONNIE: No! Literally! Look at your skin!

BENJAMIN: You know, it's very stereotypical to think that all Asian skin tones conform to a single hue.

RONNIE: You're white! Is this some kind of redneck joke or something? Am I the first person in the world to tell you this?

BENJAMIN: Oh! Oh! Oh!

RONNIE: I know real Asians are scarce in the Midwest, but . . . Jesus!

BENJAMIN: No, of course, I . . . I see where your misunderstanding arises.

RONNIE: Yeah. It's called, "You white."

BENJAMIN: It's just that—in my hometown of Tribune, Kansas, and then at school—see, everyone knows me—so this sort of thing never comes up.

(*He offers his hand.*) Benjamin Wong. I forget that a society wedded to racial constructs constantly forces me to explain my very existence.

RONNIE: Ronnie Chang. Otherwise known as, "The Bow Man."

BENJAMIN: You see, I was adopted by Chinese American parents at birth. So, clearly, I'm an Asian American—

RONNIE: Even though you're blonde and blue-eyed.

BENJAMIN: Well, you can't judge my race by my genetic heritage alone.

RONNIE: If genes don't determine race, what does?

BENJAMIN: Perhaps you'd prefer that I continue in denial, masquerading as a white man?

RONNIE: You can't just wake up and say, "Gee, I *feel* Black today."

BENJAMIN: Brother, I'm just trying to find what you've already got.

RONNIE: What do I got?

BENJAMIN: A home. With your people. Picketing with the laundry workers. Taking refuge from the daily slights against your masculinity in the noble image of Gwan Gung.

RONNIE: Gwan who?

BENJAMIN: C'mon—the Chinese god of warriors and—what do you take me for? There're altars to him up all over the community.

RONNIE: I dunno what community you're talking about, but it's sure as hell not mine. (*Pause.*)

BENJAMIN: What do you mean?

RONNIE: I mean, if you wanna call Chinatown your community, OK, knock yourself out, learn to use chopsticks, big deal. Go ahead, try and find your "roots" in some dim sum parlor with headless ducks hanging in the window. Those places don't tell you a thing about who *I* am.

BENJAMIN: Oh, I get it.

RONNIE: You get what?

BENJAMIN: You're one of those self-hating, *assimilated* Chinese Americans, aren't you?

RONNIE: Oh, Jesus.

BENJAMIN: You probably call yourself, "Oriental," huh? Look, maybe I can help you. I have some books I can—

RONNIE: Hey, I read all those Asian identity books when you were still slathering on industrial-strength sunblock. (*Pause.*) Sure, I'm Chinese. But folks like you act like that means something. Like, all of a sudden, you know who I am. You think identity's that simple? That you can wrap it all up in a neat package and say, I have ethnicity, therefore I am? All you fucking ethnic fundamentalists. Always settling for easy answers. You say you're looking for identity, but you can't begin to face the real mysteries of the search. So instead, you go skin-deep, and call it a day. (*Pause. He turns away from Benjamin, starts to play his violin—slow and bluesy.*)

BENJAMIN: So what are you? "Just a human being?" That's like saying you *have* no identity. If you asked me to describe my dog, I'd say more than, "He's just a dog."

RONNIE: What—you think if I deny the importance of my race, I'm no-body? There're worlds out there, worlds you haven't even begun to understand. Open your eyes. Hear with your ears. (*He holds his violin at chest level, does not attempt to play during the following monologue. As he speaks, a montage of rock and jazz violin tracks fades in and out over the house speakers, bringing to life the styles of music he describes.*) I concede—it was called a fiddle long ago—but that was even before the birth of jazz. When the hollering in the fields, the rank injustice of human bondage, the struggle of God's children against the plagues of the devil's white man, when all these boiled up into that bittersweet brew, called by later generations, the blues. That's when fiddlers like Son Sims held their chin rests at their chests, and sawed away like the hillbillies still do today. And with the coming of ragtime appeared the pioneer Stuff Smith, who sang as he stroked the catgut, with his raspy, Louis Armstrong-voice—gruff and sweet like the timbre of horsehair riding south below the fingerboard—and who finally sailed for Europe to find ears that would hear. Europe where Stephane Grappelli initiated a magical French violin, to be passed from generation to generation—first he, to Jean-Luc Ponty, then Ponty to Didier Lockwood. Listening to Grappelli play "A Nightingale Sang in Berkeley Square" is to understand not only the song of birds, but also how they learn to fly, fall in love on the wing, and finally falter one day, to wait for darkness beneath a London street lamp. And Ponty—he showed how the modern violin man can accompany the shadow of his own lead lines, which cascade, one over another, into some nether world beyond the range of human hearing. Joe Venutti. Noel Pointer. Sven Asmussen. Even the Kronos Quartet, with their arrangement of "Purple

Haze." Now, tell me, could any legacy be more rich, more crowded with mythology and heroes to inspire pride? What can I say if the banging of a gong or the clinking of a pickax on the Transcontinental Railroad fails to move me even as much as one note, played through a violin MIDI controller by Michael Urbaniak? (*He puts his violin to his chin, begins to play a jazz composition of his own invention.*) Does it have to sound like Chinese opera before people like you decide I know who I am? (*Benjamin stands for a long moment, listening to Ronnie play. Then, he drops his dollar into the case, turns and exits R. Ronnie continues to play a long moment. Then Benjamin enters D.L., illuminated in his own spotlight. He sits on the floor of the stage, his feet dangling off the lip. As he speaks, Ronnie continues playing his tune, which becomes underscoring for Benjamin's monologue. As the music continues, does it slowly begin to reflect the influence of Chinese music?*)

BENJAMIN: When I finally found Doyers St., I scanned the buildings for Number 13. Walking down an alley where the scent of freshly-steamed char siu bao lingered in the air, I felt immediately that I had entered a world where all things were finally familiar. (*Pause.*) An old woman bumped me with her shopping bag—screaming to her friend in Cantonese, though they walked no more than a few inches apart. Another man—shouting to a vendor in Sze-Yup. A youth, in white undershirt, perhaps a recent newcomer, bargaining with a grocer in Hokkien. I walked through this ocean of dialects, breathing in the richness with deep gulps, exhilarated by the energy this symphony brought to my step. And when I finally saw the number 13, I nearly wept at my good fortune. An old tenement, paint peeling, inside walls no doubt thick with a century of grease and broken dreams—and yet, to me, a temple—the house where my father was born. I suddenly saw it all: Gung Gung, coming home from his 16-hour days pressing shirts he could never afford to own, bringing with him candies for my father, each sweet wrapped in the hope of a better life. When my father left the ghetto, he swore he would never return. But he had, this day, in the thoughts and memories of his son, just six months after his death. And as I sat on the stoop, I pulled a hua-moi from my pocket, sucked on it, and felt his spirit returning. To this place where his ghost, and the dutiful hearts of all his descendants, would always call home. (*He listens for a long moment.*) And I felt an ache in my heart for all those lost souls, denied this most important of revelations: to know who they truly are. (*Benjamin sits on the stage, sucking his salted plum, and listening to the sounds around him. Ronnie continues to play. The two remain oblivious of one another. Lights fade slowly to black.*)

CURTAIN

PROPERTY LIST
Electric violin with bow (RONNIE)

Violin case, open, with change and dollar bills (RONNIE)

Coins (BENJAMIN)

Dollar bills (BENJAMIN)

Scrap of paper (BENJAMIN)

Pack of cigarettes (RONNIE)

Lighter or matches (RONNIE)

Hua-moi (BENJAMIN)

Velina Hasu Houston

PLAYWRIGHT AND POET

Born in Tokyo in 1957, Velina Hasu Houston is a prolific playwright, poet, professor of theater, and director of the Playwriting Program at the University of Southern California. Her signature play, Tea, *has been produced internationally. Her body of plays also includes* Necessities, Asa Ga Kimashita, American Dreams, Kokoro, As Sometimes in a Dead Man's Face, The Matsuyama Mirror, Hula Heart, Cultivated Lives, Tell Her That You Saw Me, *and* Sentimental Education. *She has published cultural criticism and poetry and written film scripts for Columbia Pictures, Sidney Poitier, PBS/KCET (Los Angeles), Lancit Media, and several independent producers. She has edited two anthologies of Asian American drama:* The Politics of Life *(1993) and* But Still, Like Air, I'll Rise *(1997). Twice a Rockefeller fellow, her other honors have included the Remy Martin New Vision Award from Sidney Poitier and the American Film Institute, three recognitions from the John F. Kennedy Center for the Performing Arts, California Arts Council fellow, Japanese American Woman of Merit 1890–1990 by the National Japanese American Historical Society, and Susan Smith Blackburn Prize finalist. A Phi Beta Kappa, she holds a master of arts degree from the University of California, Los Angeles, and is a doctoral candidate in Critical Studies in Cinema and Television at the School of Cinema-Television, University of Southern California in Los Angeles. She resides in Santa Monica, California, with her children, Kiyoshi and Kuniko-Leilani.*

RESPONSE ⌇
Observations on My Life as an Artist

On the Origins and Genesis of My Work

In terms of my inspirations, the genesis of my work lies in an emotive quality; a fierce passion for an idea, a character, or an event that crescendos inside of me. The passion must at first overwhelm the idea, event, or personage, because without that ardor and stamina, the entity that is the seed of a poem, play, or screenplay cannot be born. The intense passion is the catalyst for conception and gestation, transcending into a quieter but no less significant passion that sustains the entity through artistic growth and development. In other words, I *feel* my ideas before I *think* them.

Moreover, the emotive aspect must remain with the artistic-intellectual that drives art and craft beyond conception through the arduous and long process of refinement. I consider inspiration to be a spiritual process, one during which you must dig deep into that amorphous entity we call the soul and excavate and mine its resources for intangible cues to unlock certain doors in the mystery of the human condition.

This brings me to the second part of how I view the roots of my work. Its origins/genesis also can be explained in perhaps less ethereal terms. I am struck by what critically strikes at the human *kokoro* (heart-mind-soul), what I call the human condition. I have little interest in writing about superficial aspects of life. I must go beneath the surface, the painted masks of clay, as I say in one of my plays, to explore the genuine desires and compelling needs that we conceal out of fear, shame, pain, or greed. The mask of the exterior must be peeled away, layer by layer, until the truth stands bare and shaking, for better or for worse.

Who Is My Audience?

I do not create my work for any particular audience, because I feel that the human soul must speak to everyone and anyone.

What Artists/Art Do I Admire?

I do not admire any particular artist or musician. I admire certain works of art, usually literary works of art, but not necessarily because of the artist. I do not have any favorite novels, plays, or poems, but some of the works that have, at some time in my life, touched me or made me feel painfully alive include *The Makioka Sisters* (Tanizaki Junichiro); *Sentimental Education* (Gustave Flaubert); *The Dream Songs* (John Berryman); *The Doctor's Wife, Hishoku, The River Ki,* and *The Twilight Years* (Sawako Ariyoshi); *Ethan Frome* (Edith Wharton); *Love in the Time of Cholera* (Gabriel García Márquez); *A Personal Matter* (Oe Kenzaburo); *A Raisin in the Sun* (Lorraine Hansberry); *The Sea Gull* (Anton Chekhov); *for colored girls who have considered suicide when the rainbow is enuf* (Ntozake Shange); sometimes the poetry of Anna Akhmatova, Delmore Schwartz, Anne Sexton, Dylan Thomas, Langston Hughes, W. H. Auden, and Charles Baudelaire; and one poem ("Daddy") by Sylvia Plath. Beyond these voices, however, I have encountered contemporary voices, lesser-known poets, whose words sang for me, such as Eloise Klein Healy or Thelma Seto. You may never hear their songs, but I have eaten their words and they have fed me in one way or another with spiritual food.

Am I Part of a Tradition?

I am not part of any tradition. I am a unique individual whose writing does not fit into any prefabricated commercial mold and, I daresay, any noncommercial mold. This has something to do with the out-of-the-ordinary circumstances of my ethnicity. I am multiethnic: Japanese, Native American Indian (Blackfoot Pikuni), and African American. Furthermore, I am a multiethnic who will not compromise her triple-culture identity by passing as one ethnic group or another; I adhere to a no-passing zone. This desire to live what/who I am problematizes my ability to fit into society, because society has an obsessive need to categorize everything. When it comes to ethnicity, this need to categorize borders on the archaic and pathological, reduced to four or five "traditional" ethnic groups who fight like hell to maintain their "purity," based mostly on the need to retain or obtain federally allocated moneys. I break tradition ethnically and also statistically in terms of reproductive and marital issues. As an educated, financially independent, mature, and intellectual individual, I bore a son whom I rear on my own. The last thing that anybody can say about me is that I am ordinary. I did not set out to be curious, eccentric, and unusual; but I think that it came part and parcel with my Amerasian birthright. That ethnicity made independence (ethnically, socially, politically) a *necessity*. I did not have to try to be different; I *was*. *I am*.

When observers speak of a "tradition of artists of color" I grow cautious, because I am concerned that ethnic cleansing is rearing its ugly head. By this I mean that the mainstream society (which continues to be Eurocentric and patriarchal) may be struggling to keep the arts as mainstream as possible, focusing on European and European American arts and artists, while representing artists of color or art about people of color in only token veins. In effect, the arts are being kept clean of too many representations of life of color in these United States while an artistic ghetto is being created in which are thrust all those artists of color and their remarkable traditions and expressions, so that they re-main peripheral to what is "real" art in America. If you are a European American artist in the United States, you create art and are called an artist. If you are an artist of color, you create art, but you are never an artist; you are always an "Asian American artist," "African American artist," "Latina artist," "Native American Indian artist," and so on and so forth. These distinctions are meaningful in that the ethnic histories reflected in many of the works of these artists are important to acknowledge and include in what we think of as "American," but they also are problematic because they marginalize the artists of color.

The Asian American Sensibility

I do not believe that there is an authentic Asian American sensibility. What, after all, is "the Asian American community"? Most Asian Americans are ignorant about the diversity of Asian America, especially in economic and ethnic terms. Most Asian Americans believe that in order to be Asian American, you have to look like Connie Chung or Tritia Toyota, be at least middle-class, and have an education. What the majority of Asian Americans do not take into account is that many persons of Asian descent look nothing like Ms. Chung or Ms. Toyota, especially if they come from India, Sri Lanka, Polynesia, the Philippines, or if they are Amerasian/Eurasian/Afroasian. Second, most people do not realize that the Asian American community has a poverty rate of roughly 14.8 percent, which is twice that of "non-Hispanic" Whites. A dark-skinned Micronesian or Indian or a Laotian without a high school education shatters the image that both Asian Americans and non–Asian Americans retain about the "typical Asian American."

But even the shattering of the myth does not kill the myth. Most Asian Americans continue to believe in and perpetuate the ethnic/economic myth, trying to reflect a racial and political cohesion that simply does not exist. Because of this, I do not believe that an authentic Asian American sensibility exists. What is authentically Asian American to a nutmeg-colored doctor from Bombay is going to be very different from what is authentically Asian American to a thirteen-year-old Laotian welfare mother or to a yuppie Japanese American driving a late-model Honda or Mazda. Until those Asian Americans who feel a sociopolitical need to project the myth of an "Asian American community" face up to the intragroup racism, sexism, ethnic diversity, and economic diversity, the party line or the "sensibility" simply represents the egocentric desires of a few who have the audacity to think that they can truly represent all persons of Asian descent in America.

Role of Asian American Artist in Society

I think the role of any artist is to explore the dimensions of truth. I suppose that Asian American artists, like all artists of color throughout U.S. history, may have political desires that intertwine with artistic desires: namely, the need to dispel myth and stereotype, to document history. I do not believe, however, that Asian American artists consciously set out to accomplish these political goals. Rather, I believe that, like most artists, they mine their souls, and in the process (because they are people of color with many an untold history to share), myths and stereotype automatically are dispelled.

Because of this, I feel that Asian American artists can contribute to society's ability to survive in the long term; for whether we want to admit it or not, this country is in the midst of civil war. The battles of urban violence are ever increasing; people are divided and dividing. Peace on earth is harder to find than dinosaur skeletons. Many of these battles are catalyzed by ethnic intolerance; therefore, the more that society can understand the histories, idiosyncrasies, behaviors, and significant contributions of communities of color, the more ethnic tolerance can flourish.

I feel that all artists of color face risks and challenges that are difficult, but not impossible to overcome. First of all, all artists are marginalized in the United States. Thus, artists of color have yet another layer of difference. As I said earlier, they are seen as artists of color rather than as artists; thus, they are not taken as seriously and not given the same level of attention that a European American artist garners. The need to prove oneself is greater. Furthermore, the artist of color is rarely given the opportunity to fail. His or her success is usually considered an anomaly, the bulk of the work being relegated to fad or folk art. The work is displayed or presented as such (the token color), thereby further problematizing the integrity and perceived value of the artist of color. The artist of color must, therefore, give 200 percent and be immensely successful, because a second chance to prove oneself is rare. The only way to begin to resolve these issues is to have people of color represented in the decision-making ranks of presenters and producers of art. What is "good" and "valuable" as art must be decided by a more ethnically diverse group of individuals.

Stereotypes

I do believe that the Asian male is perceived as less than masculine by the dominant society. I also believe that the Asian female has been overly exoticized, in ways that heighten her attractiveness or demean her dignity. I believe that the popularity of martial arts and the presence of virile, manly Asian male celebrities (such as actor Jason Scott Lee) are beginning to debilitate the Asian male myths, but it is only a beginning. Because I am Asian and have dated (native) Asian men, the American views of the Asian male baffle me. It is clear that such views are born of ignorance, fear, and prejudgment. The same negative sources have stereotyped the African American male and Latino male. They are perceived as overly sexual, while the Asian male is perceived as nonsexual, the sexual stereotypes usually being based on the myths of penis size. In contrast, the Asian female is seen as overly sexual. This stereotype can be that of either the sexual innocent or the more common dragon-lady/back-rubbing bimbo-whore. I do not think there is anything to be gained from either view or, for that matter, from stereotypes in general.

In my work, I try to present genuine, dimensional portraits of men and women of color. For example, in my play *Kokoro,* a native Japanese male has two lovers, and in fact, a point is made of his penis size. While having two lovers was intertwined in the story, perhaps, in retrospect, I can say that I intentionally introduced phallic measure into the text of the play to counter the persistent stereotype that Asian men have small penises. I think it is abominable to attempt to strip an entire ethnicity of men of their masculinity, but especially to do it by, in a sense, castrating them. In terms of representations of Asian women, I must say that my plays generally offer diverse portraits of tradition-breaking Japanese, Japanese American, and Amerasian women.

Reception of Asian American Artists

The early to mid-1990s has been a receptive time for the work of Asian American artists. I feel that what is commonly known as the "multicultural movement" helped shape this receptiveness. I also feel, however, that as the term *multiculturalism* loses meaning, due to the distortions of its original intent by the political Right, society will begin to feel less of a need to diversify their palette.

Reception of My Work

I feel that my artistic career began prior to the "multicultural movement" that saw American audiences embracing the Asian American arts. Also, because I am Amerasian, I feel that the reception of my work has been very different than that of "typical" Asian American artists. I do feel that the Japanese American community has, on the whole, been very supportive of my work. Furthermore, Japanese society has been interested in my work. (There have been three documentaries about me and my work, and three productions of my play *Tea* in Japan; in addition, *Tea* is going to be published in Japanese for the Japanese market.) Beyond these communities, I also have been produced and presented in the mainstream community; furthermore, I also have worked in film and television, being hired not for what I am ethnically but for what I can write and how I write it.

I am grateful for all of the individuals who have believed in my work and supported it either by presenting, producing, or publishing it or by coming to see it. I think audience is such an important and often overlooked part of an artist's life. While I may write many a poem that is a private lyric for my loved ones, the majority of what I create is meant to be seen and heard publicly. On the down side, in the Asian American community, I also have had to deal with a lot of racism. It is more irritating than racism from European Americans because it comes from people who ought to know better, because they suffer themselves. In other words, the very hypocrisy of it is repulsive. I have experienced the same from some elements in the African American community and find it loathsome for the same reasons.

My wish for artists of the future is that they have the courage to mine their souls for truths and lay them out on the table to enlighten others.

From *Tea*

TIME AND PLACE
1968. The home of Himiko Hamilton in Junction City, Kansas, and an obscure netherworld where time moves at will.

SCENE ONE: THE ART OF TEA

Atsuko and Teruko drift to the tatami room where piles of books and a wild-looking wig are on the floor. They take off their shoes outside of the room and enter. Atsuko has brought her own booties and puts them on. She removes her sweater, and studies the room with mixed feelings of revulsion and attraction, as if she has vicariously imagined this room's experiences. She sniffs the air with displeasure, and covers her nose and mouth with a handkerchief. They set up the Japanese-style table and place four zabuton as Himiko observes from the darkness. Whenever Himiko speaks to the audience, it is as if she is on trial and offering a matter-of-fact defense.

ATSUKO: Ugh. How were you able to have tea here with this stench! (*studies the floor*) Maybe we should keep our shoes on.

TERUKO: It didn't smell here before, Atsuko-san!

ATSUKO: Yes, it did. You said it did.

TERUKO: I said it smelled like liquor and burnt candles.

ATSUKO: Well, you know that's from bringing home men and making sex.

TERUKO: (*insistently protective*) Before her husband died, Himiko lived a quiet life.

(*Atsuko picks up the wild wig as if to negate Teruko's statement. Teruko starts to exit to the kitchen.*)

I'm going to find the teapot and cups.

(*Atsuko hurriedly drops the wig and looks around the room as if she has seen or suspects ghosts.*)

ATSUKO: Don't leave me alone!

TERUKO: We must begin. (*Teruko exits to kitchen.*)

HIMIKO: (*to audience*) Yes, we must begin. . . . Tea for the soul; tea to cleanse the spirit.

(*Atsuko examines the room carefully as if afraid of getting dirty and begins to put things away. She puts on her glasses.*)

ATSUKO: Himiko was so wild after her husband died. Maybe she was like that in Japan, too. I don't know how she passed the screening tests for army brides. They took so long and the Yankee officers asked so many stupid questions.

HIMIKO: (*addresses Atsuko as if echoing a reminder, encircling her as she speaks*) "Are you a Communist? Why do you want to marry this man instead of one of your own native Japanese? Do you think moving to America will afford you personal financial gain? Are you suffering from insanity? Are you an imbecile or idiot?" (*a beat*) "Are you now—or have you ever been—a prostitute?"

ATSUKO: The nerve of that Amerikan Army! Did the army ask you if you were a prostitute?

(*Teruko returns with a teapot, cups, lacquer coasters, and two cloths—one wet and one dry—all on a lacquer tray. She handles them delicately.*)

TERUKO: Yes. I told them we weren't all bad girls just because we fell in love with Amerikans. (*looks around the room as if drinking in Himiko's life*) Poor Himiko.

ATSUKO: Where is Setsuko Banks? I thought she was the one most friendly with Himiko. (*looks around the room eerily*) I heard the tatami was covered with blood. It's funny, isn't it, how one moment someone is full of life and the next, they are ashes.

TERUKO: Atsuko-san, ne, if you're that uncomfortable, go home. Setsuko and Chiz (*pronounced like "cheese"*) and I can take care of this.

ATSUKO: As head of our Buddhist chapter, how would it look to head-quarters if I didn't do everything I could to help a member? (*feigning an innocent smile, she peers over her glasses*) Besides, I wanted to see the inside of this house.

TERUKO: Well, Setsuko-san went home to pick up o-sushi.

ATSUKO: And "Chiz" is always late. Her nickname sounds so stupid. Like food. She even wears pants now and grows her hair long like a hippy. (*removes a crocheted green-and-purple poodle toilet paper cover from the trunk and shakes her head at its oddity*) She's just as silly as Himiko was.

(*Atsuko takes out her own tea cup, admires it, and places it on the table. Teruko wipes Himiko's tea cups, first with a wet cloth and then a dry one. She carefully arranges the cups with coasters and teapot on the table. Atsuko moves Himiko's tea cups away from her own.*)

TERUKO: (*removes a folded newspaper article from her wallet; reads from it with officiousness*) Listen. I cut this out. "Death Notices. September 9, 1968. Himiko Hamilton, thirty-nine, widow of Chief Warrant Officer William Hamilton, passed away in her home from a self-inflicted gunshot wound. She was preceded in death by her husband and, recently, her daughter, Mieko, eighteen. A Japanese war bride, Mrs. Hamilton was a resident of Junction City for twenty years. She leaves no survivors."

HIMIKO: (*to audience with quiet dignity*) But, still, I ask you to listen. Please. (*a beat*) I am suspended between two worlds. There is no harmony here (*indicates the women in tatami room*) nor here (*indicates her soul*).

TERUKO: Well, she *did* leave survivors.

ATSUKO: Who?

TERUKO: Us.

ATSUKO: Not me! Just because I'm Japanese doesn't mean I have anything to do with her life. Dead is dead, Teruko-san, so what difference does it make? Who knows, ne. Maybe next it will be me. Do you think the Japanese women in this town are going to pray for my soul just because I happen to come from Japan?

TERUKO: (*shocked at Atsuko's callousness*) Atsuko-san. We must respect the dead.

ATSUKO: Only because they no longer have to fear the darkness. The rest of us must wait, without any idea of when our time will come to an end.

TERUKO: (*as if she feels Himiko's presence*) No, sometimes even the dead must wait. In limbo.

ATSUKO: (*a smile*) Well, Himiko should wait forever after what she did to her husband.

TERUKO: But you know what he was doing to her.

ATSUKO: Nobody really knows.

HIMIKO: Nobody would listen.

ATSUKO: Maybe she wasn't a good wife.

HIMIKO: I was the *best* wife.

TERUKO: He never let her out of the house and hardly let her have guests. Remember during the big snow storm? The phone lines were down and—

HIMIKO:—I didn't have any tea or rice left. Billy had gone to Oklahoma to visit his family. He said, "Don't leave the house," and took my daughter, Mieko, with him. So there I was, starving to death, standing behind—

TERUKO: (*overlapping with Himiko's last two words*)—standing behind the frosty glass. She looked like she was made of wax.

HIMIKO: (*smiles at herself*) I asked him once. I said, "Why did you marry me?" And he said he wanted a good maid, for free.

ATSUKO: Maybe she wanted too much.

HIMIKO: I never asked for anything. Except soy sauce and good rice. And dreams . . . for Mieko.

(*Himiko glows with love for her child, turns around, and seems to see her as a tot, and beckons to her.*)

HIMIKO: Mieko-chan! My little girl! (*Himiko exits as if chasing "Mieko."*)

ATSUKO: Teruko, I saw your daughter last week. She looks Japanese. (*a compliment*) That's nice. Too bad she isn't friends with my girl. My girl's always with Setsuko-san's daughter. Have you seen her? Looks Indonesian, not Japanese at all. Shame, ne.

TERUKO: But Setsuko's daughter is the only one who cooks Japanese food. My daughter likes hamburger sandwich and yellow-haired boys.

ATSUKO: My daughter always goes to Setsuko-san's house. I've never been invited.

TERUKO: Setsuko likes her privacy.

ATSUKO: She invited you to tea.

TERUKO: Well, if you're not willing to be genuine with her, how can you share the honor of tea together?

ATSUKO: She invited Himiko, too!

TERUKO: Yes, even after the incident. Even though everyone was afraid.

(*A siren wails as a deafening gunshot echoes in the air and all lights black out. Atsuko and Teruko exit to the kitchen in the darkness. Himiko, without sunglasses, drifts from the darkness and stops center stage. The siren fades out and a spotlight fades up immediately on Himiko who crouches as if shooting a pistol. She smiles and rises gracefully. She speaks matter-of-factly to the audience.*)

HIMIKO: (*imitates the sound of shots, pronounced "bahn" like in bonfire*) Ban! Ban! Ban! Yes. I am Himiko Hamilton. The murderess. I married and murdered a gentleman from Oklahoma. And they let me go on self-defense. It took one shot—right through the heart I never knew he had. Now that he's gone, I can speak freely. Please listen. I wasted my life in Kansas. The state—of mind. Not Kansas City, but *Junction City*, a stupid hick town that rests like a pimple on an army base called Fort Riley. Where the army's resettlement policy exiled our husbands because they were married to "Japs."

(*Himiko indicates her own face as Chiz and Setsuko enter from opposite corners carrying food in a basket and furoshiki, respectively.*)

HIMIKO: They won't tell you that because they're real *japaneezy* Japanese.

(*Chiz and Setsuko smile and bow formally to each other in greeting; Setsuko bows a second time.*)

HIMIKO: See what I mean? Well, . . . I'm about as Japanese as corn flakes, or so they say, and I killed my husband because he laughed at my soy sauce just one time too many.

(*Himiko smiles whimsically and turns away from the audience. Chiz and Setsuko drift downstage. They are unaware of Himiko's presence. Setsuko and Chiz stand outside of the house.*)

SETSUKO: Oh, Chizuye-san, I wish Himiko-san could have seen all the Japanese women at her funeral.

HIMIKO: (*to the audience*) All the Japanese women who were too ashamed to say hello to me in public because I was "no good."

CHIZ: (*adamant with characteristic exuberance*) Ever since she shot her husband two years ago, she's kind of haunted me. It made me remember that underneath my comfortable American clothes, I am, after all, Japanese. (*a quick smile*) But don't tell anybody.

SETSUKO: Well, after all, you were the one who went looking for her.

CHIZ: Someone had to. The rest of you were too afraid of what you would find. (*looks into space as she recalls*) I forced her door open and, there she was, paler and bluer than the sky over Hiroshima that strange August. She had pulled her kimono over her American dress, as if it might make her journey into the next life a little easier. But I took one look at her and I knew nothing was ever going to be easy for her, not in life or in death.

HIMIKO: I would have given anything to have tea with Japanese girls. I drank alone.

(*Setsuko and Chiz approach the house and remove their shoes. Setsuko straightens hers and Chiz's.*)

CHIZ: What'd you bring?

SETSUKO: Maki-zushi.

CHIZ: (*smiles to poke fun at her friend*) Figures. I brought spinach quiche, Sue.

SETSUKO: My name is not Sue. My name is Setsuko. Chizuye-san, I tell you many times not to call me by this nickname you made up.

CHIZ: But it's easier.

SETSUKO: Like "Chiz." (*pronounces it "cheese"*)

CHIZ: (*laughs; pronounces it with a short "i"*) No, Setsuko, like "Chiz." That's what my customers at my restaurant call me, but you can call me anything you like.

(*They enter the house and Chiz looks toward the kitchen.*)

CHIZ: Hello? Hello? Ah, Teruko! Hello.

(*Teruko appears from the kitchen with food, including fruit. Setsuko scurries to help her.*)

TERUKO: Hello! Hello! Look, Atsuko-san is here, too.

CHIZ: (*much surprise and a touch of contempt*) Atsuko?!

SETSUKO: Well, what an unexpected pleasure.

ATSUKO: Setsuko-san! I rarely see you, but you look younger every time I do. I was sorry to hear about your husband.

SETSUKO: Yes, well, it was his time to . . . to move on.

ATSUKO: Negroes don't live very long. The food they eat, you know.

SETSUKO: My husband ate almost entirely Japanese food.

TERUKO: Atsuko-san's husband hates Japanese food. (*giggles*) And he's Japanese Amerikan!

ATSUKO: He does not hate Japanese food! (*to Setsuko and Chiz*) Why are you both so late? We cleaned the kitchen already. And, of course, we must have tea.

SETSUKO: Oh, yes, tea sounds very good to me now.

TERUKO: Why, yes. Everything must start with tea.

CHIZ: (*laughs*) Tea is *just* a drink.

SETSUKO: Oh, it's much more than that.

ATSUKO: I couldn't live without tea.

HIMIKO: Yes, . . . it brings everything into balance.

ATSUKO: I think it improves my eyesight.

SETSUKO: (*laughing*) And my insight.

(*Teruko, Setsuko and Atsuko have a good laugh over this as Chiz looks on dead-pan. Finally she smiles and lights up a cigarette.*)

CHIZ: Hey, enough about tea. Who else is coming?

TERUKO: More than four would be too many. I stopped asking for volunteers after Atsuko-san spoke up.

CHIZ: How many were there?

TERUKO: At least fifty Japanese women!

CHIZ: Fifty? Jesus. You'd think it was a blue-light special.

SETSUKO: Chizuye-san! Shame, ne! After all, this is a difficult occasion for us: the first time a member of our Japanese community has passed on.

CHIZ: What "community"?

HIMIKO: (*again, to audience*) Yes, what community? We knew each other, but not really. . . . We didn't care enough to know.

CHIZ: Who's got time to chit-chat, right, "Ats" ? (*pronounced with a short "a," like "ahts"*) Now that I'm finally having tea with the great Atsuko Yamamoto, you get a nickname.

ATSUKO: Thank you, but you can keep your . . . gift. (*a beat*) It's obvious we're all from different neighborhoods.

SETSUKO: But we are all army wives—and we are all Japanese.

CHIZ: So what? That won't buy us a ticket to Nirvana. Let's face it, girls, after we get through dealing with our jobs and our families, we're ready to go to sleep. And, if any of us are willing to drive across town and have tea, we don't even talk about what's really on our minds—whether coming to Amerika was such a good idea. (*she smiles*) Countries last; love is mortal.

SETSUKO: But we're here today because we're Japanese.

CHIZ: We're here today because we're scared.

HIMIKO: Scared they will be next to die or their souls will be left in limbo like mine.

(*Atsuko can hardly contain her excitement at finally being able to ask a question she's pondered for years:*)

ATSUKO: Tell us, Setsuko-san. Is it true about Himiko being a dance hall girl in Japan?

SETSUKO: If that's what she said. I never really knew her until after her husband died. I would see her walking in the middle of a humid summer day in a heavy coat and the yellow-haired wig.

HIMIKO: (*reliving that day*) "Hello. I am Mrs. William Hamilton. May I have a glass of water? Oh, thank you, thank you. You are so kind."

ATSUKO: (*gesticulating that Himiko was crazy*) Kichigai, ne . . .

CHIZ: She was not crazy.

TERUKO: It is the Japanese way to carry everything inside.

HIMIKO: Yes. And that is where I hid myself.

ATSUKO: She came from Japan, but the way she dressed, the way she walked. Mah, I remember the district church meeting. She came in a low-cut dress and that yellow-haired wig, (*mocks how she thinks a Korean walks*) walking like a Korean.

SETSUKO: Atsuko-san, ne, we have something in common with all the Oriental women here, even the Vietnamese. We all left behind our countries to come and live here with the men we loved.

ATSUKO: Okay, okay. It's not that I didn't like Himiko-san. So many things she did were not acceptable. If she acted like that in Japan, people would think she was . . . well, a prostitute. Something was not right inside her head. I mean, whoever heard of a Japanese shooting her husband with a rifle? I told you that day at the cemetery.

(*Himiko, having had enough, rushes forward and the women freeze.*)

HIMIKO: (*defiantly calls them back into the past with a roll call, stamping her foot as she calls out each name*) Teruko. Setsuko. Atsuko. Chizuye.

(*Himiko exits through the kitchen as the music for "Taps" sets the mood. The women drift from the house as if answering the roll call. The lights fade out on house and fade up downstage. They stand as if around a headstone at a cemetery as Himiko enters. A black-veiled hat, black coat, and black pumps complete her widow ensemble. She carries a black bag out of which she pulls a can of beer. The women watch in shock as Himiko opens the beer and pours it over the "grave" by which they stand. Setsuko runs to her and takes the beer.)*

HIMIKO: Mah, there must be a thousand graves here!

SETSUKO: Shame on you, Himiko-san! Pouring beer on your husband's grave!

HIMIKO: I am celebrating. First Memorial Day since he "left me." He liked beer when he was alive. Why shouldn't he like it when he's dead.

CHIZ: Sounds pretty fair to me.

ATSUKO: Teruko-san, come. We've seen enough.

(Atsuko pulls away a reluctant Teruko, who beckons to Chiz. All three exit. Setsuko, concerned, lingers as Himiko suddenly looks up at an invisible object in great shock.)

HIMIKO: I'm sorry, Billy. That's right. I forgot. You like Budweiser beer. This is cheap kind, brand X. See? *(points at the can)* just B-E-E-R. Billy, what are you doing here? I believe in reincarnation, but this is a little soon. I planned on being gone before you came back. I'm sorry I didn't bury you in your favorite shirt. I couldn't fix the hole in it from when I shot you. No, no. I don't want to go with you. *(fighting)* No, I want to stay here with our daughter. She's not mad at me for what I did. She says you deserved it. No, I don't want to be alone with you anymore. I don't want to kiss and make up. *(pushes away an unseen presence)* Setchan! Help me! Billy's going to take me away. *(the presence knocks her off her feet)*

SETSUKO: *(an antithetical picture of solitude, she draws near)* Himiko-san. Let's go home now. We'll make tea and talk.

HIMIKO: Help me, Setchan. He's going to beat me up again.

SETSUKO: Come, Himi-chan. You must go home and rest.

HIMIKO: There is only unrest. It is like the war never ended.

SETSUKO: *(sympathetically)* Oh, Himi-san. *(not knowing what else to do, she releases Himiko and bows her head sorrowfully)*

HIMIKO: *(enervated, to herself)* I wish I would have died in World War II. It was an easier war than this one.

(Himiko exits offstage as Setsuko removes her shoes and returns to the tatami room and lights crossfade into Scene Two . . .)

Dwight Okita

PLAYWRIGHT AND POET

Born 1958 in Chicago, Dwight Okita continues to live in this city. A GAM (gay Asian male) and SGI (Soka Gakkai International) Buddhist who chants daily, he is the author of several plays and one book of poetry, Crossing with the Light *(1992). His first screenplay,* My Last Week on Earth, *was a finalist in the 1997 Sundance's Screenwriters Lab competition. Okita's* The Rainy Season *(a gay multicultural play) was published in* Asian American Drama: Nine Plays from the MultiEthnic Landscape *(ed. Brian Nelson and Dorinne K. Kondo, 1997); and* The Radiance of a Thousand Suns *(cowritten with Anne McGravie, Nicholas Patricca, David Zak, and composer Chuck Larkin), which won the Joseph Jefferson Citation for Outstanding New Work in Chicago Theater, was published in 1998.* Radiance *presents multiple views of the fiftieth anniversary of the atomic bomb. In 1994, HBO New Writers Project staged his plays* The Salad Bowl Dance, Richard Speck, *and* The Spirit Guide. *Okita is a resident playwright with Chicago Dramatists Workshop and a member of Independent Features Project/Midwest.*

RESPONSE

I am a Japanese American playwright and poet. The origins of my work are often autobiographical and colored by various aspects of my identity: as a gay man, as an American-born Asian American, as a romantic, as a Buddhist, as a human being.

250

Poetry-wise, my work frequently comes out of my own experiences, or sometimes out of imagining myself in unfamiliar situations. I wrote the poem "Where the Boys Were" after paging through *Life* magazine one day and seeing a photograph of a woman with AIDS sitting on the steps beside the funeral urn she had just purchased for herself. In "In Response to Executive Order 9066," I imagined myself in my mother's shoes as a teenager about to be interned.

As for my theater work, my play *The Rainy Season* grew directly out of my frustrating experiences dating Latino men. *Richard Speck* grew out of my darkly humorous recollections of growing up a block from where a mass murder took place. But sometimes, the genesis of a work comes from outside. For instance, I was recently approached to collaborate on a theater piece for the fiftieth anniversary of the bombing of Hiroshima. Since I'd just had a play produced relating to the internment camps for Japanese Americans, I was concerned about being pigeonholed as a playwright who dealt only with Asian-specific issues. But I liked the idea of collaborating with a composer on my first musical theater piece. So although the play originated from outside of me, I found a way to connect to the project that was new, exciting, and personal.

Generally, I create my work for the universal audience. As a writer, I want to create the most value I can by communicating with the largest number of people possible. But these issues vary from project to project. *The Salad Bowl Dance* was produced in 1993 by Angel Island Asian American Theater in collaboration with the Chicago Historical Society and was presented in 1994 at the HBO New Writers Project workshop in Hollywood as a staged reading. It is an absurd look at assimilation in the 1940s. I was writing, first and foremost, for the Japanese Americans in Chicago of my parents' generation who had come out of internment camps to settle here. But I was also hoping that the subject would be one that all communities of color could relate to—and that the mainstream audience might be also touched by.

Musically, I like the haunting melodies of Kate Bush and Sting and Tori Amos, the toughness and spirit of Janet Jackson, the passion of Amy Grant, the cool cosmicness of Cocteau Twins. And I am a big fan of Stephen Sondheim's musicals. They move both my mind and heart. They are both disturbing and seductive, perverse and purehearted.

As for playwrights, I love the way Tony Kushner in *Angels in America* fuses fantasy, realism, history, humor, and politics into a new kind of stew. He breaks rules and reinvents them with abandon. The thing I enjoy about John Guare's plays is that no one in his plays talks like real people. They talk in a heightened, rich, giddy kind of voice which I find compelling. In Chay Yew's *Porcelain,* I enjoyed the spareness of his language, the spiky edge it gives his characters. Magdalia Cruz's *Miriam's Flowers* has a breathless, gritty kind of poetry which engaged me. I'm very impressed with George Wolfe's writing and directorial talents. He has a grasp of theater and its possibilities that I find exciting and I want to learn from. As for film directors, I loved Wayne Wang's *Joy Luck Club* and Gus Van Sant's *My Own Private Idaho.* And of course, *Forrest Gump* was a movie I wish I'd written. I think *My So-Called Life* is an amazing TV show.

I see myself in a tradition of American artists, Asian American artists, artists of color—as well as part of a movement of gay artists and Japanese American artists. These distinctions can, at times, be meaningful. For instance, when Amy Tan's wonderful novel *Joy Luck Club* succeeded as a movie— it was a success for me, too, as an Asian American artist, even though Tan is Chinese American and I am Japanese American. But I also am aware of the wealth of Chinese American writers and artists that have risen in America, and I look forward to a similar flourishing of Japanese American talent.

It's helpful for me, at times, to see myself as part of a movement of Japanese American artists that (to the best of my knowledge) includes playwrights Philip Gotanda, Velina Hasu Houston, Wakako Yamauchi, Keith Uchima, James Yoshimura; filmmakers Gregg Araki, Steve Okazaki, Rea Tajiri; writers Cynthia Kadohata, David Mura, Kimiko Hahn, Garrett Hongo, Kyoko Mori; performers/actors Amy Hill, Sab Shimono, Cheryl Hamada, Tamlyn Tomita, Pat Morita, Suzy Nakamura, Chris Tashima, Nobu McCarthy, Lane Nishikawa, Brenda Wong Aoki; and musicians Hiroshima and Chika Sekiguchi.

It's tempting to try to describe an Asian American (AA) sensibility, though it's a daunting task, any way you slice it. Certainly, there is a valid distinction that can be made between the sensibilities of Asian national art and Asian American art. Asian national art comes out of a long tradition of artists living in Asia, where Asians are the dominant culture; while Asian American art comes out of a relatively shorter tradition of artists living in America, where Asian Americans are not the dominant culture.

But how to go about defining an AA sensibility? Well, as AAs, each of us has our unique albatrosses and breakthroughs in America. But the common grounds for an Asian American sensibility, however arbitrary, might include:

a striving toward giving visibility and voice to a vital part of American culture that has long been overlooked by Hollywood, misrepresented by the media, and underrepresented in general;

an awareness that mainstream America still has trouble distinguishing Asian Americans and Asian nationals;

a wish to express the full range of humanity, complexity, and idiosyncrasy that is Asian American life.

But then, if you ask someone else—they may give you a completely different answer.

As artists, we have entrée to the hearts and minds of the mainstream in a way that activists and politicians don't; because as Asian American artists, we don't come in the front door, we come in the back— through the subconscious. We challenge mainstream perceptions of us by giving new images of ourselves: new Asian American characters, stories, paintings, plays, and movies of Asian American life. We can— with our own hands—change the images of Asian Americans. All of us, artists or not, just by walking out the door and into the world, create Asian America each day.

There are those who would want to dismiss Asian American artists as riding the wave of affirmative action or multiculturalism. And there is definitely a wave. But I choose to focus instead on my own evolution and development as an artist. What are the challenges unique to AA artists? Sometimes institutions won't take chances on our work because they fear that it will not appeal to the general public. Once I was even told by a theater that their multicultural grant would cover only Hispanic and African American plays and would not be given for Asian American plays because they had no track record with AA works. And so it becomes a self-fulfilling prophecy: they don't produce an AA play, which only reinforces their lack of a track record of doing AA work.

Another challenge is that mainstream theaters often do not understand that when they choose to produce a Kabuki play or a Chinese fable, this does not satisfy an Asian American audience that is hungry to see Asian American life onstage. I choose to put my energy into trying to create work that is both unique and universal, irresistible and compelling.

I generally agree with the statement about our commodification and exoticization. But I am less interested in what the "dominant society" may have done *to* me, and more interested in what I, as an Asian American male, can do *for* me. I essentially confront stereotypes of Asian Americans with every AA male (and female) character I create as a playwright. Some of the strong AA male characters I've created in my plays include Harry, who stands up to Antonio's lies in *The Rainy Season;* Hank Shimizu, who struggles with Grace Komachi to make a place for the two of them in postwar Chicago in *The Salad Bowl Dance;* and atomic-bomb survivor Rev. Tanimoto, who confronts the copilot of the *Enola Gay* in *This Is Not My Life* (in development as of this writing).

I am very drawn to masculinity, both in myself and in the men I associate with. My sense of masculinity includes tenderness, forcefulness, sensuality, joy, sexiness, physical strength, and courage. As Asian American men, we can be as manly as we want to be. Pump some iron, now and then. Let your voice be heard above the noisy din. Be strong enough to be vulnerable, too. Take a chance. For me, the whole question of the image of the AA man in this country starts with me, who I see in the mirror. And it moves outward to how I interact with the world, my involvement. Ultimately, it all gets reflected back into my work as an artist.

Yes, this is a receptive moment. A multitude of voices are being heard from at this point in time in our country's evolution. Certainly, the changing demographics of this country in the next half century to a place where European Americans are no longer in the majority has something to do with it. I think people tire of the same familiar stories and are developing a taste for diversity. And movies like *Joy Luck Club* and *The Wedding Banquet,* even the television show *All American Girl,* help open doors. They give us a place at the table, on the channel selector, at the movies. The first wave of Asian American movies and plays dealt provocatively with issues often ignored by the American theater and Hollywood—cultural assimilation, what it's like to be new in America and of Asian heritage, intergenerational conflicts, the internment of Japanese Americans, and so forth. Works such as *M. Butterfly, The Dragon: The Bruce Lee Story, Come See the Paradise,* and the excellent documentary *Days of Waiting* come to mind.

I think the next generation of Asian American films, plays, and so forth, will have Asian American characters but will deal with less with traditional "Asian American issues," because people will have already processed issues of assimilation and history. Rather, they'll deal with universal human issues at their core, and ethnicity will be addressed more implicitly. Independent films such as *Shopping for Fangs* and, to some extent, *Double Happiness* do this. Even a film from Asia such as *Chungking Express* might be considered part of this new wave. A movie like *The Joy Luck Club* is perhaps the missing link between waves—with one impulse to tell of the ghosts of a Chinese past and one impulse to tell the universal story of every mother and daughter, every parent and child.

The progression from one wave to the next parallels the evolution of work other diverse groups. Initially, gay films and plays dealt with issues of coming out, AIDS, homophobia. But later, films such as *My Beautiful Launderette, Go Fish, Love Valour Compassion,* and *Beautiful Thing* broke new ground—partly by seeing the issue of sexual identity not as an issue to be "dealt" with but as an integral, implicit part of life.

As for the reception of my own work, I have been lucky. I have been very much embraced by the mainstream. The AA community has received my work with open arms. The gay community has gradually come to acknowledge me. I once said in an interview that the Asian American community embraces me in a way that the gay community doesn't. It's as if the Asian American community accepts that I'm gay more than the gay community accepts that I'm Asian American. But as I say, things are improving. As for geography, my theater work has mostly been seen in Chicago and somewhat on the West Coast. I've yet to make inroads on the East Coast. As for my poetry, since my book *Crossing with the Light* came out in 1993, my poetry has received national exposure. Also, I've been the cover story for mainstream and alternative magazines and newspapers and had some radio and TV coverage.

I don't feel, as a multicultural writer, that I must be totally answerable to my ethnic community. Nor to the gay community. Nor to men. Nor to gay Asian American men and any permutation thereof. On the other hand, I am often most interested in writing from those perspectives because I have lived them and they are most familiar to me—and least familiar to the general public.

This issue plays out somewhat differently depending on whether we're talking poetry or theater. As a poet, there are times I may write poems that do not specifically deal with being Asian American. But people who buy my poetry book know I'm AA when they see my face on the cover; people who read a poem of mine in a magazine can see my AA name. And I like that. In this way, my ethnicity comes into play in a more powerful way because it is implicit.

As a playwright of color, however, I feel there are more deliberate choices that we must make—because when an audience sits down in a theater, if they are aware of ethnicity at all, they are more likely going to be conscious of the ethnicity of the actors on stage, breathing before them, than of the playwright (who frequently doesn't have his headshot in the theater program and may or may not have an ethnic-sounding name).

Personally, it's hard for me to write a play in which my main characters are European American (Caucasian). More often than not, the protagonist will evolve out of something I've experienced, and I feel my life experiences always occur within the context of my being Asian American—as well as my being gay, an artist, a Buddhist, and so on. Besides, my AA actor and actress friends would be really pissed off at me if I didn't have some juicy roles for them. I need them and they need me.

I know AA playwrights who constantly populate their plays with all White characters, and it puzzles me. When I asked one writer why she did that, she said it was because she wasn't writing about an ethnic issue. But that's a troubling leap for me. One's ethnicity does not disappear just because you're not thinking about it for the moment or for one play. And I don't think the *absence* of an ethnic issue translates as the *presence* of a Caucasian mindset either. That seems to trivialize both Asian American and European American identities. I defend any artist's privilege to write about what moves him or her. I do, however, encourage such an artist to understand the reasons he or she makes such choices. Is there a denial of ethnicity going on, a self-hatred, or a simple commercial pandering to the White mainstream? (Which is fine, if that is a clear, conscious choice.) Or is there some other unique and valid rationale at work?

Asian Americans who write about subjects other than their cultural identity, of course, are still "Asian American writers" in my book. Whether those writers realize it or not, their perceptions are colored by their identity—even if all their characters are Caucasian. I create characters in my plays that are Hispanic, African American, Euro-American, women, heterosexual, older than me, and so forth—even though I have never been what they are. I do so because I have known intimately people of these diverse backgrounds. However, I would not personally be comfortable writing something in which the central issue was, say, the history of slavery, or a play about straight men and how they feel about women. I think my authority is questionable in these areas. But certainly, artists have the ability to imagine as well. I'm more interested in how I empower myself through what I create than in trying to tell others what they can or can't create. So if tomorrow I decide to write the history of White people in America—hey, it's a free country. Isn't it?

Does an ethnic writer become admitted into the general canon because he or she is less controversial? I don't know. But I certainly agree that strong "ethnic" and non-mainstream writers who have a serious, disturbing message clothed in a dazzling writing style also can be embraced by readers. In addition to writers like Toni Morrison and Maxine Hong Kingston, look at gay playwright Tony Kushner. His play *Angels in America* skewers racist America and Republicans, questions even the possibility of spirituality in America and the presence of angels, celebrates gay life, and mourns the loss of life from AIDS. The show has done very well in Chicago, and tickets have sold well over expectations here in "middle America." That's encouraging.

My "inspiring" words for aspiring AA artists? I feel most alive when I am creating a work of art. Do you? If so—maybe then that's what you must do. Find a way to do it, to support and nurture yourself. Concern yourself less with impressing others and more with the hard work of expressing yourself. It's important to get the energy flowing in the right direction. When I try to impress, my focus is on my feelings, my ego. When I try to express, my focus is on the audience's feelings, moving them. My energy is best when it moves outward from me—not inward.

Remember, there is not always a big pot of gold at the end of the art rainbow, so by all means, enjoy yourself. And keep your eyes peeled for that pot of gold. When it stops being fun—stop doing it. Until then, knock yourself out. Move a couple of mountains. Make your life extraordinary. Leave something behind that will outlive you. Tell them what you learned and what you loved.

If you're an aspiring artist, you're probably also an avid consumer of art. Think about what other artists (Asian American, other artists of color, "mainstream" artists, etc.) are doing that you find exciting; what aren't they doing? Can you do it better? When you go to a play, a movie, what would you love to see on stage or screen that you have never seen before? Put it there. The answer is in your hands. Create Asian America.

~~~~~~

Richard Speck

(*An Asian American woman stands on stage. She speaks directly to the audience.*)

I grew up on the east side of Chicago—no, not in the lake. That's what's my parents called it anyway: the "East Side." What I DO know for sure is that we lived exactly one block from where Richard Speck killed the eight nurses. You remember, Richard, don't you? The guy who stopped off one night and killed eight nurses, one by one. Some of them were Filipino.

I used to play in the playground behind that apartment complex, I think I was in second grade. I remember going to the park that day and seeing all these people on the lawn in front of the apartment and police cars everywhere. I think I was too shy to ask anyone what was going on, so I went to the park behind the building and played on the swings. That night, my parents told me what happened, there were pictures of the bodies on the news. "He could've stopped at ANY house," they said.

I always think about that one Filipino nurse who escaped. She hid under the bed. See, that's what I would do. She wanted to save ALL of them. "There are nine of us, we can take him!" she said. But they were too afraid, so she crawled under the bed—and she lived. I LOVE that—when people trust their instincts.

Anyway, I don't think I could ever kill anything—let alone eight people. Well, once I killed a parakeet—accidentally. I had a pet bird named Cisco. I wanted to trap it between the storm door and the wood door. I thought it'd look pretty flying there behind the glass. Like a little zoo I could show off to my friends. But when I shut the wood door, Cisco tried to fly out, and he got smashed. Red blood trickled down the door jam. Well, we got another parakeet. But this one my mother killed accidentally. She got tired of changing the newspaper in the bird's cage, so she got this bright idea to use the vacuum cleaner to clean the cage.

(*Long pause. She shakes her head.*)

It's not what you're thinking. The bird didn't get sucked up. Actually I think it died of a heart attack. All that noise! We found him on the bottom of the cage upside down, his little feet in the air like a cartoon. So I guess I come from a long line of bird killers.

I haven't thought about Speck for about twenty years. Well, last week I had this creepy dream that Speck came to my apartment and somehow thought that I was the nurse that got away!

(*Eerie music comes in under. She begins to relive the dream as if under a spell.*)

In the dream I'm sleeping on my futon, and suddenly I get this distinct feeling that someone's standing over me, watching me sleep. I open my eyes in the half dark and there's this man—just standing there. I'm terrified, but I don't scream. I pretend to be totally calm. "Can I help you?" I ask.

"I didn't forget you," he says.

"Do I know you?"

"The name's Richard," he says. "Call me Richie. You were my one mistake. You hid under the bed, but you won't hide under the bed this time." And he's right. I'M SLEEPING ON A FUTON!! (*pause*) And that's when it hits me: Richard Speck! Of course.

"I think you have the wrong apartment," I say. "But there IS a nurse who lives in apartment 211, right down the hall—"

"I've come back to correct my mistake," he says.

"Richard, you've got the wrong person! For one thing, I'm Chinese American, not Filipino. There is a difference. For another, I'm not a nurse. I don't even have insurance!"

"Look, you fooled me once. You're not gonna fool me again." And before I know it, I hear the click of a pocketknife, and he starts slashing at me, like I'm a painting at a bad art auction. But wherever he cuts me—birdseed pours out instead of blood. I open my mouth to scream and parakeets fly out, hummingbirds, toucans . . . feathers fill my apartment.

(*Pause. Music ends.*)

That's when I wake up.

(*She smiles, delighted with her story.*)

Pretty weird, huh?

Sometimes at night, I walk through the hallway of my building. You might think I'm tempting fate, but the truth is I just want to feel free to walk wherever I want, whenever I want. I don't want to be one of these paranoid urban dwellers with 22 locks on their doors—3 is plenty. It's kind of nice when you walk through the hallway. You hear TV shows, people leaving messages on answering machines, sometimes a typewriter late at night. When I walk past the doors, it reminds me of tuning in a radio station and you hear bits and pieces of things, but never the whole thing.

Those women he killed, they weren't just nurses, you know—they were Asian Americans. Most people don't think about that, but I do. Last May, for Asian American Heritage Month, I made a toast to the nurse that got away—to her courage, her wisdom, and her survival.

I think when Speck comes back in his next life, he'll come back as something harmless. Something gentle. Maybe a parakeet.

(*Woman flashes a mischievous grin.*)

I can hardly wait.

Asian Men on Asian Men: The Attraction

1.

Judy and I don't agree on many things, but two things we do agree on: There aren't enough Asian American male sex symbols; and Bruce Lee's been dead for a long time. And though Judy is only partly Chinese and the rest Euro-something, she is heterosexual after all, so her vote counts. I myself am a gay, Japanese American man who has only recently awakened to the sexiness of other Asian men, and describe myself as a recovering "Hispanoholic"—one who is obsessively attracted to Hispanic men. After a disappointing decade of Latino boyfriends, it's my experience that Asian men are similar to Latino men but with one essential difference: Asian men are stable.

2.

The first time I remember being attracted to another Asian man is while watching the Japanese art film *In the Realm of the Senses* over Christmas break. The leading man is dashing, passionate, clearly fun in bed. And how refreshing—for most of the film he isn't wearing any clothes. What a concept! Aren't Asian men (and Asian American men) born into this world fully dressed, their top shirt buttons securely buttoned? What do their bodies look like freed from the shackles of their clothes? Like fish jumping in a river? Like the ripe melons I squeeze at Treasure Island? After I leave the theater, I make a vow to sleep with an Asian man at some point during the new year.

3.

In some gay Asian circles, the derogatory term *sticky rice* is used to describe Asian men who are attracted to other Asian men. I notice that those who most often use the term are Asian nationals—not Asian American like me. For them, perhaps, loving another Asian man is nothing special, old news—or worse yet, like loving your brother, almost incestuous. But for me, being brought up on the smoke and mirrors of Hollywood, the notion of Asian men being sexy is a radical idea—and therefore appealing, fresh, downright revolutionary.

4.

The first Asian man that I find attractive, who is not in a movie, is Masaru. We meet on New Year's Eve at the Broadway Limited, a bar that you have to climb past an abandoned train car and up a wooden stairway to get to. Masaru is from Japan, but he teaches design in Chicago. He has a neatly trimmed mustache, a mischievous smile, and a stocky build. The first time we sleep together, I notice we like to touch each other and be touched in the same way, and it is at once familiar and strange and wonderful. "Do you like me because I'm so handsome?" he half jokes. "No," I say, "I like you because you're so goofy. So un-Japanese." And yet as un-Japanese as Masaru is, I'm aware he'll never be as American as I am. He is mainly attracted to White men because they are, after all, exotic ones.

5.

I tell Judy about Jason Scott Lee, a charismatic young actor who made his debut in two highly visible movies: *Dragon* and *Map of the Human Heart.* I tell her that the wait may be over. An Asian American male sex symbol may have just been born. Judy remains skeptical. "To truly qualify as a sex symbol, a man must have more than a pretty face and a statuesque physique," she insists. "He must be someone you'd want to have a beer with." I tell her I'd have a beer with Jason Scott Lee any time, any place. That his smile lights up a movie screen. That he's more than a nice package—the contents are intriguing as well. "That's not enough," she insists. "He must be more!"

6.

It's been a couple years since Masaru and I went our separate ways. We now have what must be the perfect relationship: I leave sporadic messages on his answering machine that he never returns; he sends me Christmas cards during the holidays though he knows I'm Buddhist. In my mind, I replay the last conversation we had, drinking our sodas in the abandoned train car after a night of dancing. "We were born under different stars," he said, and slowly walked away. How utterly inscrutable of him! And as I look up at the night sky making room for the coming of yet another new year, I try to remember why we drifted apart. Perhaps the truth is only an Asian American man can understand and appreciate another Asian American man. And what I need to do is find one that I can have a beer with, before another new year comes and goes.

In Response to Executive Order 9066:

All Americans of Japanese Descent
Must Report to Relocation Centers

Dear Sirs:
Of course I'll come. I've packed my galoshes
and three packets of tomato seeds. Denise calls them

love apples. My father says where we're going
they won't grow.

I am a fourteen-year-old girl with bad spelling
and a messy room. If it helps any, I will tell you
I have always felt funny using chopsticks
and my favorite food is hot dogs.
My best friend is a white girl named Denise—
we look at boys together. She sat in front of me
all through grade school because of our names:
O'Connor, Ozawa. I know the back of Denise's head very well.

I tell her she's going bald. She tells me I copy on tests.
We're best friends.

I saw Denise today in Geography class.
She was sitting on the other side of the room.
"You're trying to start a war," she said, "giving secrets
away to the Enemy. Why can't you keep your big
mouth shut?"

I didn't know what to say.
I gave her a packet of tomato seeds
and asked her to plant them for me, told her
when the first tomato ripened
she'd miss me.

Dan Kwong

PERFORMANCE AND INSTALLATION ARTIST

Dan Kwong first became known for his 1989 multimedia solo Secrets of the Samurai Centerfielder, *a disturbingly funny collage using the great American pastime of baseball as a metaphoric springboard into the treacherous undercurrent of racism in America. Many of his subsequent works, including* Tales from the Fractured Tao with Master Nice Guy *(1991),* Monkhood in 3 Easy Lessons *(1993), and* Correspondence of a Dangerous Enemy Alien *(1995), also draw strongly on autobiographical material. Kwong combines penetrating social commentary with a generous sense of humor as he explores subjects such as cultural identity in a mixed-heritage family, parodying the Model Minority Syndrome, surviving child abuse, and Asian male identity. His multimedia performances weave together visual imagery and physical movement around monologues.*

In April 1994, Kwong, one of four invited artists, launched his first internationally commissioned work in London, The Dodo Vaccine, *an installation and performance about HIV/AIDS in the Asian American community; the final version premiered in 1996 in Santa Monica, California.* Samurai Centerfielder Meets the Mad Kabuki Woman, *a collaboration duet with Denise Uyehara, was first performed in 1997. Kwong is working on a screenplay about a baseball team in a Japanese American internment camp during World War II and a new millennium multimedia extravaganza about space travel and the astronaut experience. He has performed at venues across the United States, including in theaters and*

261

at colleges and elementary and high schools. Kwong has received fellowships in performance art from the NEA and the City of Los Angeles Department of Cultural Affairs, among other granting agencies. A native Angeleno and graduate of the School of the Art Institute of Chicago, he has also studied judo, tai chi chuan, aikido, and iaido.

RESPONSE ⟝

My performance work generally begins with personal stories. I often start with memories of significant incidents from life. Oftentimes one remembers specific experiences or episodes in life as vividly as if they were yesterday. Strange details that one has never forgotten. Images, sounds, textures, feelings. A certain kind of presence. Sometimes they are significant, life-shaping events. Sometimes they seem unconnected to anything. And oftentimes these memories carry a particular emotional charge. There is a reason these things have stuck in our memories so clearly and persistently. I think of them as signal flags in the mindscape, signifying "Buried Treasure Here." The emotional charge is generally the treasure map to finding out what makes us tick (assuming you want to know). This exploration and reexamination of the past is a crucial piece in the puzzle of discovering who we are, how we got to be that way, and simultaneously charting the course for our future. The act of telling one's story can be an act of self-empowerment, an act of individual and cultural validation. This is especially true when your particular story is one that has been generally ignored, distorted, and lied about in the culture in which you grew up and live. I certainly did not see my family or my experience reflected in television, movies, books, plays, or any other cultural representations digested during my upbringing.

I am interested in examining social conditioning and its effects on people. In particular, I try to create work that sheds light on the distinction between internalized oppression and reality—that is, the reality of our intelligence, our creativity, our integrity and inherent self-worth, our full range and depth of human emotion and experience; our preciousness as unique, living-breathing-thinking-feeling entities; the reality of our place of belonging in this society and this universe. In performance, I use my own life as a "lab specimen" of human experience. I try to lay out connections between individual, personal experience and the larger social-political landscape and to portray the struggle of the individual to retain human integrity in the face of irrational society and its oppressive structures. I use my own social conditioning as an example, either as member of a "target" group (i.e., person of color/working-class) or as member of an "oppressor" group (i.e., male/heterosexual).

While my work usually approaches subjects from an Asian American perspective, ultimately I write for a general audience. Different sections of any given performance may be addressing non-Asians at one moment, Asian Americans the next. Sometimes this leapfrogs back and forth within a single paragraph. This can be difficult, because I want to retain the poetic freedom to be nonlinear, yet I don't want to lose people. There are always very specific ideas I am trying to communicate, and in doing so, I try to combine the intimately personal with the broadly inclusive.

The writer/performers I most admire and am inspired by are mainly my local peers in Los Angeles. Many of them are friends. I continue to learn different things from each of them, and each inspires me in different ways: Tim Miller, Luis Alfaro,

Amy Hill, Keith Antar Mason, Shishir Kurup, Nobuko Miyamoto, Joan Hotchkis, and many more. The fact that they are my friends and peers gives me a sense of having comrades in a common cause. They are all artists with a very strong social consciousness integral to their work. They are not just interested in entertaining people and having a "career," they are all radicals in their own ways.

In terms of how my performance work aligns with various concepts of "tradition," I think the strongest alignment is with the oral tradition of storytelling, something found in nearly every culture at some point in history, but especially among people of color. I think it can be useful to be aware of this connection with an artistic heritage, to know that one is not some isolated little island floating in time but part of a vast continuum of human experience as an artist. Oral tradition in performance is as "legitimate," "significant," and "important" as any form of expression, regardless of the dominant culture's attitudes and definitions (he said defiantly).

The idea of "authenticity" in relation to Asian American literature has, of course, been championed like no other by Frank Chin, especially in regard to accuracy of folklore and mythology. But authenticity of sensibility? I tend to practice a sensibility of hybridity as an Asian American, one in which different cultures mix and swirl into strange new recombinants, in which influences are short-circuited and one can no longer distinguish just who is in the shadow of whom— as Duke Ellington put it so eloquently. This requires us to look at the world completely fresh and anew.

Yet at the same time, I still appreciate what Frank Chin espouses (however vehemently): that it is important to know where we come from, to know the original sources of our images and mythologies; to know there is an experience that preceded "Asian American," from which we can draw strength and richness. My embrace of this confusing hybridity comes in part from being mixed-heritage Asian (Chinese and Japanese). At this point, I would describe it as an affectionately held confusion of sensibilities, a confusion I consider inherent to the process of sorting out one's life as product of an inherently irrational society. This does not mean I embrace my internalized oppression, but that I accept the feelings that accompany the process of getting free of it. I would consider "irony" to be a strong element of an Asian American sensibility, and there are as many versions of an Asian American sensibility as there are Asian Americans. Each is valid. Dig it.

In my opinion, the most pressing responsibilities/burdens/urgencies facing Asian American writer/performers today are— dumping all that urgent, burdensome responsibility shit, and quick.

I think one of the challenges peculiar to Asian American writer/performer types has to do with trying to express oneself in the face of massive public ignorance of Asian American experience. How do you just say what you want to say, without getting bogged down giving history lessons over and over again? At the same time, if you want people to know what the hell you are talking about, sometimes you gotta give some clues and information about your cultural references. This is a dynamic dance of balance. I'm not interested in explaining everything, but I try to find ways to invite people into my world, however unfamiliar it may seem to them. How can I make it interesting to them and me? This is an essential part of the artist's work. As I teach you who I am, I teach myself who I am. Ooh, that sounds so Zen. (Sarcasm is part of my Asian American sensibility.)

Many of us have gone on and on about the emasculation of Asian men and the exoticization and commodification of Asian women in America. This is part of the basic legacy of anti-Asian racism, intersecting with sexism and class oppression. It is alive and well. Most of us know it in our bones, it is so old and familiar to us. I have tried tackling the male side of this sexual dehumanization in a performance titled *Monkhood in 3 Easy Lessons*. It looks at male identity from a variety of different angles, with a distinctly Asian American perspective: from political emasculation (Japanese American internment) to physical, sexual emasculation (attitudes regarding body image), with various stops in between. I am just beginning to address issues of sexism and homophobia (my own) in performance. I find it humiliating, depressing, and crucially important to be doing this. As well as elucidating our experiences as victims of oppression, we need to acknowledge our own culpability as agents of oppression. Everyone knows both positions, both ends of the stick, in some form or another. Both are hurtful to our humanity.

There are more and more Asian American writer/performers out there doing their own work, speaking their own words, dancing their own forms, and creating their own images. One thing I have greatly appreciated here in Los Angeles is a noticeable lack of unpleasant competitiveness, especially in the performance art realm. We have been remarkably mutually supportive of each other, with a positive sense of sharing resources and information. I am deeply grateful for the sense of community I feel with Asian American performing artists. A new generation of artists is coming up, and petty careerism seems to be relatively at bay in the forefront of creative people here. At least for now. I perceive a great hunger for work that expresses "Asian American experience" in all its glorious permutations, and that hunger is slowly being acknowledged by cultural and educational institutions.

Yet at the same time, I also perceive an atmosphere of hostility toward culture-specific work that seems to be part of a backlash to multiculturalism. This gets confusing. Multiculturalism—the "M" word— that ill-fated concept promising people of color and minorities a strange new world of diversity and equity in the arts, only to wind up being (to paraphrase Guillermo Gómez-Peña) another opportunity for the powers that be to say, "Dance for us, sing for us, show us your colorful costumes. . . . " But little to nothing has changed in the decision-making processes, the power structures; arts organizations and educational institutions are, by and large, still run by Whites. People of color were invited to come out of the kitchen but often brought the heat with them. A lot of White allies got burned. When you encourage people to step out of their oppressed position, you'd better expect there will be some anger, resentment, and rage involved, and fortunately or unfortunately, if it's real, it's going to get messy. And just because you did the encouraging doesn't mean you won't get clobbered by flailing fists of fury. "Who, me racist? But I'm your friend!" People were not prepared for that.

I have witnessed the destruction of friendships and working relationships between people of different backgrounds because members of oppressed groups felt it was open season on anyone identified as part of the oppressor group, viciously attacking their own allies (who indeed carry the virus of oppressor conditioning), attacking their own community, and completely ignoring the basic human connection they had established with each other and their own perpetration of oppressor roles. Most definitely, multiculturalism and culture-specific work got a bad rap from this kind of destructive lashing out. It has been described as "new tribalism" and separatism. Instead, we are all supposed to leap to the conclusion that we are all one people, one human race, and so forth. Essentially, I agree with this point of view, but reaching for "we're all just one people" while ignoring the effects of oppression on specific groups of people is a fundamentally unsound approach. It's fake "healing," the idea of healing so passionately lobbied for after the 1992 riots in Los Angeles, which really meant "Cover it up, forget it, let's get back to the same fucked-up normalcy we're used to."

I don't have a problem with denial!

I think the process of truly aligning with "we're all one people" requires that we do "damage repair" in the areas of our identity that have been the basis for oppression. Otherwise it is like a spine with a badly injured vertebra. Damage to an individual component severely limits and deteriorates the functioning of the whole. And the process of damage repair often means creating *temporary* divisions, that is, affinity groupings, for purposes of safety; for creating a place where you don't have to explain everything and certain things are understood, where one can find relief from the relentless barrage of the "otherness" status with which we are bombarded every day in the dominant culture, where we can first go for unity and support within our groups.

An Asian American Studies department may serve such a role, an Asian American performance festival, an Asian American support group, newspaper, art exhibition, anthology—all these are forms of culture-specific activities that are increasingly under attack as "separatist" and out of line with the concept of the great American melting pot, a melting down of cultural heritage into something palatable to White middle-class America. Some of this backlash against culture-specific phenomena comes from wounded, discouraged, well-meaning White allies, and some of it is just plain ol' Eurocentric White supremacist racism. And some of it also comes from people of colors themselves, who have experienced the "multicultural thang" as another opportunity to be ghettoized by White-run institutions. "It's Asian American heritage month!" It's an old joke that my African American performer friends get the bulk of their work in February (Black History Month), while I'm busy in April or May.

There is an interesting thing happening now (spring 1994) in the entertainment industry. We are on the verge of having an Asian/Asian American–based prime-time situation comedy on the air. Perhaps one could see this as a gross indicator of a shifting cultural landscape. In reality, it is merely a shifting market strategy. Such decisions in a market economy are not driven by motivations of social transformation and human liberation but by where someone can make another buck and more of them. I am not totally rejecting these outlets of popular culture, just trying to acknowledge the built-in limitations to the structure that contains them. Bottom line, it's not about art, not about creativity, not about justice or equality or compassion. It's about turning a hefty profit. Greed is still the basic motivating force.

As curator for an annual Asian Pacific American performance festival in Los Angeles, I occasionally deal with great cynicism, resentment, and distrust from artists I invite to perform. They don't want to be in another ethnic festival. They are sick of being plugged into their little ethnic pigeonholes when it comes to programming. They want to be identified first and foremost as artists, not *Asian* artists.

Their sentiments are completely understandable. It can seem as if artists of color are given a choice between identifying as a unique, distinct human being or identifying oneself as (for example) "Asian-heritage." This is a false choice, one painfully and systematically imposed on us by oppression and then internalized—*we must choose one or the other.* It is a lie. In fact, there is no conflict between identifying oneself by culture, race, gender, sexual orientation, and so forth and being completely human. Oppression and internalized oppression continually set us up to think we are restricted to inhuman choices, irrational choices, stupid choices about who we can or cannot be. I think we get to have it all when we define ourselves and our cultures on our terms.

So in regard to culture-specific phenomena, I believe it *is* significant and important to have focused, concentrated representation of a particular community and its issues, whether it be in a book, performance festival, art exhibition, academic department, or social club. And yet, tokenization and ghettoization must be resisted and avoided rigorously. I think of it like this: "We want to be special—and we want to be just like everyone else." There is no necessary conflict in this. This requires leaders (writers, artists, editors, teachers, administrators, etc.) who continue to fight the ongoing battles against institutionalized racism, sexism, classism and gay oppression; who are willing to go with us into the nasty, messy shit of eliminating our own internalized oppression; and who simultaneously hold out a clear-cut vision of our inherent connection with each other as human beings across all dividing lines.

Song for Grandpa (from *Monkhood in 3 Easy Lessons*)

In my last semester of high school, I discovered marijuana. And I got stoned after school on a regular basis. Looking for escape from the miserable loneliness of my petrified social life, there was no alternative I could see. As with many Asians, for me alcohol produced a mild allergic reaction, turning my face a bright crimson and filling me with a strong desire to sleep. So I got stoned.

Later on I remember hearing a story about my Chinese grandfather Kwong Kwok Hing, born and raised in Los Angeles. Just like me. It seems he had the same after-school routine as me—except he got stoned in the biblical sense, white boys pelting him with rocks as he ran home to Chinatown. No student of martial arts, he. Could've used Bruce Lee. Even Brandon would've been nice to have around.

He was a lonely one too, my Grandpa. I must've been about five years old when he came to live with us. Grandpa was the kind of man who could sit in his room all day long reading newspapers or autobiographies of famous people. Scarcely a sound ever came out of that room except for maybe an occasional soft belch. He'd make himself useful every morning by rousting us up in time for breakfast.

"Ah Danny-ah, you go brush yo teeth an' come eat yo oatmeal!"

This did not make sense to me. I brush my teeth now, and *then* I eat the oatmeal?

"DANNY YOU GO BRUSH YO TEETH RYE NOW!!!"

Grandpa could definitely get in your face. It used to drive me nuts when he pronounced "margarine" with a hard "g":

"Naw Danny-ah, you pass the margarine to Maria."

He was a classic "Chinaman." A thin, wiry, round-shouldered man wearing cardigan sweaters, round horn-rimmed glasses, and a wispy goatee. Kind of looked like Mahatma Gandhi, waking up from a bad dream. Periodically Grandpa would emerge from his bedroom for trips to the kitchen or bathroom, his spindly body barely disturbing the air as he shuffled along in his plain brown leather grandpa-slippers. He would pause along the way to dispense lectures on his latest reading material, his long slender hands (like a spider monkey's, I thought) would point an endlessly bony finger at you, jabbing at some invisible elevator call-button as he talked:

"Naw, dit you know how much money he was making when he was only twenty-fi years of age? Ahhhhh!"

What kind of man was he? Growing up in Los Angeles, Grandpa's English was actually quite well-formed. He was sent back to China for an arranged marriage. Fathered seven children, came right back to America. Almost never lived with his family. Alone for most of his adult life. Believed everything he read.

What was it that lay deepest in this man's heart? Nobody knew and nobody asked. There was an emptiness in his life that I could sense, even as a child. Not the kind of "emptiness" that brings enlightened peace or freedom from worldly desire but an emptiness born of dislocation of the spirit, of bent mental framework, and too many rocks upside the head.

We used to laugh at my Chinese grandfather. My three sisters and I, we found him genuinely amusing. He would sing for us. Yeah, Grandpa used to sing the white pages of the phone book. He would sing *The Golden Book Encyclopedia*—especially Volume Six, "Erosion to Geysers." This is the one my two younger sisters would specifically request because it contained "Fruits," "Flowers," and "Flags"—lots of pretty, colorful illustrations.

"Grandpa! Grandpa! Sing the encyclopedia!"

Little Didi and Poppy would parade into Grandpa's bedroom brandishing Volume Six, in preparation for the Sacred Ritual of the Tome of Knowledge . . .

Yes, America has long marveled at the Oriental People's long tradition of academic achievement. "Those academic whiz-kids—how do they do it?" Well, for the first time, one of our most closely guarded ethnic secrets will be revealed here for you. That's right. You want a Westinghouse Award winner in your school district? Pay close attention, America.

"Ahh. Awright now, Grampa sing for you!"

Before he even uttered a note we'd be giddy with anticipation, because Grandpa was gonna get *weird*. He'd open his mouth and suddenly that wheezy, tentative voice of his transformed into a rich, resonant sound—heavy on vibrato—filling the room:

"Watermelon! Pineapple! Pomegranate! Cherry, Apple, Coconut!"

Then he'd turn to the page of flowers:

"Dandelion! Goldenrod! Poppy, Tulip, Daffodil!"

Then on to the national flags:

"Denmark, Sweden, France! Canada, Peru!"

And no matter what he sang, it always came out like Chinese music.

"Grandpa, Grandpa! Sing the phone book, sing the phone book!"

"Ah. Ah. Awright. Ah, Smith, Mariann! Smith, Martin R.! Smith, Max and Judy! Smith, Monica . . ."

And we laughed. HAAAAA! We laughed so hard we'd be rolling around on the floor. I mean, we practically peed in our pants it was so funny to us. He thinks he's actually singing! Grandpa would laugh too from the contagion of our hysteria, but he sang on unperturbed—even though I wasn't laughing with him, I was laughing *at* him.

Because that's what Grandpa was. Something to be laughed at. A kooky old man. An oddball eccentric. The "yellow sheep" of the family, lost in some sorry-ass world of sensational tabloid delusion. My Grandpa, the Chinese version of Don Knotts!

I believe, no matter how contradictory outward appearances may seem, everyone has something of the heroic inside them. Somewhere in everyone there is courage. There is spirit. There is dignity. A voice that says, "Yes, I am somebody, I am alive and my life has meaning." And looking back I wanted so much to find that something in my Grandpa, my oldest personal link to Kwong men. To find that in us, my family. Because his life looked so pathetically empty through and through. And I thought surely this must reflect on the rest of us Kwong men: my father, my uncles, my cousins and I . . .

"Please—give me something manly to be proud of! Isn't there anything, anywhere in my Chinese blood? Somewhere? Give me something. Father of my father: be a man, be a hero, be a stud, be something, anything, but don't be some wimpy CHINK! Don't be everything they say is weak about us. Don't be everything they say we are. Everything they—say . . . Because when you're young it gets under your skin, Grandpa. Gets under your skin and into your brain. I think you know. It's real gradual and sneaky, it oozes into your consciousness like some kind of slime mold, until one day you suddenly find yourself incredibly uncom-

fortable around any Asians who even remotely resemble the stereotypes. Hating not only them, *but all the ones trying so hard not to be like them.*"

Oh wow man, check it out . . . Check it out—the dude's actually got one of those plastic penholders in his shirt pocket! Oh jeezus! Ha! Hey man! I'm not like these nerd-types, okay?!? Like, I'm a real *guy,* you know. Like, I'm a jock, man. I'm a dude. Uh—I hate math! Yeah, yeah. Uh, I get laid, regular . . . Hey creep—like, stay the fuck away from me, okay? I don't wanna get hit by any shrapnel when they blow your sorry ass away . . .

"Grandpa. What was it like for you when those rocks were bouncing off your head? I'm sorry I couldn't be there to stand by your side, Grandpa. I was a helluva good rock thrower. Arm like a bazooka. I would've fired on those punks so hard and fast they'd never know what hit 'em. We would've fought 'em off, Grandpa. We would've kicked ass and stood tall and proud. Together. I would've helped you find your courage and keep your self-respect. I would've helped you. I would've held you when you felt scared and alone, let you shake and cry. I would've told you how brave and strong you were. And no one would laugh at you, Grandpa. No one would laugh at us. They would treat us right. They would see our humanity, and they would respect us. Because we got nothing to prove to anyone. And we don't take any shit . . . !"

Nah.

My Grandpa lived a strange and lonely life. He died a strange and lonely man. I couldn't find any hero in him. No "right stuff" to make him more studly.

I finished high school. Went to college, art school. Got a degree, got a job. Traveled to Asia. Hong Kong, China, and Japan, every year for five years. Started to explore the unknown, the forgotten. The ignored. Listening to unheard voices of culture, family—and self. Around that time I finally decided to try and deal with my feelings. And I quit getting stoned.

And I remembered my Grandpa's singing. Now, I remember a man who delighted in the sound of his own spirited voice, completely uninhibited. A man who, although he knew we were laughing at him, allowed himself to sing out loud and said "Yes!" to a song—songs that had never been sung before and would never again be repeated. And I thought, "How many could do that very same thing?" How many of us willing to sing *our* song, even in the face of ridicule? Because the simple delight of singing is too great to be denied. Because the moment calls for a song. Because your life is a song. And what a rich and wise lesson from a funny old man.

So I sing for you, Grandpa. In joyous recognition of your spirit, forever in my heart.

Watermelon! Pineapple! Pomegranate! Cherry, apple, coconut . . .

LEFT TO RIGHT: RICHARD EBIHARA, PERRY YUNG, WAYLAND QUINTERO (PHOTO COURTESY SLANT PERFORMANCE GROUP)

Slant

ABOUT THE GROUP ⌐

The Slant Performance Group, comprised of Rick Ebihara, Wayland Quintero, and Perry Yung, is a resident company of La MaMa Experimental Theater Club in New York City. Their energetic performance pieces combine wit, humor, slapstick, and pop music and draw on their training as actors, musicians, dancers, and choreographers. They interweave original live music on electric and acoustic guitar, bass guitar, drums and percussion, bamboo flute, and other instruments with comedic scenes and airborne choreography. Slant premiered in 1995 with their hit musical satire Big Dicks, Asian Men, *in which media and pop images and stereotypes of Asian masculinity are deconstructed and satirized.* Big Dicks, Asian Men *has been per-formed nationally on tour and was the highlight of the 1997 Belgrade Summer Festival in the former Yugoslavia. In 1996, Slant produced a fiery and politically charged musical satire* The Second Coming. *In this work, the trio journey through different periods in Asian American history by way of the recurring reincarnations and experiences of three monks. The piece ends in a grand "sperm" ballet in swim fins and goggles. In their most recent work,* Squeal Like a Pig, an Intergalactic Pop Operetta, *the men of Slant are transformed into otherworldly beings who have crash-landed in the border zone between Mexico and Texas. The three white-faced alien newcomers weave and wobble their way through border patrols, celebrity wanna-bes, con artists, sex-deprived cops, false messiahs, late-night cable-channel jocks, and more, while ex-*

posing absurdities of human behavior. In 1998, Slant released a CD of their two shows Big Dicks, Asian Men *and* The Second Coming, *available at Slant Stuff, c/o Rick Ebihara, 330 Haven Ave, Apt. #3A, New York, NY 10033.*

Richard Ebihara

Richard Ebihara is a third- and fourth-generation Japanese American from Cleveland, Ohio. He has a bachelor's degree in Music Vocal Performance from the Baldwin-Wallace Conservatory of Music. Since moving to New York City in 1991, he has performed with the Pan Asian Repertory Theatre in Cambodia Agonistes *and* Letters from a Student Revolutionary *and with Isaiah Sheffer in Symphony Spaces'* Selected Shorts *series, and he has toured with Theatreworks USA productions of* From Sea to Shining Sea *and* The Velveteen Rabbit. *Ebihara was in Theatre For a New Audience's production of* The New Americans *and has been involved with their New Voices program, which goes to New York City public schools and develops and inspires students to write dramatic plays. He has also danced and toured with Chen and Dancers'* Transparent Hinges *and the Saeko Ichinohe Dance Company's* The Tale of Genji.

RESPONSE

My personal inspiration to perform stems from an early infatuation with pop music, listening to the radio and to my mother's old 45s. While listening to the sounds of Elvis and the Platters, I would envision a drama and sing the song along with them. What's so incredibly rewarding about Slant is that it's us—Rick, Wayland, and Perry—saying what we want to say in a way that's fun for us. When performing other people's work, I've found that the truly rewarding and gratifying stuff comes few and far between, but the stuff that we come up with comes from within, and it's very real for us. I don't know if Slant

has a main message other than to show the world through our eyes—how we, Rick, Wayland, and Perry, see and experience issues that affect us and try to express those things using our collective voices and humor. Even though all three of us are very different Asian Americans, we have found mutual experiences that we feel very strongly about.

I identify myself as a performer, period. But to those who don't know who Rick Ebihara is or who need to have a place to put him, the term *Asian American performer* seems to embody a lot of what I am. I am American of Asian descent who gets up in front of people, and no matter what I do, I'm still going to have an Asian face and speak "American."

All three of us are very different. Wayland is a Filipino American who is also part Japanese, from Hawaii; Perry is Chinese American from San Francisco and Texarkana; and I am Japanese American from Iowa and Cleveland. We are all very different Asian Americans, coming from very different parts of America, and yet all of us have very similar issues about how we as Asian Americans are perceived and approached by non–Asian Americans. If there is an Asian American sensibility, I think that is its root. From the time we were children until now, we've all been placed in the same "Oriental" box. I remember being taunted as a kid with "Chinese, Japanese, dirty knees, look at these," at which the girls would lift their shirts. I remember being confused, and actually still am, as to what this actually meant, and also rather intrigued by the fact that they would expose themselves that way. I also remember being called "Chinaman." Even now, a lot of Hispanics will refer to me as *Chino*, which I gather is a derogatory, all-encompassing term for Asians. I believe that there is a sensibility that all Asian Americans have in dealing with these situations.

Asian American performers have a rising consciousness about how they represent themselves and their race to the public. With the increase in the visibility of Asian Americans in the media, slight as it may be, also comes an expansion in the spectrum and variety of Asian Americans available to the public. We as performers and actors have the opportunity of giving an audience a perspective on Asians and Asian Americans that they may have never seen. We also have the challenge of not falling into negative stereotypes, which are all too familiar. We can resolve the issue of negative stereotyping by choosing not to do these roles or by changing the portrayal.

Asian male roles in general have not been terribly sexy or masculine, because Hollywood believes that only White males personify these characteristics. However, if Hollywood is looking for an exotic they find an Asian, because we're what America sees as exotic. Slant addresses these issues through our satirical humor; we push the issue to the point of ridiculousness and, we hope, show how silly these conventions of masculinity are.

I feel our work has touched a common chord with Asian Americans and non–Asian Americans alike. Even though we may address specifically Asian American issues, they are also issues of being alienated and outside the norm, which everyone can identify with. If anyone can identify with any of the things we address and find them entertaining and thought provoking, we've contributed to mutual understanding.

Wayland Quintero

Wayland Quintero was born in the Philippines in 1964 and raised in Hawaii; he lived and performed in the Bay Area, then moved to New York in 1989. For thirteen years he was a touring member with three modern dance companies—Chen and Dancers, Gus Solomons Dance Company, Tandy Beal and Company—until 1994.

He has choreographed for New York stage productions of Berlin-Berlin *(1994),* In Ten Cities *(1995),* The Ecstasy *(1995), and the musical* Tallahassee *(with director Damien Gray, 1995), and his contemporary, experimental work has been presented in New York at Dance Theater Workshop, St. Mark's Danspace, the Gowanus Arts Exchange, and other venues. He was a 1993 recipient of the Edward and Sally Van Lier Community Trust Fellowship for choreography. As an actor he has performed in Ping Chong's* Deshima *(1995–1996), Jeff Weiss's* Hot Keys *(1995), Xavier Muhammed's* Mumia, the Judgment *(1995), Shigeko Suga's* Sotoba Komachi *(1995), Miguel Pinero's* Short Eyes *(1995), and other productions in New York City. He has just completed work on* Disoriented, *a full-length feature film directed by Francisco Aliwalas. Quintero has a bachelor's degree in political science from the University of Hawaii and a master of fine arts in dance from New York University's Tisch School of the Arts. His dance training includes ballet, modern, jazz, improvisation, Philippine folk, and composition. He has studied acting with Philip Gushee, Joe Anania, Michael Harney, Lenard Petit, and at the Atlantic Theater Company in New York City. He has worked as a volunteer with university and community service organizations in Hawaii and as an English tutor to immigrant Asian children through "Operation Manong" at the University of Hawaii. He is the drummer for the Slant Performance Group.*

RESPONSE

So much of what I do as an artist and as a member of the Slant Performance Group is influenced by my upbringing and training. A number of people and memorable experiences have contributed to my being a performing artist.

While growing up in Hawaii, I was surrounded by retired Filipino plantation laborers, old bachelors who didn't have wives or children of their own but adopted my family into their weekend partying and became my family's extended kin. These old "tatas" cheered me on and threw change at my feet as I sang and danced for them at their parties, from the time I was two until I was about four—my first performing experience and my first fund-raisers. At this age, too, I used to hang onto a house beam in my parents' kitchen and bounce around and dance to the sound of my father scrambling eggs in the morning. He would vary the beating pattern and tempo of the stainless steel fork against a hard plastic bowl. It seems that this morning ritual nurtured my sense of rhythm.

For a couple of weekends every month, from age two up until I was a teenager, my parents would take me to Filipino parties of anywhere between two hundred and eight hundred people, where whole pigs would be roasting on spits, with men and women cooking chicken *adobo, pancit, dinardaraan* (pig blood stew), and other delicacies. Lots of aromatic smells, lots of dancing, and lots of music. At these parties, ensembles of old Filipino guitarists, stand-up bass players, clarinet players, saxophonists, drummers, trumpet players, and other musicians would play traditional and folk music and what they termed American tunes—usually World War II–period Glenn Miller compositions. People admired the players, so it was accepted to be a musician in the Filipino community, and it was totally OK to mix it up with passionate Filipino love songs and festive folk tunes, popular Hawaiian music, as well as waltzes, polkas, tangos, Miller, and Elvis.

My dad used to get up, grab the microphone, and sing with the bands. He was the crooning minister and people loved it, although nobody threw money at him. When I was little, I asked my mother, "How come nobody trow money when Daddy stay singing?" She explained, "Da people probably figah dey already gave at da church for his

show ovah deah." At my father's church masses, my mother would sing her heart out, leading the mostly Filipino congregation along with my father's faithful Jamaican American acolyte, Byron Devonish, who would rock the altar with his booming voice, as I would imagine Koko Taylor or Aretha Franklin might. In this way I grew to love Anglican hymns. As a teenager, I got good enough on keyboards to play the pipe organ for the Sunday service, which taught me more about playing with people.

My first acting gig came when my third-grade Hawaiian-Filipino-Chinese teacher cast me as the lead, playing a Spencer Tracy–like old man dressed in a little powder-blue suit, with little wing tips on my feet. The audience screamed with laughter as I melodramatically struggled to move a big gray papier-mâché boulder for the little Korean girl playing my wife, followed by my inadvertently leaving my pathetic little red clip-on tie on this enormous boulder before I exited and then, in a panic, rushing back onstage to retrieve this tie, miraculously stuck to the rock, but then suddenly and accidentally knocking the boulder, which ran over the little girl dressed in a white *Little House on the Prairie* dress, who was in the middle of passionately delivering her "Hark! Hark! Spring is here!" daisy-picking monologue—my first taste of stage comedy.

In the sixth grade, my fifty-five-year-old Scandinavian teacher, originally from Kansas, cast me in a May Day play as King Kamehameha the Great. She constructed an oversized Hawaiian-replica red helmet, built to a large, protruding shape like a huge tidal wave at its peak, which I wore along with an oversized fake-feather red-and-yellow plastic floor-length cape tied around my neck and red cotton gym shorts with my first name printed on the front, as was the practice with our official school gym shorts in those days. My job as King Kamehameha? To stride in with my spear-bearing warriors and then to sit up on a gymnasium stage, on a fan-shaped bamboo chair big enough to accommodate a small sumo wrestler, in front of the whole school—"Proudly! Like John Wayne would!" admonished my well-meaning teacher. Looking at the photos, my parents and I figured out that I was probably cast for the part because I was the chubbiest and darkest kid among my Caucasian, Hawaiian, Japanese, Chinese, and Portuguese classmates. Not only that, but since I went to an all-boys school at the time, the thinnest and fairest were cast as faux hula maidens—my first experience in typecasting and experimental theater.

Other inspirations and influences are my acting, dance, and music teachers; directors I worked with; and dance companies I toured with. There were media and pop culture figures I especially paid attention to while I was growing up. Muhammad Ali was a favorite. I admired his unique eloquence, his intelligence, defiance, resilience, humor, and seeming fearlessness. I loved the music of Elton John, Led Zeppelin, Creedence Clearwater Revival; imitated the singing of Maurice White of Earth, Wind, and Fire; and dressed up like the Stylistics. Richard Pryor nailed things perfectly, with candor and incisiveness, in his stand-up work. Paraphrasing the line the first time I heard him say it in one of his shows: "So when I landed in Africa and got off the plane, I realized, there are no niggers here!" Bang! The line stuck with me as a kid and came back to me again in the summer of 1996, when I was backpacking through Malaysia. While watching a puppet show along with hundreds of proud Malaysians, it hit me: "Check it out. There are no gooks in Asia."

Here in America, I could never figure out why a Caucasian actor who seemed to look inebriated most of the time was cast as

the Chinese martial monk in the TV series *Kung Fu.* Before I ever heard the story of how and why Bruce Lee never got the part, I thought that there had to be lots of Asian actors—even the actor playing the Chinese cook Hop-Sing in *Bonanza*—who could have executed the fight moves better than "Grasshappah." I used to tell my friends: "Brah, da guy doesn't even look hapa-haole!"

I used to wonder from time to time how other actors deal with choices of auditioning for a role in something like *Miss Saigon,* where one-dimensional character images of Asian men as maniacs, crazy cult-worshiping commies, and weasely pimps are reinforced. I suppose some people do it for the money, experience, and perceived exposure. We all make our own deals.

Fortunately, there seems to be a growing presence of fresh work written by Asian Americans, performed by Asian Americans, and attractive to a wide range of audience members. With Slant, the three of us have had the opportunity to write, compose, choreograph, and perform our own material, with productions like the immensely popular *Big Dicks, Asian Men* (1995), the fiery and politically charged *The Second Coming* (1996), and our third musical satire premiering in January 1998, *Squeal Like a Pig, an Intergalactic Pop Operetta,* which, from observing audience reactions to scene previews, promises to be raucous and surreal and is a new direction in our work within our style of musical satire. The three of us like to keep it fresh and are willing to take risks and try different things.

Many times at our Q & A sessions after performance, we get questions about how we do what we do. Rick, Perry, and I are from three different regions of the United States, and each of us brings a different background in upbringing, training, and experience to the work. We work heavily through collaboration, with each of us bringing in and trying out new ideas, having differences of opinions, fun, flexibility, fun, commitment to the work and the group, fun, and having the support and encouragement of Ellen Stewart and her staff at the La MaMa Experimental Theater, our artistic home base. There are also many other people who continue to support us with their time, attendance, enthusiasm, and generosity.

Recently, while I was on vacation in Hawaii, a director friend asked me to speak to his group of high school and college actors and to answer questions they might have. Asked for suggestions by this young group about a life in the performing arts, I listed the following: Get some training in acting, movement, voice, and music. Practice often, but don't get stuck on technique. Learn an instrument. Travel and stay open to experiences and opportunities. Leave home, at least for a while. Take a few detours as they come. Accept that it is all a crap shoot. Don't get too serious. Avoid buying into a "starving artist" image. Get a job; or get a sugar daddy or sugar mama. Use lots of humor. Don't fuck anybody over. Sleep well, but get out of bed. Eat healthy. Get E-mail. Get a credit card or two. Use the cards. Minimize TV viewing. Do some volunteer work in a community at some point in your life. Get a massage every now and then. Give a massage. Return phone calls. Go and watch all kinds of shows. Go to museums and exhibits. Write, compose, choreograph, perform your own work, or get others to do it. And get some surf time in.

One student then asked if we would ever let other people do *Big Dicks, Asian Men*. I said, "Sure! As long as all three Asian American men are between their late twenties and their mid-thirties and are of at least three different Asian backgrounds. They all have to be skilled enough to act a variety of comedic and dramatic character roles, have a good sense of comic timing, and be able to dance ballet, modern, and jazz. One guy has to know how to play electric and acoustic guitar, be able to sing lead, and have a back strong enough to strap on a big, black, four-foot-long penis prop. Another guy has to be able to play bass and bamboo flute, sing backup harmonies, and be proud to strap on a midsize three-foot-long tanned penis. The third guy has to be able to sing backup harmonies and play drums and be willing to strap on a one-and-half-foot long curved white penis."

Perry Yung

Perry Yung was born in Oakland, California, in 1964 and spent his formative adolescent years in Texarkana, Texas, in the archetypal Chinese restaurant in the middle of nowhere. He received his bachelor of arts degree from San Francisco State University, with an emphasis in painting and printmaking. Since then, he has been a performer throughout the United States and on the international festival stages of Cairo, Johannesburg, Istanbul, Vienna, Milan, Belgrade, Spoleto, Dubrovnick, and Seoul. Perry is a member of La MaMa Experimental Theater Club's Great Jones Repertory Group.

RESPONSE

In 1977, when I was thirteen years old, my older brothers Peter and Paul took me to see a Kiss concert. It was the most fantastical thing I had ever witnessed. After a blazing electric bass guitar solo, Gene Simmons, in full makeup and dripping in theatrical blood, held a torch up and began to spit fire as if he were a fire-breathing dragon. The audience was in a screaming frenzy, and I wanted some of that power. Moments later, the lead singer, Paul Stanley, announced that Elvis—the king of rock and roll—had died and dedicated their hit song "I Want to Rock-n-Roll All Night" to him. Afterward, as we drove away from the concert hall, Peter turned on the radio and we heard it announced again and again: "The King is dead . . . Elvis Presley died in Las Vegas tonight . . . the King is dead." In that moment, my life changed forever. The death of one meant the birth of another. I had to become a rock star. A week later, I bought my first guitar—a Fender Stratocaster. Although I've given up that dream these days, I'd still like to think that my performance pieces are imbued with the energy of a rock concert. On good nights I sometimes leave my body, and if I can just take some of the audience with me, then it all becomes worth it. These days, I'm still searching for my fire-breathing character, one that spits fire onto the celluloid Asian face of Hollywood.

Slant is a performance group that surfs the fine "pipeline" between race and culture, between the condition of the Other and the dominant society. The Asian American references in our work create a conceptual framework that enables us to dive into a sea of cultural assumptions in search of universal truths. When we were invited to perform *Big Dicks, Asian Men* at the 1997 Belgrade Summer Festival in Yugoslavia, the Serbo-Croatian press translated the name of our piece into *Big Fire Hoses, Asian Men*. After our performance, many Serbians approached us and expressed how much they identified with our show, that they know what it is like to be used and misused by the media, to be misportrayed. "We are Asian, we are Slant!" exclaimed the producer, Ivana Vujic. "The media and news say that we are the bad ones, the rapists . . . the enemy; we are alike!" Working as a member of La MaMa Experimental Theater Club's residency group in New York City has shown me that society and culture are a merely a coat covering humanity; if we want to question and expose, we must get under the skin. Slant seeks to tell the truth across universal boundaries.

In a dream, I direct an opera: *Imagine the Purple Pyramid Dragon*. The set is by I. M. Pei, the choreography by Bruce Lee, the music by Jimi Hendrix, and the libretto by John Lennon. The leads are played by Anna May Wong and me. And let me tell you, she ain't no Cho Cho San.

Rick Ebihara and I were debating heatedly once about whether there is an authentic Asian American sensibility or not. After a few beers, we found that he, a fourth-generation Japanese American born in Davenport, Iowa, and I, a first-generation Chinese American born in the Bay Area and raised in Texarkana, Texas, had only two things in common: we both had owned and driven Camaros at one time in our lives and both our dads pumped Elvis into our living rooms daily. With Wayland Quintero, who is Filipino Japanese from Hawaii, I share the love of surfing—he on the waves of Waikiki and I on the sidewalks of Northern California. If there is an authentic Asian American sensibility, then I would say that it is close to that of an authentic American sensibility.

I got a call from my freelance agent one day. He asks, "I know you're young, but can you play a Yan Can Cook type?" Apparently, *Saturday Night Live* wanted to spoof his show and, judging from what they've been churning out these days, it already reeked of bad chop suey. "Oh come on, Michael, you know I'm too young and besides, my pony tail?" "Oh, what the heck," he says, "I thought I'd just give you a try. . . . Oh, by the way, I'm finally getting somewhere with *Kung Fu, the Legend Continues*. I think they're gonna wanna see ya soon. No kidding, talk to ya soon kid." The idea of spoofing Martin Yan's show would only work if it were done by a group like Slant.

The telephone call from Michael inspired our prison cooking sitcom, "The Le Chang Brothers' Cajun Cuisine Show." The idea is that in the future, descendants of the Golden Venture internees, born in captivity in a Louisiana internment camp, land a television deal where they share their cooking innovations, such as General Tso's Crayfish Etoufee and Sweet and Sour Gator Claws, live from prison. Rick wrote the scene to the tune of a rap song, and when we premiered it at La MaMa in December 1996, the audience went along with our joke as they were put into the role of the television studio audience, laughing and applauding every time we enacted a Martin Yan shtick. At the end, they cheered when the three Le Chang brothers froze in position after their cleaver-wok dance. Now, this is the turning point of *The Second Coming*. I deliver the lines of the technical director of the show: "Cut. It's a take. Great work guys, same time tomorrow." As the lights turn a cold blue, we march off chain-gang style, back to our cells. Sometimes the audience would continue the applause and the laughter would grow. Sometimes, the laughter and cheers would stop cold, in a realization that this really isn't all that funny: three men born in captivity, selling their ethnic secrets through an institutionalized lens that confines them to a cell of exoticism, this lens being the audience. In the end, the only thing of value is the formula to their Le Chang Brothers' Secret Asian Cajun Sauce.

Late one night my telephone went off like the bang of a gun. My Black, I mean African American, friend Darren screams hysterically into my receiver, "I'm gonna jump man! I'm jumpin . . . I'm gonna jump off the Brooklyn Bridge!" "What the hell are you talkin bout man?" A silence ensues. "I lost my erection tonight . . . I mean I couldn't get it up." I said, "You? A young Black man? Jump, it's over Holmes, you may as well jump." "This ain't funny, man . . . you ain't funny. You don't understand, I can't be impotent!" As Darren went on rambling, I thought to myself, "Oh, but I do understand." It happened to me once—well, maybe twice—but it wasn't a big deal to me, although my girlfriend did cause me some grief about it at the

time, but that's a whole other story. I was up and ready to go but she just kept on talking, "Blah, blah, blah." Anyway, back to Darren. Fortunately for him it was only a momentary dysfunction. He called the next morning excitedly to report a morning erection. "It's fine, it's fine, I'm up. Must've been performance anxiety." I wonder what's worse, a Black man with a small penis wondering if he'll ever measure up, or an Asian man with a large penis walking around with something to prove. Or maybe it's this system that keeps people of color and women down. At the end of my monologue in *Big Dicks,* my tourist character describes this situation to his Italian lover after hearing a racist remark while vacationing in Venice, Italy. "You see, Valentina, in America we talk about penis size all the time and how our sexuality is measured by the size of it. Black men have the biggest and Asian men have the smallest. And everyone else is safely in between." Besides, I told her of a saying I once heard from a wise old Black man, Richard Pryor, who said, "Take a look at China, they got one point two billion people . . . someone over there is doin some serious fuckin'!" Blackout.

My favorite response came from a senior citizen who, during a matinee, laughed so hard that he had to get up and pee.

My advice to anyone interested in pursuing a career in the performing arts is "Don't do it. Get into something that makes money then write a tax-deductible check to the Slant Performance Group and send it to P.O. Box 1424 New York, NY 10013." No, seriously, if you can't possibly be happy doing something else, and you've asked yourself all the soul-searching questions, such as "Will I be content ordering burgers instead of a juicy ribeye . . . all the time," then follow your bliss. Joseph Campbell is right. If lightning struck me now, I'd die with a smile on my face that says, "I did it my way."

~~~~~~

No Menus Please (From *Big Dicks, Asian Men*)

EDITOR'S NOTE: Three adult men fold themselves into angles onto tricycles built for two-year-olds and ride in circles on the stage—a visual metaphor for constraint. As they make food deliveries, their promotional material is rejected as litter.

(*Begins with chanting—Hooh-hah, Hooh-hah, etc.*)

DELIVERYMAN # 1
Through crowds of people I ride my bike,
Thousands are eating Chinese tonight,
Free delivery is my life, Send my money back to my wife,
To feed my family went overseas,
Only to read no menus please,
No menus, No menus please.

DELIVERYMAN #2
My tuition's due I don't get a break,
How much can I save how long will it take,
Two dollar tips are all that I get, Midterms are soon have to study yet,
I'm failing intro to Cantonese,
I should have took French,
No menus, No menus please. (*repeat*)

(*All chant*)
Soy sauce, and hot sauce, and duck sauce, Hooh!
Lobster sauce, fish sauce, and garlic sauce, Hooh!
White sauce, and brown sauce, and red sauce, Hooh!
Don't matter what color as long as it's good!

DELIVERYMAN #3
I can't stand this goddamn bike,
I'd rather be boning my girl tonight,
Dad says the restaurant needs family, But handing out menus is not for me,
It's for the family I shiver and freeze,
But inside I scream no menus please,
No menus, No menus please. (*repeat*)

(*BREAK/ Furious cycling around into a crash and slow motion fall*)

(*All*)
Through snow and rain and gloom of night,
We bring you your beef and chicken delight,
Nothing is ever quite as it seems. We litter your halls with our family dreams.

Delivery is our opportunity,
But all that we see is No Menus Please,
No menus, No menus please. (*repeat*)

~~~~~~

Diary of a Paper Son (from *The Second Coming*)

(*Beat Poem performed with an electric bass.*)

I've been on this vessel for one week now
the journey west to the gold mountain may take as long as forty days
if the winds are on our side
I can hardly move in here
I'm beginning to find it difficult to breathe.
On the twentieth day of the tenth month,
the winter storm allowed us a bath on deck tonight
the cold cold rain did what it could to wash the vomit
off our clothing
on our return we found they had swept the feces from where we are kept
in the bowels of the ship.
On the second day of the eleventh month,
there's more room to move now
as two more of my fellow countrymen have died
their bodies tossed overboard
perhaps it's a better fate that the sharks should have them
for I am becoming weak from the soup of rotten vegetables.
On the twentieth day of the eleventh month,
my head is filled thick with death and decay
as the bones of my brothers lie at the bottom of the Pacific Ocean
the stench is unbearable
even the rats won't come down here no more
or perhaps we've eaten them all.
On the twenty fifth day of the twelfth month,
a light cuts through the hull like a jagged sword
the gwei lo screams in his devil's tongue
YOU ARE AT THE GATE OF THE GOLD MOUNTAIN!
AT THE ISLAND CALLED ANGEL WHERE YOU SHALL WAIT YOUR ENTRY
ANGEL ISLAND!

(*bass solo*)
On the third day of the tenth month,

I've been on this rock now for nine moons
and I can still hope that one day
I can walk the gold mountain and pocket the gold I find
but day after day the immigration interrogation officers
question me on my family, my father, my history
YOU ARE A PAPER SON, AREN'T YOU!
YOU ARE TRYING TO BUY YOUR WAY INTO AMERICA, AREN'T YOU!
And what would you do if we allowed you on the gold mountain
how will you live
would you take the job of an american?

Some have been on this rock longer than i
some have managed to escape
some have taken their lives
rather than risk the hell journey back
while others simply died on this rock
called angel
this rock called ellis
this rock not called
plymouth.

Christine Choy

FILMMAKER

Christine Choy is an Academy Award–nominated filmmaker and recipient of the 1997 Sundance Award for Best Cinematography in a Documentary Feature. Born in Shanghai, People's Republic of China, Choy is the child of a Korean father and a Mongolian mother. She came to the United States in 1967 as a high school student, later attending Manhattanville College of Sacred Hearts, Maryville College, and Washington University in St. Louis. She has a bachelor's degree in architecture from Princeton and a master of arts degree in urban planning from Columbia.

A pioneer filmmaker in the Asian American community, Choy has been working in cinema since 1972. As a producer, director, and cinematographer, she has completed fifty-two films, including Teach Our Children *(1974)*; From Spikes to Spindles *(1976)*, Inside Women Inside *(1978)*, To Love Honor and Obey *(1980)*, Bittersweet Survival *(1981)*, Mississippi Triangle *(1982)*, Namibia: Independence Now *(1984)*, Permanent Wave *(1986)*, Who Killed Vincent Chin? *(1988)*, Monkey King Looks West *(1989)*, The Best Hotel on Skid Row *(1990)*, Korea: Homes Apart *(1991)*, Jennifer's in Jail *(1992)*, Sa-I-Gu *(1993)*, Out in Silence *(1994)*, Not a Simple Story *(1994)*, In the Name of the Emperor *(1995)*, Ain't Nothing but a She Thing *(1996)*, and A Shot Heard 'Round the World *(1997)*.

A founder of Third World Newsreel, Choy is presently executive director of Film News Now Foundation and a board member of the Associa-

tion of Independent Video and Filmmakers and the National Asian American Telecommunications Association. Among her numerous international awards are a Peabody for Excellence in Broadcast Journalism and fellowships from Guggenheim, Mellon, Rockefeller, and the American Film Institute. Currently, Choy is an associate fellow at Yale University and chair of the Institute of Graduate Film and Television at New York University.

RESPONSE ↩

I create my work because I feel close to my subjects and their lives. I make films not only to present my insights but also to record an Asian American history while it's being unfolded. I bring the perspective of a Chinese, a Korean (I'm half of each), an immigrant, a woman of color, a mother, and a filmmaker to my work. As an immigrant, I am interested in strangers on this shore and strangers in this society. I like to address women's concerns in this repressive, male-dominated environment. I have a rebellious instinct that only gets stronger. I'm a real loudmouth. I want to shake things up, point things out, but I also never want to idealize anyone or try to impose a mythic importance on any one person or cause.

I create for my mother, because she is not a very bright person but she has a big heart. She represents the type of audience I'd like to reach. She loves soaps and romantic movies from the 1950s. She has talents but never had an opportunity to express them, apart from her knitting. I create the kind of work my mother never had the opportunity to see, work that relates to her life experience. I want to switch her brain from melodrama to reality, show her her own experience.

Which filmmakers do I most admire? I look up to individuals not for their success or financial gain. The people whom I respect and admire are those who have a strong sense of humanity, who (unlike myself!) are humble and quiet-speaking, and who create a body of work that influences thoughts and emotions. Charles Burnett is one of these individuals who has integrity, creating works from his heart and soul. His filmic expressions are from his roots—Mississippi, L.A.—and yet very universal. He is one of the few artists able to be successful in the industry and yet retain his cool and his true vision.

I admire Ang Lee for his soul, brains, and creative juice; Martin Scorsese for his generosity toward the independent film community and for preserving the important work in the field; Spike Lee for his fierce fight in the filmic language and for his strong African American ideology.

Shit, all these men. I'd better mention women. I respect Jane Campion for not showing the brutality of someone's hand being chopped off in *The Piano*. I respect Lourdes Portillo for her ceaseless passion, exquisite approach, and strong political stand in documenting Latin American stories. I respect Yvonne Rainier for her daring experimentation in filmmaking and her honesty about her menopausal experience.

Nevertheless, I respect only those who give back to the community. If they don't, regardless of how great filmmakers they are, they're on my shit list.

How do I see myself? I see myself as an Asian American, American, and person of color, as well as third world, immigrant, feminist, and single, working mother. These distinctions are meaningful simply because they are how the society defines me, and I am part of society. The more labels, the better it gets. I feel sorry for WASPs who don't have such a colorful personality. The whole term *Asian American* is very misleading, and I wish I could come up with a better one. The Asian population in the United States is a complex group of people, with their distinctly different histories, cultures, languages, and looks. We don't believe in the same religion, we have vastly different philosophies. Some eat their rice with chopsticks, some with their hands, and some even imitate the West by using forks and knives. Therefore, to use a general-term "authentic" Asian American sensibility is wrong. The sensibility that we do share is not one that springs from our own cultures but from our shared experience of having our cultures misunderstood and lumped together. This is expressed in titles such as *Bamboo Baby, Yellow Chinaman's Scream, Sayonara, The World of Suzie Wong, Year of the Dragon,* or *A Little Man's Dream,* which are about the presiding culture's failure to make important distinctions.

Apart from Amy Tan's *The Joy Luck Club* and Louis Chu's *Eat a Bowl of Tea*—both books made into movies by Wayne Wang—I can't think of any Asian American literature directed by Asian American filmmakers that has made it onto the big screen in the United States. (Oliver Stone's *Heaven and Earth* doesn't count! Neither does David Henry Hwang's *Golden Gate.*) Perhaps Wayne Wang should stop making movies, start a publishing company, and hire a bunch of Asian directors for their interpretation of the material. It would be much more exciting than making *Joy Luck Club 2.*

What are the most pressing burdens/urgencies/responsibilities facing Asian American filmmakers today? Money!!! Distribution. If you make a film with a subtitle, you are fucked the rest of your life. Your film doesn't get acceptance unless it's acclaimed by the established press, the Sundance Film Festival—without that, you're ignored. The Asian population goes to see Asian films praised by non-Asians. Where are all the Asian critics? Get out of the damn closet, we need you. NAATA (National Asian American Telecommunications Association) has done a hell of a job of sponsoring film festivals, creating network and distribution. Unfortunately, through lack of funds, their catalog looks like shit. Compare it to the catalog put out by Miramax.

Are there risks and challenges peculiar to Asian American filmmakers? Yes, we are being ghettoized by the funders. We can make films about Asian Americans, but we can't make films about Whites, especially the rich Whites. At the same time, very few Asian American establishments are willing to finance films that deal with our community, not to mention films that don't. The Asian establishment is cautious about its position in the political and economic power structure in America, and they don't want to rock the boat. I bet it's going to change. It's going to take a while, but when their sons and daughters get caught shoplifting or are thrown out of school or want to make films, the experience may shake them up a bit. In fact, more and more Asian young people are applying to film schools—NYU, Columbia, UCLA, USC, American Film Institute, Cal Arts, and so on. Are they talented? Do they have anything to say? I'm not sure. There are so few Asian professors in those institutions. Who is going to validate their creativity? Who is going to understand their sensibility? Who is going to nurture them when they get off the line? Who is going to understand their wacky sense of humor or their depressing dysfunctional family stories?

I don't worry about confronting stereotypes in my work; I confront them in my own life, where I can really enjoy the fight. I trust that this battle—and my victories and my failures—appears in the work in its own way. The Asian male has been depicted as having a big brain with small equipment—that's why we don't see Asian male sportscasters.

Lily Chin, Vincent Chin's mother. Film still from Who Killed Vincent Chin? *by Christine Choy and Renee Tajima-Peña (16mm, color; Film News Now Foundation and WTVS/Detroit, 1988).*

Roger Ebens, killer of Vincent Chin. Film still from Who Killed Vincent Chin?

On the other hand, we have the roles played by Brandon Lee, Russell Wong, and Jackie Chan—they jump, contort their bodies, but they cannot speak a coherent sentence. Then there's the Asian female: classified as whores, submissive wives, endlessly bowing to the establishment—they don't have the brains, the equipment, they have nothing. To overcome this unbalanced image of masculinity and femininity, I think we should step forward following the pattern of a Madonna or a Howard Stern—speak louder than ever, and outrageously. Think of something totally grotesque: arrive in the classroom with a fig leaf on to cover your dingdong, make a seaweed hairdo, use a profanity when you address authority. Maybe this will wake a few people up. Films on Maya Lin, I. M. Pei, and Yo Yo Ma bore me and make us all look like fucking geniuses. They should make a film about a loser like Chris Choy for once. Pat yourself on your own back when no one is praising you.

I'm not married, forever single, always looking, looking, looking for the perfect companion to arrive—which is a dream. I sneak into the cracks between my daily required tasks to make my films. I challenge institutional sexism in the person of those in positions above me. I used to fight with anger, but now I fight with cunning. I document all questionable behavior on paper and then *wap*, I sock it to them.

I try to create my life with people who truly believe in the same principle and never mix my personal and my professional life. I believe in showing my own weakness and changing it, willingly and openly. I refuse to join any memberships, clubs, church organizations, study groups, isms: I try to keep my life and my mind as open, flexible, and experimental as possible.

Is this a particularly receptive moment for Asian American filmmakers? *Receptive* is a relative term. Today, with the growing economic power and population of Asia, Asian filmmakers are having an easier time than when I started in 1972 (the end of the Vietnam War)—especially if we make films that don't offend the establishment. Unfortunately, we are still "goody two-shoes"—we don't have the guts to challenge those who have oppressed and continue to oppress us. What a mess.

In Japan, the creative energy is dead. After World War II, Japan adopted so much Westernization in its culture that it lost its own identity. In the three Chinas (People's Republic, Hong Kong, Taiwan), however, there is so much exciting film emerging from the confusion and conflict and uncertainty about the future. Vietnam is gradually making headway; so is the Philippines. There is nothing, however, coming out of Singapore, Burma, Thailand, because it's all repressive regimes and severe censorship. In Korea, the young filmmakers are beginning to address the issue of the North/South division, as well as daring to criticize Japan's colonization. India makes a massive amount of films, mainly senseless melodramatic musicals, but there is definitely some interesting energy emerging.

Why are the majority of visible filmmakers in the United States from immigrant populations? Why are the films much stronger and more original when the country is in conflict, rather than in uniformity? Filmmakers are visionaries. They are able to predict what a society is moving toward, able to grasp subtleties in unseen sectors of the world, and able to push ideology or point of view by synthesizing the conflicts into a harmonious presentation. If artists are too comfortable, too sure of what they do, then their work becomes mundane or imitative. The true artists are the ones who are willing to challenge what has been unseen, unfelt, unthought.

How would I characterize the reception of my work? I would say the majority of my work has been shown on TV or in film festivals, and because it's gone through that screening process beforehand, you're pretty much assured that you step up on that podium before a satisfied audience. The reception for those films has been polite, good, but other films get neglected in that process. Some films can be appreciated only by a small group of individuals who care about a particular concern. Such films are made about battered women, women in prisons, AIDS and HIV.

My weakness is that I work so urgently, from conception to completion, and I tend to work on too many projects at the same time and don't have the luxury of concentrating on one particular project. So at times it can be sloppy. And I get frustrated and I yell for help—I bring in expertise to fix the problem, and it costs me a fortune. I need to spend more time in preproduction, and it's unfortunate that funders aren't wise enough to recognize the importance of this stage. Today, 10 percent of a budget is available for preproduction, 40 percent for production, 30 percent for postproduction, 10 percent for audience development, 10 percent for distribution, and 0 percent for promotion. With that breakdown, it's hard to get your money back.

Should Asian American filmmakers be a voice of the community or an individual voice? I think they should be both. The individual should voice personal concerns but not be a pompous, self-loving Leo type—day in day out just checking for pimples on his or her nose and worrying what other people are going to think. If filmmakers can situate their individual experiences in the context of universal compassions, I think that's cool. Then you have the busybodies, who assume that they know everyone's business, make

epic films that cover birth to grave, lump all nationalities into one experience, mingle the sexes, and pretend they are the voice of the Villages. That's why I never read the *Village Voice,* because there's something unethical about that kind of pompous assumption that you can know so much about so much experience.

Is the filmmaker who has achieved national recognition by definition one who has "sold out"? When you get national recognition I think you should follow Robert Frank's footsteps. After his national and international exhibit at the National Gallery in Washington, D.C., he decided to stop being a photographer. He put a nail through his negatives and wrapped them up with chicken wires, stuck them on the wall, and shot darts at them. So I can't speak for others, but if I had his stature and had received such national recognition—still a long way to go—I would string all my awards, plaques, lucite delibobs, and make them into a minicemetery with all the worst reviews attached to them—a Choy-a-Choy film theme park.

Selling out is everybody's innate, genetic, embedded human nature. To despise the sellout and pretend you are someone above and beyond is full of shit. I hope the successful filmmakers I know do sell out, so when I pick up a phone and dial a number they will be able to help me. Woody Allen once said: Hollywood is a dog-eat-dog world—when one dog calls another dog, the other dog refuses to respond. So as long as everybody sells out, the few who haven't can actually receive the phone call where we will praise them further. But when you fail, after you have sold out, after your name has been mud, after your wife or husband or loved one has left you—after you can't even walk your dogs to the veterinarian—you can always call me, because I remember the support you gave me when I was down and under.

Renee Tajima-Peña

FILMMAKER

Born in Chicago and reared in Altadena, California, Renee Tajima-Peña graduated from Harvard-Radcliffe, where she was chairperson of the United Front Against Apartheid and majored in East Asian Studies and sociology. Tajima-Peña has long been active as a chronicler of the Asian American scene on film. Beginning in collaboration with Chris Choy, she has written or produced more than a dozen documentary films, including the Academy Award nominee Who Killed Vincent Chin? *(1998) as well as* Yellow Tale Blues *(1990),* The Best Hotel on Skid Row *(1990), and* Jennifer's in Jail *(1992). Her latest film, a feature-length documentary,* My America . . . or Honk if You Love Buddha *(1997), represents five years on the road capturing the lives of Asian Americans all over the nation. Tajima-Peña has held a number of other po-*
sitions: film critic for the Village Voice, *editor of* Bridge: Asian American Perspectives, *cultural commentator for National Public Radio, associate editor of the* Independent Film and Video Monthly, *and founding director of the Asian American International Film Festival in 1980. Her essays have been published in the anthologies* Moving the Image, Making Waves, *and* Mapping Multiculturalism.

RESPONSE

I started out as an activist at a young age: read *The Autobiography of Malcolm X* when I was ten, considered myself a cultural nationalist in junior high. I had all of these intense beliefs, convictions about race, justice, equality.

287

But I couldn't stand it when someone disagreed with me. So I figured I could make a movie that said what I wanted to say, and no one could talk back to it. Basically, I wanted to make propaganda. That all changed when I actually started making films. I became intrigued by the gray areas, by the moral and ideological unanswerables—especially in making *Who Killed Vincent Chin?* Was it a barroom brawl or a racial attack? How is legal evidence—the facts—interpreted and colored when viewed through the prism of race? I also became addicted to the dialogue—traveling with my films, confronting and being confronted by audiences. It gives the filmmaking process a continuity. For example, I finished *My America . . . or Honk if You Love Buddha* (coproduced by Quynh Thai) a year ago (1997), but the process is still ongoing because I'm traveling with the film, getting feedback, talking with audiences about the idea of Asian America. Inevitably, the discussion generated from these screenings will feed my next film. What are Americans thinking about? What are we going to be dealing with two, three, five years down the road?

In both the production and distribution of my films, I've gone to places I could never have access to otherwise: invited into people's homes, into their lives, into their memories. It's taken me to every corner of America—which is really like one endless, edgy theme park. A biker bar on the Black Warrior River in Alabama. A Chinese debutante ball at the Disneyland Hotel. Documentary filmmaking gives me a ticket to ride. In particular. it's gotten me to places off-limits for me as a woman—places I always longed for but was never brave or stupid enough to pursue, all those male type adventures like hitchhiking across country, doing a Bukowski number writing poetry from an SRO on Skid Row.

For example, we were recently visiting Veracruz, Mexico, with a group of friends. In the middle of the night, one of the wives called our room—her husband had just gone out to the bars and strip joints and she wanted my husband, Armando, to find him and make sure he was all right. Now, I would have loved to go out prowling around the Veracruz night in search of this errant husband. We were staying right between the zocalo, the downtown square known for the *danzon,* and the Veracruz port. There had to be some incredible characters from all over the globe haunting these places. For my husband it was a big pain in the ass, getting out of bed in the middle of the night to case out the bars. He's a guy—he's seen everything, he has few of the boundaries I have as a woman. But for me, it would have been a foray into a whole new world—which, if I had a camera in hand, could give me a reason for being there as well as a protective armor. As it was, I had to stay in the hotel watching *Seinfeld* reruns.

Of course, the real joy isn't so much the voyeurism. It is the experience of entering people's lives, their memories, being a synapse in our collective consciousness as a people. And given the vagaries of racial and cultural difference, making that link from the particular to the universal is the point of filmmaking, of telling stories. A couple months ago I was standing in a tiny airport in Finney County, Kansas, at 9:30 at night. For some reason, all the Vietnamese refugees come in on that same 9:30 puddle jumper from Denver. I was there with about fifteen Laotian and Vietnamese meatpackers, men and women, waiting for a new family to arrive.

A young Amerasian woman and her two children, around five and seven years old, came off the plane in a daze. Both wore hand-scrawled name tags pinned to their jackets, only a duffel bag and a tiny suitcase between them. They'd flown a straight forty-eight hours from Vietnam for a new life in this little town, two hundred miles from Amarillo or Wichita, a company town dominated by the single biggest beef-processing factory on the planet. I drove with the new family past the cattle pens to the trailer park where hundreds of Southeast Asian families lived—almost all working in the slaughterhouses. What were they thinking of America? That it was one long, empty country road? That it smelled like cow dung? Who, what had they left behind?

The other joy about being an independent filmmaker is the camaraderie. I depend on a network of filmmaker friends around the country—we help each other on our projects, watch each other's cuts, provide moral support, help each other raise money. It's not limited to Asian American filmmakers but independents committed to socially responsible filmmaking, and to friendship. *Who Killed Vincent Chin?* for example, would never have happened without Loni Ding, who gave us our first footage she had shot of Lily Chin, then loaned us her car for production. I find documentary filmmakers in particular to be incredibly generous people, really in it for the love of the work and for their convictions. Documentary filmmaking may be a relatively poorly paid, unrewarded art, but the asshole quotient is definitely low.

I am an Asian American filmmaker. I came out of the Asian American movement and became a filmmaker specifically to be a part of building the community and culture. I never questioned that identification or saw it as being ghettoized. Instead, I always thought of it as being on the cusp of something new, of an America becoming. I don't, however, believe that self-identity must apply to all filmmakers who have an Asian American ancestry. The whole point of the movement has been artistic democracy, freedom and diversity of expression.

Wayne Wang is the director who liberated Asian American filmmaking, especially with *Chan Is Missing* (1982). It had humor, idiosyncracy, a definite filmic vision, and it was absolutely Asian American. Miné Okubo, the painter, has most inspired my decision to keep on living as an artist—and tolerating small inconveniences such as driving a ten-year-old car and being perpetually in debt. Miné is remarkable. She has a persistent, obsessive vision—every breath, every heartbeat is in the service of her work, even though she's been overlooked by much of the art world. Miné has always been in the wrong place at the wrong time. She trained in Europe on an art fellowship during the 1930s but had to flee the German invasion on the last boat from Bordeaux. Then she got a job in Oakland with the WPA, creating mosaics. But as a Japanese American, she was rounded up and interned at Topaz. She was a woman painter during the male-dominated era of the New York School. She was experimenting with abstract work during the Asian American social realist arts movement. She was an older artist during the 1980s fixation on youth in the art world. As a result, she hasn't gotten anywhere near the acclaim she deserves. She's now in her eighties, but Miné keeps on painting. She lives in the same tiny walk-up in the Village she's lived in for over forty years. I don't think she's bought a stick of furniture since the 1960s— and she literally sleeps among her canvases. She once showed me a selection of her work dating back to the 1930s—realist charcoal drawings, cubism, primitivism, abstract expressionism—it was breathtaking. Artists today work in a highly commodified, career-oriented environment. Especially filmmakers. For God's sake, there are video competitions for high school students. There's definitely a way to work the system, play the gatekeepers. But to do what Miné has done—maintain your own values, an artistic integrity, hone your craft over sixty years' time regardless of external snubs and fashion—that is the kind of artist I can only dream of becoming.

The idea of an Asian American sensibility has always been problematic. Ever since the beginnings of the Asian American movement, we've strained under the burden of aesthetics, following the politico-cultural footprints of third world nationalist movements, within and without America. As Wittman Ah Sing, Maxine Hong Kingston's *Tripmaster Monkey*, bemoaned: "Where's our jazz? Where's our blues? Where's our ain't-taking-no-shit-from-nobody street-strutting language?"

A political movement can be willed. But culture is an organic force. Culture takes root over time, bends with the weather, the tides, the ravages of history. It sings with language that exists because something needs to be said and someone somewhere liked the sound of it. Then someone else liked that sound, and then it got passed down the same way the stories did. Culture also lives and grows, thanks to God almighty, without the politicos and intelligentsia and professional culture makers necessarily sticking their hands into things.

Asian Americans never had a land base per se. Hawaii is the closest thing, and the Hawaii way is probably the closest we'll ever get to having an Asian American culture. Asia the homeland is simply too huge, too diverse as a single aesthetic source; so many languages, so many religions, so many rhythms. Our foreparents brought them all, then a new generation is born in America, then another, and another, and another. What is left, and what becomes that which is Asian American? We are essentially an

eclectic culture. And that is what makes Asian Americans so much a part of America becoming in the twenty-first century. Eclecticism defines U.S. culture—we are an amalgam of global influences.

In my film work, as I tried to define Asian American culture, it didn't make sense until I looked back on my own upbringing. What was organic to me, what came naturally? I'd been raised in an integrated neighborhood—a Japanese American girl in a culturally African American environment living in White America, with a heavy dose of southern California Chicanismo. That was the sensibility that surrounded me and became my own.

Likewise, in making *Who Killed Vincent Chin?* the iconography I wanted to use as the cultural road map for the film surfaced for me organically from my own childhood: Motown, Dinah Shore's exuberant, standing-on-top-o-the-world exhortations—"See the U.S.A. in your Chevrolet!"—the prevailing sense of America ascendant. It was how I connected to Vincent Chin and to his killer, Roger Ebens, having the shared experience of coming of age in America's go-go years when car was king, then coming face to face with the United States in its decline. I remember very clearly as a child the meat crisis and the gas crisis and the recession of the 1970s, realizing that our entitlement as Americans, that heady feeling of being a three-ton V-8 monster tooling down the highway with Wolfman Jack blasting on the AM dial, wasn't going to last.

I tried to take this idea of connecting the organic, cultural synapses of Asian American experience a step further in *My America*. In a sense, it is a chronicle of my personal responses to the American cultural landscape, both in memory and in the present tense of being on the road. The film deals with political identity in that it is a conscious search for

Asian America. But it is a cultural document because of the elements rooted in the subconscious—listening to and seeing American lives as one eclectic highway.

The conventional notion of an aesthetic, a sensibility, begs for commonality. In the case of Asian Americans—for Americans in modern society—the commonality is difference. That's one reason I used Jon Jang as a composer for the film. His development as a musician closely paralleled my coming up as a filmmaker: growing up with both Western and Asian cultural influences, the political movements of the 1960s and 1970s, being steeped in both pop and classical culture from varied sources. Jang's arrangement for the Chinese composition "Butterfly Lover's Song," for example, captures perfectly this idea of an organic, eclectic Asian American sensibility, as it moves seamlessly from the *pipa* to gospel keyboards. A new film that really encapsulates this idea is Eric Koyanagi's new feature *hundred percent*—one week with Asian American slackers in Venice Beach, California, who worship Bob Marley and Bruce Lee with equal fervor. It's a terrific farce and completely comes out of Asian America—in that there is a consciousness of race but a cultural free-for-all.

At the end of *My America,* I conclude that the question for me is no longer "How do people become real Americans?" but rather "How has America become its people?" When I was growing up during the 1960s and 1970s, the end of ethnicity was defined as assimilation—how do we as Asian Americans fit into the mainstream? With the demographic changes wrought by the post-1965 immigration reforms and the culture wars of recent years, there's been a paradigm shift. More and more, we are no longer looking at Asian Americans as marginal to the larger society but as playing a central, activist role within the whole fabric of the Republic.

Gary Okihiro sets that foundation in his book *Margins and Mainstreams,* by arguing that the marginal peoples of the United States have actually been a pivotal force in moving forward the democracy through their struggles against oppression. If you look at any number of sectors today, you'll see it. As I was researching my new film on women's labor issues, I saw that Asian American and immigrant workers groups, within and without the union establishment, have been at the vanguard of recent labor organizing. Although I began filming with the question "Who are we as Asian Americans?" by the time I'd finished, I realized the real question is "What are we here to do?" Through the Asian American movement we declared that we're no longer second-class citizens. But if we are first-class, fully enfranchised Americans, what is our role in the public life of the nation? It's not enough to come here in search of the "Gold Mountain"—to make money and raise our families. There is a social contract involved in living in a democracy. People in the film such as Bill and Yuri Kochiyama and Alyssa Kang really resonated for me. They translated their personal experiences of struggle and racism into a moral obligation to fight injustice wherever they see it—and not only for Asian Americans. They get involved—and that's what I think we're here to do.

We've entered a very interesting period for Asian American feature filmmaking. Right now, there are an unprecedented number of features in release or in the can—well over a dozen at last count, including Eric Koyanagi's *hundred percent*, Rea Tajiri's *Strawberry Fields,* Justin Lin and Quentin Lee's *Shopping for Fangs,* Chris Chan Lee's *Yellow,* Eric Nakamura and Michael Idemoto's *Sunsets,* Tony Bui's Vietnam feature, Gene Cahayon's *The Mercado Family Debut.* I hear Kayo and Mari Hatta are developing

Renee Tajima-Peña and Victor Wong. From My America . . . or Honk if You Love Buddha *by Renee Tajima-Peña (National Asian American Telecommunications Association, in association with Independent Television Service, 1998).*

Renee Tajima-Peña as a child. Photo by William Short. From My America . . . or Honk if You Love Buddha.

an Asian American surfer-girls-in-Bali film. The list goes on. But volume hasn't necessarily made for impact. I think Asian American films in general are having trouble finding a non-Asian audience because they don't fit into the hackneyed, old images of Asians that Americans have grown to love. If you look at the few films about Asian Americans that have a general theatrical release, such as *The Joy Luck Club* and *Heaven and Earth,* these are really films about Asia, which still has an exotic allure. In contrast, many of the new Asian American features are about youth in particular, coming of age right here in the United States, and that eclectic, homegrown sensibility that is essentially Asian American. It's only a matter of time before one of these films breaks through, just as *Chan Is Missing* did sixteen years ago. I hope it will happen not because the filmmakers have relapsed to the old conventions but because someone out there has figured out how to promote and distribute these films.

In *My America,* I consciously tried to de-emasculate Asian American males on screen: for instance, Bill Kochiyama as a romantic figure in his World War II love story with his wife, Yuri. The Seoul Brothers have this playful, rap machismo, not to mention Rafael looked pretty ripped in the bare-chested shaving scene. But I think there is less of a problem today with the emasculation of Asian men. It seems the screen is becoming populated far more with heartthrob types like Dustin Nguyen, Garrett Wang, Jason Scott Lee, and Russell Wong than with the geeks of yore. As for the exoticization of Asian culture, I definitely agree. As I said before, I think the new Asian American features pay a price because they are so Asian American, so today, and do not pander to that exoticism. For these directors, Asian America exists in Venice Beach, Chicago's

North Side, the Valley suburbs. *Chan Is Missing* was a fresh breakthrough film for Asian Americans because it was an expression of our new culture and community. But non-Asians could still read San Francisco's Chinatown as an otherworldly locale. (If you look for it in Blockbuster Video, *Chan Is Missing* is often cataloged in the "Foreign Film" section.)

I think you could see the groundwork being laid. Although the Asian American arts have been marginalized commercially in the United States, there is always Asia. A number of Asian American features have received production financing and distribution dollars from Asian markets—where they're not put off by an Asian face on screen. Still, in the independent filmmaking world, Asian Americans don't have much power as gatekeepers. There are only a handful of Asian American critics who get any print in major publications; we are not curating the festivals. In fact, I think many Asian American films have been hurt because they lack the sexual edginess or violence that is in vogue in independent filmmaking. But as I've said before, it's only a matter of time before someone breaks through.

I think I'm still too young to talk about my body of work. I've really just started, but of all my films, I like *The Last Beat Movie* because I did it, start to finish, in ten weeks' time. Otherwise, I find it agonizing to look at my previous films, because I want to change them.

Advice for aspiring filmmakers? Tom Vu had three magic words to his fabulous secrets to success: Don't Give Up. Half the battle is just being persistent, because filmmaking is so full of obstacles at every imaginable step of the way. You have to have a healthy dose of insanity to keep at it. I would also say to look at your career as just that—a long-term commitment to developing your craft. We exist in a very instant world—instant technology, instant fame. But there is something to be said for hunkering down, solitude, spending time thinking, imagining, experimenting, learning, and practicing technique. Even Michael Jordan still spends hours by himself practicing his free throw! Finally, remember where you came from. While I was filming *My America* in New Orleans, I met four sisters who were eighth-generation Filipino Louisianans. Even after all these years, and quite a bit of intermarriage, the family still passed along their Filipino heritage. When I asked one sister, Benita, why, she told me, "Well, if you don't know where you've been, you won't know where you're going."

Eric Koyanagi

~~~~~~~~~~~~~~~~~~~~~~~~~~~~~~~~~~~~~~~

FILMMAKER

Eric Koyanagi was born outside Toronto in August 1967 and now lives in Los Angeles. He has a bachelor of arts degree from the University of Toronto, in cinema studies and English literature, and a master of fine arts in film production from the University of Southern California. His thesis film, Angry Café, *starred France Nuyen* (The Joy Luck Club) *and Garrett Wang* (Star Trek: Voyager) *and earned him the Best Young Filmmaker Award at the 1996 Chicago Asian American Film Festival. He recently completed* hundred percent, *his feature film directorial and screenwriting debut. Produced by Jusak Yang Bernhard and Paul G. Bens Jr., the exciting new film, blending realism and camp, interweaves the lives of young L.A. Asian Americans. The cast includes Tamlyn Tomita, Garrett Wang, Lindsay Price, Stan Egi, Dustin Nguyen, Darion Basco, and Keiko Agena.*

RESPONSE ⌒

Filmmaking for me is really an exhilarating means of personal expression. At least, I think that's what initially drew me in. I remember screwing around with super 8 films when I was a teenager. Trying to realize a vision, collaborating with friends, exploring the creative process—it's really a blast. I mean, in making a film, you're not just telling a story, you're really realizing a vision, creating a whole new world from scratch. And when you're working with people you love,

295

doing what you love to do, and working on something you really believe in, I mean when things are grooving on that level, I can't think of anything I'd rather be doing. That for me is the pinnacle.

My parents have always been totally behind me. And for this, I consider myself extremely lucky. My mother is a sculptor and my father is an architect, so they understand the allure and the pitfalls of pursuing a career in the arts. Granted, they are still Asian parents with their share of old-school Asian ideals, but I have an older brother who paved the path by getting his MBA, a great job, and a bright future. I like to think he paved the path so I could stray off it.

I studied film theory as an undergrad and then I studied filmmaking in Hollywood, so I have a very open and varied spectrum of films and filmmakers that I admire and respect religiously. But I guess personally and not so specifically in terms of aesthetics, there are two filmmakers who stand out in mind as role models, or I guess more as inspiration, in that they definitely fueled my fire. Jim Jarmusch broke when I was still studying film theory as an undergrad. His fiercely independent vision and the depth he achieved through seemingly simple means awakened me to the exciting potential of just going out and making a damn movie. He made it seem possible. I guess Spike Lee broke around the same time as Jarmusch, maybe a little later. But for me, Spike Lee has been a much stronger influence in terms of his passion. Not unlike Jarmusch, he started out with a fierce vision, fresh out of NYU. But Spike Lee had a new voice to boot, and he was crusading for change, loud and proud. It's not so much the films of Spike Lee, but it's the clarity and success of his passion and purpose. He was at the vanguard of a long-overdue African American media presence. He made it clear that representation was and is a tremendous problem and, more important,

that change is possible. One of his great quotes went something like this: "When the subject matter you love is not being done right, you have to make your own movies." Dig that.

Is there an authentic Asian American sensibility? Well, I'm not exactly sure what is meant by "authentic" and, I guess, "sensibility" as well. But it's hard for me to comprehend the notion of a single definition for everything that we are. I wouldn't want to begin to define something so complex. We are such a complicated and diverse group. Attitudes and "sensibilities" in Asian America are not and cannot be unified in terms of class, gender, heritage, generation, immigration, and so forth. This, of course, can lead to frustration because it prevents the ideals of commonality and total solidarity. But in trying to define ourselves, if the findings are too didactic, we will only hurt ourselves. We are in constant flux, which is frustrating, but outrageously exciting. So, yeah, I may not know exactly what is "authentic," but I do know we are changing, growing, and getting better, damn it.

If with the term *Asian American filmmaker* we're implying a certain sense of consciousness, awareness, in that case I think the Asian American filmmaker has the opportunity and responsibility to bring about change in terms of representation. Of course, it's not only about justice in equal and fair representation, but I think it can lead to a giant leap in terms of healing a bruised psyche. As filmmakers, and all artists really, we have a very special position in that we can shine a light on a slice of Asian America and try to share in its radiance. Asian Americans, Americans, and the world, really, have yet to see us in this brilliant light. We have to continually push ourselves to show our beauty. I think that's what it's all about.

Trying to be a filmmaker is a pitfall, risk, and challenge. But in trying to make an Asian

Troy (Garrett Wang), Slim (Darion Basco), and Isaac (Dustin Nguyen) yukking it up over bones by the beach. Film still from hundred percent *by Eric Koyanagi. Photo by Huey Tran, copyright © I.C.M.I.M.*

American feature, I guess the biggest obstacle has been financial. *How do I get this made?* In Hollywood, filmmaking is all about big bucks, and let's face it, the powers that be just don't associate Asian America with big bucks.

My first feature, *hundred percent,* was pitched and shopped around town for a long time. I had a slew of harrowing experiences trying to do a song and dance for some really crusty, blank-faced executives. Trying to sell

them on a vision, a fresh look at a slice of Asian American. Believe me, it was never too pretty. Fittingly enough, in the end, financing for the picture came from an executive producer from Asia.

Aside from finances, for me, the hardest part is the writing. The screenplay is really a monster. It's the thing I hate to do and it's the thing I love to do. Very yin yang, as it were. But it really is a constant struggle, a push-and-pull, an endless tug-of-war with your cranium. But therein lies the first benchmark for the success or failure in making a good film.

Yes, I agree that the dominant society has emasculated the Asian male, commodified the Asian female, and exoticized Asian culture in general. Just turn on your TV, flip through a magazine, or go see a movie. Granted, things are changing; awareness is growing, progress seems to be happening slowly. And I guess that's the way it's going to change: slowly. I mean, we're talking about the healing of a bruised psyche, right? No one film or novel or anything is going to change that overnight. It's going to be the continued progress of Asian Americans, as individuals and as a galvanized whole, that will move us beyond these issues and into a brighter light. I try to stay conscious of these issues when I write, but it's too easy and ultimately ineffectual if anger gets the best of you creatively. It seems to work best for me when these issues are dealt with organically, but I guess that's the trick, really.

My most recent work is my first feature, *hundred percent*. It's about these three Asian American dudes who hang out in Venice, California. One guy works in a coffeehouse, one guy's a struggling actor, and the third's a Rasta. They're all after respect in their own

The cast of hundred percent *(left to right): Darion Basco (Slim), Keiko Agena (Casey), Dustin Nguyen (Isaac), Tamlyn Tomita (Thaise), Lindsay Price (Cleveland), and Garrett Wang (Troy). Photo by Huey Tran, copyright © I.C.M.I.M.*

Stan Egi as Mingus. Film still from hundred percent. *Photo by Huey Tran, copyright © I.C.M.I.M.*

individual ways, and in the end, they all learn to find their place.

The project's genesis was really in trying to examine Asian American masculinity in a comical but genuine light. Better to laugh about it than cry about it, I guess. But *hundred percent* turned out to be much more than that. I feel it's different because the thrust of the film is Pan-Asian. The experience is not defined by a specific Asian heritage. It's not a Chinese American or Filipino American or Korean American or whatever experience. I really tried to blur those lines and just set it in Venice amongst a kind of Shangri-La slice of Pan–Asian American riffraff.

But what's really exciting for me is the support that the project generated. We got a very decent budget and an amazing cast and crew. People believed in what we were doing. Something fresh, new, and important. When I'm working on something I'm totally into, and the people I'm working with are totally into it, it's the ultimate rush. Filmmaking is one of the most collaborative art forms around. So when everyone is grooving to the same rhythm, I mean really feeling it, well, that's what it should be about. That felt good. Really good.

As for other projects, I do have many in mind and partially on scraps of paper here and there. I haven't begun to gear up for something new, but as long as it's something resonant, something I love, and if I get the chance again to work with people I love, then I can't wish for anything more.

Words of advice for young, aspiring Asian American filmmakers? Challenge yourselves. Well, believe in yourself first, then challenge yourself. I think a lot of young Asian American filmmakers, myself included, are eager, optimistic, idealistic, crazy, and probably a little angry to boot. Look, we all know representation is all screwy and that Asian Americans deserve a louder, prouder voice, but nothing is going to come easy. The best way to bring about change and get your work out there is by challenging yourself. Be tougher on your-self. Make your stuff the best it can be. That also means being open-minded and continually allowing yourself to grow. I'm talking about myself here, too. We all need to get better at what we do. Writing, directing, acting, all aspects. We can demand change to a certain extent, but if we produce quality, then that's more than half the battle, right there.

Believe in yourself and challenge yourself. Whatever. Who knows for sure, really? It's an outrageously funky road, but hey, I'm diggin' the ride.

Garrett Richard Wang

ACTOR

Born in Riverside, California, in 1968, Wang grew up in Indiana, Bermuda, and Tennessee. A graduate of the University of California, Los Angeles, with a major in Asian Studies, Wang has played John Lee in Chay Yew's Porcelain *at Burbage Theater and a Korean doctor suitor of Margaret Cho on* All American Girl. *He appears weekly as Ops/Communication Officer Harry Kim on* Star Trek: Voyager. *His recent feature films include* hundred percent *(1997) and* Auteur Theory *(1998). In 1997,* People *magazine named him one of the "Fifty Most Beautiful People," and* E! Entertainment Television *selected him as one of the "Twenty Coolest Bachelors" in the country.*

RESPONSE

I decided to become an actor the summer before my junior year at UCLA. Disillusioned and disinterested in both pre-med and pre-law, I was forced to reevaluate my future. My decision to act was a direct result of what I had always loved doing: entertaining. As long as I could remember, I loved to entertain relatives, family friends—anyone, actually—with jokes, impersonations, foreign accents, stories, and the like. I find the ability to captivate an audience an extremely attractive and distinctive trait belonging to the acting profession. I suppose, in that respect, I probably would be able to make a successful transition into car sales or televangelism. In truth, nothing can compare to the sheer power and magic of separating an audience from its reality to join you on a journey that can uplift, educate, thrill or compel.

My parents staunchly opposed my decision to choose acting as a career. Like all parents, they had hoped I would choose something safe and successful. Acting was not it. There were really no successful Asian American actors that they could relate to as precedents. When I began to pursue tennis seriously in high school, they also showed no support. Reared in Taiwan and coming to the U.S. for graduate study, my immigrant father could not consider sports or acting to be viable career options. Who knows, maybe if my parents had supported my tennis game, I might have made it as a professional tennis player before Michael Chang. On that note, because of Chang's success in the professional tennis world, Asian immigrant parents across the nation are now adding tennis to the list of approved extracurricular activities, which include ice skating and violin and piano lessons.

My mother kept telling me that I should treat acting as a hobby only and to concentrate on either medical school or business school. A chance conversation with actress Bonnie Franklin further reinforced her beliefs. While waiting for a flight at the airport in Hawaii, my mother found herself sitting next to the star of the once popular sitcom *One Day at a Time.* They struck up a conversation, which inevitably led to my wanting to be an actor. Bonnie advised my mother to tell me to "get out of the business, because he'll never make it." This was the ammunition that my parents used against me in the numerous battles we were to have. Bonnie's words were transformed into scripture in my parents' household.

At one point, my relationship with my mother had become so strained that she sug-

gested I join the army to learn some discipline. All of my relatives were upset at my career-path decision, except for a few progressive aunts who attempted to persuade my parents to let me follow the career path that would make me happy. What I found the most ironic was the fact that when my mother graduated from high school, she was the number-one pick to enter the Taiwan School of Drama. She never attended because of her father's objections, but I wish she'd taken into account that I had received her creative genes.

Our disagreements intensified until I asked my parents to provide me with two years of expenses (food, rent, acting class tuition) so that I could focus entirely on my career. I had known too many would-be actors who were working so hard to pay bills that they had no energy left for acting. According to our verbal contract, at the end of the two-year period, either I would attain success and pay them back in full or I would fail miserably, pay them back in installments, and, I added, they could disown me. To my surprise, they accepted the deal. I didn't really expect any major breakthroughs for four to six years, but I was banking on booking at least one acting job within the two years. It would be enough to prove I could make a living in this business and, I hoped, extend my two-year meal ticket an extra couple of years.

Nine months into this contract, I had not booked one acting job. It was almost the halfway point, and I was growing more nervous by the day. Luckily, during the third week of my second month, I had the good fortune to book five commercials. This success led to my being hired as the guest star on the ABC sitcom *All American Girl,* which was followed by my winning the role of Ensign Harry Kim on *Star Trek: Voyager.* Exactly one year and a half after my contract with my parents began, I had "hit the big time" with *Voy-*

ager. I paid my parents back in full, and the rest is history. The unfortunate ending to this story is that I have had to work through strong resentment against my parents for not trusting me to do what I wanted and needed to do. Let my story be a lesson to all parents and future parents: Support your children in whatever field they choose to make their career.

After three months of working on *Voyager* I was invited to attend the play opening of *Woman Warrior*. While waiting outside the theater to go in, I saw none other than Bonnie Franklin. After struggling for two seconds over whether I should go over and confront her, I walked up to her and said, "Hello, aren't you Bonnie Franklin from *One Day at a Time*?" "Yes . . . ," she smiled, thinking I was some adoring fan about to pay her a compliment. Her smile turned into a perplexed look as I continued, "My name is Garrett Wang. You don't know me, but I was wondering if you remember meeting my mother in Hawaii at the airport?" Still confused, she shook her head while her husband stared at me as if I were some crazed stalker. "It was probably about four years ago, so let me refresh your memory. My mother struck up a conversation with you and told you that her son was interested in acting and kindly asked for your advice, to which you responded by telling her to tell me to get out of the business because I would never make it. Well, I just wanted to tell you that I just booked my first series, you'll be able to watch me weekly on a new show called *Star Trek: Voyager*, so you don't have to worry about me anymore." For so long, this woman's words had burned a hole in my head; but I was finally able to speak my "peace" and truly have the last word.

Another major influence behind why I chose to become an actor were my experiences growing up Asian American in a predominantly White America. I was too young to re-member, but my mother told me that when she picked me up after my first day in kindergarten and she asked me how my day went, I answered her question with a question: "Why am I different?" I was only three at the time (my parents started me in school early), but I think it is quite obvious that something or somebody made me feel uncomfortable in that Indiana classroom. This uncomfortable feeling would follow me to Bermuda, Memphis, and finally back to California, where I enrolled in college. Wherever I have lived, I have always been reminded of my minority status. Being the only Asian American, other than my sister, in grade, junior high, and high school really left some deep scars, because more often than not, it meant being the subject of ridicule. Many times I wished that I had been born to White parents.

In the summer of 1990, I finally acquired a better perspective on my ethnic background. I traveled to Taiwan to attend a six-week Chinese cultural and language program for Chinese Americans and Canadians. This program, subsidized by the Taiwanese government, was referred to as the "Love Boat," because just like the TV show, people started out single and ended up in pairs. My time in Taiwan opened my eyes to the fact that being Asian American was not something to be ashamed of. Being in a country where people who resembled me were the majority changed my views forever. I now feel that as an Asian American, I have the best of both worlds.

Although I returned to the United States a new person, I still remembered all the pain that I had endured from racist classmates. Thus, my decision to act was not only because I enjoyed entertaining but also because I wanted to help eliminate racist attitudes toward Asians in America. I felt that if I was able to portray nonstereotypical roles that young people could look up to, then maybe I would save some Asian American kid living in the Deep South the embarrassment of being subjected to racial epithets.

Role models? There really haven't been any Asian American actors who have served as role models for me as I was growing up, simply because there were so few roles for Asian American actors. The only Asians I saw on TV and film were always playing stereotypically embarrassing parts. When I first saw John Hughes's film *Sixteen Candles* with the Asian exchange student Long Duck Dong portrayed by actor Gedde Watanabe, I was horrified. This one film resulted in ongoing humiliation and name-calling as other kids often referred to me as "the donger." Even into college I was unable to evade this ridiculous moniker. For the longest time, I wanted to really lay into Mr. Watanabe for all the damage he had caused in my life. Not until I began pursuing acting as a profession did I realize that if he hadn't taken the job, someone else surely would have. An Asian American actor in the 1980s didn't have the same opportunities.

Actually, looking back, one can see that for each decade, starting with the 1960s, there has been only one significant nonstereotypical Asian American male television role; by significant, I mean a role lasting for more than one season. They are as follows: George Takei as *Star Trek*'s Sulu (1960s), Jack Soo on *Barney Miller* (1970s), Dustin Nguyen as Detective Harry Ioki on *21 Jumpstreet* (1980s), and yours truly as Ensign Harry Kim on *Star Trek: Voyager*. Although there are no actors that I consider role models, there are actors that I admire for their acting talents. Without rhyme or reason, my list runs the gamut from old to new, including Ralph Fiennes, Jack Nicholson, Sean Connery, Chow Yun Fat, James Spader, and Gary Oldman.

I identify myself primarily as an Asian American actor, although I most certainly identify with being an American actor, as well as an actor of color. I believe in the existence of an Asian American sensibility. I see it as a mixing of Eastern and Western values, myths, and culture. It is the result of having "two feet in two boats," so to speak. My parents were born in China, while I was born in the United States. I acknowledge both American and Chinese New Year celebrations. I speak both English and Mandarin Chinese. I believe in a Baptist God and I attempt to adhere to the principles of *feng shui*. I believe that as time goes on, my greatgrandchildren will probably have less of an Asian American sensibility as compared to their American sensibilities. As long as there are new Asian immigrants, however, a strong Asian American sensibility will exist.

Films and television programs have a great deal of influence because they reach large numbers of viewers; they can inspire and educate or have detrimental effects. I believe directors, producers, writers, and actors have a certain ethical responsibility to uphold. Unfortunately, serving as a role model is more than often overshadowed by the color of money. It is my hope that the role of the Asian American actor lies in educating and inspiring the masses.

I recently was asked to present an award at the annual makeup and hair stylists' awards dinner. Charlton Heston and Robert Culp, who presented awards before me, both went on ad nauseum praising the makeup stylists for their part in making them up to play Chinese in old Hollywood films. When my turn came, I said with a tinge of resentment, "Unlike my venerable fellow actors Mr. Heston and Mr. Culp, I have no amusing anecdotes about the trials and tribulations of putting on Chinese makeup, since I am Chinese."

Thus, the biggest challenge faced by Asian American actors in the past has been the loss of Asian roles to Caucasian actors. Sadly enough, this trend, although lessened, has continued to the present decade. As recently as 1992, an Italian production company filmed a movie based on the life of Genghis Khan in which Charlton Heston was once again hired to play Chinese—this time a Chinese emperor—while two other Caucasian actors starred as Mongolian generals.

Even Broadway has not escaped the miscasting of Caucasians in Asian roles. The casting of Jonathan Pryce as an Amerasian in the Broadway debut of *Miss Saigon* sparked much debate among Asian Americans. On a side note, Charlton Heston spoke publicly in favor of this casting. This controversy united Asian American actors under the banner of the newly formed APACE (Asian Pacific Americans for Creative Equality). Although their protests did not affect the casting of Pryce, all subsequent actors hired to reprise his role were Asian Americans.

Another challenge that faces Asian American actors is the small number of roles available. A 1990 survey conducted by the Screen Actors Guild reported the breakdown of acting jobs according to ethnicity in one calendar year. Of the total number of roles cast during this year, fewer than 1 percent (.08%) were cast with Asian American actors, although Americans of Asian descent make up 5 percent of the nation's population. Hollywood has most definitely been guilty of underrepresenting Asian Americans. In contrast, Hollywood has overrepresented African Americans. While African Americans comprise only 13 percent of the U.S. population, they were cast in over 21 percent of the total roles.

A perfect example of this discrepancy can be seen in NBC's medical drama *ER*. Two of the series' regular doctors are cast as African American. Visit any medical school in the country and one will readily see that Asian American medical students outnumber African Americans. *ER* actor Julianna Marguilies herself told me that while visiting a Los Angeles hospital to research for her role, she noticed the above-average number of Asian American doctors. She reported her concerns to the *ER* producers. Their ridiculous reasoning was that the high percentage of Asian American doctors was a Los Angeles phenomenon and thus did not apply to *ER*, which was based in Chicago. Even worse than medical dramas, college-based dramas have ignored the always-present Asian American college student. To this date, only science fiction has consistently given Asian Americans proper representation.

The third challenge facing Asian American actors is stereotyping. An Asian American actor friend once told me about a film where he and two other Asian Americans were playing the parts of Viet Cong soldiers. During the filming of a particular scene, the director asked the three actors to speak to each other in "Oriental." Of the three, only two had any working knowledge of an Asian language; my friend protested that he spoke only Korean, while a second actor was somewhat fluent in Cantonese. The director responded, "It's all the same thing, just do it." So off they went, running through the mock jungle terrain of Vietnam yelling back and forth in Korean and Chinese.

Once I auditioned for the part of a Japanese mafia character, which required me to speak with a Japanese accent. As an Asian American, I am very aware of the different Asian accents and am careful to reproduce them accurately. Midway through the audition, the casting director, a Jewish American woman in her mid-forties, stopped to inform me that my accent was incorrect. I told her that I was using an authentic Japanese accent;

she insisted that it did not sound right. After several minutes of debate, I realized that the accent she was probably looking for was the stereotypical nasal, high-pitched, staccato reproduction of a Cantonese Chinese accent. I was outraged but decided to test my theory. "Is this the accent you're looking for?" I asked and proceeded to belt out the most ridiculous sounding accent I could muster, to which she responded with a resounding yes. I left without finishing the audition.

On a final note, there is a disturbing trend whereby film, television, and commercial projects that have been financed by Japanese money tend to discriminate against all non–Japanese American actors in the casting of Asian roles. I have actually seen casting notices that stated in bold, black letters "No Chinese Actors." It was this type of absurd nationalistic attitude during World War II that led the Japanese into thinking they were the rightful rulers of Asia. It is entirely unfair to say only Japanese actors may portray Japanese roles. The best Asian American actor should be cast. Asian American actors have enough difficulty getting work at all without having to worry about being the "right" Asian ethnicity.

I believe that the 1990s are definitely more receptive to Asian American actors than the previous decade, but it has always been an uphill climb for Asian Americans. "One step forward and two steps back" is a saying that has held true for Asian American actors since the inception of film and television. The earliest Asian American actor to make any significant progress was Sessue Hayakawa. Hayakawa's success and popularity as a screen idol led to the start of his own movie studio, but the Japanese attack on Pearl Harbor put an end to his career. America has always had its prejudices, but none has been more consistent than its prejudice against Asian Americans. While it is true that each ethnic group landing on the shores of America has faced its share of hard-

ship and racism, through time, each group has gone on to reach a position of equality.

This equality, however, has not happened with Asian Americans because of America's history of armed engagements. In the 1940s it was the Japanese, who were replaced by the Koreans and Chinese in the 1950s, who were in turn replaced by the Vietnamese in the late 1960s to early 1970s, and once again by the Japanese in the form of trade wars in the 1980s. At least three generations of Americans have fought against Asian foes. As battles raged on, White, Black, and Latino American servicemen viewed Asian men as the enemy, while Asian women served to "ease" their homesickness and libidos with secrets of "exotic" passion. This mindset had and continues to have a direct influence on the emasculation of the Asian male and the commodification of the Asian female.

A sociology class at UCLA conducted a survey on the subject of desirability according to ethnicity. In the category of men, Black men were found to be most desirable while Asian men were most undesirable. In regard to women, it was the Asian female who won top honors while Black women were found to be most undesirable. The results of this survey are the unfortunate results of stereotypes that pervade our society. How often does one see an Asian American man and an African American woman hand in hand? As for Asian Americans in front of the camera, females have had a much warmer reception than males. When films and television shows choose to include an Asian actor, a female is usually hired to fill the quota. Even in television news, broadcasters such as Connie Chung have no Asian American male equivalent.

Despite all the drawbacks faced by Asian Americans, as time continues, negative stereotypes will eventually fade, provided the United States does not get into another fight with an Asian country. The 1990s has seen many firsts for Asian American actors: the first macho shaving commercial to feature an Asian American man, the first Asian American spokesman for a tire company, the first to be hired for a Burger King commercial (that was me), an Asian American prince and an African American Cinderella. This is only the tip of the iceberg. With the importation of successful Hong Kong directors and stars, America is well on its way to "bear-hugging" all things Asian.

My work on *Voyager* has elicited much response from all types of people, the majority of which has been positive. Asian Americans approach me with a sense of pride in their voices, telling me how happy they are to see an Asian face regularly on television. Many people have commented on my being a good role model. I've been invited to emcee several Asian American functions, I've received awards of recognition from Asian American organizations, and I've even served as the "poster boy" for OCA's (Organization of Chinese Americans) "Don't Drive Drunk" campaign. My character, Harry Kim, has often been referred to as the glue that holds the rest of the cast together: the one character who gets along with everyone else. Fans have commented on how Kim often serves as an "Everyman" character. The writers and producers of *Voyager* have done an excellent job of portraying Kim in a nonstereotypical manner. He truly comes off foremost as a citizen of the universe.

Being on *Voyager* has afforded me the opportunity to meet everyone from President Bill Clinton to Prince Abdullah of Jordan. I am constantly amazed by all the fans of *Star Trek* that I have had the pleasure to meet. From pizza delivery to CEO, they have come from all walks of life. It is always a treat to meet fellow actors who find *Trek* irresistible. One such person is Robin Williams. Robin was filming a movie on the Paramount lot, which is also where *Voyager* films, and decided to drop by our set, not once but several times, to watch us at work.

What I feel has been lacking is the reception of the show itself within the industry. Despite legions of *Star Trek* fans, critical acclaim by Hollywood insiders has eluded *Star Trek*. Except for music, special effects, makeup, and hair departments, everyone else seems to be ignored when it comes to Emmy nominations and awards. It is almost as if because *Trek* takes place in outer space, we are not considered of this earth. Even in the film world, science fiction has not received its proper recognition. Maybe when *Star Trek*'s futuristic technology becomes a reality and *Star Trek* evolves into a real-life drama, the TV industry recognition will follow.

In addition to *Star Trek,* I've had a number of other roles. On prime-time television, I played the part of Margaret Cho's traditional Korean boyfriend on *All American Girl,* ABC's now-defunct sitcom about an Asian American family. I have a running joke with a Korean American actor friend who seems to be cast only in Chinese roles while I seem to be cast only in Korean roles. I call him "eggroll" and he calls me "kimchee." My character, Raymond Han, was a young anesthesiologist and the "straight man" to Margaret's zany rebelliousness. In one scene, Margaret and I return to her home after a Korean folk-dance performance, which was Raymond's idea of a good time but definitely not Margaret's. Raymond presents Margaret with a CD recording of Korean folk-dance music. Now, I had taken a Korean traditional theater class in college, so during a rehearsal where I excitedly play the CD for Margaret, I added an improvised dance with a twist of my own zany style. I definitely got laughs, but the network executives cut out my dance. The official reason had to do with the length of time allotted the scene, but later, someone informed me that my antics could have upstaged Margaret, the star of the show.

Disheartened as I was by this unfortunate turn of events, I still had the time of my life working on *All American Girl*. Apart from the commercials, it was my first professional acting job, the first time I worked with a predominantly Asian cast, and best of all, I was able to tell my mother that I had finally become a doctor.

While I was rehearsing for *All American Girl*, I won the role of Ensign Harry Kim on *Star Trek: Voyager*, as well as roles in two feature films (*Glory Daze* and *Mortal Kombat*). Since they were all filming at the same time, I had a difficult decision to make. I still wonder what would have happened to my career if I had chosen the two features instead of *Voyager*.

I've done two films with Eric Koyanagi: the lead role in *Angry Café*, his USC graduate thesis film, and my feature film debut, *hundred percent*. In the latter, I play Troy Tashima, a struggling actor who uses alcohol to drown his career frustrations. I enjoyed working on this project because not only was it written and directed by an Asian American and all the leading roles were Asian American but *hundred percent* tackled stereotypes head-on with a vengeance.

My most difficult role to date would have to be the part of John Lee in Chay Yew's play *Porcelain*. Years before I was to Trek through the stars, I committed to four exhausting months at the Burbage Theater, playing to sold-out audiences. John Lee was a gay British Chinese teenager who had killed his bisexual Irish blue-collar lover in a crime of passion. Although the subject matter and language were racy, *Porcelain* dealt with universal issues of abandonment, exclusion, betrayal, and lost love and was met with overwhelming critical acclaim. This was one of my most memorable acting experiences because it stretched my abilities to the limit. After each night's performance, I felt as if I had been run over by a freight train, twice.

Having played many angst-ridden roles,

I now look forward to playing more comedic roles. My idea of the dream job would be working on a sketch comedy show like *Saturday Night Live*. Who knows, maybe someday I will create an all–Asian American sketch comedy show.

Words of advice for young actors? First and foremost, know your craft. Your study of acting should include scene study, technique, improvisation, stage combat, and voice and movement classes. In addition, you must have knowledge of the entertainment business. People say with good reason that acting is 10 percent "show" and 90 percent "business." An aspiring actor must keep his finger on the pulse of the entertainment industry. Daily industry newspapers such as the *Hollywood Reporter* and *Daily Variety* will inform you of significant events involving behind-the-scenes "movers and shakers." *Drama-Logue* includes listings of theater, film, and television castings, as well as helpful articles on all phases of the acting business. K. Callan has written an excellent series of books on surviving as an actor.

An actor must be patient. Talk-show hosts invariably ask a newly successful actor, "So, were you discovered eating at a restaurant or did some producer pick you out of some random crowd?" With the exception of some child actors, there are no overnight sensations and no such thing as luck in this business. "Luck" occurs when opportunity, preparation, and timing join together. While waiting for the big break, keep creatively busy. Write a screenplay, take a sculpting class, play an instrument, paint. As tough as the odds may be, it is an educated, informed, patient yet persistent actor who will find success. On a final note, I am proud to say that I made it as an actor without knowing or being related to anyone in the entertainment industry, and also without having to place myself in a compromising situation. So can you. Best wishes.

William David "Charlie" Chin

MUSICIAN, COMPOSER, AND WRITER

Born 1944, William David Chin, nicknamed "Charlie," has been performing, composing, writing, and teaching for over thirty years. He has performed, toured nationally, and recorded a wide variety of music, from folk to rock and roll to jazz to Asian American songs with Chris Iijima and Nobuko Miyamoto. As a writer, Charlie Chin contributed to the Yellow Pearl Anthology, *a collection of writings by Asian Americans published in 1972. His plays have been produced in New York, Boston, and San Francisco. His poetry has appeared in several periodicals, and his haiku won first place in the American Poetry Association's national competition in 1986. His children's book,* Hua Mu Lan, China's Bravest Girl, *appeared in 1993. His short*

story "Johnson's Store," *which follows his response in this book, was first published in the* Asian New Yorker *(June 1994). Chin has studied acting (with Mako), traditional Chinese music, Japanese* taiko *drumming, Taoist philosophy and meditation, and Shing Yi/Ba Kua Gung Fu. From 1988 to 1991, he was the education director of the New York Chinatown History Museum. He is currently working on several projects: performing as an instrumentalist and singer in Tiger Soul, an Asian American jazz group in elementary schools throughout the San Francisco Area; developing the Peninsula chapter of the Asian American Writer's Workshop; and being the artistic director for the annual San Mateo Asian Pacific Heritage Celebration.*

RESPONSE

I was born in 1944 and grew up in a United States where institutionalized racism was widespread. I left home at the age of eighteen to become a musician in New York City's Greenwich Village. As a person of color, I watched the Black/African American Civil Rights movement of the 1960s with interest. I held leaders such as John F. Kennedy, Dr. Martin Luther King Jr., and Malcolm X in high regard, and attended the first Civil Rights March on Washington, D.C. But this was an intellectual commitment, unchallenged by any direct involvement other than the occasional protest march. The American myopic view of race relations as a matter of "Black and White" left no space for others.

By 1969–1970, I had become a successful recording artist and acknowledged authority on Anglo folk music; was living with my first wife, an attractive woman of Russian Jewish ancestry; and had a circle of Greenwich Village friends that included some of the most brilliant young artists, dancers, musicians, and writers of the creative vanguard at the turn of the decade. At the risk of bragging, I was successful in the field that I had chosen to pursue and was accountable only to my own whims and interests. Since I was not directly involved in politics, I enjoyed the position that most artists adopt: that of being a cynical and clever critic of the system without offering any practical solutions.

Yet there was a deep sense of dissatisfaction that seemed to contradict my "success," and I was haunted by the fact that life up until then had been a matter of following the path of least resistance. In a racist society, I had become an artist in order to work in liberal circles, where my being racially "different" was seen as positive. There were so few Asian women in the New York City when I came of age (eighteen years old in 1962) that

it was predictable I would be in a relationship with a member of the nearest ethnic group that shared the same economic stratum and intellectual aspirations, that is, a politically liberal, college-educated Russian Jewish woman with an interest in the arts.

I knew that something was wrong with the U.S. involvement in the Vietnam War, but since the subject was distasteful, I tried not to think about it. It never occurred to me that the American attitude that Japanese/Koreans/Vietnamese were the "enemy" extended to me as well. In short, I was a classic "Banana." Then, in 1969, an incident started me on a path of discovery.

While teaching that summer at a folk music camp in the Cape Cod area, I gave a young man from Kentucky a lesson on the finer points of playing technique on the five-string Appalachian banjo. After the student left, my English-born roommate remarked, "It's strange that a young man whose people have lived in the Blue Ridge Mountains for five generations has to come to a New York City Chinese in order to learn how the play the music of his forefathers." I was instantly aware of the contradiction he was pointing out. I knew "their" music, "their" customs, "their" history so well that I could answer obscure questions with ease, and yet I knew nothing of my own people and their culture: that of the Chinese, or for that matter, of the Chinese in America.

Over the next several months I meditated on the subject, and each issue I inspected left me with ever-increasing questions about my entire position and purpose in life. Meanwhile, outside pressures and problems began to tear the fabric of my world, in rapid succession. My work on the road as a touring musician kept me away from home for weeks at a time, and my fragile marriage fell apart. My hope had been to finish that busy year with enough money to start a business or put away a substantial nest egg for my future, but at the end of the season, I discovered my manager had stolen more than $50,000 by forging my name. Like many other newcomers to the business, I had trusted him and was devastated by the betrayal.

The combination of my personal crisis and my disastrous business affairs led me to simply walk away from all that I had worked on. I was at an emotional and spiritual low point and could have been easily recruited by some religious cult, but something else entered my life.

In 1970, I was working as a bartender in a popular rock-and-roll bar in New York City and was approached by a young Asian man who asked if there were any "Asian" musicians in the house. I told him that I was a musician, and he gave me a flyer for an Asian American conference to be held the following night at Pace College. If I was interested in performing, I was to be there at 8 P.M. Having nothing else to do that night, I packed up my guitar and went to the conference on a lark.

There I saw and heard people who spoke of a very new thing they called Asian American consciousness. I was amazed and stunned. I watched excerpts from Asian American plays, heard Asian American musicians such as Joanne Miyamoto and Chris Iijima, saw Asian American pamphlets and art. For the first time in my life, I was with other Asian Americans who shared the same experiences and questions that I had been groping with. The answers that had eluded me and threatened my sanity were laid out with crushing, casual simplicity. I resolved to find out more about this Asian American "thing" as soon as possible.

I joined Joanne (now called Nobuko) Miyamoto and Chris Iijima to form a singing trio that played at colleges, community cen-

ters, and political rallies around the United States. Then I left Greenwich Village and moved into a political commune in Chinatown. For the next two years I underwent a "political reeducation." To counterbalance a lifetime of ignorance, I made a point of not leaving Chinatown for six months. I ate, slept, worked, participated in political discussions, watched movies, drank at bars, and went to parties without ever leaving the seven blocks that made up Chinatown, New York City.

The conclusions that I arrived at after this self-enforced journey to find my roots were that I was an overseas Chinese in the United States; that this is a racist country in which an Asian would always be seen as a foreigner, no matter how many generations we had been here; that whether we agreed or not, the mainstream saw all Asians as a homogeneous group; that other minorities—other people of color, women, gays, lesbians, working-class European Americans, and so forth—also suffered and were exploited by the same system; that this system of often-misapplied economics aggravated and encouraged people's traditional prejudices in order to divide and control the various groups who lived here, but while the system was not perfect, contrary to what the extreme political Left claimed, there would not be a violent revolution in this country.

Seeking a way I could help change the situation that produced the confusion and pain in my life, I took a look at the issues of the day in 1970. The United States was involved in a costly, immoral, bloody war in Vietnam, with no end in sight. The progressive element of the Afro-American community was taking an extreme posture that excluded members of other ethnic groups as well as successful, assimilated members of their own community, whom they suspected of "selling out." Latinos were forming grassroots organizations to address problems in *el barrio*. Women's groups were breaking new ground and exploring areas outside of traditional women's roles. Chinatowns in the United States were seeing a surge in new immigrants—sometimes 25 to 50 percent growth in one year—because racially discriminating quotas were eliminated in 1965. The physical, economic, and social ills of those neighborhoods were exploding. Hundreds of young Asian Americans, our "baby boom generation," were graduating from college and asking questions about identity, their role in the community, marriage, career choices.

The solution for me was obvious. If others could contribute skills, education, and money in an effort to "fight the good fight," then I could at least offer my experience as a professional musician and writer toward the same purpose. From this premise came the basis of the work I was to be involved in for the next twenty-five years.

Given the aforementioned background, my "work" is aimed at (in order of importance) other Chinese Americans, other Asian Americans and Pacific Islanders, other people of color, other minorities that share a history of oppression (women, gays, working-class Europeans, religious groups, etc.), and the mainstream society.

Of course there is an Asian American sensibility, *but*—and this is a very important but—it changes from moment to moment, decade to decade. If you wish to define it, you have the same problem the United States' legal courts have when trying to define pornography, namely, everybody claims to be able to recognize it at once when they see it, but nobody can agree on a definition of what it actually is.

The role of the Asian American artist is the same role that the artist has always had: to hold a mirror up to society, to ask ques-

tions, to introduce ideas, to reveal contradictions and injustices. The more facets a jewel has, the more brilliantly it shines.

Though not peculiar to Asian American artists, one of the major challenges artists of color have to deal with is that the society at large offers the opportunity of commercial success to artists if they are willing to compromise. There is nothing wrong with this, for only the very young and naive believe they can be successful and avoid compromise. The heart of the problem is the degree of compromise. Sometimes it's as simple as not letting your ethnic background intrude on the work or indirectly supporting something you may not totally agree with. On the other hand, the compromise may be quite serious and affect the image, status, or social position of all other Asians in America. Because 90 percent of the membership of Actors Equity is always out of work, Asian American actors are especially vulnerable to the temptation of taking questionable roles that reenforce negative stereotypes, out of a desperate need to practice their craft in any form or fashion.

The way to resolve this, I believe, is for Asian American (AA) writers to write more plays, filmmakers to make more films, and so on—and for community members to support Asian American theater and film. To address the shortage, I have written several plays that have been produced in New York City, Boston, and San Francisco, and I encourage all Asian writers I meet to add to the repertoire of AA theater. Unfortunately, middle-class Asian American communities have been historically indifferent when it comes to supporting local AA theaters. The result is that at the moment, of the four major AA theaters in the United States, none is making a profit.

While the dominant society has been reluctant to show positive examples of Asian males, it must be noted that they are following a European-based cultural pattern of attempting to eliminate any adult male of color as a serious contender for the role of dominant male. In fact, many Asian American males are secure in the knowledge that they are fulfilling their responsibilities, providing for their family, raising their children, and contributing to their communities. If any male, Asian or non-Asian, needs to be reassured by the popular media and the dominant society that he is masculine and virile, he will wait in vain. For those who feel they do need assurance, it may be that they have drifted away from a community base that reaffirms their identity in a number of ethnic social rituals. I am talking not about feudalistic practices that reenforce manhood at the expense of the women in the group but about those social passages that allow a young male to bond in student-teacher and apprentice-master relationships with positive role models and begin the journey of self-discovery. In the case of Asian Americans, this can be a pursuit of traditional or other, more "American" interests, for instance, martial arts, calligraphy, painting, meditation, Chinatown basketball, political groups.

To address the issue of Asian females being commodified, I can speak only about my observations of the women I know best, namely, the women in my own family. I was raised in a working-class background (hand laundry). As far back as I can remember, female family members have been fast-thinking, hard-working, no-nonsense women who contribute to the family income and have an active voice in family matters and decisions. I have noticed that some view as distasteful those Asian females who use the stereotypes about Asian women in order to get what they want, but at least they're consciously in control of their lives, while those who "play the game" of the China Doll, Beautiful Dragon Lady, and so forth, without understanding how they are being manipulated by popular images, are to be pitied.

The exoticizing of Asian culture was going on in Europe long before Europeans stumbled onto the New World. The two-faced coin of resentment and awe when dealing with Asia has old roots. The fantasies and fabulous tales repeated by word of mouth along the Silk Road in the time of the Roman emperors was one example. Why would we expect anything different today in a country in which Asians and Pacific Islanders represent only 3.8 percent of the population? The average American living outside a major city or the state of Hawaii has probably never even met an Asian American.

Is this a particularly receptive moment for AA artists? Let's not be silly. It is, and has been, difficult for artists of any color, at any time, anywhere, to get recognition and make a living. The only comfort we may have is that many things taken for granted by young Asian Americans today were undreamed of only twenty or thirty years ago. The recent success of a handful of AA artists is proof that things change, but they change slowly. Many older AA artists worry that the interest in "new voices" is really a preference for the novelty of Asian American culture over the depressing facts of the Afro-American and Latino communities in this country. Mainstream liberal literati can easily become enamored of these "new voices" when some of the old voices—for example, Africans complaining about social wrongs and Latinos mired in poverty and drugs—keep reminding them of problems for which they have no solutions.

And of course, don't forget, we are talking about a handful of AAs against a previous record of just about *none*! No, for old-timers such as myself, who have seen this sort of thing before, there is always the haunting feeling that we may be only the "flavor of the week" for the jaded reading and viewing American public and the liberal intellectuals of the campuses.

Over the years, my audiences (in the order of priority listed above) have always been good, with the exception of the very early 1970s when some middle-class Asian Americans, their position and status in society being based on the uneasy tolerance of the mainstream, feared that by expressing open agreement with the messages in my work they might put themselves in jeopardy (which, by the way, was one of the messages). Because my audiences have always been those I consider important—Asian Americans raising funds for community projects, unionizers, teens at risk, outreach, college student conferences, Asian/Pacific Islander cultural organizations and functions—there has never been any money to speak of. I don't regret not making more of an income in my life, but it would have been nice to do something that I believed in and make money at it too. Oh well.

What I am most grateful for is the occasional comment made by a community worker, political leader, Asian American scholar, or another Asian American artist that for him or her, it was after listening to one of my albums or attending one of my concerts or plays that this person decided to take the path in life that he or she did. This balances out the lack of income.

My advice to the next generation of artists? Art transcends craft but is firmly based on craft. Learn everything there is to know about your discipline and stay in touch with the latest developments. You will know when this is no longer necessary in the same way that a hungry man knows when he's full and ready to leave the table.

Nobody can predict the future. If you want a hint of what is going to happen, study the history of our people in this country and in Asia. Labels change like the yearly fash-

ions in the clothing business. If you're doing what you should be doing as an artist, they will make up a new label for you when the time comes, so don't waste time trying to label yourself.

Any artists of worth or real importance are at least ten to twenty years, if not more, ahead of their time. If your work is valid, you're not going to be given very much credit for it while you're doing it. If you expect money and recognition, you'll only become bitter, and being bitter is a waste of time. It is enough to know that you and those whose opinions you respect, understand what you're trying to do.

Never believe your own reviews. If you are elated by the good ones, you'll be crushed by the bad ones. Reviews are important only in terms of business and should be viewed clinically. Remember, an artist can change the way the world looks at itself, give a voice to thousands who can't speak for themselves, and inspire a whole generation to take action. It is a demonstrable fact that artists can exist without critics but critics cannot exist without artists.

Artists can only write/paint/sing/photograph/dance about what they know from their experiences and observations. If your whole day is filled with being an artist, dealing with other artists, taking about *Art,* you won't know very much about life. The label of "artist" is just as dangerous as any other, if you begin to believe that's the sum total of your being. If you make the mistake of giving your life to art, then art will take your life, leaving no time or room for anything or anybody else.

After your apprenticeship, leave the comfort and abstractions of the art world, the armchair speculations of the campus, and have real relationships; risk getting emotionally hurt, and accept responsibility for the actions you take. There are many worlds, and in most of those worlds, you're just another warm body. Get to know people from every walk and station of life so that you will be able to perceive the universal and general rules that occur in specific and unusual circumstances.

If you don't, you will have no resources from which to draw for creative ideas. The truly great ideas, which are often simple but profound, are polished in solitude, but they were first observed in the artist's direct social involvement in the lives of a wide range of people. The artists or would-be artists who don't do this are easily discerned by the lack of direction and shallow content of their work. They tend to write, paint, and so forth about themselves and their personal whims, sorrows, and interests. The hallmark of a true artist is the ability to write convincingly about somebody else, from that person's point of view, and say something important.

And in the end, remember what is always needed is "less talk, more work."

Johnson's Store

The kids were excited. Makoto kept one hand on the wheel as they drove down the highway and used his free hand to point out places he remembered. The little town had put up a few new buildings since he had left but he could still spot some familiar places. As they passed a shopping center, he commented,

"That's where the drive-in movie theater used to be."

His daughter Keiko asked a normal question for a ten-year-old.

"What's a drive-in?"

His wife nervously pulled at the long sleeves of her blouse, trying to cover the back of her hands against the bright California sunshine coming in through the passenger-side window. Being somewhat vain about her fair skin, she was always worrying about developing liverspots. She twisted around in her seat to check on their eight-year-old son. The boy glanced at her and asked,

"How much longer until we get to grandma's?"

She corrected him.

"Honey, you should call her Obaasan."

Janice turned back to Makoto and went through the ritual of pulling down her sleeves again. She talked to all of them at once.

"Is it much further, Makoto? Gary, do you need to go to the bathroom? Keiko, don't put your fingers in your mouth. You're going to get sick again and have diarrhea. You don't want to have diarrhea again, do you sweetheart?"

Without taking his eyes off the road, Makoto forced his shoulders down and twisted his head in an odd way that made a cracking sound in his upper neck bones. It was a nervous habit he used to release tension. He checked the road signs.

"The next exit is the one we want."

The kids quieted down and Makoto began to see the ghosts of his high school years. They drove on an overpass where Jimmy Oto and he used to sit and get drunk during that crazy summer. Jimmy wanted to go to San Francisco and be in a rock band. He probably ended up taking over his father's garage. The taco joint was still there. Different owners though, Miguel would never have sprung for that fancy paint job. Kimberly liked that place. He pulled onto the exit and turned onto Third Avenue.

As they passed the town's tiny park he inspected the landmarks. That stupid cannon was gone; in its place was a bronze memorial. He could just make out the word Vietnam. The big oak tree where he and Kimberly had kissed was still there.

She had worn her cornsilk hair in a ponytail that night. They left the gang at Miller's Cafe and walked in the darkness to the park. She smelled of hand soap and violets. When they stopped in the shadows under the tree, she leaned forward with her eyes closed and her lips pursed. For a second he was paralyzed by the immensity of the moment, it would be his first "real" kiss.

Her lips were soft and she made a muted moaning sound as their lips fumbled. It struck him that this was probably her first "real" kiss also. Clumsily at first but gaining skill with each embrace, they learned how to touch, to kiss, to whisper what they wanted. They didn't hear or see anything else but each other. They lost track of time.

Kimberly's father and two brothers had been driving around town looking for her since ten o'clock. They spotted the couple from the street side of the park and jumped out of their car spitting out curses. The first couple of punches confused Makoto and by then it was too late to defend himself. As he lay on the ground trying to cover his head with his arms to block the stomping kicks, he could hear Kimberly screaming,

"Stop it, stop it! We weren't doing anything."

Her father and brothers grimly went on, finishing their work with a couple of carefully aimed kicks. It was a minute or two before Makoto realized that they had stopped beating him. He chanced sitting up. His face was all wet. He looked down at his shirt and saw it was bloody and that the blood was coming from a wound on his head. Makoto tried to get up but his legs wouldn't work. He rolled over to watch them drag Kimberly away to their car. Her father was slapping her face with his hand full force and repeating the words as if he didn't believe it.

"A goddamn Jap. A goddamn Jap."

Kimberly was screaming hysterically.

"I love him. I don't care. I'll always love him."

At the hospital, Makoto lied and said he fell down in the darkness and hit his head on a sharp rock. Kimberly didn't come to school for a week. When she did come back to class, the swelling on her face was still visible. Makoto tried to send her a note through a mutual friend but Kimberly was terrified. She wouldn't even touch it. He felt helpless. The semester passed and he lost interest in school. He started to come home late and drunk. Conversations with his parents became shouting matches and finally one day, he just left.

He ended up waiting tables in a New York City sushi bar. A couple of years went by. He saved a few bucks and went in with some other waiters on a small restaurant down in the Wall Street area. The place did mostly lunch trade but it was steady.

Then one day an Asian woman walked into the place and asked if they needed someone to do flower arrangements. She gave him a card that said, "Janice Sakai-Interior Decorator." Even though the place didn't need flowers, he kept hiring her every week for a month until he got up the courage to ask her out on a date.

Two years later they married. When the kids came, they moved to the upper west side of Manhattan. His mother tracked him down by calling every Takata in the New York City telephone book to tell him that his father had passed away. He promised to come home soon to visit but something always came up.

Now after twenty-five years he was back, a middle-aged man with a wife and family. As he turned the car into the driveway of his mother's house, he reached up and touched the old scar on his left temple. It's funny how cuts on the head bleed so much.

The house front door was open and a gray-haired woman stepped out. He was shocked by how physically small his mother appeared.

"Makoto." The tiny woman was wiping away tears. He went up to her and gave her an awkward hug. He turned back to the car and motioned for his family to come out. There were shouts on both sides of "Obaasan" and "Gary, Keiko, so big neh?" After a big dinner they all settled down in the living room to look at family photo albums. His wife mentioned to him that Keiko had gone to the bathroom three times. He spoke to his mother.

"Mom, Keiko is not feeling well. Something she ate at the airport I think. Is there any Pepto-Bismol in the house?"

His mother thought for a moment and then stood up abruptly.

"I don't keep in house but I go Johnson's store. They got there."

He motioned her back onto the old sofa.

"Mom, stay here. I'll go." As he put on his jacket, his mother prattled on.

"The store on Cypress and Delaware. You know where. You went high school with the daughter." Makoto stopped at the threshold of the door and turned around slowly.

"Kimberly Johnson? Mr. Johnson owns the store?"

"Oh, the father die many year ago. Drunk car crash. The both son jail now. So tough for daughter. She very nice, neh? She run store now. She never marry."

Makoto stepped out into the street. Before getting into his car, he pushed his shoulders down and twisted his head in such a way that it made his upper neck bones crack.

Chris Iijima

LAWYER, SINGER, AND SONGWRITER

Chris Iijima was born in 1948 and reared in New York City. His parents, Kazuko and Takeru Iijima, taught him the value of political activism at an early age. In the late 1960s, at his mother's urging, he joined Asian Americans for Action, the first Asian American political community organization on the East Coast, and in the early 1970s, he worked with his father on establishing the Asian American Community Center. He worked as well with other early Asian American organizations, including the I Wor Kuen Organization, Asians in the Spirit of the Indo Chinese Organization, the Chickens Come Home To Roost Storefront, the Basement Workshop, Asian Americans for Equality, Coalition Against Anti-Asian Violence, and the New York Chol Soo Lee Defense Committee, among others.

Iijima is presently a law professor at Western New England College School of Law in Massachusetts.

A sometime lawyer, schoolteacher, and youth counselor as well as Asian movement activist and performer, Iijima was also one of a trio of notorious bartenders—along with Eddie Kochiyama and Greg Morozumi—at the late Enka Japanese Restaurant, one of the true Asian American hangouts in New York in the 1980s. He recorded the album Grain of Sand *with Nobuko Miyamoto and Charlie Chin in 1973. In 1983, he and Chin reunited to record* Back to Back. *Iijima's work has been recorded by performers such as Holly Near and published in various collections, including the* Yellow Pearl Anthology *(1972). Although no longer performing regularly, Iijima speaks*

319

about race and politics to student and community groups. He is also the father of two young sons who like to hear Daddy sing—but not for too long.

RESPONSE ⬅

Nobuko, Charlie, and I originally started singing many years ago, to document what was going on within the Asian American communities in the late 1960s and to have a mechanism to reach out to other communities to share what was going on in our communities. It was also a way to try to further organize and connect the localized APA (Asian Pacific American) activities happening around the country. We sang all over—basements, churches, community centers, storefronts, rallies, campuses, East Coast, West Coast, Midwest—wherever there were events, people, or organizations that might be receptive to "the news." My intent was to help bring a consciousness about how racism affected us and others; how many poor communities, communities of color and of Asians, needed to be given greater voice; and the ways in which we could respond, as Asian Americans and as concerned beings. Whether or not we were successful is not something I think about much now, since there were many more (I think) important things going on than our performing and traveling. I thought we contributed a small bit to the larger context of the time, and that is satisfaction enough.

In the past few decades, since the beginnings of a Pan–Asian American consciousness and identity in the 1960s, there has been much discussion/academic rambling on the definition, structure, content, borders, parameters of Asian American "identity" and culture. What is interesting to me, being an old geezer, is how acontextual the discussion

has been by so many—particularly APA artists and some academics. Indeed, it has been relatively fashionable of late for some APAs to eschew racial/ethnic labels but nevertheless be quite willing to be defined as such if it enhances their career, opportunities, and visibility.

My experience and understanding of the roots of APA identity were that it originally had less to do with who one was and more to do with for what one stood. By that I mean that APA consciousness was developed at a time of great political upheaval in the nation and the world. The construction and articulation of an APA identity at that time was a way (1) to organize other APAs around political issues; (2) to create dialogue with other racial groups around common interests; (3) to construct a basis to engage the larger public on issues of racism and subordination in the society and in government policy, particularly with respect to discrimination, education, and other poverty issues; (4) to create a "domestic" face for discussion of the larger global events (i.e., martial law in the Philippines and South Korea, the Vietnam War, recognition of the People's Republic of China, etc.). Thus, APA identity as first conceived had very little to do with having unity as "Asians" just because we were Asians. Indeed, the staunchest and most vocal opponents of many of the early APA identity constructions and its inherent politics were other (usually conservative) Asians. Some of the earliest targets of APA activism and criticism were Asians (e.g., S. I. Hayakawa).

We were able to construct an APA identity precisely because our shared experience as Asians in America—always cast as foreigners and marginalized as outsiders—allowed us to bridge ethnic lines and allowed a platform and commonality to engage and understand other people and their struggles. I think we can still do this. Somewhere along the line, the inherent link of racial identity with progressive politics got lost, and "identity" became simply "heritage." But it also has become increasingly clear that without such a political focus, APA identity is incoherent. Indeed, any racialized identity, APA or otherwise, without a political framework is incoherent.

I don't know when the break between student/academic activity and community activity took place, but there used to be a notion that scholarly, academic, and cultural pursuits could not be separated conceptually from the ongoing life, struggles, and needs of the larger communities. For those interested in pursuing this subject, I recommend two articles: Glenn Omatsu's "The Four Prisons and the Movements of Liberation," in Karen Aguilar-San Juan's book *The State of Asian America;* and Russell Leong's "Lived Theory (Notes on the Run)," in *Thinking Theory in Asian America Studies*, vol. 21 of *Amerasia Journal*. There are also some progressive approaches to Asian American activism in books such as *Dragon Ladies: Asian American Feminists Breathe Fire*, edited by Sonia Shah.

You ask whether there is an "authentic" Asian American sensibility. Asian American identity was originally conceived to allow one to "identify" with the experiences and struggles of other subordinated people—not just with one's own background. Because "heritage" rather than politics is the touchstone of so many APAs, I'm betting that a great many answers in this survey are going to be variations of (1) "Aren't we all individuals? And I hate being categorized"; (2) "I'm not sure what 'authentic' or 'Asian American' means, so I can't answer the question"; (3) "I'm proud of my heritage so whatever I do it's a part of me." These kind of answers,

it seems to me, miss the point. Is Supreme Court justice Clarence Thomas an "authentic" African American as opposed to Malcolm X? He is if politics is not a part of "authenticity." Of course, he isn't if one defines authenticity as whether one works in the best interest of eradicating African Americans' pervasive subordination. I choose the latter.

We are living in an Orwellian era, when the gap between people of color and the poor, on the one hand, and the wealthy, on the other, grows even greater, but the majority of civil rights discussions and concerns are focused on whether White males are being excluded and discriminated against or emerge when the Right rails against "political correctness" but blatantly imposes its own litmus political tests (e.g., Bill Lann Lee).

One of the reasons Nobuko, Charlie, and I decided very recently to start performing together again on a limited basis is to acquaint younger people with what we believe are the principles and traditions in our contemporary history of thirty years ago, which, ironically, in the subsequent institutionalization of APA Studies, seems to have been relatively de-emphasized.

So I guess the bottom line is that Asian American artists who are conscious and responding, either through their art or in the process of living their lives, to the racial, gender, class, and other subordination that continues to exist and to the reactionary onslaught that poor Asian and other communities of color are presently facing are, to me, APA artists who have continued the tradition of what APA culture was originally meant to be. I have always admired artists such as Tomie Arai, who combines beautiful aesthetic imagery with a true commitment to improving the conditions of how people live their lives.

Asian Song (from the 1983 album *Back to Back*)

Mr. Woo works in the laundry
    his wife sews in a shop
And each and every wrinkle tells a tale
A survivor of the hard times
    and a fighter all his life
But the twinkle in his eye has never failed
He puts a kettle on the table and he leans against the wall
He says, "Excuse my English," but his words speak for us all

He says . . .
    These hands
    Have washed the clothes
    These hands have served the food
    Heaven knows
    And this neck has felt the mob's rope
    And it's been behind barbed wire
    These arms have built the railroad track
    This back has been for hire
    And these hands have fought injustice
    And this soul has been on fire . . .

    But I'm still here
    I'm going strong
    And I'm getting tired of proving
    I belong

Mrs. Gomez works the night shift
    in the pediatric ward
By day she cooks the meals for her own
New in the big city
    she has never given up
And tries her best to give her kids a home
There's Mrs. Kim who sells the produce
    on the corner of the square
The people pass by quickly
    but we all knows she's there

And so the story goes on to another generation
A page, another chapter being turned
Tomorrow is the struggle we face in anticipation
And yesterday are lessons we have learned

Johnny, he's a young boy
    who pumps gas to pay for school
His options being cut back one by one
His father marched in Europe
    and John's mother was in camp
And each shows off the battle scars they've won
Some nights you hear raised voices
    that come drifting through the wall
But each knows deep inside them
    that what binds them binds us all
Because . . .
    Our hands have washed the clothes
    Our hands have served the food
    Heaven knows
    And our neck has felt the mob's rope
    And it's been behind barbed wire
    Our arms have built the railroad track
    Our back has been for hire
    These hands have fought injustice
    And our soul is still on fire
    And we're still here
    We're going strong
    And we're getting tired of proving
    We belong.

Nobuko Miyamoto

~~~~~~

DANCER, SINGER, AND SONGWRITER

Born in Los Angeles in 1939, Nobuko Miyamoto and her parents were relocated to a work camp (a beet farm) in 1941. After moves to Idaho and Utah, the family resettled in Los Angeles, where Miyamoto studied at the American School of Dance. She began her professional career as a court dancer in the 1955 film The King and I, *followed by* Les Girls *(1956) and* West Side Story *(1961), and was the lead dancer in* The Flower Drum Song *on Broadway. In the early 1970s, she became involved with the Asian American movement. In 1973, with Chris Iijima and Charlie Chin, Miyamoto recorded* A Grain of Sand, *the first recording of Asian American music. In 1978 she founded Great Leap, Inc., to support the creation of new works about the Asian American and multicultural American experience, and she recently started a recording company,* Bindu. *At age thirty-three she became the single mother of a Japanese-African American boy, whose father was killed during an ambush on a mosque. Since 1986, she has been married to an African American writer, Tarabu Betserai. Her latest work is a one-woman performance fusing poetic story, song, movement, and video imagery, also called* A Grain of Sand, *which follows her personal journey to find and follow her inner voice.*

RESPONSE ⤸

Coming out of a career of musical theater in both New York and Hollywood, I had the experience of working in a field that made me confront the limitations that many Asian Americans faced. All actors face a lack of jobs, but for us it was more intense. Some of the roles that we were asked to play—spies, maids, and concubines—were stereotypical and more demeaning than for other people. *West Side Story* was the first movie in which I wasn't typecast as an Asian; I played Francisca, a Shark, and I was able to do my own work. I had the privilege of working with Jerome Robbins and Jack Cole, both renowned choreographers. But the stereotyping and limitations in the business pushed me into my own music.

At the invitation of Pat Suzuki's manager, I started a career as a chanteuse, beginning with an eight-month gig at the Colony Club in Seattle, Washington. Dancers are not used to hearing the sound of their own voice, and I was so scared when asked to sing by myself that I decided I had to conquer this fear. I took singing lessons with a Black teacher, Dini Clarke, who introduced me to Black music and also to the racism that is part of everyday Black life. After eight months of singing in the nightclub every night, I began to wonder what I was doing and what would happen to my brother, who was of draft age. This was the Vietnam War era.

So I returned to Los Angeles and began working with Antonello Branca, who was making a film, *Seize the Time*, about a Black man moving from cultural nationalism into revolutionary nationalism by joining the Black Panther Party. It was later difficult to distribute the film in North America because of the split in the Panther Party, but the experience moved me around the country a great deal and I learned a lot.

While in New York, at a church the Young Lords were taking over for a breakfast program in East Harlem, I met a Japanese American woman, Yuri Kochiyama, who invited me to a meeting of Asian Americans for Action in New York, and

that was the beginning of my involvement in the movement. Her family became my second family and showed me the way to work in the Asian American struggle. At that meeting I met Chris Iijima. Initially we were doing political work, antiwar together. In the summer of 1969, we both went to a JACL (Japanese American Citizens League) convention, and we were working on a program for the elders to show them what younger people were doing and thinking. The convention brought together large numbers of East and West Coast Asian Americans, all working on similar issues. It was an incredible emotional reunion. We stayed up all night partying, singing. Chris brought out his guitar, and we spontaneously sang together. One night we wrote a song together, "The People's Beat," inspired by the words of Fred Hampton, the Black Panther who had just been murdered in Chicago, and the next day, we sang it together. People liked it very much, and that's how we began.

During the convention, a seventeen-year-old girl, Evelyn Okubo, was murdered; her throat was slit. Chris and I decided we needed to go her hometown, Stockton in California, to do a memorial. We wrote five songs, learned others, gave a concert at the Buddhist Temple in New York City, and made enough for two airfares to California. We traveled up and down California giving concerts, seeing what was going on, and getting to meet a lot of people. In 1970 we hooked up with Charlie Chin, meeting him at Pace College in New York City, and the three of us toured the country for the next three or four years. Barbara Dane, founder of Paradon Records, wanted to record us, so in 1973 we did an album, *A Grain of Sand*, the first album of Asian American songs in this country and now a part of the Smithsonian collection. In the early 1970s we cut a 45 rpm record with "Somos Asiaticos" (We are Asians) on one side and "Venceremos" (We will win) on the other. It was released in Puerto Rico and became very popular there, played on lots of jukeboxes. In fact, we did more gigs for Puerto Ricans and Dominicans in New York than for Asian Americans. They were so pleased we could sing in Spanish. Our biggest audience was when we played for the Puerto Rican Liberation Day in 1973 or 1974, to a packed house in Madison Square Garden. That concert was recorded in *Break and Enter,* a film about squatting on the Upper West Side of New York City (available through Third World Film).

How do I identify myself? Of course I see myself as part of a movement of Asian American artists, I don't mind that label, but my leaning recently has been more and more toward a more multicultural movement. If you have to put a label on it, I'd prefer person of color. My experience has been an Asian American experience, but this is mixed with all the other peoples in the United States. My work incorporates all different forms of music: reggae, jazz, classical, Latin. To me, music is a language, and even though I can't speak Swahili, I can sing and dance in those rhythms and sounds. It's in my body. It's a stereotype that Asians have no rhythm. We haven't had the opportunity to sing and dance. There are plenty of Asians with rhythm and style. Even if you go to China or Japan, you'll find people taking that rhythm into their bodies.

Music has traveled and made positive influences in distant places where politics and policies could not travel. This change is from the bottom up rather than the top down. In China they play classical European music, thinking that is high culture, but on the street level, there are musicians you've never heard of who have turned mu-

sic into something of their own. People no longer remember that we're doing African rhythms and music here. An African rhythm can travel to Jamaica or Trinidad and then go back to Africa. In this way, it's been recycled and transformed. This is, to me, authentic culture—not something that has any limits and a label on it. It's the fringes that people like and feel, that people want to take into themselves, the things that spill over the boundaries. That's authentic.

Gypsies brought their dance and made flamenco. We Asian Americans are in a swaddling stage in making this happen for ourselves. Many hands will need to work on this, and maybe by that time what results will be unrecognizable. Kenny Endo is a good example. He started out as a traps player, then took up *taiko* drums. Next he went to Japan, and after ten years, he earned a name there, and now he lives in Hawaii. He's put many influences into his music— Latin, Indian, African sounds and rhythms. *Taiko* to me is the most recognizable Asian American or Japanese American form. *Taiko* in America is different than in Japan. Kinnara Taiko in Los Angeles and San Francisco Taiko Dojo are the two oldest groups in the United States, but a player from Japan who hears them would smile and say, "You're playing African music," because of the rhythms that we all grew up with. But that's authentic music, it's authentically Japanese American music.

Who is my audience? I think Asian Americans are my first wave of audience, and especially younger people, because they are the ones who are most open and who need to hear the work. We perform to a lot of different groups, mixed groups. It's important as Asian Americans to share our music, our stories, to create a deeper understanding among all peoples, all levels of society. I've been very fortunate, being in the right place at the right time—to be part of this great wave of change, along with the movement for civil rights and cultural identity, that really brought out my voice and the voice of many others. I happened to be there with some skills and with the right people. I just gave myself to it. I never really expected to be working as a part of the establishment after I left it. From the 1970s on, my goal was to create an alternative cultural voice that grew out of the community and was connected to the community. After moving back to Los Angeles from New York, I started teaching dance at the Senshin Buddhist Temple, and I did that from 1976 to 1985. I also started a band called Warriors of the Rainbow. Benny Yee, a keyboard artist, was a member of this band. He and I started Great Leap in 1978. We combined music, dance, and story. In 1980, Mako, director of East/West Players, commissioned us to do a piece that we called "Chop Suey."

That moved me toward theater again, the tradition I'd come out of. I really believe our stories have to be told and one way of doing it is through music and theater. I created a couple musicals, *Talk Story I* and *Talk Story II,* based on Asian American stories. Then I looked around and saw young performer-writers creating and performing their own material, and that pushed me to organize "A Slice of Rice," a festival of single artist-performers such as Dan Kwong, Jude Narita, Young-ae Park. Now it's a regular show, a magazine of three or four artists who will go out to a college to do a performance. We also do a version of this for schools. The latest version is "A Slice of Rice, Frijoles and Greens," which is turning out to be more multicultural and more popular. People are looking for instances of border crossing, showing that people can and do work together.

It is challenging to be an Asian American artist, but it's also possible to turn something negative into something positive. I'm grateful that I woke up to who I am, that I didn't persist in a business that didn't want me. Creating the alternative was creating my own voice and a voice for my community, and that's been my blessing and has not held me back. It has allowed me more expression and opportunity than I would ever have had just being in show business. Of course, we're always fighting for more budget and more money. We have to push to get our work into a bigger arena. We started a record company, Bindu Records, in order to create a bigger platform and more visibility for multicultural artists of color. We're just on the launching pad with this now; we have four or five projects in the works. It is challenging to do with little money what other companies do with millions. It really pushes you to be your most resourceful.

Is this a receptive moment? Yes and no. I really think, still, it is easier for artists who are born in Asia to have confidence in themselves than for artists in the United States. It's almost as if we're brought up with the psychological barrier that we can't do it. It's the internal barriers—your parents who say, "Don't be an artist, don't be crazy." These interior barriers are what stopped us and what we need to get over.

Fortunately, my mother loved dance and visual arts, encouraged me, and made sure I had good teachers. And my father could have been a good musician. My mother was smart. When I was very little, she showed me picture of Sono Osato, a Eurasian Japanese American ballerina (her father was Japanese, her mother Irish), and she said, "See, she did it! So can you." These models were important to me.

It's important to document the movement and the culture, to show its development. I'm anxious to say, "Hey, I'm here." I'm trying to do that with *A Grain of Sand,* the work I'm presently touring. In the creation of *A Grain of Sand,* I am offering one grain in the sandbox of stories that are part of Asian Americana. I use experiences of myself and my family against America's social and political landscape since the early 1900s, giving one a lens to see the past and present. For me, its creation has been a journey in itself, challenging me artistically and personally to reach places I have not touched before. As an artist, I feel this is a journey we should all take.

Years ago, when I was asked to write music for a Buddhist festival called Obon, I found there were no separate words for song and dance. As a dancer in my early years, who then moved into the realm of song, theater, film, and video, I have come to know all of these forms as one language to tell my story. Music is at the heart because it is the silver thread that weaves through my life. I see the stage as my place of ritual, to dissolve boundaries and elevate our consciousness.

My advice for young performers? Learn your art, whatever form it is. That in itself is a journey. Connect yourself with community. Let your art be useful. We have to be cultural warriors. We have to advocate for the arts at the same time. We have to show its usefulness. We need to keep our community informed about what we're doing so that we have a support. The community is not just an audience; they are your roots, your support. People who run show business are basically twenty or thirty years behind or ignorant and representing avenues that aren't representing our interests. Whether you like it or not you're going to be fighting, so you'd better have somebody behind you!

To All Relations/Mitakuye Oyasin

This is a song for the earth, a prayer that came through me after going to a Gathering of Elders from different Native American tribes. Before each talk they used the greeting *Mitakuye Oyasin,* "to all relations" . . . from the Lakota Nation.

> to all relations
> mother earth and father sky
> to all relations
> every nation, every tribe
> every family, every stranger
> every friend and every foe
> every form and every creature
> to all relations
> > Chorus:
> > mitakuye oyasin

mitakuye oyasin
mitakuye oyasin
to all relations . . .
(the voice of Duncan Pain in Lakota:)
all my relations . . .
this sacred place, this hoop
comes from the Lakota Nation
it is from the animal nation
it comes from the wing people
it comes from the two legged
nation
this place is the place from
which all other places come
and it is good
aho (I have spoken)

one drop of water
one link in the chain
one thread, one kernel
one tiny grain
a grain, a tiny grain of sand
a world, a universe, a new
beginning
a grain, alone and yet a part
a heart within a heart
ever changing
    Chorus: mitakuye oyasin, etc.
in the circle of oneness
we dance a simple prayer
feel the beauty, know the
wonder
of the circle that we share
in the circle of oneness
a song that each one knows
in the circle of oneness
a sound from where the river
flows
    Chorus: mitakuye oyasin, etc.
we're in the circle of oneness . . .

What Is the Color of Love

For my son, Kamau

he came to me
he saw through me
and he gave me his heart
we found harmony
so much in common
though we were from worlds
apart

when I saw him
I loved him and he loved me
what could be simpler to see
but clouds of fear hovering near
coloring the simple truth
afraid to let it be . . . let it be

we had a son
and being half Black
he asked some hard questions

at six, while building sand
castles at the beach
he said, "mommy, I wonder
what people think
seeing a Black kid with a
Japanese lady?"

at seven, he watched a white
neighbor scream at me
"you should be ashamed for
having a Black child!"
and my son said
"mommy, is there something
wrong with that lady?"

at eight years old he came home
from school one day and said
"why do some people hate
Black folks so much?"

I didn't know how to answer
but I hope he never runs out of
questions

love so strong
like a simple song
it made two worlds into one
but I'm still left with a child's
question
what is the color of love?
what is the color of love?

The Chasm

on April 29, 1992, in Los Angeles
just around the corner from my
house
a Black child pours gasoline on
a store
a neighbor sees him
pleading with him to STOP! STOP!
but he can't
something has taken over his
hand
a power he has never known
he strikes a match to burn
what he thinks he will never
own
FIRE . . . FIRE!

as I watch plumes of smoke rise
around me
I wonder
is this Bosnia
is this Beirut
is this the fall of Babylon
no it's the city of lost angels

DEEP IS THE CHASM
WIDE IS THE SEA
HIGH IS THE MOUNTAIN
SO FAR IS THE DREAM

driving my car through the war
zone
I stop at a light
a young Black man looks at me
fire in his eyes
he sees in me the enemy
no time to say
hey, I loved Malcolm
or you could be my son

DEEP IS THE CHASM
WIDE IS THE SEA
HIGH IS THE MOUNTAIN
SO FAR IS THE DREAM

for 3 days my tv never slept
I watched the marathon of
madness
burn like a virus through LA's
veins
unleashing the anger old sores
pointed finger
opening new fractures
in our fragile co-existence
cracks in our spirit
faultlines in our mind

DEEP IS THE CHASM
WIDE IS THE SEA
HIGH IS THE MOUNTAIN
SO FAR IS THE DREAM

my silence grew as the tv spoke
I tried to turn it off
but it wouldn't obey me
it's still on
more marathons spilling from
the screen
flooding my room
my house . . . my brain
maybe the revolution will only
be televised
or played on the net

as I slip, as I slip into virtual
reality

life becomes a fantasy
and I'm trying to find the key
and I'm trying to find a reason
to keep on singing
what can a song do
what can a song do?
can it stop a bullet
can it tell the truth
can it help the homeless
can it talk to the youth
what, what can a song do?
can it kill the hate
can it stop the fear
can it give you hope
can it make you hear
what can a song do?

I'm losing my grip
it's like sand slipping through
my fingers
and I'm feeling so small, so
small
tinier than a grain of sand

all this fire . . . all this fire!
and where is the light?

Peggy Myo-Young Choy

DANCER AND CHOREOGRAPHER

Peggy Myo-Young Choy was born in Chicago, Illinois, and grew up in Hawaii. She danced in the womb before she began her first ballet classes at age seven. She is on the faculty of the Dance Program at the University of Wisconsin–Madison, where she teaches Asian American Movement, Asian Theater, and Javanese Dance. Her work includes Seung Hwa: Rape/Race/Rage/Revolution *(1995) and* Ki-Aché: Stories from the Belly *(1997).*

RESPONSE

My work emerges from a political and cultural commitment to telling stories of women who have been silenced or ignored, and it is inspired by the rich knowledge found in Asian dance, martial arts, and music, particularly from Korea, Java, and China. My first piece with an Asian American theme was *Sajin Shinbu/Picture Bride* (1991), which focused on the period between 1910 and 1924, when some one thousand women sailed from Korea to Hawaii to marry Korean plantation laborers after having exchanged photos. Many of these *sajin shinbu* had their hopes shattered as they met their aged husbands-to-be for the first time. Some suffered abuse and had extramarital liaisons. They carried the double burden of working in the fields alongside the men and caring for household needs. The specific genesis of this piece comes from two main sources. First, I grew up in Hawaii and came into contact with picture brides through the local Korean community. Second, the alienation and racism I experienced after moving to Madison, Wisconsin, in 1982 led to my own political awakening as an Asian American woman.

In 1985 in Madison, a group of us, including Donna Chan, Wendy Ho, Mimi Kim, Jan Miyasaki, and Joan Varney, formed a women's community group called the Pacific and Asian Women's Alliance (PAWA) . The group's energy created a lot of havoc in its wake. We were part of the illegitimate activist Minority Coalition on the University of Wisconsin–Madison campus, which pushed for increased support of ethnic studies, hiring and retention of faculty of color, as well as increased recruitment of students of color. PAWA was the engine behind the creation of the Asian American Studies Program, which was approved by then-chancellor Donna Shalala. We brought Chris Choy, Loni Ding, Maxine Hong Kingston, Nellie Wong, and Elaine Kim to campus as part of a festival, "Talking Story: Images of Asian American Women in Literature and Film." Through the solidarity generated by PAWA, I began to internalize a sense of identity as an Asian American woman. From this position of feminist strength, I first considered the possibility of telling a story about Asian American women through dance in 1993.

Since this first piece, there have been other stories about women, such as *Chongshindae/Comfort Woman*. During World War II, between eighty thousand and two hundred thousand Korean women were unwillingly abducted and forced to be sex slaves for the Japanese soldiers. Officially, they were labeled "military supplies" and were sent to the battleground, while the soldiers sarcastically called them "public lavatories." My latest work, *Ki-Aché: Stories from the Belly*, includes stories about four other women

warriors—Assata Shakur (the Black Panther), Kwon In Sook (the Korean labor organizer), Nonggae (the sixteenth-century *kisaeng*, or female entertainer), and Sarraounia (the nineteenth-century Hausa queen of Burkina Faso). Although these pieces speak for women who had little or no opportunity to tell their own stories, I create my work for anyone and everyone who wants to experience it.

The artists who have most influenced my work are those with whom I studied intensely over a number of years. Sun Ock Lee taught me not only traditional Korean dance but Son Mu/Zen dance, which she developed alongside her own practice as a Buddhist. Sasminta Mardawa, the Central Javanese dance master, taught me female style (*putri*) of Javanese dance she developed, which is strong yet subtle and refined. Suhardi tirelessly taught me Javanese music (*rebab*, the spiked fiddle) and singing (*sindenan*). There are other politically motivated artists: for instance, Ngugi wa Thiong'o, who moved the "center" with writing for the disempowered in his own native tongue. Perhaps most important are family and friends whose voices resonate with my own and who have inspired me to express my own voice with courage—my own mother, Mary Whang Choy, who lived strong and gentle compassion with fearlessness; Chan Eung Park, who introduced me to *p'ansori* (Korean storytelling/singing) and *sol changgo* (a style of Korean folk drumming); and Fred Weihan Ho, who tirelessly creates new terrain with sound.

I see myself as part of a tradition of Asian American artists only if we define "tradition" as a notion that not only extends back in time but also provides a vision for the future. I learn about "traditional forms" and, in so doing, link with traditions to create contemporary forms. I see myself not so much part of a tradition of artists per se as part of a lineage of women from whom I have learned and from whom I have received inspiration and empowerment for my life. In addition to the women I mentioned above, others include Wahyu Habib Bari (with whom I studied Javanese dance), Sung Kum Yun (with whom I studied the Korean zither *kayakum*), and Nyai Supadmi (with whom I studied Javanese singing). Others I have "met" through research and have come to "know" in my own body through my choreography. These women are the focus of my choreography. They form my imagined lineage.

If there is an "authentic" Asian American sensibility, it is not a concrete phenomenon as much as it is a process of empowerment in a changing national and global landscape. "Authenticity" means speaking with compassion and without fear not only about our own personal and political conditions and histories but about others who do not have the opportunity or time to speak out about their sufferings and injustices on their own behalf.

We as Asian American artists have an important role to play in this country. Although from an international view America may appear bullish and stable, a view from within the "belly of the beast" sees American society breaking apart at its roots. Poverty gnaws bigger and bigger holes for people of color, including Asians. Prisons incarcerate increasing numbers of African American men. Our educational institutions remain entrenched in approaches that tokenize "multiculturalism" and minimally support ethnic studies, if at all. In this context, Asian American artists need to be guerrilla teachers and spiritual warriors, particularly for the sake of our children. It is not so much whether or not we are positioned adequately to contribute to this soci-

ety. For me, it is not a matter of waiting for the right time or the right place. We are contributing as Asian American artists every moment that we are communicating to others through our work or are creating a new vision together with other artists. We contribute valuable knowledge about the process of creating linkages between cultures—not only through our artistic work but also through living our daily lives in a mindful way, whether as artists or as social activists. To me, there is no division between these paths.

There are specific challenges for Asian American dancers. Stereotypes abound when it comes to the Asian body. We are seen as exotic and inscrutable, moving in mysterious or vague ways. We are either delicate lotus-blossom women, weak and incapable of strong movements, or wicked, overaggressive dragon ladies. We are flat cardboard stereotypes of Bruce Lee or Jackie Chan, rigid and incapable of fluid, graceful movements. If we perform Asian-inspired forms or Asian dances themselves, uneducated audiences might see the movements as painfully slow or too repetitive, undynamic, and not physical enough, and thereby miss the *ki,* or *chi* (life-force energy or breath) energetics completely. One challenge for Asian American dancers is to break through constructed stereotypes that we hold about ourselves, fed us by mainstream images, and to educate ourselves about processes that support us to explore movement beyond what we thought to be our limits. To subvert stereotypes as well as to empower myself for the work I need to do, I am constantly trying to learn more about Asian forms of dance, movement, and "play" (as *tai chi* practitioners say). Right now, Korean dance, music, and theater forms are my central focus. Learning and teaching about these forms connect me to my ancestral culture. Embedded in these forms are strategies for survival and empowerment in the face of *han* (the state of continuous anguish and frustration).

I would agree that the dominant society has emasculated the Asian male, commodified the Asian female, and exoticized Asian culture in general. These dominant culture perspectives on Asians are strategies to disempower and to isolate Asian groups, not only from White society but also from other people of color. These images have far-reaching ramifications affecting Asian American politics and economics and our ability to participate actively in what we endeavor. But it's not only the dominant society that has these views of Asians; Asian Americans themselves also believe these false identities. The basis of these stereotypes is fear of or distancing oneself from the unknown. Asian Americans also fear the unknown inside ourselves. In my work, I try to create images and experiences that tell about the unknown body histories expressed through movements that are *ki* based. The body histories express stories of women who have lived in different times and spaces. I create a terrain for meetings between powerful women across space and time. For example, in my work *Ki-Aché: Stories from the Belly,* two women meet for the first time—when Nonggae, the sixteenth-century *kisaeng,* jumps from a cliff to her death in the river below, while grasping the invading Japanese general Motani. After she drowns, the body of Nonggae is lifted up by Sarraounia, the nineteenth-century Hausa queen, who leads a successful campaign against French colonial troops. Sarraounia mourns for Nonggae, and the energy of the two women warriors comes together in mutual support. Through their appearance on stage, we are informed about these two women who are different racially and culturally and yet who share uncommon courage and the

sense of justice for their people. By choreographing this work, I create the memory of these women, including both tragic and triumphant moments, expressing their stories with movement rooted in *ki* energy so that the process of performance is energizing rather than enervating.

It is up to us to seize the moment, whether there is receptivity or not in the society at large. As we look toward the twenty-first century, there are indications of a tremendous racist backlash against Asians in America. We are still seen as foreigners in this country. The persistence of the stereotypes already mentioned is an indication of our continued marginality. Some of us still believe that we can "succeed" as "model minority" and careerist artists, buying into mainstream standards, aesthetics, and measures of individualistic success. We hesitate to set our own standards and fail to measure success by the degree to which we persist, or by the degree to which we assist in the empowerment of our own communities.

As far as the reception of my work goes, I have felt great appreciation and interest from many who come to see my performances. There have been quite profound moments of communication where I have learned about my pieces in a deeper way because of insights shared by those in the audience. This dialogue is meaningful as a process of making connections and a kind of community building across gender, age, race, and ethnicity.

On the other hand, I wonder about those in the audience who have little background knowledge of Asian performance and who are ignorant about the history of political struggles of Asians in America. It remains debatable how much these people really understand the content of my work and what I am trying to forge and subvert.

To aspiring Asian American dancers, I

say two things in conclusion. The Koreans have a dish called *bibim bop*, which is basically hot rice into which you throw chopped vegetables, *kim chee* (spicy pickled cabbage), hot sauce, and any leftovers you wish. You mix everything up and then eat it. We Asian American dancers are like *bibim bop*—mixed up, but with a rich flavor that is distinctively our own. Finally, there is nothing like dance. Dance has the capacity to reveal and express profound depths and insights. It has the capacity to empower, to stimulate social change, to create imagined lineages, and it can both clarify and construct our identity as Asian Americans. It can root us in the moment, in the midst of the confusion of daily life, and can give us vision and surety when we face the insecurity of ambiguity and change in chaotic times. As Asian American dancers, we have unique stories and much to tell. But to speak with power, you have to be honest and clear. This is a lifetime challenge.

Jon Jang

COMPOSER AND PIANIST

Born in 1954 in Los Angeles, Jon Jang grew up in northern California, began piano lessons at the late age of nineteen, received his bachelor of music degree in piano performance at the Oberlin Conservatory of Music in Ohio in 1978, and has been breaking barriers and crossing genres as a composer, pianist, and artistic director ever since. A pioneer in exploring the interface of jazz and classical music, Jang has been developing original works noted for their compelling mix of influences and sounds. Jang's work has a strong lyrical quality that is informed by Chinese folk music, African American spirituals and sorrow songs, European expressionism, and French impressionism. With more than ten recordings, Jang and his ensembles have performed in major concert halls and jazz festivals in China, South Africa, Europe, Canada and the United States. As a composer, Jang has received numerous commissions from the National Endowment for the Arts, the Rockefeller Foundation, the Kronos Quartet, and others. Jang has also composed scores for theater and film, including the 1994 dramatic adaptation of Maxine Hong Kingston's The Woman Warrior and Renee Tajima-Peña's 1997 documentary My America . . . or, Honk if You Love Buddha. *He has collaborated with prominent African American, Asian American, and Latino writers and musicians; performed with the Los Angeles Philharmonic; and taught an Asian American music course at the University of California, Irvine.*

RESPONSE ⌐

Knowing Where the One Iz (in Order to Know Where You Are Going)

Through my various associations and collaborations with many musicians from the Chinese diaspora, I have based my musical language over the years on the recontextualization of Chinese sorrow songs in a "modern" jazz or classical music context from a Chinese American perspective. Some of my works reflect this concept: *Tiananmen!* (1992); *The Procession/Woman Shaman of Alishan* (1993); *Two Flowers on a Stem* (1994); *Island: The Immigrant Suite* no. 1 (1995), which featured the poetry of Genny Lim; and *Island: The Immigrant Suite* no. 2 (1996), for string quartet and a Cantonese Opera singer. However, for nearly twenty years, I had almost no direct access to Chinese traditional music and jazz.

During the early 1970s, the power of African American music and culture had a profound impact on my understanding of culture and ideology. Listening to the music of John Coltrane's late recordings, such as *Expression,* and reading books by Amiri Baraka and W. E. B. Du Bois inspired me. Du Bois's *The Souls of Black Folk* (1903) recognized the importance of spirituals and sorrow songs as the foundation of African American culture. When I first learned about the Chinese building the railroad in the United States, I wondered if the Chinese sang work songs or sorrow songs while working and what they sounded like. They must have sung traditional songs, but the context was totally different. Building a railroad in Canton was not like working for robber barons Leland Stanford and cronies; for as Amiri Baraka noted in *Blues People* (1963), "It is obvious that working one's own field is quite different from forced labor in a foreign land." In my search for the Cantonese "blues," my "uncle" Philip Choy, a

spokesperson for the Chinese Historical Society of America in San Francisco, gave me a poem written by a Chinese immigrant, expressing his lament on Angel Island; but unfortunately, Uncle Philip had no audio recordings and did not know where to find them. Much later, the 1980s, I discovered Cantonese "blues" in Cantonese Opera performances in the Chinatowns of San Francisco and New York.

Apart from my piano teacher, Wilbur Price, Dr. Wendell Logan was perhaps my most influential teacher at the Oberlin Conservatory of Music. In his African American music history course, Dr. Logan assigned us Duke Ellington's *A Tone Parallel to Harlem,* a work that expressed "a tone parallel" to the life of African Americans. Ellington's work and William Grant Still's *Afro-American Symphony* inspired me to dream about Chinese American music. Although the Black liberation and third world movements and the power of African American music through John Coltrane liberated me on a humanistic, spiritual, and political level, I could only *imagine* the possibility of my liberation through an Asian American music because I was unaware of any existing models.

The year 1981 was a turning point for me as an Asian American artist. Responding to an announcement in the Stanford University student newspaper about an Asian American music workshop, I met Francis Wong. As the only participants who attended the workshop, Francis and I discovered that we shared a number of common interests in music and politics. In October we attended the first Asian American Jazz Festival (AAJF) in San Francisco, which has since become the longest-running continuous jazz festival in San Francisco. The concert performances by Russel Baba's ensemble and United Front made me realize that my dream of creating a music so personal and powerful could become a reality. Compositions such as "Forgotten Spirits" and "I Will Be Free" by Japanese American bassist Mark Izu represented strong examples of music that is informed by a combination of traditional Asian music forms, such as sixteenth-century Japanese court music called *gagaku*, and jazz based on the African American music tradition.

The early examples of Asian American jazz, or what the musicians prefer to identify as Asian American Creative Music, can be characterized as a collaboration between Japanese American musicians who grew up in the Bay Area and transplanted African American musicians originally from the Midwest. Japanese American musicians such as Mark Izu, Russel Baba, Paul Yamazaki, and Gerald Oshita sharply redefined an Asian American aesthetic in their collaborations with African American musicians George Sams, Lewis Jordan, Ray Collins, and Eddie Moore. Another significant contributor during the early years of the Asian American Jazz movement is Dr. Anthony Brown, a composer, scholar, and multiple percussionist. Born to an African and Native American father and a Japanese mother, Anthony Brown physically embodied an intercultural collaboration, akin to his description of his chosen instrument: "The drumset is comprised of European bass and snare drums derived from North African and Turkish prototypes, tom toms which were originally Chinese Tang drums, cymbals from Turkey and China, and all assembled by an African American drummer to play jazz" (*The Development of Modern Jazz Drumset Performance, 1940–50* [Ann Arbor, Mich.: University Microfilm International, 1997], 52–53).

My second recording, *Are You Chinese or Charlie Chan?* was released in March 1984. What is significant about this recording is that it is music *about* Asian Americans, *by* Asian Americans, *for* Asian Americans, and *created from* the Asian American communities, as I explained on the liner notes:

This music is about Asian Americans.

This album is dedicated to Vincent Chin, a young Chinese American who was beaten to death by two white men in June 1982. Mistaken for a Japanese person ("they all look alike" or "are you Chinese or Charlie Chan?"), Vincent was made a scapegoat for high unemployment and the victim of racist anti-Japanese-import hysteria in Detroit. In March 1983, the murderers were set free on a 3 year probation and $3,700 in fines. The brutal murder of Vincent Chin and the exoneration of his murderers by the court is part of the history of racist, systematic violence, oppression and injustice that Asians have faced in America.

So this album is not only deeply dedicated to brother Vincent Chin, but also to his mother, Lily, and all Asian brothers and sisters who are struggling together to create a better world for all people.

This music is by Asian Americans. The Asian American musicians who appeared on the recording include: Francis Wong, Mark Izu, Anthony Brown, Fred Ho, Randy Senzaki and members of the San Jose Taiko Group.

This music is for and created from Asian American communities. Much of this music developed out of performances for Asian American events held at the Japanese Presbyterian Church on Sutter Street in San Francisco Japantown. East Wind, a nationwide progressive Asian American magazine, also organized an event in San Francisco Japantown which raised $2000 to help support the recording costs.

Asian American Empowerment!

I think that the stronger Asian American statements are being made on the West Coast.

—FRED HO, IN AN ARTICLE BY BRIAN AUERBACH, OPTION (1985)

During 1987–1988, Francis Wong and I cofounded AsianImprov Records (AIR) and AsianImprov aRts (AIR), nonprofit organizations based in San Francisco. Because of the vision and leadership of Francis Wong (AIR) and Mark Izu (AAJF), AsianImprov Records has over thirty recordings in its catalog, and the jazz festival remains the longest running in San Francisco. Wong's and Izu's persistence of vision and commitment have encouraged other Asian American musicians, such as Tatsu Aoki from Chicago and Jeff Song from Boston, to produce their own recordings under AIR and to create Asian American jazz festivals in their respective cities, events that have drawn mainstream attention. Other prominent Asian American musicians who are strongly connected to this movement include Glenn Horiuchi from Los Angeles, Miya Masaoka and Jeff Chan from San Francisco, Vijay Iyer from Berkeley, Hafez Modirzadeh from San Jose, and Kenny Endo from Honolulu. Many Asian American artists have collaborated with musicians in this movement, including performance artist Sachiko Nakamura, choreographer-dancer Paul Unbungen, poet-playwright Genny Lim, performance artist and writer Brenda Wong Aoki, actor Kelvin Han Yee, and writer David Mura. New York musicians such as Jason Hwang, Akira Tana, Sumi Tonooka, and Fred Ho have all performed at the Asian American Jazz Festival in San Francisco. They, too, were inspired to hold an Asian American Jazz Festival in New York, which unfortunately lasted only a few years during the mid-1980s.

Audience and reception? Music is an expression of my life and is an offering. My deepest experience is when the music comes *through* me rather than to me. I do not expect everyone to experience the music in the same way as I do. I just hope that the music will help move the audience in some meaningful way.

When I was preparing for my senior piano recital at the Oberlin Conservatory of Music during the summer of 1978, there were no pianos available because the conservatory building was closed. I posted a request for a piano at the town's only bank, and an African American woman, who was the music director and pianist at the Rust Methodist Church, responded. About to undergo surgery, she wanted me to replace her as the Sunday service pianist for the summer in exchange for use of the church piano.

As the only non–African American participant in the church, I found this experience very meaningful. On the last day before the minister's retirement, we all held hands and sang "Precious Lord, Take My Hand." Tears streamed down the minister's face, and I could feel the power of spiritual elevation. When it was time for my senior recital, the entire African American church community helped pack the hall. Although I did not perform Doris Akers's "Sweet, Sweet Spirit," the church joined the conservatory student audience in giving me a standing ovation after my hour-long recital of Beethoven, Ravel, Schoenberg, and Thelonious Monk. Throughout my undergraduate years at Oberlin, I had heard nothing but derisive remarks about the townspeople, who were often referred to as "townies." But the African American church community took "just a closer walk with" me in proud step through the halls of the conservatory. When you give something meaningful to the community, they will give back something meaningful.

Since then, one of my goals as an artist has been to dismantle "arts apartheid" and bring as many different kinds of people to the table as possible in some meaningful way. When the world premiere of *SenseUs— The Rainbow AnthemS* was performed at Davies Symphony Hall in San Francisco in 1990, the audience of color gave us a standing ovation. *SenseUs* is a music and poetry collaboration that also featured Max Roach, John Santos, Sonia Sanchez, Genny Lim, and Victor Hernández Cruz. The purpose of the work is to question the present national anthem by creating a body of anthems that will express a multiplicity of voices, as a way to expand democracy for people of color. Because most people do not know all the words and cannot sing the difficult national anthem, which was based on an eighteenth-century British sex and drinking song, *The Star-Spangled Banner* is essentially undemocratic.

When the world premiere of my work *Tiananmen!* was performed at the Julia Morgan Theatre in Berkeley in 1992, the sold-out audience of four hundred, made up of "Asian Americans, African Americans, and other communities," gave us a standing ovation. Before the world premiere of *Tiananmen!* there was a free outdoor work-in-progress performance at Portsmouth Square, the center of San Francisco Chinatown, where elderly Chinese men congregate and play chess in the park. When they heard the familiar Chinese folk songs in a jazz context, they sang along to the songs and applauded in a boisterous and celebratory manner. They then grabbed my CDs and proceeded to sell them to people on the street.

After a concert I organized including some of the leading African American and Chinese musicians in United States, at the University of California, Berkeley's Zellerbach Hall, a nationally respected spokesperson from the arts community remarked on the "rainbow" audience of fourteen hundred, who gave a standing ovation to my sextet. In my continued pursuit of dismantling "arts apartheid" and developing mixed audiences of color, James Newton and I have been commissioned by Cal Performances and the Walker Art Center in Minneapolis to collab-

orate on a new piece. We are currently composing *When Sorrow Turns to Joy,* a tribute to Paul Robeson and Mei Lanfang. Newton and I had a highly successful residency in Minneapolis during the summer of 1997, under the sponsorship of the Walker Art Center, Asian American Renaissance, and Penumbra Theatre. Our workshop performances drew a balanced mix of audiences from the communities of African Americans, Asian Americans, and European Americans.

Two Flowers on a Stem
During the past eight years, I have been listening to Chinese folk songs, from both the northern and southern regions of China. When I was creating *Two Flowers on a Stem,* I composed a melody for the *erhu* that had characteristics very similar to Chinese folk songs, but I placed it in a jazz ballad context. In counterpoint to the elegant and lone voice of the *erhu* melody, the other musicians are free to contribute toward creating a panorama of sound that I associate with silken watercolor paintings. As part of a distinct generation of Chinese Americans who are trying to recast the Chinese phrase *Xungen wenzu* (searching for one's roots and ancestors), coined by Professor L. Ling-chi Wang as an expression of ethnic pride and consciousness, I wanted to compose a love song that would allow conflict to become tenderness, to express a desire for beauty and strength. But underneath the beauty are tragic overtones.

Two Flowers on a Stem is dedicated to my mother. Her American dream was shattered when my father died tragically in the worst airline disaster during the 1950s. My mother, who was four months pregnant at the time, was denied funeral services for my father at the Glendale Cemetery in southern California because he was Chinese American—even though he had been burned to ashes. Two years later, my mother suffered a nervous breakdown and had to take electroshock treatment in Belmont, California. Despite these hardships, my mother survived and raised three children by herself. *Two Flowers on a Stem* is the about the lily that can endure in the swamp.

Chen Jiebing is featured on erhu as the voice penetrating the heart of tragedy and transforming it into the embodiment of beauty. There is a strong connection in the relationship between tragedy and beauty in an earlier work, *Tiananmen!* as there is in *Two Flowers on a Stem*. This connection can be traced to the early composers for the *erhu*, such as Hua Yan-Jun, when he responded to his losing his sight by composing *Moon Reflected over the Autumn Lake* as a way to remember the beauty of life.

EDITOR'S NOTE: The album *Two Flowers on a Stem* (Soul Note, 1996) is performed by the Jon Jang Sextet: Jon Jang, piano; James Newton, flute; David Murray, tenor sax, bass clarinet; Chen Jiebing, erhu (Chinese two-stringed violin); Santi Debriano, bass daluo (Chinese large gong); Jabali Billy Hart, drums.

Island: The Immigrant Suite *No. 2 (for String Quartet and Cantonese Opera Singer)*

I owe a lot to the Chinese immigrant poets who lit the first candles. Their poetry not only represents a testimony to the indignity they suffered coming here, but it is also an affirmation of the truth about institutional racism in the United States. During the Chinese Exclusion Act (1882–1943), the Chinese in the United States were targets of racist exclusion laws for nearly sixty years, and they continue to be among the disenfranchised in this society. In an atmosphere of anti-immigrant bashing and racist scape-goating, "it depends on all of us together to roll back the wild wave."

Island: The Immigrant Suite no. 2 for string quartet and Cantonese Opera singer (1996) is inspired by the poetry carved on the walls by Chinese immigrants who were incarcerated on the Angel Island Immigration Station in San Francisco Bay. I selected nine poems from the book *Island: Poetry and History of Chinese Immigrants on Angel Island, 1910–1940*, edited by Him Mark Lai, Genny Lim, and Judy Yung (1980), and programmed them into five movements, placed in partially chronological order. The early movements feature the poetry supported by the accompaniment of the string quartet, while the later movements feature the string quartet. The five subtitles of the movements are derived from the English translations of various lines from the poems.

Mvt. 1—"Sadness kills the person in the wooden building"

Mvt. 2—"The sad person sits alone, leaning by the window"

Mvt. 3—"What happiness is there in this?"

Mvt. 4—"I grieve for my native land"

Mvt. 5—"It depends on all of us together to roll back the wild wave"

Stop anti-immigrant exclusion laws!

EDITOR'S NOTE: *Island: The Immigrant Suite* no. 2 for String Quartet and Cantonese Opera Singer was commissioned by the Kronos Quartet through Chamber Music America with funding from the Pew Charitable Trusts and the CAC Challenge Program. It was performed by the Kronos Quartet (David Harrington, violin; John Sherba, violin; Hank Dutt, viola; Joan Jeanrenaud, cello) and Eva Tam, Cantonese Opera singer.

Island: the Immigrant Suite No. 2
Mvt. I

"Sadness kills the person in the wooden building"

Jon Jang
Zhang Music ASCAP
C.P. 1996

Mvt. V

"It depends on all of us together to roll back the wild wave"
Stop anti-immigrant exclusion laws!

18

PHOTO COURTESY FRED HO

Fred Ho

~~~~~~

MUSICIAN AND COMPOSER

Born in Palo Alto, California, in 1957, Fred Wei-han Ho grew up near Amherst, Massachusetts, and attended Harvard, where he was alienated by the Eurocentric curriculum and the academic elitism. After graduating with a bachelor's degree in Sociology in 1979, Ho became a construction worker for two years. During periods of unemployment, he picked up the baritone saxophone, his high school instrument, and found himself happiest playing music (sometimes six hours a day). He moved to New York City with no contacts and has been making a living from his music ever since.

Self-styled as "a revolutionary socialist Chinese American baritone saxophonist, composer/arranger, leader of the Afro Asian Music Ensemble and the Monkey Orchestra, a longtime activist in the Asian American Movement," Ho has five

recordings to date: Tomorrow Is Now! *(1985)*, Bamboo That Snaps Back *(1986)*, A Song for Manong *(1988)*, We Refuse to Be Used and Abused *(1989), and* The Underground Railroad to My Heart *(1994). His honors and awards include Harvard University, Peter Ivers Fellow, 1987; Duke Ellington Distinguished Artist, 1988; Chinese for Affirmative Action Honorees, 1990; a National Endowment for the Arts Music Composition Fellowship, 1993; and a Rockefeller Bellagio Residency, 1998.*

RESPONSE ⌐

My music is a synthesis of African American musical influences with Asian folk musical elements, first explored as an activist

347

in Boston's Chinatown in the late 1970s to early 1980s. I wanted to pursue artistic/aesthetic forms that were *not* Eurocentric.

The Black revolution of the late 1960s and early 1970s, when I was a teenager, inspired my own awakening in terms of cultural identity, political and cultural consciousness. I immediately plunged into the most radical politics, music, and literature of the day: Malcolm X, the Black Panthers, Archie Shepp, Amiri Baraka and the Black Arts Movement, Sonia Sanchez, and so forth. Writing and playing music, writing poetry, became an outlet for the explosion of ideas and emotions I was going through as an Asian American, realizing that my pain and troubles with White racism were not my fault (the blaming myself as the victim syndrome) but the result of a racist society that profited from slavery, contract labor, a divided working class—a whole system of inequality and injustice. The Black liberation struggle gave a framework and reference to understanding my own oppression and struggles. Soon, as I got involved in Asian American activism, I began a process of learning about the histories and cultures of the Asian/Pacific peoples in the United States.

As one of the founding organizers of the Asian American Resource Workshop in Boston's Chinatown, I learned the folk songs and music of the immigrant workers. This is how I began to forge both African American and Asian musics. My music is simply a reflection of my own development, as well as a larger socio-cultural-political vision of dismantling Eurocentrism and White supremacy and implementing a new, genuine, revolutionary Afro-Asian multicultural musical expression. It is neither American nor Asian but quintessentially Asian American.

I create for all open-minded, justice-loving people. My validation and legitimation is oriented not toward the (White) main-stream but among oppressed nationalities (primarily African and Asian Americans). My work is revolutionary, therefore "experimental" and not mainstream, conventional, easily digestible because immediately familiar. I don't expect everyone to understand or embrace it. If that were the case, then it wouldn't be provocative and challenging the status quo—the existing state of things, ideas, and sounds. I seek to inspire oppressed peoples, particularly Asian American and African American people who want to struggle against our common oppression. Those who don't want to struggle or who may not have come to that position yet will have a difficult time with my stand and views, but they might respect and appreciate my artistic craft. If they continue to connect with the music, they may begin to change and realize that my politics can't be divorced from my music—because both will continue to be very, very strong!

My sources of individual artistic inspiration include, but are not limited to, John Coltrane, Charles Mingus, Archie Shepp, Ngugi wa Thiong'o, Aretha Franklin. I am moved by profound cultural rootedness (grounding) and soulful expression and originality, as well as attendant social consciousness.

Conversely, I do not admire or have much tolerance for insincere opportunists, trying to cash in on fads, who exploit and steal the cultural resources of others, aim for mainstream success, lust after White critical anointment, and lack serious talent and creativity. I am most impressed by sincerity and depth, which is measured not necessarily by technique, production values—that is, quantitative measurements—but rather by qualitative efforts and results, the soulfulness and emotional and intellectual profundity of a good story, a down-to-earth fullness about life, ideas, and human experiences.

My traditions are African and Asian

American in artistic form. My philosophy is internationalist and revolutionary socialist.

What is "a tradition of Americans" if it isn't multicultural and hybrid? "American" is not mostly White or European except in terms of power and control of institutions and resources and wealth. I am in the tradition of rebels, guerrillas, agitators, heathens, that is, all those rejected, despised, hated, and opposed by the White patriarchal bourgeoisie.

What makes Asian American art and culture Asian American? Is it simply the ethnicity of the artist? Or is it the cultural forms and traditions contained either explicitly or implicitly in the works? No single Asian American sensibility exists, because Asian Americans are a plurality of nationalities and national heritages, cultures, and languages. Furthermore, I reject the notion that anything by an artist who happens to be Asian American makes it Asian American art. "Asian American authenticity" is both the content (explicit) and the form (implicit). It is not genetic! (That would be racialist!) Many of today's modern Asian American artists, while trying to express Asian American themes and experiences, don't know the first thing about Asian cultural traditions and forms as carried to the United States by the immigrants. They merely ape or imitate Western (mostly White European) forms and traditions. However, there are also a number of Asian American artists who have embraced Asian American cultural forms and traditions, either practicing it close to tradition or seeking to synthesize new forms. Some of these artists are Peggy Choy, Music from China, H. T. Chen, Genny Lim, Mark Izu, Brenda Wong-Aoki, Dan Kwong, the various *taiko* groups, Frank Chin, Mu Theater, Kulintang Arts, Silkroad Theater.

Q: What are the most pressing burdens/ urgencies/responsibilities facing Asian American artists today?

1. Creating our own standards of excellence and aesthetic criteria by developing *independent* criteria and standards of cultural excellence based upon commitment to community, to struggle and liberation from Eurocentric and White supremacist standards and values. Asian American cultural and arts journalism needs to be more than ethnic cheerleading or hype but must critically examine the content and forms of our artistic works.

2. Institution building or cultural empowerment to produce and disseminate our own work. The "nonprofit" grants hustling has created a sector of cultural pimps, of arts brokers and accommodationists who are literally dependent upon mostly government and (some) corporate "benevolence." This dependency has gutted our cultural movement and weakened our artistic efforts. Even the word *empowerment* has been coopted by these hustlers (cf. several Bay Area Asian American arts groups), who espouse the rhetoric that funding "is our share of tax dollars." As they get more grants, their work gets weaker and weaker, their politics less militant and critical. Grants qua grants are not wrong or pernicious, but the ideological and political dependency upon them is simply tokenism and co-optation. Our own independent institutions and forms can be a mixture of grants as well as community support. We need more grassroots, militant, bold, and daring organizations, collectives, and enterprises.

3. Uniting activists, artists, intellectuals toward a movement for our collective liberation from White racist national oppression. Without a movement, we are simply individuals struggling and trying to do our work up against tremendous obstacles and booby traps. A movement collectivizes above points 1 and 2 and provides the base of support, direction, clarity, and vision for us to succeed both artistically and financially (i.e., more of

us rather than a few superstars). This movement can only be built by the most conscious and committed core, rather than a diluted democracy that starts at the lowest common denominator and goes nowhere.

What are the risks and challenges peculiar to Asian American artists? To avoid the trap of seeking White critical and financial acceptance and dependency. Too often, if the White media certify one of us as legitimate or "good," our communities finally recognize us. This is simply internalized oppression: We wait until our oppressors say it's OK, then it's OK. We will be trapped in this syndrome until we become more independent and liberated, develop our own arts and cultural journalism and media grounded on militant struggle.

How do I, individually, resolve this? First, I'll never become a nonprofit entity! (I don't believe in nonprofit, since the money is based on the state and the superprofits of imperialism, and nonprofit success is increasingly replicating the for-profit models, e.g., boards of directors, slickness, marketing, etc. I guess I'm antiprofit!) I earn my money the honest way: I work and sell my creative labor power, and I occasionally get aid from sympathizers inside institutions. Second, I don't read or care about what the mainstream arts media say. Third, I accept that I am a revolutionary artist, that my path will be of tremendous hardship and sacrifice, and that I will fight by any means necessary for victory and progress. My goal is clear, my commitment and spirit are strong, my integrity uncompromising.

As part of our systematic oppression, we cannot define our own identity or control our representation. To confront this oppression, we need not only to oppose stereotyping but more actively to generate our own cultural production, *independent* from White mainstream legitimation and support, whether it

be funding (NEA, PBS, Rockefeller, et al.), critics (*New York Times*, White academia, et al.), or careers.

"Emasculation" vis-à-vis what values of "manhood"? "Manhood" is equated to the Big White Man! As part of the destruction of patriarchy, much of social life and meaning has to be degendered, especially as gender intersects with power. In a sexist society, there is very little chance of being nonsexist. Both men and women have to be antisexist. Violence against women will end only when women defend themselves. Male monopolization of the means of violence is the primary pillar of women's oppression.

With more revolutionary Asian American men and women who transform both their personal and political lives, we will reject our oppressor's sexual commodification, internalized oppression, and feelings of inferiority.

I am one of the few Asian American male artists who has created such a vast, explicit body of work about the struggles of Asian and Asian American women: *Bound Feet*, "What's a Girl to Do?" "Earth Is Rockin' in Revolution/Drowning in the Yellow River" (poems by Janice Mirikitani), "Song of a Slave Girl," "Lan Hua Hua" (an anti–arranged marriage Chinese folk song), the opera *Warrior Sisters: The New Adventures of African and Asian Women Warriors*, the suite *Yes Means Yes, No Means No, Whatever She Wears, Wherever She Goes!* (commissioned by the Brooklyn Women's Anti-Rape Exchange and Women's Health Action and Mobilization), and many others. I have collaborated with Genny Lim, Janice Mirikitani, Marina Feleo-Gonzalez, Alleluia Panis, Peggy Choy, Cindy Zuoxin Wang, Sonia Sanchez, Alma Villegas, Esther Iverem, Didi Dubelyew, and many others.

Regarding my brothers, I take the position put forward by Ms. Pearl Cleage in *Mad at Miles* (i.e., Davis, the jazz icon): Those who beat us (women) can not be our cultural heroes! In my "jazz" profession, objectification and exploitation of women are rampant; for instance, there's this big-name jazz flute player who keeps score of his more than two hundred sexual conquests, and there's an Asian American pianist who secretly admires this and confers his respect and friendship on such men. These men are not my heroes nor my friends nor my professional colleagues anymore. How many men can break off their professional or personal relations with men who disrespect and abuse women? I have and will do so. More of us must. The whining cries of the "emasculated Asian man" need to be silenced, with even a fist to the mouth if it comes to that. We haven't the energy to waste on such patriarchal rubbish, because we should be fighting the patriarchal, White racist capitalist system.

Is this a particularly receptive moment for Asian American artists? No, only for those who are "safe" and "polite" to the White gatekeepers. The small "gains" (really token), such as *Vanishing Son,* Margaret Cho, the writers (tell me, who really makes $40,000 a year off their creative writing?), one or two filmmakers (most are still in "nonprofit"), don't amount to anything significant. We still don't own or control or have decision-making power in any corporate communications companies, entertainment conglomerates, or anything else, except for some tepid and "safe" nonprofits. Anti-Asian violence hasn't diminished; on the contrary, it has skyrocketed. Instead of Bruce Lee, we now have the revival of an aging and potbellied David Carradine, a Russell Wong who can't fight, John Lone as a pulp-era "Yellow peril" buddy, a whole bunch of Asian American actresses who can't act and are always the love object of White men (on screen and in real life), the continual ped-dling of Asian as exotic by Asian Americans. This *is* a particularly receptive moment for co-optation of Asian Americans.

How would I characterize the reception of my work? Reception by whom? I *hope* the White bourgeoisie doesn't like it. I *hope* oppressed and justice-loving people find it provocative, interesting, and possibly inspiring and catalytic. What is most "lacking" is the disappointing level of Asian American arts journalism and cultural criticism/studies.

Because I don't expect justice and fairness from the system, whatever I've achieved has been a victory. I am able to live off music, which even for Whites in my profession is rare! I've paid off the mortgage to my beautiful duplex loft at the age of thirty-seven. So my shelter expenses are pretty much met. Recently, despite a serious personal injury, I've been able to exceed my personal best and can now do five hundred meters of the butterfly, three hundred sit-ups, three hundred push-ups, sixty chin-ups. I design my own clothes, cook wonderful meals, enjoy both monogamous and open relationships, and only a handful of baritone saxophonists in the world can do what I do technically on the instrument. I have won numerous highly competitive awards, and not the least, I am still a revolutionary socialist. I am very grateful for the revolutionary movement of the late 1960s and early 1970s for changing my life forever, giving me a profound life purpose, and challenging me with the questions "Who am I?" "Am I who I am?" "Am I all that I ought to be?" (Frantz Fanon).

Q: How do African American influences contribute to an Asian American musician's work?

In terms of my cultural references and standards, I have looked to the leading and principal oppressed nationality in this society: the African Americans. Despite persisting institutional racism, American music is quintessentially African American. So-called classical music is really Western European concert music. American "classical" music is jazz, American "popular" music is blues, rhythm and blues, soul, funk, rap/hip-hop, et cetera. So the American aspect of being Asian American in the context of music must connect with the African American musical traditions and forms.

Furthermore, the themes and ethos of African American music and culture are more readily resonant and relevant to us as oppressed nationalities: themes such as hope, struggle, redemption, celebration of resistance and perseverance, the triumph of the spirit and soul despite persecution, oppression, and injustice, et cetera. As a young Asian American, Black music spoke to my pain, suffering, struggle, and gave me joy, hope, the spirit of struggle, the moral fortitude that made me affirm that the oppressors are not our superiors but, indeed, morally inferior and repugnant.

Too many artists and intellectuals trained by the Academy have internalized European values, standards, methodology, aesthetics, and paradigms, including those who claim to be "critics" but tail Foucault, French philosophy, European art history, et cetera, et cetera.

Up until 1986, I characterized my music as "jazz" with Asian American thematic and musical references (i.e., "Asian American jazz"). During many years of committed cultural work within the "movement," I was struggling with the question: What makes Chinese American music Chinese American? What would make for an Asian American musical content and form that would be transformative of American music as well, and not simply be subsumed in one or another American musical genre, such as "jazz"? I began to embark upon a course which I now articulate as creating "an Afro-Asian new

American multicultural music." Taking Mark Izu's significant leadership in the incorporation of traditional Asian instrumentation (in his case, mostly in improvised or incidental approaches), I began to explore such an incorporation in a composed, orchestrated manner. With no desire to be a Sinophile or Asian traditional music academic, yet recognizing the importance of studying and drawing from traditional formic structures, I wanted to capture and evoke the spirit of folk music in both (solo and ensemble) performance and in composition.

Earlier in 1985, in New York City, at the request of Jodi Long, then a member of my Asian American Art Ensemble, I had composed music for her multimedia work *Bound Feet*, which incorporated the Chinese double-reed *sona* and the Chinese two-stringed fiddle, the *erhu*, orchestrated with Western woodwinds, contrabass, and multiple percussion. I wrote the *sona* and *erhu* parts in Chinese notation, an ability I had acquired from my days leading a Chinese folksinging group. Though *Bound Feet* was only performed twice, I was personally excited by the musical results of this embryonic integration of Eastern, nontempered, and Western, tempered, instruments. While employing my own "jazz" voicing in the harmonization of the parts, I had struck upon some new, fresh, and unusual timbral qualities from this combination. This synthesis of Chinese and African American components seemed to be a musical analogy for the Chinese American identity, or even further, something Afro-Asian in sensibility.

In 1986–1987, I then embarked upon composing what was to become the first modern Chinese American opera, *A Chinaman's Chance*. I wanted this new opera to be an extension of the traditional Chinese opera in America that was once so active in the Chinatown communities before World War

II. My concept was to utilize the wood-fishhead and syllabic verse chants as episodic narration. I collaborated with the Chinese musicologist Guang Ming Lee, whom I had met at a "Jazz and World Music" symposium at Wesleyan University in the summer of 1986. We utilized both Cantonese and Beijing opera melodic styles, integrated with African American rhythmic, harmonic, and orchestrational influences. I wrote the bilingual libretto (with sections drawn from historical narratives and the epilogue based on a Genny Lim poem), which was more of a history lesson than a conventional plot/story, though it is a story of the transformation of the Chinese immigrant god, Kwan Gung, as metaphor for the transformation of the Chinese to becoming Chinese American. It was a major struggle to fund a stage production. In April 1989, a one-time full-stage performance finally happened. The Celestial Orchestra did not perform in the pit as per Western opera tradition but was situated right on stage in accordance with Chinese opera practice—part of the drama itself. Along with *erhu* and *sona,* the orchestra consisted of "jazz" players on saxophones, bassoon, Western strings, and jazz rhythm section with Chinese opera percussion. (Since Chinese music lacks brass, I only employed strings, woodwinds, and percussion.)

In the process of realizing this opera, I struggled with two major vexing issues that confront the creation of a truly multicultural synthesis. First, the integration of two vastly different musical traditions requires bi- or multicultural musicians and artists, willing to stretch beyond their traditional roles and approaches. As such experimental works sorely lack financial resources, it is hard to sustain the years of rehearsal and interfacing needed to forge such an interactive musical dialogue and exchange. Such projects, aimed at forging a multicultural music, have taken many years of effort, working with a stable core of musicians who are themselves in the process of understanding the concept for which I am striving. The Chinese artists with whom I work are not only master musicians within their own traditions and context but are also open to playing my music, which they call *jen chi gwai* (literally, "very strange"). Their initial skepticism toward combining Chinese and jazz music has since given way to genuine excitement and commitment. Also, among the "Western" players, I have found a musical and socio-political comradeship with Iranian American tenor saxophonist Hafez Modirzadeh, whose own "chromodal discourse" conception toward both saxophone performance and composition is a shared theoretical and practical approach to synthesizing tempered and non- and variably tempered music—in his case, between Persian and African American. I also share comradeship with the world music and jazz percussionist Dr. Royal Hartigan. His astounding comprehensive fluency in percussion tradition from all around the world has achieved such a multicultural synthesis in the world of rhythm.

Q: How can music contribute to political agendas, such as making known little-known histories of the oppressed and the forgotten, or internationalist and revolutionary socialism?

Music, like art, does not exist or stand above society, but is a part of society, part of a culture of a group of people. Music alone cannot make a new society or produce a social revolution. But music has been used in and been a part of social movements that, when organized, have created social change. Music expresses the spirit, emotions, and ideas of change, struggle, of rebellion and discontent with the established social order and cultural status quo. Music evokes a cultural, aesthetical, spiritual, and intellectual challenge both from its forms and its content. Music becomes a material force when it interconnects with movements, activists, and organizers: when it becomes the sounds of social unrest and revolutionary vision. Musicians and artists assist and become part of a revolutionary process in several ways: from the works they create, from their own political practice, from how their works are embraced by social movements, irrespective of their intention or conscious activity.

Advice for aspiring musicians? I don't give advice, since I'm self-taught and stumbled into a music career. I still don't put much thought or energy into a "career." I just do what I do. Just keep struggling and never be complacent as long as people are oppressed and exploited.

EDITOR'S NOTE: Parts of the above response are taken from an essay by Fred Ho, "'Jazz,' Kreolization and Revolutionary Music for the Twenty-first Century," in *Sounding Off! Music as Subversion/Resistance/Revolution* (Brooklyn, N.Y.: Autonomedia, 1995), 140–41. Fred Ho's recordings are available by writing to Fred Ho, 443 12th Street #1H, Brooklyn, NY 11215.

PHOTO COURTESY JAMEZ CHANG

Jamez Chang

HIP-HOP AND RAP ARTIST

*Born in 1972, Jamez Chang is a radio person-
ality, hip-hop artist, and poet. He hosts the
New York radio show* Sori: Korean Traditional Music *on AM 930. Jamez also composes
and performs his own music, fusing Korean folk
music with hip-hop. He has spoken at Harvard
and Yale, among other colleges. Jamez is currently working on the music for the documentary* 7-Train, *directed by Hye Jung Park and
J. T. Takagi. He has toured extensively on the
East Coast for various Asian American bene-
fits and in 1998 released his debut album,* Z-
Bonics. *Jamez lives in Flushing, Queens,
where he is a member of the renowned Korean
drumming troupe Binari.* Z-Bonics *can be ordered at www.Jamez.iama.com.*

RESPONSE

My artistic work comes from a desperate
need to communicate. Growing up, I was always expressive. I was like the class clown,
clamoring for attention, telling teachers and
principals what was on my mind. Unfortunately, these "acts of expression" often got
me in trouble, and the next thing I knew, I
was trying to explain to my parents why I got
suspended from this school, expelled from
that one. But I couldn't get through to them;
the cultural and generational gap seemed like
a canyon between us. Enter musical outlet.

So I traded in my childhood baseball-
card collection for an acoustic guitar, and I

started to write. At the age of fifteen, I wrote my first song, "Black Man Singing in a White Man's World." It was like a fusion of reggae, folk, and hip-hop. But more important, it was a metaphor for the alienation that I, as a young Asian kid, felt but could never elegantly express—until that moment. Since Bruce Lee was dead and Margaret Cho wasn't big back then, I found my role models in the Black community. Chuck D., Run, Malcolm X, and Alex Haley guided me through adolescence and later inspired me to delve into my own roots, my own musical heritage.

My only exposure to Korean music as a teenager was the slow, lofty court music you hear when people light incense. Not to dis on court music, but most classical music buggs me out. I guess it goes back to my mom wanting me to be the Azian Vivaldi, her wrapping a violin around my umbilical cord. So I was turned off at an early age. But the summer of my junior year in high school changed everything. I went to Korea for the second time in my life. The first place I wanted to visit wasn't the Buddhist temples but the record stores. What a disappointment! The Michaels ruled all— Michael Bolton and George Michaels. Even in Korea the market was flooded with Western cultural hegemony (at the time, I didn't know what this meant). I took extreme measures and tried to find the most "Korean-looking" CD I could find. I went to the folk section and picked out a *Pansori* album, attracted by the "authentic" Korean costumes.

That day I was introduced to the Korean oral tradition. *Pansori* is like the rap for Koreans. It tells a story, introduces characters and settings, and satirizes the ruling class. It has elements of improvisation and relies heavily on call and response. From then on, I became a collector. While DJs in the hip-hop community were collecting funk and jazz records, I was searching coast to coast for Korean folk music. I felt like Indiana Jones Chang, digging up the lost archives—the culture that my parents, my community, never bothered to show me. For me, this retrieval symbolized my search for an identity. In the past I had always tried to be someone else (Black, White, Latino, etc.) because I never felt comfortable speaking in Korean. I spoke other people's experiences, listened to other people's dialects. Learning about Korean music was like learning my native tongue, albeit musically. This education continued throughout my college years and was seasoned by an introduction to Asian American activism.

I got hip to Asian Americanness when I started reading the histories of Chinese and Filipino laborers in the United States. The indignities these people suffered reminded me of the hardships of African and Native Americans. Believe it or not, it wasn't until college that I learned that this country of ours herded Japanese Americans into concentration camps. In the next four years I was showered with awareness, meeting other Asian Americans who wanted to know more about their contributions, their history in the United States. A great catalyst for this growing campus activism was a musician named Fred Ho. It was Fred who convinced me to combine my interests in Asian American issues with my music. If I was to advocate Asian American awareness on the social, economic, and political levels, why not infuse my music with an "Asian American attitude"? This "attitude" evolved into my first experiments with mixing Korean folk music with hip-hop.

It is this fusion or search for an "Asian American aesthetic" that continues to be the most challenging and rewarding experience for me as an artist. For five years now, I've been "creating Asian American culture," so to speak. It almost feels like I'm a mad scientist, constructing make-believe sound gardens for Asian American tears. The challenge: How to convince people that it's OK to listen to your native music, that it actually can be fun. When I say "native," that pretty much gives away my notion of what Asian American music should contain. Do we really want Philip Glass to represent Asian American music?! Or do we want to reclaim the music that for so long has been background music for Jean Claude Van Damme flicks? So there's an element of anti-appropriation involved in my work. Borrowing themes and rhythms from the Korean tradition myself, I sometimes work out of reaction: reaction to the brazen appropriation of our music by racist, yellow-face muzakkkologists.

Creating Asian American culture has been rewarding in two ways. First, I never have the luxury of "falling back" on whatever's accessible, marketable. I could be a Mountain Brother (God love 'em) and stick to representing strict hip-hop style. But my experiences with the Korean rap scene both here and in Korea tell me that we need more than imitation to get Asian America on the cultural map. Now, some say that true hip-hop artists shouldn't wear their ethnicity on their sleeves but should instead represent everyday life. Does that mean we can't talk about power and politics? 'Cuz the minute you open your mouth about the cops, you beg the question of power relationships, injustice, and oppression. Isn't race just as loaded with "-ships and -isms"? For Asian Americans to make any real impact on the hip-hop scene or make a scene of their own, we gotta make contributions to both form and content.

That's where challenge starts turning into responsibility. The moment an Asian American artist begins to advocate innovation in both form and content, he crosses an imaginary line called "authentialism" (cute fusion of authenticity and essentialism). Who

really wants to drag out the skeletons of the Frank Chin–Maxine Hong Kingston debate? Is it real or the fake—live or Memorex? Whosoever opens her mouth about what Asian American could be or should be faces the responsibility of defending herself, her new tautology, her treatise. Let's face it, that's what we start sounding like when we talk about "creating Asian American culture." People are so comfortable with the stultifying numbness of conformity that when a group of artists start talking about Asian American aesthetics, all hell breaks loose. It's almost as if we're geneticists engaged in discussions of cloning sheep. One side says, "I'm hybrid, my identity is multiplicity," while another side says, "Conception of a brave new cultural species at all costs: resistance is futile." These heated, sometimes comically self-absorbed debates highlight one thing: Our culture must be pretty damned vapid if we have to have panel discussions every time Steve Park appears on *In Living Color*.

That's one reason I do rely heavily on my Korean roots and identity to inform my music. At least there isn't a vacuum; I can go learn Korean drums, study the *kayagum,* or read about *Pansori*. I'm not trying to advocate reactionary nationalism or anything, but for form's sake, I can't seem to find a concrete Asian American aesthetic in this backyard. As far as content is concerned, there's a wellspring of issues and everyday experiences that provide lyrical abundance for yours truly, Aziatic Spazmatic. I even believe we have a kind of language and hidden transcript of our own. I call it Z-Bonics. From M. Society Seekers to F.O.B.'s, and from Zipperhead cliques to RIBS (Rotten Banana Syndrome), we have our own cute phrases we play with. Maybe what Azian Americans need is an Oriental William Upski Wimsatt to translate it all. That way, we can begin to Bomb the Suburbs of our minds.

Indiana Jones Chang

I sample from the source of Lyrics Past
These lyrics be the instrumentals in the back—
Ground be the surface coverin' up the water
Sound be inertia 'till I wake 'em up from

History, or this day
Point is, I am Indiana Jones Chang
Searchin' for my lost mail
Buried under rock n'
Rolling like a stone
I never gather *mas o menos*

just the right amount to make a statement:
My Letters ain't written, instead they're spoken
Culture is my excavation site, ya see
My strategy be givin' voice to Koreans

Longing for Home

Tales of searches for grails; they never got me anywhere
My holy hell be holdin' on to more than Holden Caulfield
A Catcher undecided, of the Rice of the Left of Center
Sent-a-Meant-to-say, the existential come by way of pain

I realize that economics be another key
for puttin' the world in perspective
lets us understand our meals, or lack of meals
Now I'm feeling like I'm caught up in between
four syllable messiahs and supply and demise

Feels like
We longing for a place we never lost but never found
I need to find some kind of home
I need to become, belong

I learned to decipher, an eye-for-an-eye-for
only applies to those with the cry for freedom
or for those who own the freedom of another man
You stand up for your rights, but then signs ride by
"Sit quietly while we try thee, fry thee"

And now it's back to me I'm in between, I'm in the middle
of a vast race war, at my door, a rap a little about
Why I gots to speak, Malik
And why I write a treatise 'bout a fetus of a voice
that gets unborn from every side, side

Feels like
We longing for a place we never lost but never found
I need to find some kind of home
I need to become, belong

The Silence that crosses our mind, I mind this "yellow horde, go back"
But how can I go back when I was brought up in your morgue
My country tis of thee, sweet land of misery
Louder than an ABK, second-gen, Seoul to babble-on

History, oh "sa-la-ve" but you must say S-L-A-V-E
Cuz you Know Conquistadors Conquistadored
the name of your street, Art for art's sake
means the art of war, a liquor store resides in between
a raisin and the bright . . .
Sun will help me clear my vision,
Sensify my every decision
as I reach the end of my rope,
I hope I learn to cope
with the struggle of the "other," I'm the "other," always was a
Sojourner of the Truth, a foreigner ta Boot

Home is where the heart is
But my heart is turning into stone, Fast, quick, grab a piece
I'm turning sunlight into stone
At times I get like crazy-sad
I never felt I had a home
I'm longing for a place
that I can truly call my own

Feels like
We longing for a place we never lost but never found
I need to find some kind of home

I need to become, belong

Sa-i-ku, April 29

Racial politics melting on my mind
Race to the fire
Sometimes I can't take generalizations unrefined
So I stylize my vision in a rhyme
Let's start with the crime . . .

Committed by the city of indelible force
of Evangelical Sorts
They say they treat you like a KING this time
Whose THRONE to the ground—but nothing more
or so they still say, after years in court:
"Your Blackness, we divorce."

Soon after that the demonstration was had
Some called it UPRISING
While my people called it something worse than biases:
Was The Season that the Fire Breathes
And burns to the ground

I stack the type of facts that cast a face to the name
Cuz the blanket that giveth the blame
Lies and covers up the real stains
Trying to tell you how I feel: PAIN
Turn to the ground

They beat you by: paste, paste voila!
say,
"hit-me-now" and the video will play
Lies, lies, "lie down your face, hey"
Lies lies, "lie down your face, hey"
"Don't you feel afraid?"

They both turn around and the pistol plays
The lethal bass
The judge kind of frowns and says,
"You gotta look away" (astraight)
"Buy, buy, bow down your pain, hey"
"Buy, buy, bow down your pain, hey"
The system for sale

Burning everything you know when there's no hope
Learning that you'll never get a chance to know . . .
Your real name here or why Conquistadors were named here

But I never thought I was going to be the foe, be the foe
Never knew the MIDDLE was a place to go, a place to go
Until it rained here
or should I say
Until we came here

These are the days
These are the heavy nights
But did you know that there's a TWILIGHT
in between the corporation and the violence.
Or are they the same?

These are the players,
Multi-national looters (lootars)
Who can say in many languages
For profit we abandon you
Supply and we'll be damned of you
It's epidemic

Plastac-tinsel-tack
Relax, relax
That which abhors you
The INS minors you
Ethnici-piss.

Tou Ger Xiong

~~~~~~

HIP-HOP AND RAP ARTIST

Born in Laos in 1973, Tou Ger Xiong, his parents, and nine siblings settled in St. Paul, Minnesota, in 1979, after four years in a refugee camp in Thailand. In 1992, Xiong was crowned "Mr. Teen Minnesota," judged on leadership, personality, academic achievements, community service, and athletics. Xiong began performing in college and graduated from Carleton in Northfield, Minnesota, in 1996 with a major in political science and a concentration in American politics. With some background in theater, he incorporates large puppets, rap music, and traditional Hmong stories in high-energy performances that have brought audiences to their feet all over the United States. His purpose is to instill self-respect in young people, especially Hmong teenagers, and to bring about greater intercultural understanding among all people. In 1996, Xiong was the subject of a half-hour documentary, Hmong Means Free, *by International Cable Channel, and in 1998 he participated in a film for IPBS television, the first on the Hmong experience, called* Portraits from the Cloth. *In addition to writing and performing rap songs, Xiong works as a Hmong family and youth consultant.*

RESPONSE ↩

To put it succinctly, the origin of my work is the hardship and discomfort of growing up a first-generation Hmong American in Minnesota. Like most new immigrants to this country, I came into an environment where I didn't have a voice, an identity. I can remember when we first arrived and there were no more than a handful of Asian kids in the public schools. We were "fresh off the boat," as they say, poor, dumb (so they thought), and therefore we were vulnerable. How were the other kids supposed to react toward us when even the teachers didn't know what to say or do? So the anti-Asian bashing crusade began and created a bandwagon effect. "Pick on the gooks; they won't fight back—they can't! Chink! Gook! Go back to your country, Chinaman." To many Westerners, the only "Asians" that exist are either Chinese or Japanese, and because some people believed that *all* Asians have yellow skin, dark-colored hair, and slanted eyes, they figured the term *gook* or *chink* was proper. What did I do? Exactly as my parents advised—I turned the other way, pretended not to hear them, and kept my distance from other kids. And if they spat at me, I just wiped it off. I tried to remember that the "American" kids were better than me. I was supposed to be thankful that they let me come to their country and that I didn't have to live in a country of war anymore.

The violence didn't stop when I left school. In our first few years in America, over forty times our windows were broken by kids deliberately throwing stones at our house. If we didn't know any better, we'd think that Minnesota had winter snow and falling rocks. I also remember how my mother would come home terrified and in tears because someone at the bus station threatened or harassed her. On several occasions, I witnessed others mocking my father because he didn't speak English or because he was a foreigner. Each time that I was denied entrance to a public shopping mall, stopped by the police, or harassed because of the color of my skin, I hurt. And each time I hurt, I remember. A person can endure only so much. After a while, he or she finds a way to get out the pain. My work with young people, my

storytelling, and my performances are ways of releasing much of the anger and pain of growing up with racism and prejudice.

When I first began, I created lyrics and songs for certain audiences. As I performed, I realized that there's a universal message for everybody, regardless of race, gender, culture, or creed. In trying to promote respect, I would contradict myself if I limited my message to certain groups or individuals. To respect others is to regard every person with high esteem. Some may ask why I emphasize the importance of Asian culture and history in my work and not other cultures. I teach others about what I know—the Hmong culture—not only so more people can know who we are and why we came to this country but, more important, because I want people to feel the magic of what happens when one revives with a liberated heart, thinks with a free-spirited mind, and a speaks with a loud and proud voice—his own. My pride in my heritage is merely a reflection of my "respect" for self. I then go on to stress the importance of how respect for self and respect for others go hand in hand.

Depending on where I am or with whom I am speaking, certain aspects of my identity shine. My father always talked about being respectful of the environment in which I walk. Respect others who share that space. "Be humble, quiet, and maintain peace of mind," he would say. In the various spaces in which I reside and function, I try to be respectful of that space. I am a son, a brother, a student, a mentor, an activist, a teacher, an apprentice, a friend, and at times I may even be a fool. Currently and with respect to my occupation, I am a Hmong American artist. I am Hmong because my parents and my ancestors are Hmong. My Hmong cultural heritage can be traced back four generations to the mountains of Laos, where many Hmong still reside and practice traditional customs. I am Hmong

American because although I was born in Laos, I grew up in America and am now a naturalized American citizen. I consider myself an artist only to the extent that my work has an artistic style. I would much prefer the label "educator" or "activist" because my work does have a mission, and that mission is to inform, inspire, and motivate others to take action.

The term *Asian American*, in my opinion, is useful for one main reason: to categorize members of the U.S. population whose heritage can be traced back to the continent of Asia or the islands of the Pacific, thereby distinguishing them from other racial groups, such as African, Caucasian, Indian (Native), and Latino. In other words, the label gives us a box to check. At the same time, the term can be problematic if it is misinterpreted. The label "Asian American" includes over 140 ethnic groups from the Asian countries and crosses more than five generations of Asian immigrants in the United States. Using the label "Asian American" to lump these various groups together can be culturally misrepresenting and often leads to negative misunderstandings by outsiders, thereby creating racial tension and hostility. Since I can trace my Hmong heritage back four generations to a little village in Laos, I prefer to be identified as Hmong American. For convenience's sake, I sometimes use "Asian American" to avoid having to provide a detailed explanation of what Hmong is.

The role of any "Asian American" artist, or that of any Asian American professional in the larger American society, is to educate all people about the unity as well as the diversity within the Asian American community and among all people. Although most Asian Americans may share a common agenda for political reasons when it comes to issues like immigration reform, affirmative action, and welfare reform, we differ in many other ways, mainly in our choice of spiritual beliefs and cultural practices. Artists' roles are to promote the realities of living between these cultural and ethnic boundaries.

I agree that we live in a world of stereotypes and that Asian Americans, like other minority groups, have been misrepresented in the past and still face misrepresentation today. The lack of media and literature showing the Asian male with masculine traits has led many to believe that Asian men are weak, not only physically but sexually. Asian women in the movie industry have mostly been shown as seductive, sexy, and submissive. On a general note, Asian cultures have been and still are stereotypically portrayed as exotic and mysterious. Although there is a grain of truth in every stereotype, the fact is, it is limiting to label the entire group based on the actions and characteristics of a few. As an Asian American performer, my work challenges these stereotypes in many ways. I use rap music, a form of expression stereotypically perceived as African American. I use loud, obnoxious, and an almost crazy sense of humor to depict the immigrant experience, challenging the belief that all Asians are quiet, passive, and lack a sense of humor.

It is a receptive moment in history for Asian American artists or any artists of a minority culture simply because of the recent trends to move toward a more multicultural nation. Government legislation, educational institutions, and historical events in recent decades all support the idea that we are, inevitably, a nation of diverse peoples and that we have no other choice but to live together. In general, social attitudes have helped the emergence of artists of every minority culture or race. However, it often frightens me to think that there are also groups in this country who promote hate based on skin color or religion, White supremacy groups such as the Ku Klux Klan. Maybe I'll write a song for them with a message: "I'm here to stay, Jack, and I ain't goin' nowhere so you gots to deal wit me."

The initial reception of my work was not very encouraging. Not even my parents supported my endeavors. I couldn't blame them. What were two Hmong adults who were born and raised in houses made of bamboo and grass, and who lived in secluded villages in the mountains of a third world country, supposed to think? In the past two years, however, it seems they've come around to appreciate my work. Now they say, "As long as it pays the bills and you're not bringing shame to the family, do as you please." From general audiences, I have heard nothing but praise and support. At times, I've received very surprising responses. I've brought groups of more than four hundred Hmong elders, many of whom do not speak English, to their feet to dance and chant my chorus "Go Hmong Boy Go Hmong Boy Go." I've received standing ovations from an audience of sixteen hundred high school students in a predominantly White community. I've been approached by audiences, both young and old, who were in tears because my message has touched them in one way or another. I've had teachers and counselors tell me that what I accomplished in two hours was more than what the staff at one high school could do in one year. I've had audience members voluntarily hand me twenty-dollar bills because they liked what they saw. As a performer and educator, I could not ask for anything more than to know that my work has had that sort of impact on people.

I am most grateful for the optimism that my parents instilled in me as a child. My family lived on welfare because my parents couldn't speak English well enough to get a decent job. What people called the ghetto we called home. My entire family of twelve shared a public housing apartment of four bedrooms. We often received clothing and food donations from local charities. With ten children to raise on a budget of no more than $1,000 a month, my parents had it tough. Yet I don't think a single day went by when they couldn't find a reason to be appreciative of life and of what they had. No matter what, they always found a reason to give thanks. Their philosophy was "We are poor, but we are alive. We are not educated, but we have our hands and our feet to work with."

A multicultural artist has to balance between serving as the voice of his ethnic community and finding his own voice. Sometimes these two voices coincide, and at other times they differ. I believe an artist can take on the voice of community when his work builds positive change, understanding, and friendship with other communities. An artist should distinguish his community voice from his own voice when he is in a potentially hostile environment. When he fears that his voice may cause misunderstanding of his community, then he should hold back from using that voice. Most of the time, whether or not an artist represents the voice of a community is determined by the audiences' responses and critiques. For example, if his work is received well by audiences inside his community as well those from the outside, then it is logical to conclude that he brings fair representation to his community. Therefore, if an artist is unsure of whom his work speaks for, he should pay close attention to the responses of his audience. A disclaimer I often make is "I don't speak for the 120,000 Hmong Americans in the United States." However, my life stories of acculturation, my experiences with racism, my view of life in America, and my view of the world are similar to those of many Hmong in this country, simply because we arrived recently as refugees of war; we came into a new and often hostile setting. The advantage to being an artist is in choosing not whose voice to represent but the message and the medium through which this message is conveyed.

Personally, I chose rap music, stand-up comedy, and dramatic storytelling to educate about the Hmong people and our struggles.

If Asian Americans write about subjects other than identity and community concerns, of course they should still be called Asian American writers. Who are we to question the identity of other artists or writers? The point of writing and performing is that one can express his own voice and own his identity as he chooses. For example, an Asian American writer who writes about the hardships of growing up in Chinatown in the 1920s is no more or less "Asian American" than one who writes about discovering his gay identity. On the one hand, the Asian American writer who discusses his coming of age in Chinatown will probably provide more background on his identity as an Asian American. On the other hand, the writer who discusses his gay identity can choose, as a writer, whether or not to downplay his "Asian-ness" or to conceal it completely. Nonetheless, he's still an Asian American to his audiences. I have a hard time believing that whether or not the author claims his Asian American identity will have a big impact on the number of copies he will sell. Furthermore, who's to say a Caucasian writer who writes about the experiences of growing up in Chinatown can not call himself an Asian American writer? I, for one, may contest it, but nonetheless, he has that right to identify with what he pleases.

Since it is in human nature to err, as Asian Americans we have an obligation to correct any wrongdoing to our cultural heritage. We have a responsibility to correct these faults particularly when we feel that we have ownership in what has been misrepresented. To give you an example, I began performing Hmong folktales because I was frustrated after watching a Caucasian performer tell Hmong folktales. As a child I grew up listening to my father tell Hmong folktales in the native Hmong language. Because I still speak Hmong and remember life in the native country, I listened to these tales with a Hmong ear. Hmong tales to me were beautiful, magical, captivating. The flow of the language was like music. The play with words and sounds added suspense and excitement to each turn in the story, bringing me to a world of endless imagination. When I heard and saw this Caucasian storyteller tell Hmong tales in English in the same boring manner as a grade school librarian, I felt cheated and angry. I told myself, the next time I see somebody telling Hmong tales, it's going to be me.

Another example was when I attended a conference on Hmong youth issues. The topic at hand was Hmong students and their struggles in school. Here we were in a room filled with social service providers and teachers and students. We were listening to a Caucasian professor talk about his findings about Hmong students and their struggles in education. Throughout the entire time I thought, "If we're talking about Hmong, youth, and education, duh, I live the life everyday and so do the thirty other students in the room. We've got concerns. How come I'm not up there?" I later submitted a workshop proposal titled "Let Us Speak: A Workshop about Hmong Youth Issues by Hmong Youth."

There's a saying in the Hmong culture that translates "No matter how smart you are, I am wiser than you because I have eaten more rice than you." This proverb illustrates the importance of wisdom, which is gained from living and doing. I call it the "human experience," and no one can articulate it better than the person who lived it. It can be told over and over again through books, from generation to generation, from storyteller to storyteller, and the effect would not replicate that of the original storyteller.

Let us not be fooled that because we Hmong come from a culture without a formal written language, without history books to document our ancestry, without educational degrees and credentials to validate our perspectives, our views are not as important. Traditional oral histories, cultural practices, rituals, spirituality, and cultural beliefs are what have kept us alive for centuries. Too often in this time and age, we are misled to pass judgment on ourselves based on how we compare with others in our level of "formal" education, our familiarity with technological advances, and our possessions of material wealth.

Go Hmong Boy Go Hmong Boy Go: A Rap

as you can see i'm asian and i'm not black
what i'm about to say may sound like slack
but just lend me your ears and hear me out
i come to tell you what i'm all about
yes my name is Tou and i come to say
that i'm special, talented in many ways
yes i know kung-fu and martial arts
you try to go against me and i'll tear you apart
say i'm bad, mean, tough is my game
they call me the master, yes that's my name

(Chorus)
go hmong boy go hmong boy go
go hmong boy go hmong boy go
bite that spicy eggroll
dip it in the soy sauce and put it in your mouth, uh

well you might think it's weird to see that i'm asian
bust'n some rhymes on such an occasion
let me tell you how i came to be
i was born in Laos ne, ne ,ne, nineteen-seventy-three
in the hmong culture we sing and dance
but i'm na start rapping and take my chance
even though this is my first rap
you don't have to like it you don't have to clap
for those of you listening it might be nice
to think this hmong boy's kicking it like Vanilla Ice ice ice

(Chorus)

i fled my country at the age of four
all because of the Vietnam War

my family was moving from place to place
running from the guns at a very fast pace
my people was dying here and there
dead women, children everywhere
when I think about these tragedies
thank God for my life and my family's
now that i live in the U.S.A.
I'm proud to be and glad to say

(Chorus)

sometimes i face resentment from others
and feel only the hmong are my sisters and brothers
wherever i go people give me the eye
just because i'm an "oriental" guy
with my round face and my dark hair
it still doesn't give you the right to stare
deep down inside i'm just like you
with emotional feelings and affection too
i'm not asking for a favor of yours
i don't need it now and i didn't before
say everybody knows what's right and wrong
all we got to do is get along

(Chorus)

i want to say thanks to those who accept me
for who i am and not for who i should be
i want to say thanks for those beautiful smiles
i'll make it worth your time and i'll make it worth your while
until then peace and universal love
soaring through the sky like a beautiful dove

yo i am outta here . . . peace . . .

We Are Hmong: A Rap

this is chapter one
yo my Hmong brothers and sisters, listen up listen up
cause i'll say it once, i might say it twice
this is a valuable piece of advice
now you all know that we are hmong

originated from a long long history of the strong
way way back some thousand years ago
we lived in the mountains of China or so
our lives were happy we were farming the land
we took our matters into our own hands
and if there was a problem that we couldn't hack,
we had our clan members watching our back
cause back in the village, yo love was the way
and if you didn't like it you didn't have to stay
we ate rice with cow, chicken, and pig,
we shared a common song, we had our own gig
you were who you were and there was no shame
everywhere you went, they knew you by the last name

and if you threw a party, everybody came
if you ua neeg, everybody came
if you hais ntsoob, everybody came
if you muaj mob, everybody came
if you hu plig, everybody came
and why is that? cause it's in your last name

movin on, movin on to chapter two
soon the word got out to the chinese
they began to wonder who the hell are these
uncivilized people living in the mountains
hunting the land and drinking nature's fountains
they called us barbaric, savage, and raw
cause we didn't abide by chinese law
so the chinese came to raid our village
but we weren't gonna just give up our image
we fought and fought til we couldn't fight no more
we were outnumbered and losing the war

movin on movin on to chapter three
from southern China, we went down south
and settled in the mountainous regions of Laos
some to Vietnam and some to Thailand
but wherever we went, we settled in the highland
in southeast asia there was peace again
we made more babies and we made more friends
but for whatever reason I couldn't see how
we were still mistreated by the native Lao

they called us meo,
but we didn't give a damn
cause we had each other and we had our clan

movin on movin on to chapter four
soon in southeast Asia the conflict occurred
as all of you have probably heard
when the communist power was on the rise
the american forces began to get wise
they sent the C.I.A. to recruit the hmong
having heard we were brave and we were strong
we knew the jungle and guerrilla warfare
we were capable of tasks that nobody dared
under the leadership of general Vang Pao
we fought with courage and the know how
for 15 years we were the U.S. foot soldiers
fought long, hard, and tough like boulders
from the camp of Long Chieng to camp Pa Dong
everyone had heard of these warriors named hmong
we were the secret army fought undercover
in a secret war not meant to be discovered

But, the war came to an end in '75,
Americans returned many hmong left to die
some hmongs continued to fight the communist
but nevertheless the brothers got dissed
they were fighting another man's war
left alone and behind to settle the score

movin on movin on to the final chapter
maybe it was luck or maybe it was fate
that you and i made it to the United States
but for what ever the reason was
you and i have got a mission because

in our name we are Hmong
in our blood we are Hmong
in our souls we are Hmong
in our minds we are Hmong
in our hearts we are Hmong
and forever we are Hmong

when I was little my father said to me
son no matter where you go or who you'll be

you can change your clothes but you can't change your skin
you can lie to others but you can't lie to him
he's the hmong inside you and he's everything you are
if you remember that son you will go far

so now i say to you
you may be short but you're tall at heart
so don't let no one say "you're not smart"
you're rich in culture, spirit, and soul
anyone who tells you different, well they gots to go
so my brothers and my sisters i've shared with you
a piece of history that has helped me through
it's about courage, pride and love for oneself
it's about our people, our culture, and our gracious wealth
so before I go, I say "you got a mission"
to spread the legacy and to make others listen
to show your talents and that you are strong
cause in your blood, mind, and soul, you are HMONG.

Peace. Love each other but more importantly love yourselves . . .

Permissions

We would like to thank the following for permission to include works here: "The Short Short That Changed My Fate," by C. Y. Lee, used by permission of the author. "Home Again, 1945," an excerpt from *Gourd Hollow Dance* by Kim Yong Ik, originally appeared in the *Mid-American Review;* reprinted by permission of Faith M. Leigh. "That Man" and "In Some Countries," by Mitsuye Yamada, used by permission of the author. "The Oriental Contingent," by Diana Chang, originally appeared in *The Forbidden Stitch: An Asian American Women's Anthology,* ed. Shirley Geok-Lin Lim, Mayumi Tsutakawa, and Margarita Donnelly (Calyx Books, 1989); reprinted by permission of the author. Excerpt from *Year of Impossible Goodbyes,* copyright © 1991 by Sook Nyul Choi; reprinted by permission of Houghton Mifflin Company; all rights reserved. Excerpt from *Tripmaster Monkey: His Fake Book,* by Maxine Hong Kingston, copyright © 1987, 1988, 1989 by Maxine Hong Kingston; reprinted by permission of Alfred A. Knopf Inc. "A Family Gathering" originally appeared in *Dark Blue Suit and Other Stories,* by Peter Bacho (University of Washington Press, 1997); reprinted by permission of University of Washington Press. "In Your Honor" and "The Redshifting Web," by Arthur Sze, originally appeared in *The Redshifting Web: Poems 1970–1998,* copyright © Arthur Sze, Copper Canyon Press, 1998; reprinted by permission of the author. "Imagining Dora," by Meena Alexander, used by permission of the author. "Paint," by Darrell Lum, originally appeared in *Pass On, No Pass Back* (Bamboo Ridge Press, 1990); reprinted by permission of the author. "Ministry: Homage to Kilauea," by Garrett Hongo, used by permission of the author. "The Colors of Desire," from *The Colors of Desire* by David Mura, copyright © 1994 by David Mura; reprinted by permission of Doubleday, a division of Bantam Doubleday Dell Publishing Group, Inc. "Siamese Twins and Mongoloids," by Karen Tei Yamashita, reprinted by permission of *dIS*orient Journalzine* and the author. "Clothes," by Chitra Divakaruni, originally appeared in *Arranged Marriage: Stories* (Anchor, 1996); reprinted by permission of the author. "Firoze Ganjifrockwala," from *Love, Stars, and All That* by Kirin Narayan (Pocket Books, 1994), reprinted by permission of the author. "The Brick," by Katherine Min, used by permission of the author. "Roughie," by Stewart Ikeda, originally published in *Glimmer Train Stories,* Issue 7, Summer 1993; reprinted by permission of the author. *Made in USA: Angel Island Shhh, My Mother's Baggage,* and *Baby Jack Rice Story: The Corner Beckoned,* by Flo Oy Wong, used by permission of the artist. *From Lake Minidoka to Lake Mendota, Black Diamond, Rooting for Coal, Fairgrounds Called Camp Harmony?* and *Gathering the Lost Tribes under Blue-Spot-Tailed Golden Eagle Wings,* by Munio Makuuchi, used by permission of the author/artist. *98.6—A Convergence in 15 Minutes,* by Ping Chong, used by permission of the author. *Trying to Find Chinatown,* by David Henry Hwang, used by permission of Writers and Artists Agency and the author. Excerpt from *Tea,* by Velina Hasu Houston, reprinted by permission of Harden-Curtis Associates. *Richard Speck,* "Asian Men on Asian Men: The Attraction," and "In Response to Executive Order 9066," by Dwight

Okita, used by permission of the author. "Song for Grandpa," from *Monkhood in 3 Easy Lessons* by Dan Kwong, used by permission of the author. "No Menus Please" (from *Big Dicks, Asian Men*) and "Diary of a Paper Son" (from *The Second Coming*) used by permission of Slant Performance Group (Richard Ebihara, Wayland Quintero, and Perry Yung). Stills from *Who Killed Vincent Chin?* by Christine Choy, *My America . . . or Honk if You Love Buddha* by Renee Tajima-Peña, and *hundred percent* by Eric Koyanagi used by permission of the filmmakers. "Johnson's Store," by William David "Charlie" Chin, used by permission of the author. Lyrics from "Asian Song," by Chris Iijima, used by permission of the author. Lyrics from "To All Relations/Mitakuye Oyasin," "What Is the Color of Love?" and "The Chasm," by Nobuko Miyamoto, used by permission of the author. Excerpt from *Island: The Immigrant Suite* no. 2, by Jon Jang, reprinted by permission of the composer. Lyrics from "Indiana Jones Chang," "Longing for Home," and "Sai-i-ku, April 29," by Jamez Chang, used by permission of the author. Lyrics from "Go Hmong Boy Go Hmong Boy Go: A Rap" and "We Are Hmong: A Rap," by Tou Ger Xiong, used by permission of the author.